Heritage Language Education

Heritage Language Education

A New Field Emerging

Edited by

Donna M. Brinton, Olga Kagan, and Susan Bauckus

Routledge
Taylor & Francis Group

NEW YORK AND LONDON

First published in 2008
by Routledge
270 Madison Ave, New York, NY 10016

Simultaneously published in the UK
by Routledge
2 Park Square, Milton Park, Abingdon, Oxon OX14 4RN

This edition first published in paperback in 2009

Routledge is an imprint of the Taylor & Francis Group, an informa business
© 2008, 2009 Taylor & Francis

Typeset in Minion by EvS Communication Networx, Inc.
Printed and bound in the United States of America on acid-free paper by Edwards Brothers, Inc.

Library of Congress Cataloging-in-Publication Data
Heritage language education : a new field emerging / edited by Donna Brinton, Olga Kagan, and
Susan Bauckus.
p. cm.
Includes bibliographical references and index.
ISBN 978-0-8058-4803-8 (hardback : alk. paper) — ISBN 978-0-415-99588-7 (paperback: alk.
paper) — ISBN 978-1-4106-1887-0 (e-book) 1. Native language—Study and teaching.
2. Linguistic minorities—Education. 3. Education, Bilingual. I. Brinton, Donna. II. Kagan, Olga.
III. Bauckus, Susan.
P53.H47 2008
418.007—dc22   2007023610

ISBN 10: 0-8058-4803-7 (hbk)
ISBN 10: 0-415-99588-4 (pbk)
ISBN 10: 1-4106-1887-0 (ebk)

ISBN 13: 978-0-8058-4803-8 (hbk)
ISBN 13: 978-0-415-99588-7 (pbk)
ISBN 13: 978-1-4106-1887-0 (ebk)

To Russell N. Campbell

Contents

Part III
Program Development and Evaluation

In Conclusion

Preface

We dedicate this volume to Professor Russell N. Campbell (1927–2003) who was a colleague, friend, and mentor to many of us, and who was instrumental in advocating for the creation of the field of heritage language education. Russ had the intuition, enthusiasm, and vision to encourage a new way of thinking about heritage students, who speak a language other than English at home but are educated in English.

While these students have always been present in language classrooms, they have sometimes been treated with indifference or even hostility because they bring non-academic varieties and non-standard vocabulary and grammar into the classroom, thus disrupting the established routine of foreign language teaching. Even when they are welcome in foreign language classes, they present a challenge, as foreign language instructors are not prepared to teach these students and the instruction is typically organized around the needs of foreign language learners.

Russ understood that "there is a serious need for Americans who are highly competent in languages other than English, especially languages that, historically, have rarely or never been taught in our schools and universities" (Campbell & Rosenthal, 2000, p. 177) and he believed that the preservation of heritage language competence would contribute to satisfying this need. Moreover, Russ knew that heritage speakers required a different type of instruction than foreign language learners, and he proposed what he called "commonsense guidelines" (2000, p. 177) for implementing heritage language programs. His early work and advocacy formed part of the foundation for heritage language education.

Although heritage language education is now its own field, it is still "atheoretical" (Valdés, 2000), and like any new field, it needs both research and hands-on innovation. Because of this need for both theoretical and practical insights, for this volume, we chose the multi-disciplinary approach recommended by the UCLA Heritage Language Research Priorities Conference (University of California, Los Angeles, 2001) convened by Russ Campbell and colleagues. The chapters explore policy and societal issues, present linguistic case studies, and discuss curricular issues.

Overview

As an introduction, Nancy H. Hornberger and Shuhan C. Wang position heritage learners along the continua of biliteracy. Their continua model suggests that biliteracy may develop non-linearly on the intersection of "oral-to-written, and receptive-to-productive" capabilities. This chapter poses questions regarding the goals and content of instruction, the medium of language use outside of the classroom, and the learners' language expertise. These questions, asked of both teachers and learners, may serve as a blueprint for designing a heritage language program. They also provide a framework for the themes explored in this volume.

Heritage language proficiency is the result either of migration or of societal changes when an indigenous population becomes a minority. Consequently, understanding heritage language learners' needs requires knowledge of their demographics, history, and community. In the opening chapter of Part I "Heritage Speakers: Demographics, Policy, and Identity," Richard Tucker posits that multilingual ability is becoming the norm in many countries where foreign languages are a mandated subject in elementary school. He surveys various models of foreign language instruction and recommends that educators implement programs that would create multilingual personalities with the ensuing "cognitive, social, personal and economic benefits."

Joseph Lo Bianco analyzes the representation of intergenerational language maintenance in political discourse and gives examples of language policies in Scotland and Australia. The case of Australia may be of particular interest to readers in North America as the author describes creating an infrastructure for encouraging linguistic diversity. In his discussion of the relationship between citizenship and language policies, Lo Bianco distinguishes between legal and participatory citizenship, and makes the provocative proposition that heritage language advocacy may be vulnerable to accusations of nation undermining.

An example of a long-standing policy of multilingualism practiced in Canada is provided by Patricia Duff. Duff calls the policy "official multiculturalism" and contrasts it with the American "melting pot." She surveys the demographics, policies, history, and research directions of Canadian bilingual education and includes her personal reflections of the situation in British Columbia.

Terrence Wiley presents the linguistic history of a heritage speaker of Taiwanese and Mandarin, who attempted to study Mandarin in college, and the difficulties that led him to decide not to continue. Although the chapter reports on an individual case study, the learner's history would be familiar to countless heritage learners who are ill served by an inflexible or even punishing educational system.

Guadalupe Valdés, Sonia González, Dania García, and Patricio Márquez examine the role of educational institutions in teaching heritage languages. Based on the interviews they conducted with members of a Spanish department at an American university, they catalogue and analyze assumptions of three language groups—native speakers of Spanish, foreign language learners, and U.S. Latinos—towards academic Spanish. The chapter documents a negative attitude to the language of U.S. Latinos, and concludes that foreign language professionals need to develop understanding and tolerance of language contact varieties.

Mary McGroarty and Alfredo Urzúa report on a study of three Mexican nationals who were raised and fully educated in Spanish in Mexico and then moved to the United States. At present, they use English and Spanish in their professional lives as middle managers in U.S. corporations. While their job descriptions did not require knowledge of Spanish, they found themselves using two languages on the job. The study examines their use of language as well as their self-identification.

The next section, "Heritage Speaker Profiles and Needs Analysis," presents case studies of speakers of several languages. Because these speakers typically are exposed to their first language before or simultaneously with acquiring English, we need to understand which features of their heritage language they retain once they become English dominant.

Maria Polinsky explores the structure of heritage speakers' narratives, establishes a methodological framework for studying how speakers use the language, and discusses implications for language acquisition studies. Her research suggests that heritage speakers' grammar is not fossilized at a childhood stage of acquisition, but rather represents a reanalysis of what the speaker, later in life, remembers of the language.

Kazue Kanno, Tomomi Hasegawa, Keiko Ikeda, Yasuko Ito, and Michael Long examine the variations in the linguistic performance of learners of Japanese whose speaking proficiencies are within the range of Advanced to Advanced-Plus on the American Council on the Teaching of Foreign Languages (1989) scale. The study subjects include heritage and non-heritage, those who learned the language in the classroom only, and others who acquired it naturalistically. The study shows that even though the learners have advanced proficiencies, their mastery of certain linguistic features varies.

Debra Friedman and Olga Kagan compare the use of relative clauses and temporal cohesion in the written discourse of Russian heritage speakers, educated Russian speakers, and advanced foreign language learners. The analysis shows that heritage learners are situated between educated native speakers and advanced foreign language learners on the literacy continuum.

Claudia Parodi discusses the Spanish vernacular spoken in the Los Angeles area and its stigmatization both by monolingual speakers in Latin America and, more importantly, by Spanish instructors in the U.S. Parodi proposes a model of language teaching to speakers of Spanish vernacular that builds on rather than devalues their knowledge of the language.

Masako Douglas's chapter evaluates the benefits of a curriculum created for heritage learners of Japanese that focuses on developing autonomous learning strategies. She shows that this approach resulted in a significant gain in the knowledge of kanji.

The volume's final section, "Program Development and Evaluation," opens with Scott McGinnis's chapter on teaching Chinese as a heritage language. McGinnis demonstrates that the heritage education sector is a "significant trendsetter" in Chinese instruction in the United States. His analysis of curricular developments in the heritage schools illustrates both the successful innovations of the community whose goal is to preserve the heritage language and the failure of the public educational system to provide adequate language instruction to heritage speakers.

Joy Kreeft Peyton describes a 1999 National Endowment for the Humanities Summer Institute for teachers of Spanish to Spanish speakers that was held at UCLA and directed by Russell Campbell. Peyton provides a comprehensive set of suggestions for heritage language education in areas including heritage speaker characteristics, teacher education, programs and instruction, assessment, and policy.

Donna Christian focuses on two-way immersion programs in English and a heritage language. While Christian asserts the benefits of such programs, she stresses the need for research to identify the role of communities, resources, and the conditions under which these programs could be more successful.

Sung-Ock Sohn and Craig Merrill report on a Korean/English dual language program in the Los Angeles Unified School District. Enrollment in the program included Korean-dominant and English-dominant pupils. In addition to learning another language, both groups demonstrated accelerated English language development when compared to the children in a modified bilingual or English only program.

The next two chapters describe immersion programs. While not all the participants in these studies are heritage learners, immersion studies approximate a heritage language context and thus provide useful information for the heritage field, which so far is lacking a large body of research.

Andrew Cohen and Tania Gómez report on a pedagogical intervention conducted with the goal of improving elementary school pupils' knowledge of academic language. The pupils were taught strategies including the use of the inner voice in the target language, which resulted in improved academic performance.

Merrill Swain and Sharon Lapkin show that language production can be an entry into learning, and that students can improve understanding through speaking or writing. The authors do not claim that production should always be the first step in learning, but rather that production helps acquisition and assists the learner in understanding the meaning through externalizing the inner speech.

The final chapter in this section addresses heritage language program evaluation. Brian Lynch outlines an approach to program evaluation centered in the community. He argues that a heritage language program should strengthen students' ties to the community and he advocates the use of community resources in conducting program evaluation.

Terry Kit-fong Au's chapter is a fitting conclusion to the volume. Au is a cognitive psychologist and her approach may point to some future directions for the field of heritage language acquisition. In her chapter, Au discusses whether

childhood language memory is accessible in adulthood and whether adult learners can recapture some of the linguistic material they were exposed to in their
early childhood. She explores why childhood language experience seems to be
beneficial in some cases but not in others. Au concludes that to acquire and retain
their heritage language, "children need to speak it beyond early childhood."

As can be seen from the summaries above, this volume's contributors come
from a variety of fields and perspectives. We hope that the chapters represent a
step towards the maturity of heritage language education and will contribute to
the goals of formulating theory and developing informed classroom practices,
as well as creating enlightened programs for students who bring knowledge of
the home language into the classroom.

In the summer of 2006, as the manuscript was being prepared to send to the
publishers, UCLA and the University of California Consortium for Language
Learning and Teaching (UCCLLT) learned that they had been awarded a new
National Language Resource Center under Title VI of the U.S. Department of
Education. The Center's mission is to advance heritage language education; to
that end, its research agenda was developed to contribute to the development
of curricula, materials, and teacher preparation in the field of heritage language
education. We are happy to note that many of this volume's contributors are associated with the new center as project directors, evaluators, or advisory board
members.

References

American Council on the Teaching of Foreign Languages. (1989). *ACTFL proficiency guidelines.*
Hastings on Hudson, NY: Author.
Campbell, R. N., & Rosenthal, J. W. (2000). Heritage languages. In J. W. Rosenthal (Ed.), *Hand-
book of undergraduate second language education* (pp. 165–184). Mahwah, NJ: Lawrence
Erlbaum.
University of California, Los Angeles. (2001). *Heritage language research priorities conference report.*
Los Angeles: Author. Available at: http://www.cal.org
Valdés, G. (2000). The teaching of heritage languages: An introduction for Slavic-teaching profession-
als. In O. Kagan & B. Rifkin (Eds.), *The learning and teaching of Slavic languages and cultures*
(pp. 375–403). Bloomington, IN: Slavica.

Acknowledgements

We would like to thank several people for an abundance of help in preparing this book for publication. Rachel Pratley helped with editing in the early stages, Lisa Mikesell and Brieta Marie Fass with the bibliographies and references, and Diane Childs at the UCLA Young Research Library with references. Vanda Suvansilpakit entered contributors' revisions and helped with copy editing, and Alan Paul placed all the papers into a single manuscript and prepared the index. Agazit Abate was a great help in choosing an image for the cover.

We would also like to thank Naomi Silverman and Lynn Goeller of Routledge for their help and collegiality through all stages of preparation. Finally, we are grateful to all the contributors for their patience and willingness to answer many queries and make multiple changes at our request.

An Introduction

1

Who Are Our Heritage Language Learners?
Identity and Biliteracy in Heritage Language Education in the United States

NANCY H. HORNBERGER AND SHUHAN C. WANG

Introduction

While the term *heritage language* (HL) has been in use, particularly in Canada, since the early 1970s, it has been gaining significant ground in U.S. research, policy, and practice only since the 1990s. Pedagogical approaches to HL instruction are being suggested and implemented on a large scale. Yet, there is still no general consensus on who U.S. HL speakers and learners are, which in turn has hindered the field from advancing pedagogically or theoretically (also see Wiley, 2001). This chapter represents our attempt to tackle this complex task of describing heritage language learners (HLLs).

In the first full-length edited volume about HLLs (Webb & Miller, 2000), Draper and Hicks define a HLL as:

> ...someone who has had exposure to a non-English language outside the formal education system. It most often refers to someone with a home background in the language, but may refer to anyone who has had in-depth exposure to another language. Other terms used to describe this population include "native speaker," "bilingual," and "home background." While these terms are often used interchangeably, they can have very different interpretations. (p. 19)

While this definition applies to many HLLs, it contains two weaknesses. First, it is overly broad, including both those who have had home exposure to a HL and those who have had extensive exposure to a second language (e.g., an American expatriate's child who grew up in Japan speaking Japanese). At the same time, the definition is overly narrow in that it seems to favor those with a high degree of proficiency in the HL (e.g., those typically found in bilingual classrooms). As we will demonstrate later in this chapter, this definition leaves out many other HLLs.

Scalera's (2000) definition of HLLs as individuals who have learned a language other than English somewhere other than in school seems to imply that any language learner in a naturalistic setting is a HLL. This ignores the connection between a HLL and the HL (Fishman, 1991, 2001), a connection also acknowledged by other researchers. For example, Campbell and Peyton (1998) define HL speakers as individuals "who speak their first language, which is not English, in the home, or are foreign-born" (p. 38). Their definition, which highlights the individuals' ability to speak the HL, directly links individuals to their home language and includes both native and foreign born.

One commonly accepted definition comes from Valdés (2001), who defines HL students in terms of two types: (1) individuals having historical or personal connection to a language such as an endangered indigenous language or immigrant language that is not normally taught in school; or (2) individuals who appear in a foreign language classroom, who are raised in homes where a non-English language is spoken, speak or merely understand the HL, and are to some degree bilingual in English and the HL (Valdés, 2001, pp. 37–38).

Her definition is broader than those cited above by differentiating the source and degree of students' development in the HL. Her focus, however, is on planning instruction and developing pedagogical theories for HL speakers (Valdés, 2001).

In contrast to Valdés' and other researchers' linguistically-oriented definitions, Fishman (1999, 2001) categorizes HLLs based on their socio-historical relationships with the United States into three major groups:

1. *Indigenous languages* spoken by Native American tribes that existed before the arrival of European settlers; many of these languages are now endangered;
2. *Colonial languages* such as French, German, Italian, or Spanish, which earlier European settlers brought; and
3. *Immigrant languages* such as Arabic, Chinese, Japanese, Vietnamese, Cambodian, or Korean that came along with more recent influxes of immigrants.

Fishman's categories are useful in defining the majority of HLLs in terms of a group and its historical relationship with the Unitd States, thus acknowledging HLLs' ancestral heritage and extending their ties to the HL and heritage culture (HC) beyond immediate families. On the other hand, Fishman's definition, like those offered by Valdés (2000, 2001), Draper and Hicks (2000), and Campbell and Peyton (1998), does not pay enough attention to HLLs' cultural and socio-psychological struggles. In this respect, it is typical for HLLs in the United States not only to find themselves frequently in sites of contestation of the dominant language (English) and their HL, but also needing to negotiate the use of the HL in its standard or dialect forms. Moreover, their HC often has to compete against the dominant culture, and their local (home and ethnic) ideologies must compete with the dominant ideologies (Heath, 1983; Ogbu, 1996; Street, 1995; Tollefson,

1991; Trueba & Zou 1994). These individuals must constantly choose, construct, and perform their social identities (Erickson & Shultz, 1982) vis-à-vis the different groups of people with whom they interact. In other words, defining HLLs requires far more than simply assessing their linguistic abilities and determining the relationship between their dominant and home languages.

Furthermore, the above definitions do not adequately assist individuals faced with a complex reality to answer the basic question "Which language is my heritage language?" For instance, there are many other "types" of HLLs who do not belong to any of Fishman's categories, including children of interracial or multi-racial marriages and adoptions (Root, 1996, cited in Schwartz, 1998). One such example is that of Families with Children from China (FCC), the fastest-growing phenomenon in the landscape of interracial/intercountry adoption. According to figures released by this nondenominational organization of families in the United States, Canada, and the United Kingdom, there were 23,903 such adoptions in the year 2000, mostly of girls (Families with Children from China, n.d., p. 5.).

Because many of these parents want their adopted children to continue their ties to their HL and HC, they appear at the doors of Chinese HL schools every weekend. The schools, in turn, must open new classes for these children, who are different in nature from conventional HLLs at Chinese schools (Betty Foo, personal communication, February 10, 2000; Man-Li Kuo Lin, personal communication, May 25, 2002; Chen & Chung, 2002). In the case of FCC, the adopted children may grow up to claim Chinese, English, or both as their HL(s), just as they may decide to stay within one ethnic/racial group or cross both groups (Rampton, 1995).

But children adopted by people residing in the United States come from many other countries besides China. According to Zhao (2002), Americans adopted about 19,000 children from abroad in 2001, almost three times the number adopted in 1992.[1] A host of questions arise in connection with these multiracial adoptive families. First, what is the role of intergenerational language and HC maintenance (Fishman, 1991)? Likewise, for children whose birth parents come from different ethnic, racial, cultural, and language backgrounds, which language (mother or father tongue) is considered their HL? Can we consider as HLLs monolingual, English-speaking third, fourth, or multi-generation indigenous individuals? Are immigrant offspring eager to re-establish their ties with their ancestral languages and cultures? For speakers who live and interact in two languages and cultures (e.g., Latinos in the Southwest), how do we identify which language and culture are their HL and HC? Answers to these questions can provide pertinent information concerning the so-called outsider versus insider status and the language proficiency versus ethnicity distinction—i.e., what Wiley (2001) has called the "politics of identity" (p. 30).

These questions are at the heart of HLL education. Regardless of how we categorize them, HLLs do not learn or use one, two, or more languages in isolation.

Consequently, there is no single profile of HLLs. Taken from this perspective, these individuals, their interactions with the people around them, and their dynamic interface with the social, educational, cultural, economic, and political institutions constitute an ecological system. In such a system, individuals are the center of inquiry, but they are also always a part of the larger system in which they shape and are shaped by various factors in the system.

In this chapter, we adopt an ecological view of HLL identity. Specifically, we view HLLs as individuals with familial or ancestral ties to a language other than English who exert their agency in determining if they are HLLs of that language. We take into consideration their wider group's social, economic, and political positioning in the United States. We also distinguish between HL speakers and HL learners, framing our discussion in terms of HLLs who may or may not be HL speakers. Furthermore, we do not differentiate HLLs in terms of bilingual, foreign, heritage, or indigenous language programs. Instead, our attention is focused on the identity and biliteracy development of HLLs in the ecological systems they inhabit. Specifically, we examine the multiple identities of HLLs and the multiple paths of biliteracy development and use they adopt. By so doing, we provide a basis for understanding individual biliterate educational experiences.

Our goal coincides with Valdés' (2001) call for "a coherent body of pedagogical theories about what can be accomplished in a classroom setting relative to out-of-school acquisition, functions, and rewards." (p. 50). The development of these theories requires us to understand who HLLs are in various contexts and how they see, perceive, interpret, present, and represent themselves in those contexts. We must also differentiate among different language groups with which HLLs are affiliated, and the relationship of those groups with the society at large. Only with this knowledge can we come up with effective practices or theories for classroom settings.

In this chapter, we apply the continua of biliteracy model (Hornberger, 1989a; Hornberger & Skilton-Sylvester, 2000; Hornberger, 2003) as an analytical framework for understanding the ecology of HL learning. The chapter is divided into three main sections. In the first, we explain our views on identity and biliteracy and briefly describe the continua of biliteracy. Next, we analyze how HLLs position themselves and are positioned in the continua of context, content, media, and development. Finally, we offer suggestions for dealing with these learners in our classrooms.

Conceptual Framework

Identity

Taking an ecological perspective, we use the terms *self-concept* or *self-system* interchangeably with *identity*, a hierarchical and multidimensional construct involving the perceptions, descriptions, and evaluations of one's self in relation to significant others, the social environment, and specific contexts.[2] Because of the complex web of relationships surrounding individuals and their environments, identity is crucial in a child's development and learning (Erikson, 1968; Yawkey, 1980). As such, identity contributes to children's sense (or lack thereof) of belonging, worth, competence, and achievements. The notion that there are multiple selves/identities, which are situated and contextually defined, regulated by self and others, and constantly negotiated, contested, shaped and reshaped, becomes central in the learning of a HL and HC.

Biliteracy[3]

Biliteracy, the conjunction between bilingualism and literacy, can be defined as "any and all instances in which communication occurs in two (or more) languages in or around writing" (Hornberger, 1990, p. 213). This definition follows from Heath's (1982) definition of literacy events as "occasions in which written language is integral to the nature of participants' interactions and their interpretive processes and strategies" (Heath, 1982, p. 50). As in Heath's definition, the centrality of communication in and around writing, via processes and strategies of interaction and interpretation, is viewed as key to defining and understanding biliteracy. However, unlike Heath's definition, our definition refers to the use of two or more language varieties and encompasses not only literacy events, but also other literacy instances, e.g., the actors, practices, and sites involved (Hornberger & Skilton-Sylvester, 2000; Hornberger, 2000). Furthermore, by biliteracy we mean not only schooled literacy, but also "the community funds of knowledge" (Moll, 1992, p. 20) in HL students' homes and communities. While HLLs need to acquire the literacies of the dominant society, their biliteracies in Standard English and the HL and HC should become part of their empowering tools as well.

Our view is in concert with the goals proposed by the New London Group (1996)—namely "creating access to the evolving language of work, power, and community, and fostering the critical engagement necessary for [learners] to design their social futures and achieve success through fulfilling employment" (p. 60). The Group defines traditional literacy pedagogy as "teaching and learning to read and write in page-bound, official, standard forms of the national language" (pp. 60–61). As such, literacy pedagogy has been restricted to "formalized, monolingual, monocultural, and rule-governed forms of language" (p. 61). In place of this restrictive view, the Group advocates broadening literacy teaching and learning to include negotiation of multiple discourses. Its emphases on enabling learners to seek access in the language of power, taking into account the context of our diverse societies, and engaging in the negotiation of multiple discourses mirror much of the theoretical grounding of the continua of biliteracy framework.

The original impetus for Hornberger's (1989a) review of the literature on biliteracy was an ethnographic research project initiated in Philadelphia in 1987, the Literacy in Two Languages Project.[4] Searching for a framework to underpin that research and finding little scholarly work attending explicitly to biliteracy, Hornberger looked instead to the literatures on bilingualism and the teaching of second/foreign languages and the literatures on literacy and the teaching of reading/writing. Although we often characterize bilingualism and literacy in terms of polar opposites—such as first language (L1) versus second language (L2), monolingual versus bilingual individuals, oral versus literate societies—-what emerges from these two bodies of literature is that such polar opposites represent only theoretical endpoints on a continuum of features (cf. Kelly, 1969). Further, when we consider biliteracy as the conjunction of literacy and bilingualism, it becomes clear that these continua are interrelated dimensions of one whole. In fact, it is in the dynamic, rapidly changing, and sometimes contested spaces along and across the intersecting continua that most biliteracy use and learning occur. These insights became the basis for the continua of biliteracy model, which Hornberger (1989a) first proposed and which has since informed her own and her students' research, as well as colleagues' research nationally and internationally (Hornberger, 2003). Following is a brief introduction to the continua framework.

Continua of Biliteracy Model

The continua of biliteracy, proposed in Hornberger (1989a) and revised in Hornberger & Skilton-Sylvester (2000), offers a framework in which to situate research, teaching, and language planning in linguistically diverse settings. The continuum model conveys the notion that points on the continuum are not finite, static, or discrete. Further, the model portrays the four continua as intersecting and nested, demonstrating the multiple interrelationships between bilingualism and literacy in the development of biliteracy.

Figure 1.1 illustrates how HLLs are positioned and how they position themselves in terms of: (1) the macro and micro *contexts* in which they learn and use their HL; (2) their HL *development* in terms of proficiency, expertise, and affiliation (Rampton, 1995); (3) the heritage and identity *contents* they express; and (4) the standardization and status concerns surrounding the HL *media* they acquire and use.

Each of the four sets of continua has three dimensions. Specifically, the model depicts biliteracy as it occurs in contexts encompassing micro to macro levels and characterized by varying mixes along the oral-literate and bilingual-monolingual continua. It further depicts the development of biliteracy along intersecting receptive-productive, oral-written, and L1-L2 language skills continua and as it occurs with content ranging from minority to majority perspectives and experiences, vernacular to literary styles and genres, and contextualized to decontextualized language texts (Skilton-Sylvester, 1997; Hornberger & Skilton-Sylvester, 2000). Finally, it illustrates how development occurs when the biliterate individual's exposure varies from simultaneous to successive, the linguistic structures vary from dissimilar to similar, and the scripts range from divergent to convergent.

Figure 1.2 and Figure 1.3 further illustrate the continua of biliteracy, characterizing the nested and intersecting nature of the four sets of continua. Figure (less powerful) ⇔ (more powerful)

Context

micro	⇔	macro
oral	⇔	literate
bi(multi)lingual	⇔	monolingual

Content

minority	⇔	majority
vernacular	⇔	literary
contextualized	⇔	decontextualized

Media

simultaneous exposure	⇔	successive exposure
dissimilar structures	⇔	similar structures
divergent scripts	⇔	convergent scripts

Development

reception	⇔	production
oral	⇔	written
L1	⇔	L2

Figure 1.1 Continua of Biliteracy

1.2 shows the nested relationships among the continua; Figure 1.3 depicts the context continuum as a cluster of its intersecting sub-continua.

The model suggests that the more learners and users are able to draw from across the whole of each continuum, the greater are the chances for their full biliterate development and expression (Hornberger, 1989a). Implicit in this suggestion is the recognition that there has usually *not* been attention paid to all points. In fact in educational policy regarding biliteracy, there tends to be an implicit privileging of one end of the continua over the other such that it is associated with more power (e.g., written over oral development, literary content over vernacular content). Hornberger & Skilton-Sylvester (2000) suggest the need to contest this privileging by paying attention to, granting agency to, and making space for actors and practices at what have traditionally been the less powerful ends of the continua.

So far, we have defined what we mean by identity and biliteracy and have introduced the continua of biliteracy model. We will now use the model to analyze the issues that HLLs face.

Applying the Continua of Biliteracy Model to HLLs

In our discussion of each set of continua, we highlight a theme that helps make the HLL issues salient. The theme for the context continua is *E Pluribus Unum*,

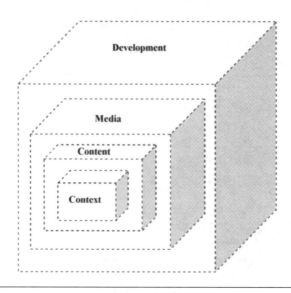

Figure 1.2 Nested Relationships among the Continua of Biliteracy

building on Lo Bianco's (2001) analysis of the "official English" debates in the 104th U.S. Congress. Here we look at how the creative tension in U.S. language ideology has affected the contexts in which HLLs find themselves. In the content continua, we highlight the theme *Bringing Heritage Forward*. Here we question the kind of content HLLs are exposed to and the extent of their engagement with this content. In the media continua, the theme "*Who*" *Needs* "*It*"?, draws attention to HLs as a critical medium of communication and instruction on both societal

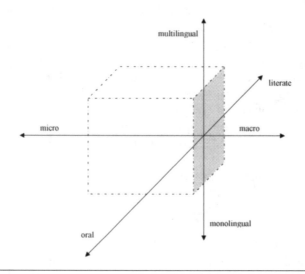

Figure 1.3 An Illustration of Intersecting Relationships: The Context Continua

and individual levels and explains why their maintenance is vital. Finally, in the development continua, the theme *I Pledge Allegiance* alludes to Rampton's (1995) typology for characterizing language proficiency.

Context Continua: E Pluribus Unum

The context continua include three sub-continua. The first is the *micro-macro continuum*, in which factors from individual to societal to global are seen as affecting the development of bilingualism or biliteracy. The second is the *monolingual-bilingual continuum*, which concerns the use of the L1, the L2, or both. The third sub-continuum, the *oral-literate continuum*, involves the extent a language is used in the oral and/or literate modality. In our application of the context continua to HLLs, we examine both how society positions HLLs and how HLLs position themselves. This is consistent with our view that identity means not just how one sees oneself but also how one is viewed by others.

How society positions HLLs

Heritage Language Education (HLE) in its "purest" form would refer to education targeted at heritage language learners. This would include "classic" forms of HLE such as *ethnic mother tongue schools* (e.g., Fishman, 1980; Fishman, Gertner, Lowy, & Milán, 1985), also increasingly known as *heritage language schools* or *community language teaching* (Clyne, 1991; Horvath & Vaughan 1991; S.C. Wang 1996, 1999; X. Wang 1996), and *heritage language teaching in foreign language departments at the college level* for second or third-generation immigrant students studying their own ancestral language as a foreign language (e.g., Gonzalez Pino & Pino, 2000; Valdés, 2000). It would also include *indigenous or aboriginal language revitalization* initiatives such as heritage language teaching at *tribal colleges* or in *language nests* (following the Maori *Kohanga Reo*) (Dune, 1999; May, 1999, 2002; Spolsky, 2003), *immersion camps*, or *mentor-apprentice partnerships*; as well as most *immersion, two-way, maintenance* (and some *transitional*) *bilingual education programs* in K–12 education; and conventional foreign language programs in the K–12 setting. All of these programs and the policies that undergird them position HLLs in particular ways.

The events of September 11, 2001, have led to a heightened sense of urgency about promoting an ecological, resource view of the diverse languages spoken in our communities. Lo Bianco (2001) analyzes *unum* (assimilationist) and *pluribus* (pluralist) discourses in the political debates surrounding "official English" in the 104th Congress of the United States. Both discourses have arguably always been present in the United States, waxing and waning with the times. The resulting ideological tension is captured in the United States motto, *E pluribus Unum* ("out of many one") from which Lo Bianco takes his designations. This tension has been played out in U.S. foreign language, bilingual, indigenous, and community immigrant language education, in all of which HLLs are increasingly being recognized.

Because of our monolingual ideology, English and foreign languages have always been strange bedfellows. For example, for most of the nineteenth century prior to World War I, foreign language education was often offered in the form of bilingual education to heritage language learners (Castellanos with Leggio, 1983). Each international conflict (World War I, World War II, the Korean War, the Vietnam Conflict, and the Cold War) changed the nature of ethnic language education (Lantolf & Sunderman, 2001). The Americanization Movement through education (Farrell 1980; Castellanos with Leggio, 1983; Crawford, 1989) made assimilation its ultimate goal. Language ideology increasingly favored English only.

The case in bilingual education is equally complicated, with a vast difference between overt and covert language policies and ideologies. On the surface, bilingual education appears to advocate the learning of both the native and English languages. However, most programs are transitional, geared toward the acquisition of English language proficiency and literacy.[5] Throughout the 1960s and 1970s, the country was caught in heated debates over bilingual education, culminating in the case of *Lau v. Nichols* (1974). Ironically, although the *Lau* remedy recognized bilingual children's rights to a meaningful education, it did not acknowledge their home language. The discourse of *Unum* has been gaining ground, with a growing number of states passing English-only legislation (California in 1998, Arizona in 2000, Massachusetts in 2002; Crawford, 2003).[6]

So far, our discussion points out that, although there is no official language policy in the United States, the language ideology underlying all language education has been guided by the spirit of *E pluribus Unum*. For a language minority child, the end goal is to learn English at the expense of maintaining the heritage language. As a result, despite empirical evidence showing the benefits of developmental maintenance bilingual programs in which native language is simultaneously developed alongside English (Fishman, 1968; Otheguy & Otto, 1980, cited in McKay, 1993; Conklin & Lourie, 1983; Freeman, 1998), most bilingual programs in the United States are transitional (Fishman, 1968; Ruiz, 1988; McKay 1993) and set the learning and use of English as the ultimate goal.

On the other hand, an interesting phenomenon co-exists with this shift toward English—namely that although most community languages are not encouraged or taught in schools, they are not prohibited in private spheres of community lives (Macías & Wiley, 1998) and continue to be used side by side with English in immigrant communities. However, because there are powerful educational, social, economic, political, cultural, and linguistic forces leading toward the shift from ethnic language to English (see Conklin & Lourie, 1983; Gal, 1979; Kroon, 1990), many educators of these community schools find themselves constantly battling to "revers[e] language shift" (Fishman, 1991) or, in other words, preserve the "pluribus" under "Unum."

How HLLs position themselves

We shall now turn our attention to how HLLs position themselves in social contexts, with specific reference to their choice of learning or using either English or the HL.

We have previously defined identity as consisting of hierarchical, multidimensional, but ever-changing images, descriptions, projections, and evaluations of self and self in the eyes of others. Closely connected to this notion of multiple selves is the notion of performed social identity and co-membership (Erickson & Shultz, 1982). Each of these multiple selves carries with it a set of rights, obligations, norms and behaviors. In social interaction, participants evaluate and perform each social role, communicating these roles through shared codes (e.g., dressing, ways of speaking, thinking, behaving, and acting). The more codes or attributes one shares with other participants, the more co-membership one feels. This sense of belonging is the basis of social membership, which Erickson and Shultz (1982) further divide into primary and secondary membership. Primary membership refers to the full knowledge of appropriate ways of interaction inside and outside the family or speech community to which one is connected, while secondary membership refers to partial knowledge of ways of interaction of the groups with which one is not intimately connected.

Here, we may extend Erickson and Shultz's notion of primary and secondary membership to the case of HLLs. On one end of the spectrum are those who grow up with a home language other than English. These individuals may be said to be primary HL members. On the other end of the spectrum are those who come from multiracial adoption or who are fourth or fifth generation. These individuals may be said to be secondary HL members. Falling between these two ends of the spectrum are those who grow up with two or more home languages and who may identify themselves as either primary or secondary HL members—or somewhere in between. The opposite is also true: If HLLs identify their primary membership with English and the dominant society, their membership in the HL and HC community may become secondary. In other words, identification as primary or secondary members may be an exercise of personal choice.[7] It is important to note in this respect that group membership is not static but instead changes according to the conditions of interaction (i.e., with whom, in what situation, and with what purpose the interaction occurs.)

Without the recognition that HLL identity is as much chosen as assigned, the efforts of language educators to instruct these learners may not be maximally effective. Norms of group interaction are not uniformly shared across language, race, ethnicity, gender, or class lines. Furthermore, the desire to belong to or dissociate from a group may prompt individuals to either acquire or mask knowledge about how to act, talk, and behave in a given group. The literature on social group boundaries helps to illuminate HLL identity. By definition, boundaries entail inclusion or exclusion, integration or isolation, alliance or alienation, sharing or division, thus exerting sanctioning power to group members (Erickson & Shultz,

1982). Bucholtz (1995) suggests the notion of "passing" in the case where one's race, ethnicity, gender, or class is ambiguous to others but where one actively constructs an image of self as a member of a desired group. Similar to this is the notion of "crossing" in situations where one clearly is not a member of the group, but strives to cross the line with a ticket of linguistic, cultural, or any other identity marker (Rampton, 1995). As research has demonstrated (Eckert, 1989; Erickson & Shultz, 1982; Gumperz, 1977, 1982; Gumperz & Hymes, 1972; Myers-Scotton, 1993; Rampton, 1995; Zentella, 1997), group members frequently use code-switching, cultural style switching, or dress-code switching to change identity (i.e., when passing or crossing group boundaries) or simply to manifest existing group membership.

Many studies of language choice, use, and identity confirm this sense of group membership and illustrate the agency that learners exert in determining and demonstrating who they are. For example, Peirce's (1995) study of social identity in adult English as a second language (ESL) learners documented that, in addition to the traditional constructs attributed to learning a second language (e.g., personality traits, motivation, opportunities to practice), perceived relations of power between speakers (e.g., racism, sexism, classism) play a significant role. Similarly, McKay and Wong's (1996) study of Chinese-speaking ESL students in California also illustrated that learners establish their changing identities within specific conversations while simultaneously engaging in multiple discourses that reflect their memberships with the dominant and the ethnic communities.

To resist being viewed as powerless by outsiders, learners may reject unidimensional identities imposed on them. For example, adolescent Southeast Asian refugees often negotiate among at least four identities: Southeast Asian, American, refugee, and adolescent (Ascher, 1989). Similarly, Mexican American gang members express a deep sense of multiple marginality, displacement, isolation, and alienation (Vigil, 1997; see also Huff, 1996; Klein, 1971). Gangs offer membership in a protective, nurturing sub-culture, thus allowing their members to assume active and powerful identities. Further evidence that learners may reject mainstream values is shown in Nagle's (1999) study of her basic writing class at a vocational high school. In this study, Nagle reports that her students reject her version of the American Dream, demonstrating that due to their working class identities and perspectives they have their own, differing, version of the American Dream.

A clear example of resistance to an imposed identity is documented in research conducted in a HLL classroom at the University of Texas at San Antonio (Gonzalez Pino & Pino, 2000). The researchers found that many students identified by the university as HLLs do not show much interest in registering for HL classes (Gonzalez Pino & Pino, 2000, pp. 29–30). They also found that the students generally: (1) do not see themselves as HLLs; (2) show lack of confidence in their language abilities and skills; (3) need a more in-depth analysis of their linguistic skills and curricular needs; (4) have internalized societal negative attitudes toward their language; and (5) resist being separated/segregated into the heritage tracks. Potowski (2002) had similar findings in a study of Spanish HL students at the University of Illinois. The HL students' sensitivity about their language ability is particularly telling: "While nonnative Spanish students are corrected often by TAs [teaching assistants], [heritage language] students experience 'correction' differently because it is tied in with their personal and cultural history" (p. 40).

Clearly, the decision to learn and use English or the HL represents the dynamic interface of ability, opportunity, incentive, individual and social constraints, and personal choices. Given this state of affairs, we contend that language educators, language planners, and language users must make concerted efforts to address these issues.[8] In other words, we take an inclusive view of those who should be involved in determining the courses of action for HLE and HLLs. A first step in trying to help HLLs is finding out how these individuals view themselves. Freire's (1970, 1974) problem-solving and self-discovery approach to examining ethnic, racial, gender, linguistic, and cultural relationships with one's own group and the dominant society would work well in helping HL students define themselves. It would also help them understand that multiple memberships are necessary and possible in their negotiation of self-identity and empowerment.

Content Continua: Bringing Heritage Forward

The content continua include three intersecting sub-continua. The first is the *minority-majority continuum*, which refers to the extent that minority voices and literacies are accepted or incorporated in the majority literacies. The second is the *vernacular-literary continuum*, which refers to the extent that "personal," "outside," and "unofficial" texts are allowed to be part of the schooled, mainstream, and standard knowledge. The last is the *contextualized-decontextualized continuum*, which refers to the extent of contextualization of what is taught and learned, as well as whether or not the information that students learn contributes to building a coherent knowledge base.

In this section, we highlight the theme *Bringing Heritage Forward*, focusing on academic content first, followed by popular culture/mass media content. By academic content, we refer to the multiple discourses embedded in the curriculum, textbooks, classroom practices, peer interactions, school structure, and educational and societal expectations. By popular culture/mass media content, we refer to the topics, messages, images, and stereotypes of different language groups in the mass media and popular culture. The sub-continua of content are addressed in these two foci.

How HLLs position themselves and are positioned through academic content
Schooling has traditionally privileged majority, literary, and decontextualized contents. The continua model, on the other hand, posits that *what* (i.e., the content) biliterate learners and users read and write is as important as *how* (i.e.,

the development), *where* (i.e., the context) or *when* and *by what means* (i.e., the media) they do so. It therefore argues for greater curricular attention to minority, vernacular and contextualized whole language texts in academic contexts.[9] Assumptions in this model about their importance in the learning of biliteracy parallel other developments in literacy research that emphasize content. These developments are informed by critical perspectives on language and literacy, such as critical discourse analysis (Fairclough, 1995; Norton, 1997), critical language awareness (Clark, Fairclough, Ivanic, & Martin-Jones, 1990; 1991), critical literacy (Lankshear, 1997; Shor & Pari, 1999), critical ethnography (May, 1997), and critical pedagogy (Goldstein, 1997).

The continua model highlights the importance of contextualized texts and discourses that allow learners to draw on and express minority identities/perspectives and vernacular genres/styles. There are many possible ways of being in the world, or in Gee's (1996) term, Discourses: "gangs, academic disciplines, bar gatherings, ethnic groups, friendship networks, types of men, women, gays, children, students, classrooms, workers, workplaces, etc." (Gee, 1997, p. xv). Yet, educators must be aware that these Discourses are not equally available to their biliterate students: instead, they are ordered hierarchically within the politics of daily life (Lankshear, 1997).

Moll and González (1994) have argued that "community funds of knowledge" (sometimes called household or local funds of knowledge)[10] are a resource that can be drawn on in schooling for language minority populations. In the words of one teacher collaborator, "the teacher mediates by creating curricula that reflect both the standard curriculum and the themes, languages, and culture of students' lives… when teachers incorporate household funds of knowledge into the curriculum and use dialogic teaching methods, students are liberated to direct their own learning" (Floyd-Tenery, 1995, p. 12).

How HLLs position themselves and are positioned through popular culture/mass media content

As we discussed above, the academic content in the educational system often privileges official, institutional, and decontextualized texts and literacy practices. The popular content in mass media exhibits the same privileging. For example, the cultural stereotypes of various groups are usually unidimensional, as seen from the perspective of an Anglo person. To an average HLL, the struggle of determining the content—the identity—of who they are and how they should project themselves is real and ongoing in daily life. In short, there are many "possible selves" (McGinnis, 2002) to assume, and different spaces—linguistic, cultural, temporal, and physical—to fill. The politics of these identities and spaces will bring both intended and unintended consequences to the individuals in education, work place, and personal and social life.

Another content issue challenging all HLLs, regardless of the language group to which they belong, is that the term "heritage" sometimes carries a negative connotation, pointing to the (ancient, primitive) past rather than to a (modern, technological) future (Baker & Jones, 1998).[11] As Hodgkinson (1992) suggests concerning the current condition of Native Americans:

> The current generation of American Indian and Alaska Native youth have a genuine choice between being proud to be an American and being proud to be a Native. As stated, those choices appear mutually exclusive. If they wish, they can live a tradition-oriented Native lifestyle, or they can move completely into the mainstream American middle class. Or (and this is the more complex choice) they can lead lives that include productive elements of both (p. 4).

The challenge of finding an alternative way of living with both the heritage and mainstream languages and cultures is the heart of the whole HLE issue. Therefore, some of the fundamental questions that HLLs should ask themselves are: "What are the meanings, purposes, and functions of HL and HC in my life? What identities do I assume with which language? How would my decision to use and learn which language affect my relationship with my own family, my group, and groups to which I would like to belong?" Perhaps when we recognize the need to approach English language learning and the HL from the standpoint of the significance and representation of societal and individual identities, we will be able to convince those in the mainstream of the importance of and need for maintaining the HL alongside English. In this way, both individuals and society will be able to enjoy the benefits of bi(multi)lingualism and bi(multi)culturalism.

Media Continua: "Who" Needs "It"?

The media continua consist of the actual communicative repertoires, or language varieties and scripts, through which multilingual literacies are expressed. Also of importance are the sequences or configurations in which these literacies are acquired and used. Three sub-continua are examined: the sequence of exposure to or acquisition of the languages/literacies (ranging from simultaneous to successive); the linguistic structures of the languages involved (ranging from dissimilar to similar); and the relationship of their orthographic scripts (ranging from divergent to convergent).

In this section we consider what language(s) HLLs need for which purposes, asking the big question: "Who" needs "it"? Our discussion seeks to encourage scrutiny of commonly made assumptions about the nature of languages and their structures/scripts; the relationship between various languages; the ways that two or more languages may be learned and used; the functions that different languages play for individuals engaging in personal and social changes; and finally the language needs that individuals may have in order to "get by" in life.

For example, in the United States bilingual ballots are often provided so that all citizens may exercise their right to vote.[12] However, not all states have bilingual ballots; and in those states where they are provided, not all languages are available. The question, then, is who gets included and who gets excluded? How is the decision to have bilingual ballots made? A host of similar questions can be asked about other domains such as in the workplace or at school. Who makes the decision whether bilingual use in the workplace is welcome or prohibited? Who enforces such a decision? Who has the right to tell whom which language to use or learn? How are decisions made (and by whom) about the language of instruction and assessment of language minority students? These are questions to which there are no simple answers. Our purpose here is to point out several ways to examine these issues, while at the same time advocating a case-by-case approach and the collaboration of decision makers and their grass-roots counterparts, the HL communities.

How HLLs position themselves and are positioned through medium of communication

Consistent with both the ethnography of communication (Gumperz & Hymes, 1972; Hymes, 1974) and the conceptions of the New London Group (1996) consideration of the media of biliteracy entails attention not just to different languages, but also to different dialects, styles, discourses, and communicative modes (including technological ones) as they are acquired and used—not in a dichotomized sequence but more often in criss-crossed, hybrid mixes. We do not mean to suggest that incorporating multiple varieties, scripts, communicative modes, and criss-crossed paths of acquisition and use proceeds unproblematically in schools or other biliteracy learning contexts. Indeed, given that biliteracy implies the intersection of biliterate learners' multiple literacy worlds in particular literacy sites (cf. Hornberger, 2000), some implicit conflict in norms, practices, and identities is inevitable. It is precisely in contexts of cross-cultural or intercultural communication, where "notions of group membership and community can no longer be accepted as fixed characteristics and well-defined totalities" (Rampton, 1992, p. 54), that relationships among differing language and literacy practices are most evident.

Research into sites of cross-cultural interaction and biliteracy practices brings to the fore notions of mediation and hybridity[13]—"the productive tension between official and unofficial discourse" (Cahnmann, 2001, p. 175). The role of literacy mediator (Reder, 1987) is a recurring one as local people negotiate with outsiders, government bureaucracies, or other national or globalizing agencies, and their languages and literacies. Hybridity is evidenced by teachers' and students' acceptance and encouragement of multiple languages and registers, unauthorized side-talk, movement, and spontaneous interaction and collaboration. Examples of hybridity have been captured in a study by Gutiérrez, Baquedano-López, and Tejeda (1999) of a second–third grade two-way Spanish immersion classroom in Los Angeles. Gutiérrez and co-authors show how the participants in this classroom reorganize the activity and incorporate local knowledge, thereby creating third spaces "in which alternative and competing discourses and positionings transform conflict and difference into rich zones of collaboration and learning" (Gutiérrez, Baquedano-López, & Tejeda, 1999, pp. 286–287). Mediation and hybridity are useful, indeed essential, constructs in understanding the role of multiple varieties, scripts, communicative modes, and criss-crossed paths of acquisition and use in cross-cultural and intercultural communication.

How HLLs position themselves and are positioned through medium of instruction

As noted previously, the impetus for the continua of biliteracy model was the "Literacy in Two Languages" project, a long-term comparative, ethnographic research project in two language minority communities of Philadelphia (Hornberger, 1989a, 1992). We draw on some examples from this project to illustrate how the media of biliteracy can inform HL educational practices.

In two-way bilingual programs in the Puerto Rican community, Hornberger and her associates found that faculty and staff continually face challenging media-related decisions with regard to: (1) the placement of students in English-dominant and Spanish-dominant streams; (2) the distribution of English and Spanish in the program structure and the classroom; and (3) the co-existence of various standard and nonstandard varieties of English and Spanish and the implications of this for instruction and assessment. In terms of the continua, the first two issues relate to the question of simultaneous versus successive exposure to (or acquisition) of the languages/literacies, while the third touches on language varieties' structures and scripts. The continua model helped the researchers to understand that, given the myriad constellations of language use, ability, and exposure in a community where ongoing circular migration from Puerto Rico to Philadelphia and back is a fact of life for nearly everyone, the categories "English-dominant" and "Spanish-dominant" were not self-evident. Most Puerto Rican children do not grow up with just one mother tongue and then acquire the L2 in school. Rather, they are constantly crossing back and forth between both languages.

The study also shed light on challenges to two-way bilingual program structure and classroom interaction. Students arriving (and re-arriving) at school with widely different constellations of biliterate expertise, affiliations, and inheritances challenge schools seeking to develop a two-way bilingual program that builds on both languages for all students (cf. Hornberger & Micheau, 1993). Hornberger (1990) studied how one fourth/fifth-grade homeroom teacher at Potter Thomas School created successful learning contexts for her students' biliterate development and, specifically, how she built students' interaction with text. The study highlighted how the homeroom teacher "allows small-group peer interaction to occur spontaneously and asystematically as a natural outgrowth of shared cultural values, emphasizes her students' community-based prior knowledge, and seeks to help her students to 'connect and transfer' strategies across languages" (Hornberger, 1990, p. 227). This teacher had found ways to build successfully on her students' biliteracy. Such an approach made a strength rather than a weakness out of students' criss-crossed, simultaneous (rather than successive) acquisition of two languages and literacies.

A third *media*-related challenge that Hornberger and her associates uncovered is the co-existence of standard and non-standard varieties of English and Spanish within the school community's repertoire. The continua model shed light on the implications of these co-existing varieties for instruction and assessment. From the beginning, their fieldwork documented Puerto Rican, Cuban, and other Latin American varieties of Spanish as well as school standard and African-American varieties of English all in use within one school.[14] However, the research initially focused on (1) the relative similarities between Spanish and English and (2) the convergences between their writing systems, as potential resources for transfer of literacy from one to the other. The continua model helped the researchers understand that dissimilarities and divergences across varieties *within* each language (which might well impede literacy development even in the case of acquiring only one language) require attention just as much as the similarities and convergences between the languages.

To pose a not entirely hypothetical example: After many years of English language standardized testing, a school with a two-way program serving Puerto Rican children in Philadelphia decided to inaugurate Spanish language standardized testing in an effort to obtain a more representative picture of their students' biliterate accomplishments. However, the only testing materials available reflected Mexican, not Puerto Rican, language varieties and identities; thus they could not render a true picture of Puerto Rican students' expertise in Spanish. Similarly, another school elected to develop portfolio assessment in Spanish and called in an English-language expert on the subject. This expert was stymied by the discovery that the teachers in the school, who spoke varieties of Puerto Rican, Cuban, and other Latin American Spanish, could not agree on the "correct" form of Spanish to use. The continua model seeks to shed light on these kinds of contested spaces in HLE.

Development Continua: I Pledge Allegiance

The development continua consist of three intersecting sub-continua: reception-production, oral-written, and L1-L2. The first of these involves the sequence of biliteracy development along the continuum of receptive (listening and reading) to productive (speaking and writing) skills. The second involves the similar development along the continuum of oral and written skills. Finally, the L1-L2 continuum pertains to the closely interrelated development of the L1 and the L2, as well as the extent to which the knowledge of one language aids or interferes with the acquisition of the other (Hornberger, 2003). To explicate the development continua, we have selected the theme *I Pledge Allegiance* in allusion to Rampton's (1995) discussion of HL expertise and allegiance.

In his study of adolescent groups of African-Caribbean, Punjabi, and Anglo descent in Ashmead and South London, Rampton (1995) noted that regardless of their language inheritance, these adolescents used linguistic "crossings" (i.e., varieties of Creole, Punjabi, and stylized Asian English) to differentiate or solidify their group membership and culture, in the process often transcending cultural or ethnic boundaries. Based on these findings, he suggests that we view bilinguals' language proficiency in terms of their *expertise* on the one hand (i.e., their skill, proficiency, and ability to operate with a language) and their *allegiance* (i.e., their identification with a language and the values, meanings, and identities it stands for) on the other.

His research led him to question the adequacy of the concept *native speaker*. In its place, he proposes the dual concepts of expertise and allegiance as a "simple and workable set of terms that try to recognize rather than obscure the dynamic social and institutional processes through which sociolinguistic identities are defined" (Rampton, 1995, p. 344). He then distinguishes allegiance as consisting of *affiliation* and *inheritance*, both of which refer to language loyalty and the attitudes of a speaker toward a certain language. However, while affiliation refers to "a connection between people and groups that are considered to be separate or different," inheritance concerns itself with "the continuity between people and groups who are felt to be closely linked" (Rampton, 1995, p. 342). That is, affiliation takes place across social or ethnic groups and inheritance occurs within the group. Thus according to Rampton, individuals may develop a social identity linked to a language whether or not they are native speakers of that language.

While Rampton analyzes individual attitudes toward language, Ruiz (1988) views them from a societal standpoint, or *language orientation*: "a complex of dispositions toward language and its role, and toward languages and their role in society" (p. 4). According to Ruiz, because much of the activity in language planning in the 1970s and 1980s had been carried out in newly independent nations formed from formerly-colonized states in Africa, Asia, and elsewhere, the emphasis tended to be on "language as *problem*" [italics added] (1988, pp. 6–10). In the United States, however, the problem orientation stems from a different circumstance, i.e., our assimilationist stance toward learning English. As previously discussed, this stance is not a recent phenomenon, having been prevalent throughout U.S. history. However, since the 1950s, many social concerns (such as underachievement in schools, poverty, and civil rights issues of minority groups) have split this orientation into two: the *language as problem* orientation (including linguistic, cultural, and racial problems) (Bereiter & Engelman, 1966; Ravitch, 1983; Bernstein, 1972; Tyack, 1996; August & Hakuta, 1998) and the *language as right* orientation (including civil and human rights) (Leibowitz, 1971; Ruiz, 1988). In recent years and in the international arena, proponents for Linguistic Human Rights (see Phillipson, Rannut, & Skutnabb-Kangas, 1995) argue that an individual should be able to identify positively with their mother tongue and that it should be respected by others, thereby strengthening the camp of the rights orientation. Finally, since the late 1980s and early 1990s, the *language as resource* orientation has been gaining support (Simon, 1980; Ruiz, 1988, pp. 14–18; Brecht & Walton, 1994; Brecht & Ingold, 2002).

Using Rampton's notions of expertise and allegiance and Ruiz's orientations toward language as problem, right, and resource, we now turn our attention to how society positions HLLs and how HLLs position themselves on these issues related to the biliteracy development of HLLs.

How society positions HLLs' expertise and allegiance as a problem

As we have previously pointed out, HLLs' underdeveloped language ability in either language has been viewed as a problem in the educational system. For example, in a bilingual or ESL classroom, HLLs are often referred to as Limited English Proficient (LEP) students, although the current effort has re-labeled them as English Language Learners (ELLs) (e.g., see August & Hakuta, 1998). Furthermore, the lack of English language ability exhibited by many immigrants often has been framed as an allegiance issue or a refusal to learn English, as many letters in the op-ed columns of newspapers show (e.g., Hariton, 2005; Pavia, 2005; Pierce, 2005; Weiss, 2003). That these immigrants may face insurmountable obstacles in their social, economic, political, family, or educational lives is often omitted or ignored.

In a foreign language classroom, HLLs are sometimes called "false beginners" (Christensen & Wu, 1993), as if they enter the classroom with the intention of cheating the system. Or, as a French teacher vividly puts it, they are "Swiss cheese," whose language performance is full of unpredictable holes (Corine Termonia, personal communication, October 10, 2000). The goal of instruction has been to convert the Swiss cheese into American cheese, standardized in form and without holes.[15]

How society positions HLLs' expertise and allegiance as a right

In bilingual and ESL education, the HLLs' right to a better education through L1 instruction has been increasingly acknowledged, along with the rights and resource orientations. More two-way bilingual, developmental, and immersion programs, in which both HLLs and children from other groups learn from one another, provide the evidence for this acknowledgement. On a deeper level, unfortunately, the goal of most bilingual programs is still English language proficiency and literacy development, along with the underlying ideology of assimilation. The HL is generally used only as a vehicle of arriving at that goal, not as a goal in itself.

Viewing language as a symbol of allegiance will continue to prevail in the current climate of post-9/11 patriotism and the Standards-based education movement. The former equates the ability to speak English with allegiance to the American identity, while the latter puts English proficiency and literacy as the center piece of the No Child Left Behind Act of 2001 (U.S. Department of Education, n.d.). Although Standards-based educational reform started with the admirable goal of raising all students' academic achievements, it has made Standard English the official language and literacy. In particular, given that foreign language learning remains outside the five assessed core areas (Math, Reading, Writing, Science, and Social Studies) in most states, literacy in another language, culture, or non-standard variety becomes even more marginalized under the pressure of high stakes testing.

How society positions HLLs' expertise and allegiance as a resource
Since the late 1980s and early 1990s, the rhetoric for economic competitiveness and national security has helped foreign language education gain new ground (Brecht & Ingold, 2002; Lambert, 1986; Tucker, 1984). Given their ability to achieve a high level of proficiency and literacy in the target language (particularly in the less commonly taught languages),[16] HLLs are finally being recognized as a resource rather than a problem. Consequently, language educators are now searching for ways to improve HLLs' motivation, proficiency and literacy in the HL and to develop appropriate materials, curriculum, and programs for them.

Regardless of the progress in these areas, however, Ricento (1998, cited in Valdés, 2000, p. 239) reminds us that the "deep values" within our society have not recognized immigrant and indigenous languages as a resource whose main-tenance is intrinsically valuable to our social well-being. At the same time, the arguments from foreign language education focused on the resource orientation have not interested all constituents, particularly members of the mainstream group, in taking part in the HL movement (Wang, 2004). According to Wang, there are two major flaws in the current resource argument. First, it does not acknowledge and, hence, has not sufficiently addressed, the nation's English only ideology. Second, not all HLs and their speakers in the United States are perceived by the dominant society to have equal status, nor are they viewed with equal sentiment. Thus, members of those language groups whose status is less valued have tended to find the rhetoric of economic competitiveness and national security irrelevant or counterproductive in their efforts to maintain and develop the HL and HC in the young.

Advocating for a HL without first mentioning English immediately raises concerns for those members of the dominant society who view multilingual-ism as a divisive rather than a unifying tool. Whether we admit it or not, in the United States there exists a hierarchy of value for languages other than English. Spanish, French, German, Japanese, or Chinese, for example, are viewed as economically useful and therefore important to learn; other languages (e.g., Hmong, Hungarian, or varieties of Creole) are not. However, placing the value of HL primarily in terms of economic utility in this manner ignores one of HLL's most important assets—cultural and familial inheritance. It also excludes many HLLs of indigenous language groups whose HL does not lend itself to global market economy. On the other hand, the national security argument seems to suggest that HLLs may be the best candidates for American spies, which not only puts the group's and perhaps individuals' allegiance to the United States to the test but also simultaneously marginalizes the group's position in the dominant society, depicting them as members of "the other side." Rather than focusing on economic and national security rationales, then, Wang advocates the notion of *"English Plus Heritage,"* arguing for a more inclusive and humanistic HL policy that includes consideration of economic, political, social, educational, and personal elements.

How HLLs position their own expertise and allegiance as a problem

Both educators and HLLs tend to view HLLs' language expertise and allegiance as problematic. Building on previously-cited research (Gonzalez Pino & Pino, 2000), Potowski (2002) conducted a qualitative study of 100 HLLs and seven teaching assistants (TAs) at the University of Illinois, Urbana. Like Gonzalez Pino and Pino, Potowski noted identity and confidence issues with the HLL, citing students as saying, for example, "I learned ghetto Spanish" and "they [non HLLs] know all these rules" (pp. 37–38). Many of the participating students identified advantages of being HLLs (better oral fluency, pronunciation, and comprehension), but more disadvantages were mentioned (nonnative students had a better understanding of grammar; teachers had higher expectations for correctness and fluency from HL speakers; and HLLs may fear being seen as incompetent). This last point coincides with Krashen's (1998) notion of "language shyness." According to Krashen, HLLs who know the HL fairly well but lack late-acquired aspects of language (e.g., politeness, social class markers) tend to avoid interaction with native speakers in the HL to avoid the embarrassment of being corrected or ridiculed. This decreased interaction reduces the input they may receive from more competent speakers, and hence lessens the chance of increased proficiency. Further, because language marks social group membership, one of the implications of language shyness is alienation on the part of the HL group.

Language shyness is only one issue that HLLs face in language development. While they may view themselves as HL native speakers, their handling of form and function may be nonstandard or hybrid.[17] Much research points to the fact that a HL acquired as a child may not develop further once the onset of schooling begins in regular American schools where English is the only language of instruction. As such, HLs may show signs of attrition or fossilization (Celce-Murcia, 1991; Ellis, 1994; Hyltenstam, 1988; Selinker, 1972). Or, as Krashen (1998) and Valdés & Geoffrion-Vinci (1998) have noted, HLLs may not develop the necessary sociolinguistic repertoire or cognitive language proficiency (Cummins, 1981) to perform in an adult-like or academic setting. HLLs need help in identifying the strengths and weaknesses of their language abilities, including language awareness training to notice the similarities and differences between the HL (and its varieties) and English (Rampton, 1995). It is also possible that the teacher values and teaches only the standard variety of the language and devalues HLLs' proficiency in a nonstandard variety of the HL. These are only a few of the possible scenarios, but they are enough to illustrate the many complex issues that HLLs face.

The most severe outcome for HLLs is language loss, with possibly irreversible consequences. Cho and Krashen (1998) and Fillmore (1991) document numerous such cases in the Korean and Spanish communities. Similarly, Cho (2001) profiles immigrant families in which parents and children are "separated by a wall of words" (p. A01) that results in intergenerational conflict or communication breakdown. Many individual HLLs studied also reported having feelings of isolation and exclusion from members of their own ethnic group or with native speakers outside the United States (Cho & Krashen, 1998). Most importantly, what is lost are opportunities for intimacy, socialization, and the transfer of wisdom and experience from elders to children (G. Cho & Krashen, 1998; Fillmore, 1991). In short, family and community heritage are lost, with repercussions that affect the entire society.

How HLLs position their own expertise and allegiance as a right
The rights orientation can be seen to operate on at least two different levels. The first of these is HLLs' right to inherit their HL and HC. This means that individuals should have the opportunities and means to learn and experience the HL and HC, either from their families, communities, or at schools. Certainly this has not been the case in most U. S. schools, where bilingual education is geared toward the acquisition of English, foreign language education is limited in its language and course offerings and curricular design (e.g., Campbell & Rosenthal, 2000), and general education does not allow much space for someone from a different linguistic or cultural background.[18]

Meanwhile, community HL schools exemplify the paradox of this rights orientation. Some language groups historically do not organize HL schools (Fishman, 1991), relegating the right to educate their children to mainstream education. For those who do exercise their right and establish HL schools,[19] there appears to be a de facto "don't ask, don't tell" policy operating between public education and HL schooling. In other words, HL schools do not ask the formal educational system for assistance, nor do mainstream educators offer it. There is as yet no established mechanism for assessing the HLLs' achievement in the HL or for measuring the efficacy of these HL schools; moreover, we have no data about these schools on the local, state, or national levels.

The second rights orientation—who has the right to be the expert, to correct whom, and to claim allegiance to a particular language and culture—can be seen at the classroom level. As previously mentioned, Potowski's (2002) study indicates that while HLLs often do not mind receiving error correction from a native TA, they may resent it from a non-native TA. Gambhir (2001), in discussing truly less commonly taught languages such as Hindi, Bengali, Punjabi, Sinhala, and Zulu, describes such a classroom phenomenon: "Students who find their teachers' analyses of the target language puzzling, their nonnative errors amusing, and their discourse unnatural and slow, may have a less-than-satisfying classroom experience. For their part, teachers may find it uncomfortable to have in their class students who in some respects are more proficient in the language than they are" (p. 217).[20]

How HLLs position their own expertise and allegiance as a resource
The continua model posits the following: (1) that the development of biliteracy may start at any point on any of three intersecting continua of L1-L2, oral-to-written, and receptive-to-productive language and literacy skills, uses, and practices; (2) that biliteracy learning may proceed in any direction along those intersecting continua; and (3) that it may do so by backtracking, spurting, or criss-crossing just as readily as by progressing linearly. In addition to comprehensible input, second language learners need opportunities to produce comprehensible output (Pica, Holliday, Lewis, & Morgenthaler, 1989; Swain, 1985). Biliterate learners not only learn to read and write through heavy reliance on oral language, but also have been observed to learn to read by writing and to write by reading (Goodman & Goodman, 1983; Hudelson, 1984), to spell words in the L2 based on the L1 sound system (Edelsky, 1986), and to read their L2 beyond the level of their L2 speaking knowledge (Moll & Diaz, 1985). There is, in fact, an infinite potential for transfer of skills across any of the three continua. However, by the same token, understanding or predicting transfer is elusive if not impossible, precisely because the three continua are interrelated.

In the ethnography of communication, communicative competence is understood as situated within communicative events (Hymes, 1972; Hornberger, 1989b). Consistent with this view, the development of biliteracy in individuals occurs along the continua in direct response to the contextual demands placed on them. Using the framework of the National Foreign Language Content Standards (National Standards in Foreign Language Education Project, 1996; National Standards in Foreign Language Education Project, 1999) as an example, HLLs can draw on existing resources in various bi(multi)lingual and bi(multi)cultural contexts in their daily lives to use the HL in the following communicative modes: interpersonal (i.e., oral or written channels in which two-way negotiation of meaning takes place); interpretive (i.e., reading, listening, or viewing channels when only one-way interpretation of meaning is possible); and presentational (i.e., speaking, writing, or other channels through which individuals convey their meanings). How they achieve this and how their biliteracy development aligns with the National Standards merit further research.

Assisting HLLs to advance their language expertise requires understanding what these learners *can do with*, instead of what they *do not know about*, the HL. With this in mind, Campbell and Rosenthal (2000) compare HLLs and traditional FLLs in university FL programs, paying special attention to their phonology, grammatical rules, vocabulary, sociolinguistic rules, culture, literacy skills, and motivation. Augmenting this research base are several action plans: (1) to assist teachers in designing appropriate curriculum and materials for HLLs, Webb and Miller (2000) propose a six-category framework in linguistic proficiency, motivation, academic preparedness, cultural connectedness, emotional factors, and societal factors; and (2), to prepare teachers to deal with this population, Schwartz (2001) makes recommendations to ensure that teachers receive adequate training or professional development to teach HLLs effectively. Together, these recommendations provide practical steps for moving HLLs forward in their HL expertise while simultaneously strengthening their allegiance to their chosen group(s).[21]

Conclusion: Educational Implications for Practitioners

Drawing on a wide range of literature, we have proposed an ecological model to examine the identity and biliteracy issues of HLLs. We intend this framework to serve as a means for educators to analyze specific HLL cases and develop their own answers to the questions of how to teach HLLs effectively.

We have reviewed various definitions of HLLs and proposed our own: In the U.S. context, HLLs are individuals who have familial or ancestral ties to a particular language that is not English and who exert their agency in determining whether or not they are HLLs of that HL and HC. We argue that the education of HLLs cannot begin and end with a linguistic perspective and with a focus on classroom practices alone. Rather, the *context, content, media,* and *development* dimensions of HLLs must be closely studied and understood by both the learners and educators. We advocate participatory pedagogy whereby learners take an active part in making informed decisions with regard to languages, cultures, and identities and chart their own paths in reaching these goals.

To conclude this chapter, we pose the following questions with regard to each of the sets of continua in the model:

Context

- In what kind of language programs does the society or educational system place the HLLs?
- What are the overt and covert goals of these programs?
- How do these HLLs, their families, and their communities view themselves?
- What goals do they aspire to regarding HL and HC maintenance and development?
- What are their goals toward English, HL, and school achievement?
- To which language or language variety are they exposed? What opportunities exist for learning this language?

Content

- What is the content of instruction?

- What is being taught and learned in homes, neighborhoods, schools, and communities?
- What are the messages in the official and schooled discourses vis-à-vis unofficial and personal discourses?
- What are the community's and individuals' attitudes toward the language and culture of the HLLs?
- What do teachers and other students know about the HLLs' language and culture?
- To what extent have schools incorporated HLLs' funds of knowledge and literacy practices into the curriculum?
- To what extent are HLLs encouraged to learn the American ways of speaking, thinking, and being while sharing their cultures with others?

Media

- What is the medium of communication in various aspects of the HLLs' lives (i.e., when do they use which language, with whom, and for what purpose)?
- What variety of the HL do they use?
- If they do not use the Standard variety, what do they use and how do their varieties differ from the Standard?
- To what extent are the HLLs aware of the power and socialization of both English and the HL?
- What is the medium of instruction and learning for the HLLs?
- Are HLLs able to go in and out of the dominant and HL groups and still feel a sense of belonging to these groups?

Development

- What kind of language expertise do HLLs possess (i.e., what can they do with the HL)?)
- To what extent are they bilingual and biliterate?
- Do they feel allegiance to English and/or the HL and to the speakers of these languages?
- If so, what are their feelings, sense of ownership, and sense of expertise?

These questions are not easy to answer. The biliteracy model puts learners squarely in the center of the inquiry, provides an analytical matrix, and enables educators and learners to pose searching questions about who they are and what they value as the heritage that they would like to cultivate and pass down to the next generation.

Notes

1. The majority come from China, Russia, South Korea, and Guatemala.
2. Identity includes factors such as the individual's appearance, behaviors, beliefs, abilities, weaknesses, achievements, race, gender, ethnicity, language, and culture (see also Brinthaupt & Lipka, 1992; Marsh, Byrne, & Shavelson, 1992; Oosterwegel & Oppenheimer, 1993).

3. The three figures are reprinted with slight modifications from Hornberger & Skilton-Sylvester, 2000, with permission from and grateful acknowledgement to Multilingual Matters in Clevedon, England.

4. Through participant observation, interviews, and document collection in school and community settings in the Puerto Rican community of North Philadelphia and the Cambodian community of West Philadelphia, the project sought to understand attitudes and practices toward biliteracy in both the classroom and the community. It also examined their fit with local, state, and national policies and programs addressing them.

5. There are exceptions, e.g., the case of two-way bilingual, developmental or immersion programs that strive to develop bilingualism in children.

6. The State of California spearheaded this movement with the passage of Proposition 227 (Unz & Tuchman, 1997).

7. For example, many Asian HLLs refuse or are reluctant to learn the HL because they want to use their native-like English language identity to mark their membership in the dominant society.

8. "Language educators" refers here to linguists and language education researchers, language teacher educators, language teachers, and others; "language planners" includes organizational and individual agents of language planning; and "language users" includes learners, parents, community members, and others.

9. Minority texts include those by minority authors, written from minority perspectives; vernacular ways of reading and writing include notes, poems, plays, and stories written in everyday non-school contexts; contextualized whole language texts are those read and written in the context of biliteracy events, interactions, practices, and activities of the biliterate learners' everyday lives.

10. Funds of knowledge are "those historically accumulated and culturally developed bodies of knowledge and skills essential for household or individual functioning and well-being" (Moll & González, 1994, p. 443).

11. For many HLLs, especially young children, it is difficult to find meanings and relevance in historical ghosts and tombs or pyramids located in a far away land (cf. Kingston's *The Woman Warrior*, 1975).

12. A similar case can of course be made for obtaining driver's licenses and for the availability of bilingual brochures in social and health services.

13. This notion is derived from the work of the Russian philosopher Bakhtin (1981).

14. See also Zentella (1997) on the repertoire of Spanish and English varieties on New York City's *el bloque*.

15. Native American students' language "problems" in learning either English or the HL has always been a haunting issue for the indigenous groups as well as the society as a whole (McCarty & Zepeda, 1995).

16. This is the term commonly used to refer to languages that are (1) linguistically and culturally distant to American students; (2) usually not offered in schools or universities; and (3) perceived to be difficult to acquire by an average non-heritage student.

17. A commonly-noted phenomenon is that HLLs tend to overestimate their knowledge of the HL. As a result, they either (1) do not learn as much as non-native learners because they do not put in as much effort; (2) find their speed and effectiveness in learning the HL disappointing because they or their teachers may overestimate their abilities in the HL; or (3) are satisfied with only oral and aural skills and do not further their development in reading and writing skills.

18. Mike Rose's (1989) book *Lives on the Boundary* is a classic example of the barriers faced in academia by those from different linguistic/cultural backgrounds, as is Caroline Pari's (1999) account of her struggle to assimilate in the academy—a journey that took her from "Italian American" to "American," then from "American" to "Italian American" again.

19. These include Chinese, Arabic, Japanese, Korean, Greek Orthodox, and Hebrew HL schools.

20. Everson also mentions that, in his Chinese language classes at the University of Iowa, his Chinese HL students and he, a White native speaker of English, often have to negotiate the ownership of Chinese and English languages and cultures (Michael Everson, personal communication, November 17, 2001).

21. See also important discussions of educational issues for HLLs in the K–12 educational system (Wang & Green, 2001), higher education (Kono & McGinnis, 2001), and in the truly less commonly taught languages in the United States (Gambhir, 2001).

References

Ascher, C. (1989). *Southeast Asian adolescents: Identity and adjustment*. Washington, DC: Center for Applied Linguistics. (ERIC Document Reproduction Service No. ED306329)

August, D., & Hakuta, K. (Eds.). (1998). *Educating language-minority children*. Washington, DC: National Academy Press.

Baker, C., & Jones, S. P. (1998). *Encyclopedia of bilingual education and bilingualism*. Clevedon, England: Multilingual Matters.

Bakhtin, M. (1981). *The dialogic imagination*. Austin: University of Texas Press.

Bereiter, C., & Engelmann, S. (1966). *Teaching disadvantaged children in the preschool*. Englewood Cliffs, NJ: Prentice-Hall.

Bernstein, B. (1972). A sociolinguistic approach to socialization with some reference to educability. In J. J. Gumperz & D. H. Hymes (Eds.), *Directions in sociolinguistics* (pp. 465–497). New York: Holt, Rinehart and Winston.

Brecht, R. D., & Ingold, C. W. (2002). *Tapping a national resource: Heritage languages in the United States* (Report No. EDO-FL-02-02). Washington, DC: ERIC Clearinghouse on Languages and Linguistics, Center for Applied Linguistics. (ERIC Document Reproduction Service No. ED464515)]

Brecht, R. D., & Walton, A. R. (1994). National strategic planning in the less commonly taught languages. *The Annals of the American Academy of Political and Social Science, 532*, 190–212.

Brinthaupt, T. M., & Lipka, R. P. (Eds.). (1992). Introduction. In *The self: Definitional and methodological issues* (pp. 1–11). Albany: State University of New York.

Bucholtz, M. (1995). From mulatta to mestiza: Passing and the linguistic reshaping of ethnic identity. In K. Hall & M. Bucholtz (Eds.), *Gender articulated: Language and the socially constructed self* (pp. 351–373). New York: Routledge.

Cahnmann, M. (2001). *Shifting metaphors: Of war and reimagination in the bilingual classroom*. Unpublished doctoral dissertation, University of Pennsylvania, Philadelphia.

Campbell, R., & Peyton, J. K. (1998). Heritage language students: A valuable language resource. *The ERIC Review, 6*(1), 38–39. Retrieved February 10, 2003, from http://www.eric.ed.gov/resources/ericreview/vol6no1/heritage.html

Campbell, R. N., & Rosenthal, J. W. (2000). Heritage languages. In J. W. Rosenthal (Ed.), *Handbook of undergraduate second language education* (pp. 165–184). Mahwah, NJ: Lawrence Erlbaum.

Castellanos, D. (with P. Leggio). (1983). *The best of two worlds: Bilingual-bicultural education in the U.S.* Trenton: New Jersey State Department of Education.

Celce-Murcia, M. (1991). Grammar pedagogy in second and foreign language teaching. *TESOL Quarterly, 25*, 459–480.

Chen, D. K., & Chung, G. (2002, May). *Key factors to the successful implementation of pre-school and early elementary bilingual Chinese language programs in weekend Chinese language and heritage schools*. Paper presented at the annual conference of the Association of Chinese Schools, Washington, DC.

Cho, D. (2001, April 11). Separated by a wall of words. *The Washington Post*. Retrieved February 4, 2003 from http://washingtonpost.com/wp-dyn/articles/A2205-2001Apr10.html

Cho, G., & Krashen, S. D. (1998). The negative consequences of heritage language loss and why we should care. In S. D. Krashen, L. Tse, & J. McQuillan (Eds.), *Heritage language development* (pp. 31–39). Culver City, CA: Language Education Associates.

Christensen, M., & Wu, X. (1993). An individualized approach for teaching false beginners. *Journal of the Chinese Language Teachers Association, 28*(2), 91–100.

Clark, R., Fairclough, N., Ivanic, R., & Martin-Jones, M. (1990). Critical language awareness part I: A critical review of three current approaches to language awareness. *Language and Education, 4*(4), 249–260.

Clark, R., Fairclough, N., Ivanic, R., & Martin-Jones, M. (1991). Critical language awareness Part II: Towards critical alternatives. *Language and Education, 5*(1), 41–54.

Clyne, M. G. (1991). *Community languages: The Australian experience*. Cambridge: Cambridge University Press.

Conklin, N. F., & Lourie, M. A. (Eds.). (1983). *A host of tongues: Language communities in the United States*. New York: The Free Press.

Crawford, J. (1989). *Bilingual education: History, politics, theory, and practice*. Trenton, NJ: Crane.

Crawford, J. (2003). *Hard sell: Why is bilingual education so unpopular with the American public?* EPSL-0302-102-LPRU. Language Policy Research Unit, Education Policy Studies Laboratory, Arizona State University, Tempe, AZ. Retrieved March 11, 2006, from http://www.asu.edu/educ/epsl/LPRU/features/article8.htm

Cummins, J. (1981). Four misconceptions about language proficiency in bilingual education. *NABE Journal, 5*(3), 31–45.

Draper, J. B., & Hicks, J. H. (2000). Where we've been; what we've learned. In J. B. Webb & B. L. Miller (Eds.), *Teaching heritage language learners: Voices from the classroom* (pp. 15–35). Yonkers, NY: American Council for the Teaching of Foreign Languages.

Durie, A. (1999). Emancipatory Maori education: Speaking from the heart. In S. May (Ed.), *Indigenous community-based education* (pp. 67–78). Clevedon, England: Multilingual Matters.

Eckert, P. (1989). *Jocks and burnouts: Social categories and identities in the high school.* New York: Teachers College Press.

Edelsky, C. (1986). *Writing in a bilingual program: Había una vez.* Norwood, NJ: Ablex.

Ellis, R. (1994). *The study of second language acquisition.* Oxford: Oxford University Press.

Erikson, E. (1968). *Identity: Youth and crisis.* New York: Norton.

Erickson, F., & Shultz, J. (1982). *The counselor as gatekeeper: Social interaction in interviews.* New York: Academic Press.

Fairclough, N. (1995). *Critical discourse analysis: The critical study of language.* London: Longman.

Families with Children from China. (n.d.). Retrieved April 2, 2004, from http://www.fwcc.org/news. htm.

Farrell, J. J. (1980). *The immigrant and the school in New York City.* New York: Arno Press.

Fillmore, L. W. (1991). When learning a second language means losing the first. *Early Childhood Research Quarterly, 6,* 323–346.

Fishman, J. A. (1968). Sociolinguistic perspectives in the study of bilingualism. *Linguistics 39,* 21–48.

Fishman, J. A. (1980). Bilingual education in the United States under ethnic community auspices. In J. E. Alatis (Ed.), *Georgetown University Round Table on Languages and Linguistics 1980: Current issues in bilingual education* (pp. 8–13). Washington, DC: Georgetown University Press.

Fishman, J. A. (1991). *Reversing language shift: Theoretical and empirical foundations of assistance to threatened languages.* Clevedon, England: Multilingual Matters.

Fishman, J. A. (1999). *Handbook of language and ethnic identity.* Oxford: Oxford University Press.

Fishman, J. A. (2001). 300-plus years of heritage language education in the United States. In J. K. Peyton, D. A. Ranard, & S. McGinnis (Eds.), *Heritage languages in America: Preserving a national resource* (pp. 81–97). Washington, DC/McHenry, IL: Center for Applied Linguistics/Delta Systems.

Fishman, J. A., Gertner, M. H., Lowy, E. G., & Milán, W. C. (1985). *Ethnicity in action.* Binghamton, NY: Bilingual Press/Editorial Bilingüe.

Floyd-Tenery, M. (1995). Teacher as mediator. *Practicing Anthropology 17*(3), 10–12.

Freeman, R. (1998). *Bilingual education and social change.* Clevedon, England: Multilingual Matters.

Freire, P. (1970). *Pedagogy of the oppressed.* New York: Continuum.

Freire, P. (1974). *Cultural action for freedom.* Cambridge, MA: Harvard Educational Review (Monograph Series No.1).

Gal, S. (1979). *Language shift: Social determinants of linguistic change in bilingual Austria.* New York: Academic Press.

Gambhir, S. (2001). Truly less commonly taught languages and heritage language learners in the United States. In J. K. Peyton, D. A. Ranard, & S. McGinnis. (Eds.), *Heritage languages in America: Preserving a national resource* (pp. 207–228). Washington, DC/McHenry, IL: Center for Applied Linguistics/Delta Systems.

Gee, J. P. (1996). *Social linguistics and literacies: Ideology in discourses* (2nd ed.). Bristol, PA: Taylor & Francis.

Gee, J. P. (1997). Foreword: A discourse approach to language and literacy. In C. Lankshear (Ed.), *Changing literacies* (pp. xiii–xix). Philadelphia: Open University Press.

Goldstein, T. (1997). Language research methods and critical pedagogy. In N. H. Hornberger & D. Corson (Eds.), *Research methods in language and education* (pp. 67–77). Dordrecht: Kluwer.

Gonzalez Pino, B., & Pino, F. (2000). Serving the heritage speaker across a five-year program. *ADFL Bulletin, 32*(1), 27–35.

Goodman, K. D., & Goodman, Y. (1983). Reading and writing relationships: Pragmatic functions. *Language Arts, 60*(5), 590–599.

Gumperz, J. J. (1977). *The sociolinguistic significance of conversation code-switching.* (University of California Working Papers, 46). Berkeley: University of California Press.

Gumperz, J. J. (1982). *Discourse strategies.* Cambridge: Cambridge University Press.

Gumperz, J. J., & Hymes, D. H. (Eds.). (1972). *Directions in sociolinguistics: The ethnography of speaking* (pp. 407–434). New York: Holt, Rinehart and Winston.

Gutiérrez, K. D., Baquedano-López, P., & Tejeda, C. (1999). Rethinking diversity: Hybridity and hybrid language practices in the third space. *Mind, Culture, and Activity: An International Journal, 6*(4), 286–303.

Hariton, S. (January 17, 2005). The split over bilingual education. [Letter to the editor], *Los Angeles Times*, p. B10. Retrieved April 10, 2006, from ProQuest database.

Heath, S. B. (1982). What no bedtime story means: Narrative skills at home and school. *Language in Society, 11*(1), 49–76.

Heath, S. B. (1983). *Ways with words: Language, life and work in communities and classrooms*. Cambridge: Cambridge University Press.

Hodgkinson, H. (1992). *The current condition of Native Americans*. Charleston, WV: ERIC/CRESS. (ERIC Document Reproduction Service No. ED348202)

Hornberger, N. H. (1989a). Continua of biliteracy, *Review of Educational Research, 59*(3), 271–296.

Hornberger, N. H. (1989b). Trámites and transportes: The acquisition of second language communicative competence for one speech event in Puno, Peru. *Applied Linguistics, 10*(2), 214–230.

Hornberger, N. H. (1990). Creating successful learning contexts for bilingual literacy. *Teachers College Record, 92*(2), 212–229.

Hornberger, N. H. (1992). Biliteracy contexts, continua, and contrasts: Policy and curriculum for Cambodian and Puerto Rican students in Philadelphia. *Education and Urban Society, 24*(2), 196–211.

Hornberger, N. H. (2000). Afterword: Multilingual literacies, literacy practices, and the continua of biliteracy. In M. Martin-Jones & K. Jones (Eds.), *Multilingual literacies: Reading and writing different worlds* (pp. 353–367). Philadelphia: John Benjamins.

Hornberger, N. H. (Ed.). (2003). *Continua of biliteracy: An ecological framework for educational policy, research, and practice in multilingual settings*. Clevedon, England: Multilingual Matters.

Hornberger, N. H., & Micheau, C. (1993). "Getting far enough to like it": Biliteracy in the middle school. *Peabody Journal of Education, 69*(1), 30–53.

Hornberger, N. H., & Skilton-Sylvester, E. (2000). Revisiting the continua of biliteracy: International and critical perspectives. *Language and Education: An International Journal, 14*(2), 96–122.

Horvath, B. M., & Vaughn, P. (1991). *Community languages: A handbook*. Philadelphia: Multilingual Matters.

Hudelson, S. (1984). Kan yu ret an rayt en Ingles: Children become literate in English as a second language. *TESOL Quarterly, 18*(2), 221–238.

Huff, C. R. (Ed.). (1996). *Gangs in America* (2nd ed.). Thousand Oaks, CA: Sage.

Hyltenstam, K. (1988). Lexical characteristics of near-native second-language learners of Swedish. *Journal of Multilingual and Multicultural Development, 9* (1-2), 67–84.

Hymes, D. H. (1972). On communicative competence. In J. B. Pride & J. Holmes (Eds.), *Sociolinguistics: Selected readings* (pp. 269–293). Harmondsworth: Penguin Books.

Hymes, D. H. (1974). *Foundations in Sociolinguistics: An ethnographic approach*. Philadelphia: University of Pennsylvania Press.

Kelly, L. G. (1969). *The description and measurement of bilingualism: An international seminar*. Toronto: University of Toronto Press.

Kingston, M. H. (1975). *The woman warrior: Memoirs of a girlhood among ghosts*. New York: Vintage International.

Klein, M. W. (1971). *Street gangs and street workers*. Englewood, NJ: Prentice-Hall.

Kono, N., & McGinnis, S. (2001). Heritage languages and higher education: Challenges, issues, and needs. In J. K. Peyton, D. A. Ranard, & S. McGinnis. (Eds.), *Heritage languages in America: Preserving a national resource* (pp. 197–206). Washington, DC/McHenry, IL: Center for Applied Linguistics/Delta Systems.

Krashen, S. D. (1998). Language shyness and heritage language development. In S. D. Krashen, L. Tse, & J. McQuillan (Eds.). *Heritage language development* (pp. 41–49). Culver City, CA: Language Education Associates.

Kroon, S. (1990). Some remarks on ethnic identity, language and education. In R. Pohoryles, R. Kinnear, & G. Muskens (Eds.), *Multi-linguism, Self-Organisation and Ethnicity* (pp. 421–435). Vienna: Indian Council for Cultural Relations.

Lambert, R. D. (1986). *Points of leverage: An agenda for a national foundation for international studies*. New York: Social Science Research Council.

Lankshear, C. (1997). *Changing literacies*. Philadelphia: Open University Press.

Lantolf, J. P., & Sunderman, G. (2001). The struggle for a place in the sun: rationalizing foreign language study in the twentieth century. *Modern Language Journal, 85*, 5–25.

Lau v. Nichols, 414 U.S. 563 (1974).

Leibowitz, A. H. (1971). *Educational policy and political acceptance: The imposition of English as the language of instruction in American schools.* Washington, DC: ERIC Clearinghouse for Linguistics. (ERIC Document Reproduction Service No. ED047321)

LePage, R., & Tabouret-Keller, A. (1985). *Acts of identity.* Cambridge: Cambridge University Press.

Lo Bianco, J. (2001, February). *What is the problem? A study of official English.* Paper presented at the annual meeting of the American Association for Applied Linguistics, St. Louis, MO.

Macías, R. F., & Wiley, T. G. (1998). Introduction. In H. Kloss (Ed.), *The American bilingual tradition* (pp. vii–xix). Washington, DC/McHenry, IL: Center for Applied Linguistics/Delta Systems.

Marsh, H. W., Byrne, B. M., & Shavelson, R. J. (1992). A multidimensional, hierarchical self-concept. In T. M. Brinthaupt & R. P. Lipka (Eds.), *The self: Definitional and methodological issues* (pp. 44–95). Albany: State University of New York.

May, S. A. (1997). Critical ethnography. In N. H. Hornberger & D. Corson (Eds.), *Research Methods in Language and Education* (pp. 197–206). Dordrecht: Kluwer.

May, S. (1999). Language and education rights for indigenous peoples. In S. May (Ed.), *Indigenous community-based education* (pp. 42–66). Clevedon, England: Multilingual Matters.

May, S. (2002). *Accommodating multiculturalism and biculturalism in Aotearoa/New Zealand: Implications for language education.* Unpublished manuscript.

McCarty, T. L., & Zepeda, O. (1995). Indigenous language education and literacy. *Bilingual Research Journal, 19*(1).

McGinnis, T. (2002). *Khmer-American youth in an urban migrant education program: Discourses, literacies and possible selves.* Unpublished doctoral dissertation, University of Pennsylvania.

McKay, S. L. (1993). *Agendas for second language literacy.* Cambridge: Cambridge University Press.

McKay, S. L., & Wong, S. C. (1996). Multiple discourses, multiple identities: Investment and agency in second-language learning among Chinese adolescent immigrant students. *Harvard Educational Review, 66*(3), 577–608.

Moll, L. (1992). Bilingual classroom studies and community analyses: Some recent trends. *Educational Researcher, 21*(2), 20–24.

Moll, L., & Díaz, S. (1985). Ethnographic pedagogy: Promoting effective bilingual instruction. In E. E. Garcia & R. V. Padilla (Eds.), *Advances in bilingual education research* (pp. 127–149). Tucson: University of Arizona Press.

Moll, L., & González, N. (1994). Lessons from research with language-minority children. *Journal of Reading Behavior, 26*(4), 439–456.

Myers-Scotton, C. (1993). *Social motivations of code-switching.* Oxford: Clarendon Press.

Nagle, J. (1999). Social class and school literacy. In I. Shor & C. Pari (Eds.), *Critical literacy in action: Writing words, changing worlds* (pp. 159–165). Portsmouth, NH: Boynton/Cook.

National Standards in Foreign Language Education Project. (1996). *Standards for foreign language learning: Preparing for the 21st century.* Lawrence, KS/Yonkers, NY: Allen Press/American Council on the Teaching of Foreign Languages.

National Standards in Foreign Language Education Project. (1999). *Standards for foreign language learning in the 21st century: Including Chinese, classical languages, French, German, Italian, Japanese, Portuguese, Russian and Spanish.* Lawrence, KS: Allen Press.

New London Group. (1996). A pedagogy of multiliteracies: Designing social futures. *Harvard Educational Review, 66*(1), 60–92.

No Child Left Behind Act of 2001. (2001). Retrieved February 24, 2003, from http://nochildleftbehind.gov/next/overview/index.html

Norton, B. (1997). Critical discourse research. In N. H. Hornberger & D. Corson (Eds.), *Research methods in language and education* (pp. 207–216). Dordrecht: Kluwer.

Ogbu, J. U. (1996). Variability in minority school performance: A problem in search of an explanation. In E. Jacob & C. Jordan (Eds.), *Minority education: Anthropological perspectives* (pp. 83–111). Norwood, NJ: Ablex.

Oosterwegel, A., & Oppenheimer, L. (1993). *The self-system: Developmental changes between and within self-concepts.* Hillsdale, NJ: Lawrence Erlbaum.

Otheguy, R., & Otto, R. (1980). The myth of static maintenance in bilingual education. *Modern Language Journal, 64*, 350–355.

Pari, C. (1999). Resisting assimilation: Academic discourse in the writing classroom. In I. Shor & C. Pari (Eds.), *Critical literacy in action: Writing words, changing worlds* (pp. 103–125). Portsmouth, NH: Boynton/Cook.

Pavia, H. (October 16, 2005). If you move here, speak English. [Letter to the editor], *New York Times* (Late edition (East Coast)), p. 13. Retrieved April 10, 2006, from ProQuest database.

Peirce, B. N. (1995). Social identity, investment, and language learning. *TESOL Quarterly, 29*(1), 9–31.

Peyton, J. K., Ranard, D. A., & McGinnis, S. (Eds.). (2001). *Heritage languages in America: Preserving a national resource.* Washington, DC/McHenry, IL: Center for Applied Linguistics/Delta Systems.

Phillipson, R., Rannut, M., & Skutnabb-Kangas, T. (1995). Introduction. In R. Phillipson & T. Skutnabb-Kangas (Eds.), *Linguistic human rights* (pp. 1–22). New York: Mouton de Gruyter.

Pica, T., Holliday, L., Lewis, N., & Morgenthaler, L. (1989). Comprehensible output as an outcome of linguistic demands on the learner. *Studies in Second Language Acquisition, 11*, 63–90.

Pierce, T. J. (January 17, 2005). The split over bilingual education. [Letter to the editor], *Los Angeles Times*, p. B10. Retrieved April 10, 2006, from ProQuest database.

Potowski, K. (2002). Experiences of Spanish heritage speakers in university foreign language courses and implications for teacher training. *ADFL Bulletin, 33*(3), 35–42.

Rampton, M. B. H. (1992). Scope for empowerment in sociolinguistics? In D. Cameron, E. Frazer, P. Harvey, M. B. H. Rampton, & K. Richardson (Eds.), *Researching language: Issues of power and method* (pp. 29–64). London: Routledge.

Rampton, M. B. H. (1995). *Crossing: Language and ethnicity among adolescents.* London: Longman.

Ravitch, D. (1983). *The troubled crusade: American education 1945–1980.* New York: Basic Books.

Reder, S. M. (1987). Comparative aspects of functional literacy development: Three ethnic American communities. In D. Wagner (Ed.), *Future of literacy in a changing world* (pp. 250–270). Oxford: Pergamon Press.

Ricento, T. (1998). National language policy in the United States. In T. Ricento & B. Burnaby (Eds.), *Language and politics in the United States and Canada* (pp. 85–115). Mahwah, NJ: Lawrence Erlbaum.

Root, M. P. P. (1996). A significant frontier. In M. P. P. Root (Ed.), *The multicultural experiences: Racial borders as the new frontier* (pp. xiii–xxviii). Thousand Oaks, CA: Sage. (Eric Document Reproduction Services ED 393956)

Rose, M. (1989). *Lives on the boundary.* New York: Penguin Books.

Ruiz, R. (1988). Orientations in language planning. In S. L. McKay and S. C. Wong (Eds.), *Language diversity: Problem or resource?* (pp. 3–25). Boston: Heinle & Heinle.

Scalera, D. (2000). Teacher beliefs and the heritage language learner: What will you teach your students? In J. B. Webb & B. L. Miller (Eds.), *Teaching heritage language learners: Voices from the classroom* (pp. 71–82). Yonkers, NY: American Council for the Teaching of Foreign Languages.

Schwartz, A. M. (2001). Preparing teachers to work with heritage language learners. In J. K. Peyton, D. A. Ranard, & S. McGinnis (Eds.), *Heritage languages in America: Preserving a national resource* (pp. 229–252). Washington, DC/McHenry, IL: Center for Applied Linguistics/Delta Systems.

Schwartz, W. (1998). *The identity development of multiracial youth* (Report No. EDO-UD-98-7). New York: ERIC Clearinghouse on Urban Education. (ERIC Document Reproduction Service No. ED425248)

Selinker, L. (1972). Interlanguage. *International Review of Applied Linguistics, 10*, 209–231.

Shor, I., & Pari, C. (Eds.). (1999). *Critical literacy in action: Writing words, changing worlds.* Portsmouth, NH: Boynton/Cook.

Simon, P. (1980). *The tongue-tied American: Confronting the foreign language crisis.* New York: Continuum Press.

Skilton-Sylvester, E. (1997). *Inside, outside, and in-between: Identities, literacies, and educational policies in the lives of Cambodian women and girls in Philadelphia.* Unpublished doctoral dissertation, University of Pennsylvania, Philadelphia.

Spolsky, B. (2003). Reassessing Maori regeneration. *Language in Society, 32*(4), 553–578.

Street, B. V. (1995). *Social literacies: Critical approaches to literacy in development, ethnography, and education.* London: Longman.

Swain, M. (1985). Communicative competence: Some roles of comprehensible input and comprehensible output in its development. In S. Gass & C. Madden (Eds.), *Input in second language acquisition* (pp. 235–253). Rowley, MA: Newbury House.

Tollefson, J. W. (1991). *Planning language, planning inequality: Language policy in the community.* London: Longman.

Trueba, H. T., & Zou, Y. (1994). *Power in education: The case of Miao University students and its significance for American culture.* Washington, DC: The Falmer Press.

Tucker, G. R. (1984). Toward the development of a language-competent American society. *The International Journal of the Sociology of Language, 45,* 153–160.

Tyack, D. B. (1996). *The one best system: A history of American urban education.* Cambridge, MA: Harvard University Press.

Unz, R., & Tuchman, G. (1997). *California Proposition 227: English language education for children in public schools.* File No. SA 97 RF 0009.

U.S. Department of Education. (n.d.) *No child left behind.* Retrieved March 11, 2006, from http://www.ed.gov/nclb/landing.jhtml.

Valdés, G. (2000). The ACTFL-Hunter College FIPSE Project and its contributions to the profession. In Webb, B. J. & Miller, B. L. (Eds.), *Teaching heritage language learners: Voices from the Classroom* (pp. 235–251). Yonkers, NY: American Council on the Teaching of Foreign Languages.

Valdés, G. (2001). Heritage language students: Profiles and possibilities. In J. K. Peyton, D. A. Ranard, & S. McGinnis (Eds.), *Heritage languages in America: Preserving a national resource* (pp. 37–77). Washington, DC/McHenry, IL: Center for Applied Linguistics/Delta Systems.

Valdés, G., & Geoffrion-Vinci, M. (1998). Chicano Spanish: The role of the "underdeveloped" code in bilingual repertoires. *Modern Language Journal, 82,* 473–501.

Vigil, J. D. (1997). *Learning from gangs: The Mexican American experience* (Report No. EDO-RC-97-1). Charleston, WV: Educational Resources Information Center Clearinghouse on Rural Education and Small Schools. (ERIC Document Reproduction Service No. ED405157)

Wang, S. C. (1996). Improving Chinese language schools: Issues and recommendations. In X. Wang (Ed.), *A view from within: A case study of Chinese heritage community language schools in the United States* (pp. 63–67). Washington, DC: National Foreign Language Center.

Wang, S. C. (1999). Crossing the bridge: A Chinese case from mother tongue maintenance to foreign language education. In M. Chu (Ed.), *Mapping the course of the Chinese language field* (pp. 271–312). Kalamazoo, MI: Chinese Language Teachers Association.

Wang, S. C. (2004). *Biliteracy resource eco-system of intergenerational language and culture transmission: An ethnographic study of a Chinese-American Community.* Unpublished doctoral dissertation, University of Pennsylvania.

Wang, X. (1996). Introduction. In X. Wang (Ed.), *A view from within: A case study of Chinese heritage community language schools in the United States* (pp. 1–6). Washington, DC: National Foreign Language Center.

Webb, J. B., & Miller, B. L. (Eds.) (2000). *Teaching heritage language learners: Voices from the classroom.* Yonkers, NY: American Council on the Teaching of Foreign Languages.

Weiss, M. (April 15, 2003). Seeking the right words. [Letter to the editor], *New York Times* (Late edition (East Coast)), p. F4. Retrieved April 10, 2006, from ProQuest database.

Wiley, T. G. (2001). On defining heritage languages and their speakers. In J. K. Peyton, D. A. Ranard, & S. McGinnis (Eds.), *Heritage languages in America: Preserving a national resource* (pp. 29–36). Washington, DC/McHenry, IL: Center for Applied Linguistics/Delta Systems.

Yawkey, T. D. (1980). Through the looking-glass self: An introduction. In T. D. Yawkey (Ed.), *The self-concept of the young child* (pp. 1–6). Provo, UT: Brigham Young University Press.

Zentella, A. C. (1997). *Growing up bilingual: Puerto Rican children in New York.* Malden, MA: Blackwell.

Zhao, Y. (2002, April 9). Living in 2 worlds, old and new: Foreign-born adoptees explore their cultural roots. *New York Times,* p. A1.

I
Heritage Speakers
Demographics, Policy, and Identity

2

Learning Other Languages

The Case for Promoting Bilingualism within Our Educational System

G. RICHARD TUCKER

Introduction

Available data indicate that there are many more bilingual or multilingual individuals in the world than there are monolingual. In addition, many more children throughout the world have been, and continue to be, educated via a second or a later-acquired language, at least for some portion of their formal education, than the number of children educated exclusively via a first language (World Bank, 2000). And we know that innovative educational programs involving some form of bilingual education have been with us for at least five millennia, for example, since 3,000 B.C., in ancient Mesopotamia, when Sumerian and Akkadian were used as the two languages for training scribes. In many parts of the world, bilingualism or multilingualism, and innovative approaches to education that involve the use of two or more languages, constitute the normal everyday experience (see, for example, Dutcher, 1994; World Bank, 1995).

Every European country has a national policy for introducing at least one foreign language into every child's elementary school curriculum (cf., Dickson & Cumming, 1996; Pufahl, Rhodes, & Christian, 2001). And, in a provocative study commissioned by the British Council, Graddol (1997), after examining an array of economic, demographic, and political indicators, concluded that by the middle of the 21st century the linguistic monopoly of English will give rise to an oligopoly in which Arabic, Chinese (Mandarin), English, Hindi, and Spanish will compete for attention, with bilingual proficiency becoming an absolute necessity for participants in the global economy.

Pervasive Domestic (American) Monolingualism

Within this broad global context that supports and encourages innovative language education for a majority of students, I find it to be an enduring paradox of American life and American education that bilingualism, becoming bilingual, and the encouragement of innovative language education programs within the core or basic curriculum of public education are so often viewed as problematic, difficult, and undesirable. Why should this be, and what is the likelihood for change? Consider the following observations:[1]

- When Columbus is reputed to have first visited, approximately 700 indigenous languages were spoken in North America; linguists estimate that only 187 are still spoken, and children are learning only 38.
- Our country is historically very rich linguistically. At the time of confederation, the German-speaking population was almost as large (roughly 9%) as the Spanish-speaking portion of our population today.
- In the period from the middle 1800s until about 1915, almost 75% of our secondary school students studied a foreign language. In addition, many public schools in cities such as Baltimore, Boston, and Cincinnati offered bilingual education as a regular part of the schools' educational offering.
- By the First World War there was a precipitous decline in the proportion of students studying foreign languages, particularly German, in our schools, and in fact the state of Nebraska banned the teaching of foreign languages in the public school system in 1919. It was not until 1923 that the U.S. Supreme Court overturned that ruling (*Meyer v. Nebraska*, 1923), once again permitting the teaching of German as well as other languages.
- From 1925 until the early 1980s, foreign language enrollments among secondary school students hovered around 20–25%, with enrollments in German in particular suffering.
- Although enrollments have rebounded slightly, they are still markedly below earlier levels, a situation to which I return in a subsequent section.
- During the decade of the 1980s and continuing to the present day, there has developed a seeming groundswell of support for federal and state legislation designed to promote the use of English-only (see Tucker, 1997). This move seems to have been fueled by a tide of escalating anti-immigrant sentiments throughout the country. The vitriolic rhetoric surrounding these discussions significantly undermines attempts to discuss, define, and implement a coherent, broadly-based national language policy. The discussion led by those advocating English-only legislation focuses on the supposedly debilitating effects of bilingualism, on the negative social and economic consequences that seem to accompany bilingual policies, and on the harm to national unity and well being that inevitably accompanies the encouragement of individual and societal bilingual proficiency.

At present, a large majority of American students and recent graduates—a major source of new entrants to the service-industry workforce—do not have sufficient bilingual proficiency or cross cultural competence to be able to offer their services to international clients. Foreign university graduates and workers, however, almost all of whom speak English in addition to the language(s) of their country, are able to penetrate the American market effectively.

Evidence from Innovative Language Education Research Worldwide

Nadine Dutcher (1994) and I carried out a comprehensive review for the World Bank of the use of first and second languages in education. In this review we examined, in some detail, the literature from research conducted in three different types of countries: (1) those with no (or few) mother tongue speakers of the language of wider communication (e.g., Haiti, Nigeria, the Philippines); (2) those with some mother tongue speakers of the language of wider communication (e.g., Guatemala); and (3) those with many mother tongue speakers of the language of wider communication (e.g., Canada, New Zealand, the United States).[2]

My reading of the available literature together with the personal research that I have conducted over the past three decades in varied language education settings throughout the world leads me to a number of relatively straightforward conclusions:

- The language of school is very different from the language of home.
- The development of cognitive/academic language requires time (four to seven years of formal instruction).
- Individuals most easily develop literacy skills in a familiar language.
- Individuals most easily develop cognitive skills and master content material that is taught in a familiar language.
- Cognitive/academic language skills, once developed, and content-subject material, once acquired, transfer readily.
- The best predictor of cognitive/academic language development in a second language is the level of development of cognitive/academic language proficiency in the first language.
- Children learn a second language in different ways depending upon their culture, their group, and their individual personality.

Therefore, if the goal is to help the student ultimately develop the highest possible degree of content mastery and second-language proficiency, time spent instructing the child in a familiar language is a wise investment (i.e., Lambert's notion (1980) of "additive" bilingualism).[3]

The results from published, longitudinal, and critical research undertaken in varied settings throughout the world indicate clearly that the development of multiple language proficiency is possible, and indeed that it is viewed as desirable by educators, policy makers, and parents in many countries. The findings summarized above (based largely upon a review of international literature) are clearly also consistent with those reported by researchers in the United States and Canada (see, for example, Brisk, 1998; Christian, 1996; Lindholm-Leary, 2001; Thomas & Collier, 1997).

Education and Our Changing Demography

The move toward monolinguality by the native-born English-speaking population is occurring at a time of rapidly changing national demography, and concomitantly a rapidly changing demography for our school systems and for the workplace. As a nation, we are becoming markedly more culturally and linguistically diverse (Roberts, 1993). The number of foreign-born individuals as a percentage of the total population, and the percentage of individuals who typically speak a language other than English at home, have increased significantly since 1980. An ever-increasing number of entrants to our schools and our workforce are so-called language minority individuals, and this trend will continue for the foreseeable future. Consider the following observations (adapted from Crandall, 1995):

- During the 1980s, more than nine million individuals immigrated to the United States—more than at any time in the 20th century except for the period from 1905–1914.
- Between 1980 and 1990, the Asian-American population more than doubled, and the Hispanic-American population grew by more than 50%.
- In the five years from 1986 to 1991, the nation's school-age population grew by approximately 4%, but the percentage of limited-English-proficient youngsters in our schools rose by more than 50%.
- It is estimated that in 1990 approximately 30% of all students and 12% of all teachers were minority group members; by the year 2000 the share of pupils who are minority group members rose to 38% but that of teachers fell to 5%.

Analyses of the 2000 U.S. Census (U.S. Census Bureau, 2000) indicate that these trends have continued throughout the 1990s, with the Hispanic population increasing by nearly 60% and the Asian population again doubling.

Clearly, as the composition of the American population continues to change, individuals with at least some degree of even latent bilingual proficiency will increasingly compose the pool of students and members of the workforce. However, if present educational practices continue, these individuals will not be encouraged, nor in many instances will they even be assisted,[4] to nurture or to maintain their native language skills as they add English to their repertoire (see, for example, Nunberg, 2001). These individuals will likely comprise a rapidly expanding pool that Wallace Lambert (1980) has characterized as subtractive bilinguals.[5] I turn now to offer a few comments about language education programs for students in American schools.

Language Education for Minority Students

For the most part, we have failed to develop or implement educational policies designed to conserve the heritage language resources of our language-minority students (see, for example, Brecht & Ingold, 2002; Peyton, Ranard, & McGinnis, 2001). In addition, the available data suggest that language minority students (and, in particular, the so-called limited-English-proficient youngsters) do not perform as well academically as their language majority counterparts (del Pinal, 1995). They often do not develop the academic English language skills that they need to participate effectively in educational instruction and drop out of school in disproportionately higher numbers than their English-proficient counterparts. Those that remain in school are less likely to proceed to colleges or universities, or if they proceed to college or university, are less likely to study professional subjects such as engineering or medicine. Once employed, they are less likely to be retained and more likely to earn lower wages than their counterparts. The prognosis is not positive particularly in light of prevailing educational practices, although many (e.g., August & Hakuta, 1997; Brisk, 1998) argue persuasively for a change in current policies.

Language Education for So-called Majority Students

What are the prospects for developing bilingual language competence in our language-majority students? By all accounts we are not achieving the level of success in foreign or second language teaching programs necessary for these students to compete effectively in the commercial world of the 21st century. Although the absolute number of students enrolled in modern foreign language programs at the post-secondary level increased substantially from 1960 to 2000, enrollments in relative terms actually fell from 16.1 per 100 college students in 1960 to 7.9 per 100 in 1998 (Brod & Welles, 2000). Moreover, fewer than 10% of American post-secondary students study abroad. In the 1998–1999 year, approximately 490,000 international students were studying in the United States, but only 114,000 American students were studying abroad, and a large proportion of those were studying in English-speaking countries or in English-medium programs in other countries (Desruisseaux, 1999).

The picture is equally bleak at the elementary and secondary levels. There it is estimated that fewer than 30% of our elementary schools (reaching approximately 15% of the population of elementary school students) offer any foreign language study. Although a majority (approximately 85%) of our secondary schools offer some form of foreign language instruction, the programs enroll fewer than 50% of the students, and then the most common sequence of study is for two years. Thus, a majority of the relatively modest number of individuals who do have an opportunity for foreign language study achieve disappointingly low levels of proficiency in their chosen languages (Rhodes & Branaman, 1999). As Richard

Lambert (1993) has observed, "the foreign language effort in the United States is a mile wide but an inch thin" (p. 184).

Yet another indicator of the marginalization of foreign language study within the American core curriculum is the observation that, to date, the evaluation of language proficiency has not been included as a part of the National Assessment of Educational Progress (NAEP). The NAEP governing board adopted a recommendation to assess the Spanish proficiency of 12th grade students for the first time on a trial basis in 2003 (Kenyon, Farr, Mitchell, & Armengol, 2000).

A great deal of discussion has been held in professional educational circles in recent years about the effectiveness of so-called foreign-language-immersion programs and of developmental bilingual education programs. These do appear to be pedagogically effective;[6] to date, however, it is estimated that fewer than 50,000 American youngsters participate in one or the other of these types of programs (i.e., fewer than one hundredth of one percent of the youngsters enrolled in public or private elementary and secondary schools in the United States). Nevertheless, pedagogically, such programs hold great promise and I shall return to this topic in a later section.

Thus the evidence available at present suggests that U.S. schools and colleges have been strikingly unsuccessful in either expanding or in conserving our country's language resources. At the same time, our schools are being called upon to develop in all students a sophisticated repertoire of literacy, numeracy, problem-solving and decision-making skills while simultaneously assisting them to develop, or to conserve, bilingual language proficiency and cross-cultural competence. Fully two thirds of our gross domestic product is now accounted for by "services," and the service providers must be able to speak the target language with a high degree of fluency and have basic comprehension of the cultural assumptions and norms of the society in which they are operating. While this requirement has not proven problematic for foreign professionals wishing to enter the American marketplace, it has virtually paralyzed U.S. workers wishing to gain access to foreign markets (Brecht & Walton, 1995).

Addressing the Need

This problem must be attacked on at least four fronts: (1) by developing intensive, yet flexible, options for second language study by students in elementary and secondary schools and in colleges and universities, that draw upon students' often-ignored linguistic and cultural resources; (2) by implementing basic interdisciplinary cross-national and cross-linguistic research to investigate and describe more thoroughly the process of second language learning and teaching, both in the classroom and in natural language learning environments; (3) by developing innovative and coherent graduate training programs to prepare students to do the types of research called for or to teach in the proposed programs; and (4) by the broad diffusion of practical, timely, and relevant information to educational practitioners and policy makers. I should add here that longitudinal studies of innovative language educational programs are sorely needed (cf., Tucker, 2000).

In the section that follows, I turn to a brief discussion of the relevance of so-called two-way or developmental bilingual education programs for heritage language students. As the numbers of American-born Arabic, Chinese, Filipino, Latino, Korean, Japanese, and other youngsters continue to increase, two-way immersion programs hold enormous potential for helping such students to develop bilingual language proficiency and content mastery in both English and in the heritage language.

Two-Way Bilingual Education with Special Reference to Programs for Puerto Ricans

In her presentation at the Heritage Language Research Priorities Conference in Los Angeles, Christian (2000) described the general features of two-way bilingual programs and observed that they may well prove to be an interesting educational model for consideration by various heritage language communities, including but not restricted to Hispanic communities. Specifically, she noted that

> Two-way immersion programs integrate English-speaking and non-English-speaking students for all or most of the instructional day, and provide content and literacy instruction to all students in both languages.... This approach can provide an effective means for heritage language (HL) learners to develop high levels of proficiency in the HL.... There has been a surge in popularity of these programs in the last ten years and they are currently receiving a great deal of attention.... Many questions are coming up as more schools and communities seek to implement two-way programs that have relevance for HL learners.

By way of a broad overview, the number of programs has grown during the past decade, a large majority of programs are Spanish/English, a majority are located within the public school system, three states have the highest concentration of such programs (California, Texas, and New York), and the results of program evaluations that have been conducted in such programs have generally been positive (see, for example, Christian, 1996; Christian, Montone, Lindholm, & Carranza, 1997; Christian & Genesee, 2001; Cloud, Genesee, & Hamayan, 2000; Howard & Sugarman, 2001; Thomas & Collier, 1997; see also the Center for Applied Linguistics (n.d.) Directory of Two-Way Bilingual Immersion Programs).

I recently became intrigued with the potential contribution(s) of a type of two-way bilingual program that might utilize resource people from the migrant stream as paraprofessionals, professionals or student peer models to enhance the academic and language development of Puerto Rican students on the mainland as well as on the island.

According to reports from the 2000 census, the current population of Puerto

Rico is approximately 3,800,000 of which 98.8% are estimated to be Hispanic or Latino (U. S. Census Bureau, 2000). In addition, the Census Bureau has estimated that approximately 32,800,000 Latinos resided in the United States in the year 2000 representing about 12% of the total U.S. population (residents of Puerto Rico per se were not included in the population survey of the "mainland"). Of the 32,800,000 Latinos, the bureau estimated that approximately 9% were Puerto Rican with the largest concentrations being in urban areas in the northeastern United States (e.g., in Massachusetts, New York, New Jersey, and Pennsylvania with a substantial minority in Illinois). The bureau reported that Hispanics are more geographically concentrated than non-Hispanic whites, more likely to live inside central cites of metropolitan areas, and more likely to be less than 18 years of age. In addition, Hispanics are less likely than non-Hispanic whites to be employed or to have graduated from secondary school (Thierrien & Ramirez, 2001).

Census data (U.S. Census Bureau, 2000) further document the relatively large numbers of Puerto Ricans who reside for briefer or for longer periods of time on the mainland. In fact, when one talks informally with educators or policy makers in Puerto Rico, the usual estimate is that more than 50% of the Puerto Rican population is abroad at any one time, and that many are in a fairly constant state of seasonal movement between the island and the mainland. These data give rise to the intriguing possibility that a substantial number of those "in movement" may be trained educators or may be individuals who could serve as peer tutors in either English or Spanish.

As educators and policy makers in Puerto Rico and on the U.S. mainland wrestle with the important question of how to improve the quality of instruction and educational attainment for students, the possibility emerges that their plans for assessing their students' language needs and current levels of proficiency as well as the current "capacity" of the educational system will provide important baseline information about patterns and durations of residential mobility as well as changes in language use, language attitudes, and language proficiency in relationship to factors such as age of mobility, place of residence, length of residence, participation in formal schooling, etc. The following questions are especially pertinent:

- Who are the participants in the so-called migrant stream? At what age(s) do they move from Puerto Rico to the mainland? Where do they reside? How long do they remain there? What experiences do they have with formal education? What experiences do they have in the work force? What language needs do they face? What language skills do they develop? What are their own attitudes toward Spanish and English? What are their parents' attitudes? Which community-wide attitudes exist?
- Who are the returnees to Puerto Rico? At what age(s) do they move from the mainland to Puerto Rico? Where do they reside? How long do they remain there? What experiences do they have with formal education? What experiences do they have in the work force? What language needs

do they face? What language skills do they develop? What are their own attitudes toward Spanish and English? What are their parents' attitudes? What community-wide attitudes exist?

- What tools are currently available to provide accurate and useful documentation to questions such as those raised above? What tools need to be developed?

Information such as that identified above should be collected and analyzed in an attempt to understand some of the factors that affect the academic performance (achievement) of Puerto Rican pupils. With a view toward crafting a purposeful set of planned-variation studies to examine diverse factors associated with improving the quality of language teaching and learning in Puerto Rico, the following types of questions emerge:

- What types of innovative educational programs could be developed and implemented in Puerto Rico designed to take advantage of the presence of returning students with varying levels of proficiency in English and in Spanish?
- What program factors or variables could be manipulated in an attempt to seek optimal program design features, absolute numbers or proportions of returning students, language proficiencies of returning students, literacies of returning students, and inclusion of returning professionals or paraprofessionals?
- What types of innovative educational programs have been developed and implemented on the mainland designed specifically to take advantage of the inclusion of participating students with varying levels of proficiency and literacy in Spanish? How can existing programs be improved?
- How can trained teachers or paraprofessionals who themselves move from Puerto Rico to the mainland and back be better utilized to educate Puerto Rican students? Can this continuing flow be drawn upon regularly?
- How might partnerships be developed, or extended and enhanced, among schools and communities in Puerto Rico and schools with large numbers of Puerto Rican students on the mainland? Can one envision technology-enhanced two-way bilingual programs in Puerto Rico and the United States that are linked interactively to permit synchronous communication among teachers and students in real time?
- How will such programs enhance the language development and the educational attainment of participants? What assessment instruments will need to be developed to facilitate such program evaluation?

These and doubtless numerous other questions could be explored productively. I believe that such a framework offers a possibility for conducting cross national comparative research. Although I am not in a position to comment knowledgeably on the demography of similar "flows," in other countries, I can imagine an at least partially parallel set of questions that could be raised in other similar contexts.

For example, what role can the development of two-way bilingual education programs play in the education of immigrant children to Australia? Moreover, could two-way programs be designed in Japanese-English, Chinese-English, or Bahasa Indonesian-English and link them, electronically or otherwise, with programs and communities in countries in Southeast Asia? Likewise, could two-way Greek-English, German-English, Spanish-English or other such programs be linked, electronically or otherwise, with European schools and communities?

Work by Australian researchers (see, for example, Clyne, 1991; Elder, 1997) has already moved far beyond a consideration of questions such as these, but surely there should be areas for collaborative exploration.

Concluding Observation

The cumulative evidence from research conducted over the last three decades at sites around the world demonstrates conclusively that cognitive, social, personal, and economic benefits accrue to the individual who has an opportunity to develop a high degree of bilingual proficiency when compared with a monolingual counterpart. The message for educators is clear: draw upon community resources and involve diverse stakeholders in all phases of program planning and implementation, design carefully planned and well-articulated sequences of study, utilize trained, committed teachers, and begin innovative language education programs that will lead to bilingual or multilingual proficiency for participants as early as possible. The graduates of such programs should be culturally rich, linguistically competent, and socially sensitive individuals prepared to participate actively in our increasingly global economy. Two-way bilingual or dual immersion programs seem to hold particular promise for helping heritage learners and other students to develop bilingual proficiency and cross cultural competence.

I would like to conclude by noting my belief that the implementation of the multiple agendas described above should be a collaborative activity with teachers, administrators, policy makers, and researchers—university based as well as those working in the non-profit private sector—serving as equal partners in the enterprise, and that the concerns of disparate audiences should be represented equally in the research process. From my vantage point, the optimal planning, implementation, and dissemination of research involves, of necessity, a continuing dialogue among the diverse stakeholders in the various phases of teaching and learning.

Notes

1. Many of these observations are well documented historically. However, I wish to acknowledge Conklin and Lourie (1983), from whom some observations have been adapted.
2. What follows are a few (possibly familiar) highlights of our review—findings that are also consonant with those contained in the splendid volume edited by Cenoz and Genesee (1998;

especially the section on "Case Studies in Multilingual Education") as well as with the chapters in the special issue of the *Journal of Multilingual and Multicultural Development* (Jones, 1996) and selected chapters in two of the volumes of the *Encyclopedia of Language and Education* (Cummins & Corson, 1997; Tucker & Corson, 1997). Interested readers may also wish to review the excellent case study by the Center for Applied Linguistics (Center for Applied Linguistics, 2001) as well as the volume by Baker and Jones (1998).

3. Additive bilingualism is a term used to refer to a situation whereby the individual's first language is a socially dominant and prestigious one, and in no danger of replacement when a second or additional language is learned.

4. See, for example, the discussion surrounding the implementation of Proposition 227 in California. Information and references on this proposition are contained in the winter and spring (2000) special issue of the *Bilingual Research Journal, 24 (1/2)*.

5. Subtractive bilingualism is a term used to refer to a situation whereby the individual's first language is a minority, non-prestigious one such that the study and addition of another language would likely result in the loss (i.e., subtraction) of the first language.

6. See, for example, the endorsement by Secretary of Education Richard Riley reported in Sack (2000) as well as research data reported by Christian, Montone, Lindholm, & Carranza (1997), Howard & Sugarman (2001), and Lindholm-Leary & Borsato (2001).

References

August, D., & Hakuta, K. (Eds.). (1997). *Improving schooling for language-minority children: A research agenda*. Washington, DC: National Academy Press.

Baker, C., & Jones, S. P. (1998). *Encyclopedia of bilingual education and bilingualism*. Clevedon, England: Multilingual Matters.

Brecht, R. D., & Walton, A. R. (1995). *Meeting the challenge of GATT: The impact of cross-cultural communications on the U.S. balance of trade* (NFLC Policy Issues). Washington, DC: National Foreign Language Center.

Brecht, R. D., & Ingold, C. W. (2002). *Tapping a national resource: Heritage languages in the United States* (Report No. EDO-FL-02-02). Washington, DC: ERIC Clearinghouse on Languages and Linguistics, Center for Applied Linguistics. (ERIC Document Reproduction Service No. ED464515).

Brisk, M. E. (1998). *Bilingual education: From compensatory to quality schooling*. Mahwah, NJ: Lawrence Erlbaum.

Brod, R., & Welles, E. (2000). Foreign language enrollments in United States institutions of higher education. *ADFL Bulletin, 35*(2–3), 7–26.

Cenoz, J., & Genesee, F. (Eds.). (1998). *Beyond bilingualism: Multilingualism and multilingual education*. Clevedon, England: Multilingual Matters.

Center for Applied Linguistics. (n.d.). *Directory of two-way bilingual immersion programs in the U.S.* Washington, DC: Author. Retrieved January 20, 2003, from http://www.cal.org/twi/directory

Center for Applied Linguistics. (2001). *Expanding educational opportunity in linguistically diverse societies*. Washington, DC: Author.

Christian, D. (1996). Two-way immersion education: Students learning through two languages. *The Modern Language Journal, 80*, 66–76.

Christian, D. (2000, September). *Two-way immersion education for heritage language learners: Issues and research needs*. Paper presented at the Heritage Languages Research Priorities Conference, Los Angeles, CA.

Christian, D., & Genesee, F. (Eds.). (2001). *Bilingual education*. Alexandria, VA: Teachers of English to Speakers of Other Languages.

Christian, D., Montone, C. L., Lindholm, K. J., & Carranza, I. (1997). *Profiles in two-way immersion education*. Washington, DC/McHenry, IL: Center for Applied Linguistics/Delta Systems.

Cloud, N., Genesee, F., & Hamayan, E. (2000). *Dual language instruction: A handbook for enriched education*. Boston: Heinle & Heinle.

Clyne, M. G. (1991). *Community languages: The Australian experience*. Cambridge: Cambridge University Press.

Conklin, N. F., & Lourie, M. A. (Eds.). (1983). *A host of tongues: Language communities in the United States*. New York: The Free Press.

Crandall, J. (1995). Reinventing (America's) schools: The role of the applied linguist. In J. E. Alatis (Ed.), *Georgetown University Roundtable on Languages and Linguistics 1995* (pp. 412–427). Washington, DC: Georgetown University Press.

Cummins, J., & Corson, D. (Eds.). (1997). *Bilingual education: Vol. 5. Encyclopedia of language & education.* Dordrecht, Netherlands: Kluwer.

Del Pinal, J. (1995). *Hispanics-Latinos: Diverse people in a multicultural society.* Washington, DC: Bureau of the Census.

Desruisseaux, P. (1999, December 10). 15% rise in American students abroad shows popularity of non-European destinations. *The Chronicle of Higher Education*, pp. A57–A62.

Dickson, P., & Cumming, A. (Eds.). (1996). *Profiles of language education in 25 countries.* Slough, Great Britain: National Foundation for Educational Research.

Dutcher, N. (with Tucker, G. R.). (1994). *The use of first and second languages in education: A review of educational experience.* Washington, DC: World Bank, East Asia and the Pacific Region, Country Department III.

Elder, C. (1997). *The background speaker as learner of Chinese, Italian, and Modern Greek: Implications for foreign language assessment.* Unpublished doctoral dissertation, University of Melbourne.

Garcia, E. (Ed.). (2000). Implementation of California's Proposition 227: 1998-2000 [Special Issue]. *Bilingual Research Journal, 24* (1/2). Retrieved on May 24, 2006, from http://brj.asu.edu/archive.html

Graddol, D. (1997). *The future of English?* London: The British Council.

Howard, E. R., & Sugarman, J. (2001). *Two-way immersion programs: Features and statistics* (Report No. EDO-FL-01-01). Washington, DC: ERIC Clearinghouse on Languages and Linguistics. (ERIC Document Reproduction Service No. ED452739)

Jones, G. M. (Ed.). (1996). Bilingualism through the classroom: Strategies and practices. [Special issue.] *Journal of Multilingual and Multicultural Development, 2/4,* 87–320.

Kenyon, D. M., Farr, B., Mitchell, J., & Armengol, R. (2000). *Framework for the 2003 foreign language national assessment of educational progress.* Pre-publication edition adopted by the National Assessment Governing Board (May 13, 2000). Washington, DC: Center for Applied Linguistics.

Lambert, R. D. (1993). Language learning and language utilization. In S. J. Moore & C. A. Morfit (Eds.), *Language and international studies: A Richard Lambert perspective* (pp. 179–185). Washington, DC: National Foreign Language Center.

Lambert, W. E. (1980). The two faces of bilingual education. *NCBE Forum* (Focus Paper 3). Washington, DC: National Clearinghouse for Bilingual Education.

Lindholm-Leary, K. J. (2001). *Dual language education.* Clevedon, England: Multilingual Matters.

Lindholm-Leary, K. J., & Borsato, G. (2001). *Impact of two-way bilingual elementary programs on students' attitudes toward school and college* (Research Report No. 10). Santa Cruz, CA: Center for Research on Diversity, Education and Excellence.

Meyer v. Nebraska, 262 U.S. 390 (1923).

Nunberg, G. (2001, December 17-23). The answer is on the tip of many tongues. *The Washington Post National Weekly Edition*, p. 23.

Peyton, J. K., Ranard, D. A., & McGinnis, S. (Eds.). (2001). *Heritage languages in America: Preserving a national resource.* Washington, DC/McHenry, IL: Center for Applied Linguistics/Delta Systems.

Pufahl, I. U., Rhodes, N. C., & Christian, D. (2001, Winter). Foreign language teaching: What we can learn from other countries. *Learning Languages*, 4–13.

Rhodes, N. C., & Branaman, L. E. (1999). *Foreign language instruction in the United States: A national survey of elementary and secondary Schools* Washington, DC/McHenry, IL: Center for Applied Linguistics/Delta Systems.

Roberts, S. (1993). *Who we are: A portrait of America based on the latest U.S. census.* New York: Random House.

Sack, J. (2000, March 22). Riley endorses dual-immersion programs. *Education Week, 19.*

Therrien, M., & Ramirez, R. R. (2001). The Hispanic population in the United States: March 2000. *Current Population Reports*, P20-535. Washington, DC: U.S. Census Bureau. Retrieved January 23, 2006, from http://www.census.gov/population/socdemo/hispanic/p20-535/p20-535.pdf

Thomas, W. P., & Collier, V. (1997). *School effectiveness for language minority students* (NCBE Resource Collection Series, No. 9). Washington, DC: National Clearinghouse for Bilingual Education. Retrieved February 8, 2003, from http://www.ncela.gwu.edu/pubs/resource/effectiveness/thomas-collier97.htm

Tucker, G. R. (1997). Developing a language-competent American society: Implications of the English-only movement. In T. Bongaerts & K. de Bot (Eds.), *Perspectives on foreign-language policy: Studies in honour of Theo van Els* (pp. 89–98). Amsterdam: John Benjamins.

Tucker, G. R. (2000). The importance of longitudinal research for language educators. In B. P. Sibayan, M. L. Bautista, & T. Llamzon (Eds.), *Festschrift in honor of Andrew Gonzalez* (pp. 161–169). Manila: Linguistic Society of the Philippines.

Tucker, G. R., & Corson, D. (Eds.). (1997). *Second language education: Vol. 4. Encyclopedia of language & education*. Dordrecht, Netherlands: Kluwer.

U.S. Census Bureau. (2000). Retrieved February 17, 2003, from http://www.census.gov/prod/2001pubs/p20-535.pdf

World Bank. (1995). *Priorities and strategies for education*. Washington, DC: The International Bank for Reconstruction and Development.

World Bank. (2000). *Distance learning course on the language of instruction (LOI) in basic education*. Washington, DC: Human Development Division, World Bank Institute.

3
Policy Activity for Heritage Languages
Connections with Representation and Citizenship

JOSEPH LO BIANCO

Introduction

Most writing on language maintenance and language shift, as well as on heritage language, uses the conceptual apparatus of sociolinguistics, and is located under the category Language in Society. As such it is linked to analysis and data about language use patterns, code variation, endogamous and exogamous marriage, bilingualism and parenting, and diglossia and the identity-language correlations, with social psychological perspectives sometimes informing the sociolinguistic orientation. Language policy and planning theory, which straddles applied linguistics and sociolinguistics, is sometimes drawn on as an informing sub-discipline. The effect is that heritage languages are typically discussed from perspectives informed by applied and socially influenced linguistics, both rather code-centered, as well as by language policy and planning, which also reveals the influence of code-based language sciences.

Less common are analyses of how language maintenance issues are constructed, represented and positioned in political discourse, i.e., discursive representation, and explorations of how the policy sciences could contribute to enhancing the prospects for the intergenerational retention of heritage languages. This latter approach is adopted here, hence the present discussion concerns how policy documents and policy discourses characterize the interests and intended policy treatments towards languages of minority communities ("heritage" or "community" languages, of both indigenous and recent immigrant origin) in societies where these languages do not have active territory-based political separatism claims. This is a discussion, then, of how heritage languages are represented in texts that announce public policy and the desirability of heritage language support.

My examples are drawn from recent developments in Scotland and Australia. Both share English as the powerful other language in relation to which advocacy responds, thereby adding problems of global modernity to the challenges of dealing with intra-national questions of identity and loyalty that face all minority language advocacy. Scotland is particularly interesting because political devolution in the UK in 1997 has produced a sense of national revival, and a kind of state-making practice is in evidence there. The Australian section discusses how with the post-Second World War immigration program language policy was undertaken in the context of new citizenship created in 1948, extended to indigenous people from 1967, and culminated in the permitting of dual citizenship from 2002. Each of these liberalizing moves in formal citizenship connects to a policy moment and offers insights into how "heritage" itself is construed as a cultural commodity.

Previous work on policy representation for heritage languages has discussed the United States (Lo Bianco, 1999), Australia (Lo Bianco, 2001a), the United States, the UK, and Australia in comparison (Lo Bianco. 2001b), and Scotland (Lo Bianco, 2001c). In this work it was suggested that intergenerational language maintenance implies and requires institutional supports, ethnic loyalty, ideological beliefs about nation-state-person, and makes heritage language policy different from other kinds of language education advocacy.

Attitudes and Discourse as Language Policymaking Practices

All policy involves both "texts" (the legislative or administrative, policy report, form) and "discourse" (persuasive talking and writing that precedes, succeeds and accompanies policy texts) (Ball, 1993).

The dominant perspective in official policy is statist, and in many Europeanized countries it links to ideologies and traditions of monolingual state making, of a unitary notion of national culture expressed by a single and ethnically expressive national language. This set of associations makes one language co-terminus with national identity and citizenship, and has the effect of separating civic from ethnic identity, designating the latter as a pre-modern identification practice of minorities. This separation in turn represents the social interaction required for intergenerational maintenance of heritage languages as marginal, atavistic, or even nationally divisive.

The result is that the efforts towards revitalizing threatened languages or sustaining heritage languages are vulnerable in policy discourse because they are often associated with anti-modern atavism. In policy debates, these arguments can be abstract and hypothetical. However they have a direct analogue in educational settings in the differential evaluations attributed to bilingualism. Heritage language-based bilingualism, for example, is often devalued by comparison with majority-community bilingualism that attracts celebration. Zelasko (1991) has called this phenomenon a "bilingual double standard." Writing about the United States, she observed that the bilingualism attained by speakers who learn English and maintain their minority language is rarely appreciated as a skill, whereas the acquisition of foreign languages by majority English speakers is treated as a demonstration of talent and is celebrated as an achievement. Variations on this differential evaluation of a two-language skill are also noted by Roca (1999), who finds that minority speakers are seen to constitute difficulties for the majority, and Shannon (1999), who notes that English-speaking children acquiring Spanish receive more praise than Spanish-speaking learners' attainments in English (p. 193).

In these examples, we see ideology becoming policy, and the practice and habits of language operating as default policy.

Sedition and Parochialism

In *Can Threatened Languages Be Saved?* (2001) Joshua Fishman surveys the range of obstacles that beset language revitalization efforts, asking: "Why is it so hard to strengthen threatened languages?" (p.1). He offers five reasons:

1. Language loss follows already advanced processes of cultural attrition and substitution of rival identities that are not based on active intergenerational maintenance of the language;
2. Advocating for language maintenance is seen as competing with the replacing language, opposed to social mobility, and as parochial and anti-modern;
3. Stable intergenerational language maintenance requires some social and institutional differentiation;
4. Retained minority language functions require constant reinforcement; and,
5. Opposed to language maintenance is a statist and supra-statist discourse that characterizes language maintenance as "simultaneously disruptive of local civility and of higher order international advantage" (p. 21).

Fishman comments that advocates of reversing language shift are susceptible to criticisms of "sedition" and "parochialism" (p. 21). This vulnerability does not face other kinds of language advocacy. Deployed against efforts to reverse language shift is an overarching discourse that Fishman labels "incorporative modernity" (p. 21).

In related work on Canadian First Nation languages, Fettes (1997) articulates three criteria for sustaining threatened languages: critical awareness, local knowledges, and living relationships. Critical awareness means contesting negative characterizations of threatened languages. The second dimension, local knowledges, involves re-invigorating local, intra-family and intra-community use-functions for threatened languages. Essentially this means finding spaces in the daily lives of communities and families in which the minority language is the natural and exclusive medium of conducting at least some differentiated affairs of life. Living relationships involve children and adults recreating intact discourses in the language.

Spolsky (2002) discusses the rarity of conjoining in a single language policy heritage language, national security issues in relation to language (i.e., strategic interests), and traditional foreign languages. The latter are usually sustained by humanistic rationales; the strategic interest generates its own, usually separate, policy, and heritage languages are treated to separate processes of policy determination, though more often are relegated to the realm of policy neglect. Spolsky proposes that an "ecological view" would be able to overcome the competitive interests that preclude comprehensive language planning (p. 103). Like the points made by Fishman and Fettes, we have here a sense that underlying the lower priority given to heritage languages is a discursive representation that aligns heritage language advocacy with interests contrary to or at least dissonant with "the national interest," even, *in extremis*, potentially disrupting "national security."

Language Policy Texts in Post-Devolution Scotland

In 1997 a large majority of Scots voted in favor of a devolution package proposed by the British government of Prime Minister Tony Blair. The result was that the administrative control vested in Scotland, compared to Westminster, expanded in range and depth, and, most importantly, that a directly elected Parliament was established at Edinburgh, the first since the Union of the Parliaments in 1707. The state or semi-state emerging from this process provides an important experience of language and nation connections for language planning analysis.

The political devolution within the United Kingdom supplies evidence of how implied policy (i.e., policy as a collection of prevailing attitudes) is transformed into explicit and overt policy attention at moments when political jurisdiction more closely aligns with specific linguistic and territorial associations. Although, by comparison with other parts of the UK, Scotland had enjoyed a relatively high degree of administrative autonomy before 1997, since devolution the "question" of Scottish Gaelic, and of language policy in general, has repeatedly surfaced for prominent attention.

In Scotland the context of devolution is evident in the number and range of policy investigations, reports and analyses commissioned by the new Parliament. In addition there are active committees devoted to language issues and Parliamentary debates on language questions. Among the language issues that have been considered for policy treatment are English (child and adult literacy, English as a second language), British Sign Language, Scots and its regional varieties, Gaelic, immigrant origin community languages, and foreign languages (especially the official languages of the European Union). Of these issues progress from discourse to text and resources has been easiest for adult literacy and hardest for Scots, most embellished for Gaelic, and least productive for modern and community languages. In what follows I discuss some key texts and debates in these areas trying to unravel both process and outcome.

A Policy on Culture

Creating our Future... Minding our Past: Scotland's National Cultural Strategy (Scottish Executive, 2000) is at base a policy text for distributing public finance to the arts. It also devotes considerable attention to identity, language, ethnic pluralism and cultural production, and has made available and legitimated a way to discourse on state, culture and nation in the post-devolution context. The Strategy deployed makes difference a central organizing idea: "This strategy takes a broad view of Scotland's culture" (p. 4); "everyone contributes" (p. 5); "Celebrating Scotland's cultural heritage in its full diversity" (p. 23). At the same time, the Strategy makes explicit connections between Culture and Economy via creative industries.

The Strategy lists among its key aims "Promoting Scotland's languages as cultural expressions and as means of accessing Scotland's culture," and identifies English as "both asset and threat" in its impact on Scotland's "other languages and dialects" and on the motivation of Scots to learn other languages (p. 23). The Strategy is very positively disposed towards Gaelic, identifying initiatives for its support, and also for the support of the Scots language, about which it says: "The Scots language continues to be widely spoken today and has a long and important history" (p. 24). Similarly supportive statements are made for "other languages." Within this discourse of celebration of diversity the Strategy is also shaped by an understanding of the "practical benefits" that can be seen to derive from the active use and transmission of heritage languages, and so it explicitly argues an economic connection for languages.

In effect, *Creating our Future... Minding our Past* constitutes a framework for conservation of the linguistic heritage and resources of Scotland and for integrating language diversity into wider state and national objectives and policies. It also offers legitimation for public participation around issues of difference and diversity as unthreatening to the new state, contributing rhetorical tools and support for community advocates to engage in citizenship-based policy conversations.

Gaelic

In 1901, 5.2% of the population, or 210,677 persons, declared that they were regular users of Scottish Gaelic (McKinnon, 1991). Scotland's Census 2001 revealed that of the population of 5,062,011 Scots, 27,219 responded that they understand spoken Gaelic but cannot speak, read, or write it; 31,235 that they speak, read, and write Gaelic; 19,466 that they speak and read but cannot write Gaelic; 7,949 that they speak and read but cannot write Gaelic; 4,758 that they read but neither speak nor write Gaelic; 901 that they write but neither speak nor read Gaelic; 1,435 that they read and write but do not speak the language; and 319 that they have some other combination of Gaelic language skills, while 4,968,729 have no knowledge of the language at all (Scotland's Census Results on Line, 2001). Effectively these figures signify a dramatic decline in active proficiency so that only 58,650 persons claim spoken skill in Gaelic, a decline of almost 70% since 1901. The census figures reveal three levels of reduction and restriction: decline in absolute numbers of speakers; restriction in the age profile so that fewer younger people acquire Gaelic in their homes; and decline in the proportion of the overall population represented by Gaelic speakers.

The Scottish Parliament has devoted the most energy to Gaelic, although action on behalf of the language had begun prior to devolution, with the major public examination, "Cor na Gàidhlig" (The State of Gaelic) in 1982, leading to the formation of the organization "Comunn na Gàidhlig" (Society for the Gaelic Language) to supervise initiatives to support the language. The new Parliament appointed a Minister, among whose other responsibilities resides Gaelic, and established the MacPherson Taskforce (Scottish Executive Taskforce, 2000) to enquire into the state of the language. The Taskforce report, *Revitalising Gaelic: A National Asset*, concluded that: "Gaelic is in a precarious, even critical, condition and ... without significant Government support it will not survive beyond the mid-point of the 21st century" (p. 14).

In commissioning the MacPherson examination, then Minister Alasdair Morrison made the association between Scottish national identity and Gaelic paramount:

Gaelic is a precious jewel in the heart and soul of Scotland. It is not constrained within strict boundaries or herded into tight corners. Gaelic is national, European and international. It is fundamental to Scotland; it is not on the periphery or on the fringes. It must be normalised and its rights must be secured. (as cited in Taskforce Report, iv)

The MacPherson Taskforce used the metaphors of illness and fragility to characterize Gaelic; it was as "a critically ill patient on life support" (p. 14) and "It is hanging on by a thread which is getting more frayed by the day. Despite occasional signs of remission, the prognosis is bleak" (p.15) and described its historical treatment graphically: "The history of the Gaelic language has been a chronicle of dereliction: official negligence; malicious intent; deliberate denial; and, perhaps most damaging of all, benign neglect. The language has suffered from stigmatization and from attrition through outward migration, loss of population and decline of community" (p.16). The taskforce also commented on public perception "that the Gaels do not have their act together, that resources are being duplicated, and that public money is not being prudently apportioned or spent. While much of the 'Gaelic debate' is candid, open and healthy it occasionally generates more heat than light and the rhetoric sometimes assumes greater importance than the language itself" (p. 16).

In response to MacPherson, an additional group was convened, the Ministerial Advisory Group on Gaelic, which reported in May 2002 (the Meek Report, Scottish Executive Advisory Group, 2002). This report, *A Fresh Start for Gaelic*, proposes a series of measures in keeping with the broad approach of MacPherson, focused on a Gaelic Language Act "to establish secure status for the language," and the creation of a new Gaelic Development Agency with national powers to require public sector bodies to collaborate in supporting Gaelic, as well as providing a *National Plan for Gaelic*, combining strategic priorities, key actions, targeted research, and a call for a *National Policy for Gaelic* to be prepared by February 2003. After delays the Cultural Policy Division of the Scottich Executive issued a new consultation report in January 2007 entitled "A Strategy for Scotland's Languages" which includes references to Scottish Gaelic and Scots as well as other language issues It is too early to determine what will result.

The MacPherson and Meek reports are impressive in coherence, consistency and sophistication of analysis and sober and serious assessment of the prospects of success. They are also impressive rhetorically, making available to the public ways to constitute Gaelic's role in the emergent polity.

The authorizing remit for this intensive period of heritage language planning is the *Programme of Government* (Scottish Executive, 1999) that followed devolution and which commits Scotland to support the revitalization of Scottish Gaelic. Contained in *Revitalising Gaelic: A National Asset* is a discourse seeking to express the vision driving these efforts:

> a foundation-stone in the building of the new Scotland, the Gaelic language will be an integral and dynamic component of a self-assured community with economic and social stability and pride in its linguistic and cultural identity. (p. 2)

Work on behalf of Gaelic occurs in concrete community level regeneration activity, in schools, media, culture, and industry (McLeod, 1998), as well as in the policy discourses. There has been considerable success in some areas of revitalization. Whereas in 1984 there were probably no students undertaking a Gaelic-medium education, by 1999 some 1,850 pupils were enrolled in such programs. In 2000 the first-ever graduates in Gaelic-medium higher education took degrees from the College set up by the University of the Highlands and Islands, *Sabhal Mór Ostaig*, through the Open University. Also in 2000 the first full Gaelic-medium school (primary level) commenced operations in Glasgow, and Gaelic-medium secondary units are planned. Success has also been achieved in broadcasting, both radio and television. Finally, the Gaelic Language (Scotland) Act of 2005 received Royal Assent in June 2005 and came into effect in February 2006. The Act established a Gaelic Language Board with advisory functions and aims to develop a Language Plan as well as other strengthening proposals.

Scots

For Scots, both the action and the prose are missing (Scott, 1998). Thus far the Scottish Executive has not produced any major policy-related documentation for the Scots language that would compare with MacPherson and Meek for Gaelic, with Mulgrew for modern languages, with the activity on behalf of British Sign Language, or with adult literacy. Moreover, the amount of national funding directed to the Scots language is minute in comparison to what is provided nationally for Gaelic, for modern languages through schooling, or indeed for any identifiable language category. There has also been a refusal thus far to have Scots language signage in the Parliament to accompany existing English and Gaelic signs.

Scots advocacy devotes considerable time responding to questions about whether Scots is a separate language, "just a dialect," or "English without the Norman invasion." Often the discursive effect is to erode seriousness of purpose and mobilization. However, the new Parliament may have instigated a move forward, in the form of a cross-party grouping of interested Parliamentarians that meets with representatives from the Scots language community. The transfer from community to Parliament, two orders differentiated by their capability of resource disbursement, of a mandate to commission formal investigative texts on Scots, holds promise that devolution may yet produce language planning for Scots too. A new and different discourse would surely result, given that Scots is more readily associated with separatist Scottish nationalism than Gaelic, less restricted geographically, being mostly urban-based, widely used, and prominent in many academic institutions. The policy principle proposed under "A Strategy for Scotland's Languages" is simply that "…the Scots language will be treated with respect and pride," at least acknowledging its status but making few concrete steps for improvement.

Adult Literacy

Adult literacy is perhaps the single most effective language policy activity under-taken since devolution, in which the progress from an initial policy investigation process, subsequent policy determination, and resource allocation and program implementation has been very fast. The process has manifested a language more transactional or propositional, less persuasive and rhetorical, more reflective of the businesslike approach of public administration, with most talk about economy and social inequality.

The advocacy put forward for action used staple talk of economic transforma-tion under globalization, the knowledge-basis of production and the resultant labor market demands and declining occupational prospects for older workers, as well as the serious consequences for the young with literacy difficulties. The result is a potent mixture that aligned the mainstream and expected language of contemporary governance with professional advocacy for literacy provision in a series of funded, publicly supported initiatives governed by an overall policy of provision and review.

The importance of literacy, print, and working in globalizing economies oc-cupies education everywhere since most education and training systems operate within a framework that sees education as investment in human capital (OECD, 1998). Adult literacy therefore is a kind of mainstream language planning, in Scotland as elsewhere, working within parameters shaped by existing government priority, even if challenged by some practitioners, researchers and minority language communities (Hamilton, MaCrae, & Tett, 2001).

Shared assumptions about human capital, the technical economy, and literacy in Standard English reveal the officially sanctioned hierarchy among languages. The use of English for most literacy action has considerable consequences for Scots speakers (Addison, 2001), but these have been mostly ignored, and virtually no attention has been paid to language literacy in other minority languages.

Modern Languages

In school languages education, as in adult literacy (but without its conspicuous success) the new Parliament has also been active. First, a 1999 report by Her Majesty's Inspectorate, Standards and Quality in Primary and Secondary Schools 1994–1998: Modern Languages (Scottish Office, 1999) and then a full scale Ministerial investigation, the Action Group for Languages (Ministerial Action Group 2000, the Mulgrew Report) indicate the effort devoted to the field.

Although the proportion of students taking languages is greater in Scotland than in England (Nuffield, 2000) the range of languages offered is narrower, mostly the official European Union languages, predominantly French, some German, less Spanish and Italian, and some community languages, mainly Urdu and Chinese (Powney, McPake, Hall, & Lyall, 1998).

The Mulgrew Report (p. 5) deploys a rationale for languages that seeks to go beyond "conventional reasons" to associate the case for an enhanced place in Scottish education with "the major changes ... sweeping across Scottish and international society." These changes are noted as: European mobility, social inclusion, citizenship and democracy, the "age of information", cultural diversity and the "evolving identity" of Scotland. The Report addresses "economic regeneration" of Scotland and benefits for individual learners. Mulgrew's recommendations center on the proposal that all students should be entitled to a continuous and serious experience of learning a modern language and that heritage and community languages, including Scottish Gaelic, feature prominently. Since its release, the Report has become mired in administrative changes; devolution to local areas and the implementation of its policy goals have been stalled. The Report's aim of diversification of offerings away from mostly French appears unlikely to succeed, and its attempt to recruit a discourse of economy, citizenship, European integration and Scotland's global connections to a reinvigorated interest for languages in general seems equally challenged.

In Mulgrew the Minister for Education, Europe and External Affairs drew attention to the need for continual improvements in the quality of teaching and learning of languages, commenting that the European Union constitutes a kind of inevitable internationalization for Scotland, in which multilingual proficiency will be prominent (McConnell, 2000). But the wider educational devolution to local authorities has depleted the case for modern and community languages at a national level, and deprived a place in the national conversation about the future of Scotland and its identity. Worst affected are heritage languages of recent immigration without claims to place, territory, or ancestral history. Thus far the arguments mounted for these languages succeed best when connected to enhanced educational outcomes for learners and, to a lesser extent, to stemming the waste of linguistic proficiency, and the skills of language competence that minority language speakers donate to their community.

British Sign Language

An important debate on the rights and opportunities of hearing-impaired Scots took place in the Scottish Parliament on February 16, 2000. Some speakers suggested that British Sign Language (BSL) is an ancient heritage of the nation; others talked about the need to deliver public services more effectively, others spoke of social inclusion, or welfare, opportunity and rights (S1M–529; *Sign Langauge*, 2002).

Users of BSL number some 100,000 though this is likely to be an underestimate given the use of BSL by hearing members of the families, friends, and co-workers of the hearing impaired. According to the Royal National Institute for Deaf People, about one in seven persons in the UK have hearing loss, or well over nine million people, over half probably being over the age of 60. The profoundly deaf number about 698,000, and an additional 450,000 are unable to use a voice telephone.

The survival of BSL in the face of strong assimilative pressures in favor of speech over signing recalls struggles of other language minority groups for recognition of linguistic legitimacy in societies of which they are an integral part. BSL users are a community with a history of struggle for recognition as a component group of society, a distinctive community culture, and therefore a heritage language community.

BSL advocacy includes a range of discursive representations similar to those for other heritage languages: some positions stress community and ethnicity, its distinctive modes of expression, and identity; others locate the issue within welfarist understanding, some medicalize deafness, and some are dismissive and rejecting of culture and community-based representations. In addition, policy discussions about deafness and sign language are rarely constructed as language planning, or as cultural and citizenship entitlements, for sign language users. The Parliament has made signing an issue of language rights, as well as social opportunity, but appears still to be seeking a principled way to integrate this perspective into the array of other representations that jostle for prominence.

Nations and Languages

Scholars who write on national feeling and identity have long worked with a distinction between civic and ethnic national bonds. Civic nationalism is sometimes considered a political variety and ethnic nationalisms a blood-ancestry variety. Greenfeld (1992) applies these distinctions to combinations of individualism and collectivism to propose three ways that a sense of nation can be experienced: an individualistic and civic sense of nation, a collectivist and civic sense of nation and a collectivist and ethnic sense of nation. Combining individualism with civic bonds underlying national belonging means that political sovereignty is a compact of free and equal individuals. Combining collectivist identity with civic identity produces a nation that is imagined as a "collective individual" in which the state's interests are independent of human individuals and take priority over them. And combining a collectivist nation with ethnicity-based nationality produces a pronounced ethnic nation. Greenfeld identifies England and the United States with the first type, and nominates France as an exemplar of the second and Germany and Russia of the third.

The civic and the ethnic are a dichotomy and each expresses a powerful characterization of state and nation histories. However, exclusively associating national identity with ethnicity fails to account for the emergence of civil society in many originally ethnic-based nations, which may even transcend the original ethnicity basis of state-making nationalism or reduce it to ritual. Relatedly, stressing the civic basis of nations obscures persisting, invented, or recovered ethnic bonds.

For much of the 20th century, modernists have had the upper hand in thinking about nations and nationalism. It seemed that either cold war politics or global capital would bring about the obsolescence of nationalism. The latter part of the 20th century, however, has shown a resilience and re-emergence of nationalist advocacy utilizing language, ethnicity, and religious markers of identification. These are as vibrant and persisting as those encountered in any previous era. We cannot sensibly theorize the existence of national states entirely within modernist parameters, with only civic and no ethnic dimensions.

Europe and Passports

Citizenship, the connection between a state and its people, is manifested in the passport. The European Union represents the most evolved example of declining sovereignty. Its constant use of the term *citizenship* is interesting in that it does not formally issue citizenship, though it does makes possible shared citizenship among its still sovereign member states. The EU is concerned therefore with a kind of supra-national substantive citizenship, and in this light its language policies are particularly important. The EU's language policies have made smooth progress when justified by economically motivated mobility, but policy development has been far more problematical for regional languages. Language policy reports often use the term *passport* as a metaphorical claim for languages: as in a "language is a passport to the world." In fact, the connection is close and meaningful. The EU regularly invokes the idea of passport and citizenship, language that brings the individual legally and culturally into a union of states, nations, and peoples (Council of Europe, 2001; European Commission, 1996; European Commission, Eurostat, and EURYDICE, 1995).

Janoski (1998) has examined the meaning of citizenship in this more elaborated form identifying four general types of citizenship rights: legal rights (e.g., rights to equal treatment, expressive rights such as freedom of speech, right to own property); political rights (right to vote, right to hold office, right to form or join a political party); social rights ("enabling" rights such as access to health care, "opportunity rights" such as access to education); and participation rights (rights to job security, collective bargaining) (p. 31).

European integration is found most concretely in its human mobility entitlements. It is a right of all citizens of the EU to seek employment, education, recreational, and residential opportunities across the Union. In a 1995 Policy the European Commission set the objective of all EU citizens being proficient in three European languages. It stated: "Proficiency in several Community Languages has become a precondition if citizens of the European Union are to benefit from the occupational and personal opportunities open to them in the border-free single market. This language proficiency must be backed up by the ability to adapt to working and living environments characterised by different cultures" (European Commission, 1996, p. 67). In 2001 the specification that the languages should be official languages of member states was removed. The European Charter for Regional or Minority Languages has, by contrast, encountered a slower, more contested, path. Despite being adopted in 1992 by the EU, it was only signed into law by the UK Government in March 2000 and ratified in July 2001. The Charter makes specific mention of both Scottish Gaelic and Scots. The specific consequence is the required provision of Gaelic in certain defined civil proceedings in geographic areas of Scotland where Gaelic speakers predominate (Council of Europe, 1992).

The Passport, Australian Citizenship and Heritage Languages

The period from the late 1940s to the late 1990s not only provides a symmetrical pattern but also frames remarkably well major developments in notions of language as heritage and identity in Australia. Each development is signaled by a practical alteration to the passport, in turn signaling a wider social, cultural and language change.

An Australian Passport

During the celebrations of its 50th anniversary, the Adult Migrant English Program (AMEP) was described as a "passport" to the future, and its anniversary conference was entitled "50 years of Nation Building." By any criterion the AMEP is Australia's most successful language policy initiative. More than 40,000 new arrivals from nearly 90 language backgrounds were learning English under the program in 2001, and more than 1.5 million people since it commenced. That the policy and program are also associated with nation building is not surprising; many nation-states have used language criteria for self-definition. The link with passports was more than metaphorical, since at the same time national citizenship was created with the introduction of a national passport. This convergence of citizenship, language policy and population-building was a result of the national impetus stimulated by a sense of vulnerability experienced during the Second World War, producing a commitment to a larger population, one unable to be generated domestically.

The progressive new passport was denied to the Indigenous population, who did not even count in censuses, and non-Whites were excluded from the nation building by being excluded from immigration (Jupp, 2002). At all stages, the building of a new and bigger permanent population was accompanied by the assertion of the national identity to which new settlers would be expected to accommodate, but this national identity was itself not static; based initially on the evolving identity of existing Australians, it came to include the new Australians and eventually even those excluded initially.

An Inclusive Passport

A period of remarkable growth in linguistic and cultural pluralism characterizes the early 1970s. The creation of the Applied Linguistics Association of Australia indicated a professionalized appreciation towards language problems. The extension to children of specialist English, the formalization of the adult provision with the Immigration (Education) Act of 1971, and the granting of initial language rights to indigenous Australians signaled new pathways to incorporative policies for minorities. The emergence and success of the community languages movement make this period one of productive change.

These changes, especially those relating to first-language maintenance for immigrants, the community languages movement, the beginnings of the Asian languages movement, and new discourses of identity and participation that were pluralist and civic, made possible "heritage talk" in relation to languages. In Australia policy agitation for heritage languages has always been conducted under the term "community languages." This term was used to distinguish immigrant and indigenous languages from foreign and classical languages and to suggest that locally used languages should have priority, or at least equality, of esteem. This was all part of an emerging, and ultimately successful, discursive politics that linked pluralism to the state, eventually becoming a shared political project of all mainstream political parties.

Australian bilingual education, which had enjoyed a flourishing nineteenth century history (Clyne, 1991), had fallen victim to a 1917 cultural policy that defined Australian identity in terms of English language and the British Empire. In 1973, for the first time since 1917, Australian primary schools started to teach languages. Until then, only elite European languages were taught, and then not for speaking and daily usage, but for writing and reading, and, in fact, for selection into higher education. But in 1968 institutional changes removed the requirement for language study as a criterion for university entry, resulting in a collapse in numbers. By the mid-1970s schools were expected to get close to their communities, and many of the communities were multilingual and made up of newly confident citizens. Heritage language advocacy became prominent, but the term *community languages* was and is preferred. Inserted into policy discourses was new imagery about national multilingualism.

The post-war immigration program had wanted a larger population of Australian-passport-carrying-Australians, but not a plural, diverse, and multi-ethnic population, with communication needs for which the state was unprepared. The infrastructure for such diversity was created in the 1970s, led by second generation new Australians, professional language experts, and the newly enfranchised original Australians. This policy phase produced the world's first Telephone Interpreting Service, which provided language mediation, first for emergencies and later for more general assistance, in health and medical situations, in courts of law, and policing.

Over time, both conservative and social democratic parties embraced multiculturalism in their distinctive forms. The result was far-reaching. Relatively liberal citizenship laws, combined with compulsory voting, contributed to the emergence of a large urban constituency that the political classes appealed to with cultural politics and a discourse of heritage and pluralism.

Critically, this decade also saw radical revision of the Asia-Australian relationship. The signal moment was Britain's accession to the then European Economic Community. This move cost Australia its guaranteed markets for many export items, but its cultural importance lay in the pragmatic and urgent need to communicate with its regional neighbors. The face of language education in the 1980s and 1990s underwent a consequent revolution, from elite European foreign tongues, for elites and elite purposes, to community languages for community purposes, including indigenous languages for indigenous purposes. Trade and geo-politics shifted language education towards Asian languages, again elite ones, and often for foreign purposes too. Immigration policy eventually caught up with geographic location, and language policy did likewise.

Dual Passports

Being able to belong to more than one state extends profoundly what 50 years ago was the invention of local citizenship, separate from Britain's. The expansion has involved three major shifts. An endogenous citizenship in 1948, its extension to inclusion of indigenous Australians in 1967, and, in 2002, the granting of multiple citizenship rights. On April 9, 2002, the Minister for Citizenship and Multicultural Affairs announced the repeal of Section 17 of the Citizenship Act of 1948 (Hardgrave, 2002) which precluded multiple citizenships. What had been instituted as a device for arresting potential disloyalty was discarded as a consequence of "the reality of global labour markets" and international consistency. Multiple citizenships, as Schuck (1998) shows, represent a growing pattern resulting from increasingly plural populations, and they have considerable language policy implications, globalizing the structure and experience of a "homeland" and "diaspora" for most language and ethnic groups.

Today the AMEP brings immigrant and indigenous Australians into contact as well. They encounter each other as part of Reconciliation processes in the *Wanyaarri* program, which teaches new arrivals about Aboriginal culture and its traditions. This type of contact suggests a new kind of citizenship, extending beyond a binary "yes" or "no'" to include certain attitudes, knowledge and ideas, moving towards a notion of substantive knowledge and attitudes for public participation.

Concluding Remarks

In the history of constitutionalism, Tully (1997) identifies the present time as the "Age of Diversity." According to his analysis, plural populations are challenging constitutional practice, especially the past practice in constitutions that imply or make explicit the idea of a cultural union between rulers and ruled. This cultural union invariably made use of a single distinctive national language.

Globalization has produced increasingly fluid and multiple identities in all parts of the world. The vast international movement of peoples under globalization has made citizenship status an area of contention and debate. Formal (legal) citizenship may include evidence of the adult new arrival's ability in the national/official language and is usually defined and conferred by a national authority. This kind of citizenship is undifferentiated, i.e., it applies to all equally. In reality, however, participatory citizenship calls on the skills, knowledge, and capabilities of citizens to claim citizenship rights and fulfill their citizenship duties, which are highly differentiated. This *normative* citizenship challenges states to ensure that the language for public participation is available widely. What are the implications for heritage languages in policy?

The struggle to constitute Scottish Gaelic in Scotland and community languages in Australia as proper objects for policy attention is in one powerful sense a struggle to find a language of advocacy, a persuasive discourse that contests such deeply entrenched public belief and operates as policy even in the absence of overt and formal policy. Under the conditions of new constitutionalism, claims to heritage have been universalized, but new citizens are expected to separate their claims to heritage since these are seen to attach to other nations, possibly rival ones.

As long as nations associate language with the corporate identity of the nation, and then link nation with state, heritage language advocacy is vulnerable to accusations of nation undermining, or sedition. And as long as modernity is associated with consumerism, capital and individualism, heritage language advocacy risks being declared parochial.

Both criticisms are powerful, and new discourses that reconcile civic identity with continuing attachments of heritage and origins will be required to ground productive policy measures in society, institutions, policy texts, and policy conversations. Notions of participatory citizenship create both new challenges and new possibilities to make heritage attachments consonant with civic identity and participation.

References

Addison, A. F. P. (2001). Using Scots literacy in family literacy work. In J. Crowther (Ed.), *Powerful literacies* (pp. 155–165). Leicester, UK: National Institute of Continuing Adult Education.
Ball, S. J. (1993). What is policy? Texts, trajectories and toolboxes. *Discourse* 13(2), 10–17.
Clyne, M. G. (1991). *Community languages: The Australian experience*. Melbourne: Cambridge University Press.
Council of Europe (1992), *European charter for regional or minority languages*. Strasbourg: Council of Europe.
Council of Europe. (2001). *Common European framework of reference for languages*. Cambridge: Cambridge University Press.
European Commission. (1996). *White paper on education and training: Teaching and learning—towards the learning society* (COM (95) 590). Brussels: Author.
European Commission, Eurostat, and EURYDICE. (1995). Key data on education in Europe, 1994. Luxembourg: Office for the Official Publications of the European Communities.
Fettes, M. (1997). Stabilising what? An ecological approach to language renewal. In J. Reyhner (Ed.), *Teaching indigenous languages* [Electronic version], (pp. 301–318). Flagstaff: Northern Arizona University. Retrieved June 7, 2004, from http://jan.ucc.nau.edu/~jar/TIL_25.html.
Fishman, J. A. (2001). *Can threatened languages be saved? Reversing language shift revisited: A 21st century perspective*. Clevedon, Avon, UK: Multilingual Matters.
Gaelic Language (Scotland) Act. (2005, ASP 7). Available at: http://www.opsi.gov.uk/legislation/scotland/acts2005/2005007.htm.
Greenfeld, L. (1992). *Nationalism: Five roads to modernity*. Cambridge, MA: Harvard University Press.
Hamilton, M., MacRae, C., & Tett, L. (2001). Powerful literacies: The policy context. In J. Crowther, M. Hamilton, & L. Tett (Eds.), *Powerful literacies* (pp. 23–42). Leicester, UK: National Institute of Continuing Adult Education.
Hardgrave, G. (April 9, 2002). Minister for Citizenship and Multicultural Affairs, Media Release. *Changes to citizenship laws (H36/2002)*. Parliament House, Canberra, Australia.
Janoski, T. (1998). *Citizenship and civil society*. Cambridge: Cambridge University Press.
Journal of Parliamentary Proceedings. Sign Language. Edinburgh: Scottish Parliament, Number 52, Item 7, S1M-529 (2000).
Jupp, J. (2002). *From white Australia to Woomera. The story of Australian immigration*. Cambridge: Cambridge University Press.
Lo Bianco, J. (1999). The language of policy: What sort of policy making is the officialization of English in the United States? In T. Huebner & K. A. Davis (Eds.), *Sociopolitical perspectives on language policy and planning in the USA* (pp. 40–65). Amsterdam: Benjamins.
Lo Bianco, J. (2001a). Policy literacy. *Language and Education*, 15(2-3), 212–227.
Lo Bianco, J. (2001b). From policy to anti-policy: How fear of language rights took policy making out of community hands. In J. Lo Bianco & R. Wickert (Eds.), *Australian policy activism in language and literacy* (pp. 11–45). Melbourne: Language Australia Publications.
Lo Bianco, J. (2001c). Language policies: State texts for silencing and giving voice. In P. Freebody, S. Muspratt, & B. Dwyer (Eds.), *Difference, silence, and textual practice: Studies in critical literacy* (pp. 31–71). Cresskill, NJ: Hampton Press.
McKinnon, K. (1991). Language-retreat and regeneration in the present-day Scottish Gaidhealtachd. In C. H. Williams (Ed.), *Linguistic minorities, society and territory* (pp. 121–149). Clevedon, Avon, UK: Multilingual Matters.
McConnell, J. (2000, December 12). McConnell Outlines Support for Languages [Press release]. Edinburgh: Scottish Executive, Press Releases, SE3197/2000.
McLeod, W. (1998). Scotland's languages in Scotland's parliament. *Scottish Affairs 24*, 68–82.
Ministerial Action Group on Languages. (2000). *Citizens of a multilingual world*. [The Mulgrew Report]. Edinburgh: Scottish Executive.

The Nuffield Foundation (2000). *Languages: The next generation–The final report and recommendations of the Nuffield languages inquiry.* London: Author.

Organization for Economic Co-Operation and Development (OECD). (1998). *Human capital investment: An international comparison.* Paris: Author.

Powney, J., McPake, J., Hall, S., & Lyall, L. (1998). *Education of minority ethnic groups in Scotland: A review of research.* Edinburgh: The Scottish Council for Research in Education.

Roca, A. (1999). Foreign language policy and planning in higher education. In T. Huebner & K. A. Davis (Eds.), *Sociopolitical perspectives on language policy and planning in the USA* (pp. 297–313). Amsterdam: Benjamins.

Royal National Institute for Deaf People. (n.d.). *Facts and figures about deafness.* Available from: http://www.rnid.org.uk.

Schuck, P. (1998). Plural citizenships. In N. Pickus (Ed.), *Immigration and citizenship in the twenty-first century* (pp. 149–191). Lanham, MD: Rowman & Littlefield.

Scott, P. H. (1998). Review essay: The future of the Scots language, *Scottish Affairs, 24,* 83–97.

Scotland's Census Results Online (SCROL). (2001). Analyzer, Scotland's Census. General Register Office for Scotland. Available at: http://www.scrol.gov.uk/scrol/common/home/jsp.

Scottish Executive. A Strategy for Scotland's Languages. (2007). Available at: http://scotland.gov.uk/Publications/2007/01/24130746/0.

Scottish Executive. (2000). *Creating our future…minding our past: Scotland's national cultural strategy.* Edinburgh: Author.

Scottish Executive (1999). *Making it work together: A programme for government,* Edinburgh: Scottish Executive.

Scottish Executive, Ministerial Advisory Group on Gaelic (Donald E. Meek, Chair). (2002). *A fresh start for Gaelic* [Meek Report]. Edinburgh: Scottish Executive.

Scottish Executive, Taskforce on Public Funding of Gaelic. (2000). *Revitalising Gaelic: A national asset / Gaidhlig ag ath-bheothachadh Gaidhlig neamhnuid naiseanta.* [Macpherson Report]. Edinburgh: Scottish Executive.

Scottish Office, Education and Industry Department, Her Majesty's Inspectorate of Schools. (1999). *Standards and quality in primary and secondary schools 1994–98: Modern languages.* Edinburgh, London: The Stationery Office.

Shannon, S.M. (1999). The debate on bilingual education in the US. In J. Blommaert (Ed.), *Language ideological debates* (pp. 171–201). Berlin: Mouton.

Spolsky, B. (2002). Heritage languages and national security: An ecological view. In S. Baker (Ed.), *Language policy: Lessons from global models* (pp. 103–115). Monterey, CA: Monterey Institute for International Studies.

Tully, J. (1997). *Strange multiplicity: Constitutionalism in an age of diversity.* Cambridge: Cambridge University Press.

Zelasko, N. F. (1991). *The bilingual double standard: Mainstream Americans' attitudes toward bilingualism.* Unpublished doctoral dissertation. Georgetown University, Washington, DC.

4
Heritage Language Education in Canada[1]

PATRICIA A. DUFF

Introduction

Although there is considerable interest now in policy, research, and professional development in heritage language (HL) education in the United States and other countries featured in this volume, Canada has for several decades attracted attention for its proactive policies and initiatives supporting minority and heritage language instruction and maintenance. Indeed, according to Baker (2001), the term *heritage language education* seems to have originated with Canadian programs, despite the existence of comparable programs in the United Kingdom, Australia, and other countries that have gone by other names, such as community, ancestral, ethnic, immigrant, minority, original, non-official, or second/third language programs.

In this chapter, I describe research on HL education in Canada and also outline current and future issues. Because education in Canada is provincially governed, it is not possible to discuss the HL situation in all ten provinces and three northern territories here. Instead, I provide examples of research, policies and issues that have arisen from different regions in a variety of HL program contexts over the past three decades. I then conclude with some reflections on the British Columbian HL education situation based on my involvement in Ministry of Education and university committees, and identify topics that require further research and professional development activities.

Minority Languages in Canadian Education: Historical and Current Perspectives

Canada's national focus on minority languages is linked to the historical status of the French-speaking community in Canada, the largest linguistic minority nationally. It is also responsive to the aboriginal (Native) and other languages spoken by many Canadians. In addition to the protection and promotion of Canada's two official languages, English and French, and thus Canada's so-called linguistic duality, there has been legislative support for other languages since the late 1960s. Comprehensive reviews of policies governing official, aboriginal, and heritage language education and programs within a historical context can be found in several volumes by Jim Cummins and his colleagues published in the 1980s and 1990s (e.g., Cummins, 1983, 1989, 1991, 1992; Cummins & Danesi,

1990; Cummins & Swain, 1986; Danesi, McLeod, & Morris, 1993), as well as in Shapson and D'Oyley (1984) and Ashworth (1998). Yee and Sodhi (1991) also provide a brief description of heritage language projects funded by the government from 1973 to 1990.

The dearth of scholarship on HL education in Canada since the early 1990s probably reflects the decline of federal funding for programs and research in the 1990s. However, a new wave of research is now being undertaken in relation to such topics as the development of minority students' multiple literacies in and out of school, the divergent linguistic profiles of HL and non-HL children and adult students in modern language courses, issues of language and identity, and sociolinguistic aspects of code-switching, heteroglossia, and trilingualism among urban immigrant youth (e.g., Lamarre, 2003; Shinbo, 2004).

Technically, in Canada the term *heritage language* refers to languages other than the *official* languages (English and French) or the *aboriginal* (indigenous or "First Nations") languages (Cummins, 1992). Some writers interpret the term differently, either including or excluding the aboriginal languages of Canada's Native population. Ashworth (1988) provides a historical sketch that shows how the term *third language* was used from the late 1800s up to the 1970s to describe HLs and HL programs. Canadian political, social, and educational initiatives have emphasized the value of having speakers learn and retain their HLs for a variety of reasons: to validate multiculturalism in this country and recognize people's multiple cultural and linguistic identities, to help minority children gain strong L1 language and literacy skills that will in turn support their second language (L2) schooling, and to provide public relations and policies to help encourage immigrants to settle in this country, knowing that their cultures and languages are valued.

A policy of official multiculturalism, sometimes criticized as the superficial, celebratory showcasing of ethnic foods and festivals, has prevailed in Canada since 1971. This policy was put in place to highlight Canada's aspirations of ethnic inclusiveness and of becoming a truly multicultural, pluralistic "mosaic" as opposed to what has often been referred to, stereotypically, as an American-style assimilationist melting pot (Baker, 2001). A branch of the federal government currently called Canadian Heritage still carries out the business of official multiculturalism by developing and advocating for official language, HL, and multicultural programs, as well as other programs promoting citizenship participation, mutual understanding across diverse communities, fine arts and culture, and so on (Canadian Heritage, 2005). Although multiculturalism features prominently in Canadian public discourse and in policy statements as a core Canadian value, and one that is often linked with HL education, the clichéd discourses of multiculturalism have been critiqued by many Canadian scholars in the sociology of education who instead favor discourses surrounding diversity, anti-racist education initiatives, and critical cultural studies (e.g., Bannerji, 1995; Dei, 1993).

Canada's two official languages have enjoyed official recognition from the time of confederation in 1867, but in 1969 the Official Languages Act was designed to highlight and legislate support for national bilingualism and the rights of English or French minority groups in different regions of Canada to education and services in their first language (L1) (Canadian Heritage, 2005). The Act also ensures that Canadian students have opportunities to learn both official languages at school, through English or French second-language (alternatively, intensive or immersion) courses, and suggests that there might be economic and not just social, cultural, or political advantages in knowing both languages. Whereas, as earlier stated, provincial governments control most curricular matters, official bilingualism at the national level is a policy that impacts provincial practices, funding, and priorities to a certain extent, as well. "Minority-language instruction" in Canadian national policy documents (e.g., Canadian Heritage, 2005) generally refers to provisions for L1-medium education for French-speaking minorities living in English-speaking provinces and for English-speakers in Quebec.

Many provinces have legislated and funded opportunities for people to learn HLs, that is, languages other than English or French and typically associated with local immigrant populations. Baker (2001) contrasts two types of HL programs: those that involve after-school or weekend classes taught by community volunteers, in which students receive about 2.5 hours of instruction in the HL each week, and bilingual-heritage programs in which the HL is the language of instruction for about 50% of the day and the programs are staffed by professional teachers. In the latter, minority-language communities can lobby for education in both English and their HL.

Support for HL education across Canada and the languages selected have varied regionally but what they have in common is the underlying belief that learning the languages is an important form of educational and community enrichment and not just a way of transitioning students into monolingual programs in one of the official languages. In Quebec, the Programme d'Enseignement de Langues d'Origines (PELO) historically involved, though on a much smaller scale than in its neighboring English-dominant province Ontario, the teaching of Italian, Portuguese, Greek, and Spanish to children for a half hour a day during regular school hours (Cummins, 1984). There were also (and apparently continue to be) private schools for Jewish, Greek, and Armenian Quebecers and community-operated supplementary schools.[2]

Outside of Ontario and Quebec, both of which are major immigrant-receiving provinces that have had many forms of HL teaching and hundreds of thousands of HL learners over the past three decades, the prairie provinces of Alberta, Saskatchewan, and Manitoba have shown enthusiastic support for HLs and bilingual HL programs (Cummins, 1992). Ukrainian and German have been especially vital HLs on the prairies. Edmonton, the capital of Alberta, has had Hebrew, Yiddish, Mandarin, Arabic, and Polish HL programs in addition to Ukrainian and German. Manitoba has had bilingual heritage programs in English-German, English-Hebrew, English-Ukrainian, and after-school HL courses in a variety of other languages as well (Manitoba Education, Citizenship, and Youth, 2005). In Winnipeg, the most popular language courses taken during school hours are currently Spanish, Filipino, and Japanese (mostly HLs), plus the aboriginal languages Ojibwe and Cree (Manitoba Education, Citizenship, and Youth, 2005). In Saskatchewan, Bujea (1989) described the growth of HL schools in the late 1980s, featuring up to 18 languages in 1989, including Cambodian, Spanish, Chinese, and Tigrigna, the official language of Eritrea. Also in Saskatchewan, Rincker (1991) reports on community-sponsored out-of-school HL programs and personnel funded by provincial grants from 1974 to 1990, highlighting both the problems with implementing such programs—problems that face programs nationwide (e.g., lack of available teaching materials, lack of in-service teacher training for volunteer teachers, multi-level classes, teacher turnover, and unmotivated students)—and the benefits.

In the maritime province of Nova Scotia on the east coast of Canada, the major heritage languages in which students can receive instruction both in school and in out-of-school programs and at the college level are German and Gaelic. Nova Scotia also provides French official-language support for its Acadian francophone population and Mi'kmaw language support for its Native population (CASLT, 2005).

HL programs have generated far less controversy on the prairies than in the more populated urban centers of Toronto and Montreal, where some people have feared that HL programs would undermine social cohesion and harmony and impede the acquisition of English or French by new Canadians. Despite such fears, statistics unfortunately show otherwise: there has been a continuing high incidence of HL loss among second-generation Canadians with the shift to official language adoption (Swidinsky & Swidinsky, 1997).

Demographics

According to Statistics Canada (2005a), the Canadian population in 2001 was just over 30 million, of whom nearly 17.4 million people claimed English as their L1 (58%), 6.7 million French (23%), and the rest an assortment of other European and non-European languages. Table 4.1 lists the 10 largest "mother tongue" groups in Canada, after English and French in 1971, 1991, and 2001. The top five HLs in 2001 included various dialects of Chinese (over 850,000 speakers), Italian (about 469,490), German (438,085), Polish (208,375), and Spanish (245,495). The two largest aboriginal languages (not shown in the table) in 2001 continued to be Cree (72,880, mostly in Manitoba and Saskatchewan, but declining in numbers) and Inuktitut (formerly "Eskimo;" 29,005 speakers and increasing primarily in the new northern territory of Nunavut and in Quebec).

This national linguistic profile marks interesting shifts from previous census data (e.g., Statistics Canada, 2002), and reflects several demographic factors over the past three decades: (1) the immigration of large numbers of South and East Asians to Canada since the early 1980s, which has greatly increased the number of

Table 4.1 Canadian Language Groups Described as "Mother Tongue Other than Official Language" (Allophones)

Rank	1971	1991	2001
1	German	Italian	Chinese (all)
2	Italian	Chinese (all)	Italian
3	Ukrainian	German	German
4	Dutch	Portuguese	Punjabi
5	Polish	Ukrainian	Spanish
6	Greek	Polish	Portuguese
7	Chinese (all)	Spanish	Arabic
8	Hungarian	Punjabi	Polish
9	Portuguese	Dutch	Tagalog
10	Yiddish, Croatian, etc.	Greek	Ukrainian

Source: Statistics Canada 2002, 2005a, 2005b census data

Chinese, Punjabi, Tagalog, and Vietnamese speakers nationwide relative to earlier waves of immigrants from Western or Central European language backgrounds; (2) a concurrent increase in the number of Arabic-speaking immigrants from the Middle East and Spanish speakers from Latin America, most of whom reside in Ontario and Quebec, although numbers of Spanish speakers in the West is also increasing; (3) a significant generational shift from non-official-language (L1) use in the home to English or French use among Dutch, Ukrainian, German, Greek, Italian, and Yiddish speakers; and (4) the growing proportion of Canadians who speak neither official language as their mother tongue or home language, often referred to as *Allophones* in Canada and especially in Quebec.[3]

Besides asking respondents about their L1 ("mother tongue"), the Canadian census now also asks them about their home language, their ethnic identification, other languages they know and how often they use them, "language(s) of public use," whether they speak their HL, and what language they speak in their workplace (Statistics Canada, 2005a).[4] The inclusion of these items allows a statistical comparison of L1 to home language in any given census year, and then every five years, thus providing a measure of language vitality/retention versus language shift. The inclusion of the additional information also acknowledges that one's HL is not necessarily one's L1 and that the HL can be learned subsequent to an L1 (Jedwab, 2000).

Research on Heritage Language Education in Canada

Formative/Summative Program Evaluation Studies

Since the early 1970s, research has been conducted on a variety of heritage bilingual programs in Canada: for example, an Italian kindergarten transition program in Toronto, Italian and Portuguese transition programs in Grades 4–6, English-Ukrainian kindergarten (K)-elementary programs in Edmonton and Manitoba, and Hebrew-French-English elementary programs in Montreal (see Ashworth, 1988, pp. 190–193 for details of the studies; and Cummins, 1993; Cummins & Danesi, 1990; Danesi, McLeod, & Morris, 1993). Most of the studies were formative and/or summative evaluations, designed to reassure program participants that the students were not disadvantaged linguistically or academically by virtue of their enrollment in bilingual programs. The studies collectively looked at such topics as teachers' and parents' satisfaction with the bilingual programs (generally showing high levels of satisfaction), classroom participation (showing advantages for students who had participated in the HL programs in comparison with their peers who had not), students' attitudes toward the HL (better than those of students from the same ethnic background who had not been in such programs), academic attainment (equal to or better than those not in HL programs in subjects like mathematics), high levels of HL and English proficiency and particularly fluency, no disadvantages (and in some cases definite advantages) for trilingual or bilingual students in their English performance compared with monolingual English speakers by Grades 4-5, and feelings of increased self-esteem, cultural identity, and intra-family communication as a result of HL programs.

These results mirror those that have been reported over the years for French immersion as well, and were precisely the sorts of outcomes that program participants and scholars had hoped for (Cummins, 1989).

Research on the Experiences of Bilingual and Trilingual HL Students

There has in recent decades been an increasing recognition by many educators (if not by all parents and school board representatives, see Cummins, 1993) that use of HLs by parents at home with their children, for example in literacy activities, supports them academically, even if the academic work is conducted at school in English or another non-HL target language. Thus, although seemingly counter-intuitive, information and skills do transfer from L1 (HL) to L2 or L3 (Cummins, 1989). Indeed, Danesi (1991) suggests three interpretive frames to help explain such findings:

1. the aforementioned principle of *linguistic interdependence* (i.e., positive transfer of knowledge and skills from HL to L2)—that "the L1 and the school language are not at all antagonistic contenders for 'cognitive air time and space,' so to speak, but cooperative systems in the child's linguistic and cognitive development" (Danesi, 1991, p. 653);
2. the principle of *narrativity*, whereby "children who are exposed to two culturally specific forms of storying through HL training are in a better position to increase their mental versatility" (p. 655); and

3. the principle of *cognitive enhancement* (cf. additive bilingualism) which holds that "language lies at the base of cognition and, therefore, the presence of more than one language in the child leads to a broadening of this base" (p. 656).

Another area of research on HL students in Canada is studies of trilingual Canadians' motivations, experiences, and outcomes in French immersion or Francophone contexts. The studies tend to be situated in cities with large urban immigrant populations, such as Toronto, Montreal, and Vancouver (e.g., Swain & Lapkin, 1991; Lamarre, 2003; Lamarre & Dagenais, 2004; Dagenais & Berron, 2001). For example, Swain and Lapkin (1991), based on a two studies conducted by them and their colleagues, concluded that students in French immersion school programs who have maintained their family HL outperform those who have either not maintained their HL or who are Anglophones without a HL other than English:

for minority language children who have maintained their heritage language and supported it with literacy knowledge, we can expect superior third language performance relative to other minority language children who do not read or write in their heritage language. Moreover, we can expect superior performance for them also in relation to the French language skills of majority Anglophones for whom French is a second, rather than a third language. (p. 640)

More recent research reviewed by Swain and Lapkin (2005) concerning minority students in immersion programs who are learning through the medium of their third language (e.g., Vietnamese learners of French in Canada or Spanish learners of Korean in the U.S) suggests that in addition to their successful academic and linguistic performance, the HL speakers also were able to retain important aspects of their HL ethnic identification.

Retrospective Studies of HL Education

Another area of research has examined the retrospective perceptions of students and teachers regarding aspects of HL teaching, learning, and maintenance. Feuerverger (1991) conducted a study with 148 students studying HLs at the University of Toronto to learn more about their past HL learning experiences. The languages included Italian, Portuguese, Chinese, Korean, Japanese, Hebrew, Ukrainian, and Yiddish. A questionnaire was administered to each student, and two students from each language group were also selected for in-depth interviews. Some of the findings from the quantitative analysis were that the Japanese-Canadians, of all the groups, had the lowest ethnic identity maintenance, a finding attributed to Japanese-Canadians' internment and migration in Canada during and after World War II, which did not enable them to maintain or have pride in their HL. However, with the favorable economic position of Japan in the 1980s, Feuerverger noted that some third-generation Japanese-Canadians in her study had now become more interested in learning Japanese. As for identification with their ethnic homeland, the Italians ranked highest, with Portuguese and Jewish respondents following them. This finding was attributed to the recency of the groups' immigration and thus their ongoing ties with the country associated with their HL. Goldstein's (1997) study of Portuguese immigrant women's intense Portuguese linguistic and cultural social networks in Toronto and their HL maintenance strongly corroborates the claim of strong HL vitality among many Portuguese families in Toronto. At the other end of the ranking were Ukrainians, who, in the late 1980s at the time of Feuerverger's (1991) study, could not easily visit the Soviet Union and maintain ties with the Ukraine. That situation was anticipated to change though with the dissolution of the Soviet Union, with a concomitant expected increase in Ukrainian-Canadians' ethnic cohesion and homeland ties. Thus, students' investment in the languages depended in large measure on their perceptions of the past, present, or future sociopolitical context and status of the language locally and internationally, and the opportunities the language might afford them in the future.

However, many students' retrospective levels of satisfaction with past HL programs were relatively low. They cited such reasons as poor HL teacher training and materials, and a lack of coherence and organization in the programs. Also emphasized was the importance of maintaining HL literacy at home and at school, and family HL literacy practices, not just oracy. Unfortunately, the study provided little information about the students' current university-level experiences learning their HL or about the levels of proficiency and cultural or personal insights they had achieved. A subsequent study by Feuerverger (1997), investigating HL teachers' experiences as teachers and their relative status in public schools, documented issues of low morale among the teachers based on their own low status (as non-mainstream course teachers sometimes lacking professional certification) and the low status of the languages they taught.

Chow (2001), a sociologist, also conducted a retrospective study of Canadian university students' experiences as HL learners, using questionnaire data. Focusing on Chinese-Canadians in particular, he reported a negative correlation between age and early arrival as immigrants, on the one hand, and their experiences as HL learners, on the other hand, in part because the programs were not very successful in developing students' oral and written HL proficiency.

Studies of HL Students' Linguistic Profiles and Experiences in Comparison with Non-HL Learners of the Language

Several recent studies in British Columbia have examined HL students' current experiences in university courses, some of which were designed for second-language learners rather than HL learners specifically. Two studies examined

Japanese L2 university courses (Shinbo, 2004; Nakamura, 2005). Shinbo (2004) analyzed Japanese HL learners' areas of greatest perceived need in their language and literacy skills, their advantages and strengths over non-HL learners in mixed courses, their in-class language use, and teachers' challenges in accommodating them in these "foreign language" classes. Focusing on third- and fourth-year university students, she observed three courses (nine times in total) and gave questionnaires to teachers, non-HL students, and HL students, and also interviewed teachers and students (23 students, of whom 14 were HL learners). The HL students' experiences were quite typical: they reported that their reasons for studying Japanese at university were to improve their proficiency, especially grammar and reading/writing (Japanese characters in particular), to enhance their identity as Japanese-Canadians, to speak more fluently, to increase the range of registers in their repertoire, and to maintain and build on their existing Japanese skills. The need to improve their Japanese characters and writing, first and foremost, was strongly felt by both teachers and the HL students. They also expressed confusion about Japanese grammar and about grammatical terminology, which are usually learned in the first two years of undergraduate Japanese study. Their initial placement in higher level courses based on proficiency tests meant that the students had certain gaps in their metalinguistic knowledge and also were unused to doing literal translations from Japanese to English.

Many described their desire to use Japanese in their careers, in Japanese language education and business, for example, and realized that suitably developed literacy skills would be important in those contexts. Most of the HL students had previously attended HL classes as children, for just over four years, on average, and for as long as 12 years in two cases. Most deemed their listening comprehension to be reasonably good (again, fairly typical of the standard HL profile), followed by speaking and reading, but it depended to some extent on the type of material and sophistication of discourse encountered. A common observation was that the students lacked a full sociolinguistic repertoire of honorific, humble, and polite forms for use in formal settings. For those who reported having used Japanese mainly at home or with family and friends outside the home, most also said that they mixed Japanese and English or resorted to English; in fact, most of them opted to be interviewed for the study in English rather than Japanese, although the researcher was a native speaker of Japanese.

Shinbo also observed that in class discussions, the HL students initiated more turns and expressed more opinions than their non-HL partners did, and in questionnaires, the non-HL learners conveyed their sense of unfairness and discomfort being in classes with more proficient and fluent HL students. HL learners, on the other hand, expressed concern that they were being judged more harshly by teachers because of their backgrounds. Often the teachers and students were unaware of the challenges faced by others in the same class coming from different backgrounds and that the HL students weren't only there for "easy credit"—that they were legitimate language learners.

A second study (Nakamura, 2005) did not focus on HL learners in Japanese courses exclusively but did describe the case of one such learner in a class with mainly Chinese-L1 learners of Japanese, a common demographic in Western Canadian Asian-language courses in public schools and postsecondary institutions. Again, the advantage of the HL learner was her oral fluency and cultural knowledge, especially when speaking about everyday topics (though she often spoke in English in class). However, the Chinese classmates had a better command of literacy skills, due to their superior knowledge of Chinese characters, which are used in Japanese literacy as well.

Finally, Li's (2005) survey of HL learners of Chinese at a Western Canadian university, like Shinbo's (2004) study, revealed that although HL learners are by no means homogeneous in terms of their language and literacy profiles, on the whole they do share common features, particularly the need to work on advanced, as opposed to basic conversational, aspects of language, pragmatics, and literacy. The population of university Mandarin language students in the program she described was 92% HL learners. She conducted a survey of 695 students (8% of whom were non-HL) and did follow-up interviews with 20 HL students, from a range of Chinese national backgrounds (five each from Taiwan, Mainland China, Hong Kong, and ethnic Chinese from other locations). Sixty-four percent of the students had arrived in Canada between the age of six and 15, many of them between the age of 11 and 15. The study revealed that most were studying Mandarin for both integrative and instrumental reasons: to learn more about themselves and their ethnic cultures and to increase their future career opportunities related to the burgeoning Chinese economy, rather than for purely academic reasons. Unlike their university HL experiences, which they described using positive terms, such as *enjoyable, fun, rewarding, satisfying, important, helpful, interesting,* and *fascinating,* their childhood HL learning experiences were described in negative terms: *difficult, annoying, bothersome, unwilling, painful, isolated, lonely, uncomfortable, scared, (teacher) intimidating, embarrassed, not free, stuck, a burden.* Li also examined their preferences for the simplified versus traditional (more complicated) script and reasons for the preferences, stemming primarily from their country of origin. Finally, she analyzed students' attitudes toward different varieties (dialects) of Mandarin (e.g., Beijing, Taiwanese) and their reasons for affiliating with one or another variety, and the connection between these varieties and their evolving identities.

Studies of Language Loss, Maintenance, and Identity

Research on language shift, language loss, and language-related identity issues has been another important focus in Canada (e.g., Kouritzin, 1999; Edwards, 1993; Pendakur, 1990). Space does not permit a review of all of this research here but several recent studies are outlined. Kouritzin's (1999) study is innovative because it uses life history interviews with 21 Western Canadians who were asked to reflect on the personal impact of their HL loss (or, alternatively, lack of HL acquisition or its latent acquisition) on their lives and identities. Unlike language shift research that examines groups and their HL retention or loss over one or more generations and focuses especially on linguistic or statistical aspects of this shift based on census data, Kouritzin's study (following Fillmore's, 1991, study highlighting the social and psychological impact of HL loss on individuals, families, and society) examined the individuals' HL versus English identification through narrative accounts of their experiences and perceptions. Kouritzin included five in-depth life histories with people of Cantonese, Cree, Finnish, Korean, and Hungarian descent and identified cross-case themes gleaned from 16 others in her study. Those themes included the breakdown and thus aversion to extended family relationships resulting from L1 (HL) loss, the reluctance to invite school friends home, and the personal dissonance of not even understanding oneself speaking in the now-forgotten L1 in home videos at a younger age. Participants reported feeling anger, frustration, shame, and disappointment with such outcomes, thus experiencing negative self-image and negative views of their ethnic cultures and a feeling of identifying with neither their HL nor the dominant English culture.

A subsequent multiple-case study of HL maintenance versus loss was conducted by Guardado (2002), who is also currently conducting a larger-scale study of L1 language and literacy maintenance among a larger sample of Hispanic immigrant families in British Columbia. His original study examined four Spanish-speaking immigrant families' maintenance or loss of Spanish, and particularly the HL experiences of their school-aged children. The parents had been in Canada from eight to 17 years and each family had at least one child over the age of six years. Two of the families had children who had successfully maintained Spanish and two families had children who were already losing the language as they shifted to English dominance. Guardado examined some of the causes and consequences of both HL maintenance and loss based on his semi-structured interviews and observations. He also described parents' perceptions of the home language situation. Promoting a strong, positive L1 identity was one of the factors associated with HL maintenance, though parents conceded that this is difficult when there is not a large vibrant local community of Spanish-speakers, a situation that is gradually changing in the region. All four families recognized possible economic and social benefits for the children if they maintained their L1, but those whose children were losing the L1 expressed optimism nonetheless that the children would develop their HL later.

Finally, Chumak-Horbatsch (1999) documented a longitudinal study of children's successful L1 maintenance by Ukrainian-speaking parents living in Toronto. The children had attended an HL nursery school and later a Ukrainian Catholic school. The children reportedly attained bilingual status and also perceived themselves as bilinguals, despite the lack of opportunities to use the language more widely in Canada. This, then, is a case of HL resilience because of church/school community support for the language.

Controversy and Change

As described above, much of the early support for multilingualism was framed by a discourse of ethnic identity, diversity, tolerance, and multiculturalism. However, it is important to note that positive views of multilingualism and multiculturalism officially touted in Canada since Pierre Trudeau's tenure as prime minister are in sharp contrast with earlier policies of Anglo-conformity and racism in the late 19th century. They also contrast with the majority of policies in the 20th century, which resulted in the suppression and even extinction of some languages and the mistreatment of their speakers as well as members of other minority groups, regardless of their languages (e.g., Blacks, Jews, Japanese-Canadians, the Deaf; see Cummins & Danesi, 1990).

In fact, aboriginal languages and peoples have not fared as well in Canada historically. Only in recent years (typically from the early 1970s) has there been federal assistance to fund aboriginal language programs and preserve what remains of the aboriginal linguistic and cultural capital of the various First Nations peoples in Canada (Canadian Heritage, 2005). In Quebec, similar controversy has existed in relation to Franco-assimilation, particularly when it is implied that Allophones (those who speak neither French nor English) are not true Quebecers and undermine Quebec's racial and cultural homogeneity.[5] In addition, there have been restrictions placed on who is allowed to study in Quebec's English-medium schools, with parents of new immigrants in many cases being required by provincial policies to send their children to Francophone schools, despite possible preferences for Anglophone schools (Cummins & Danesi, 1990). Finally, when HL programs were first introduced (primarily in Francophone schools), there was distrust of the motives behind them, with some groups fearing that this was an attempt by politicians to attract "the ethnic vote" and also to take away control of language programs from the cultural groups themselves. However, such fears have abated and currently three types of HL programs exist in Quebec and appear to be growing.

Current rhetoric focuses to a greater extent on antiracist education, pluralism, multilingualism, and, as the following excerpt (Canadian Heritage, 2002) illustrates, on the economic potential of a multilingual citizenry because of globalization and international telecommunications:

> Recent advances in technology have made international communications more important than ever. Canadians who speak many languages and understand many cultures make it easier for Canada to participate globally in areas of education, trade and diplomacy. (p. 1)

The term *heritage languages* in recent government documents as well as in provincial educational curricula is therefore being replaced by *international languages* to reflect a more forward-looking global focus as opposed to one that harks back to the ethnolinguistic roots of certain sectors of the population

(Baker, 2001). For example, Cummins (1992) points out the problems with perception of the erstwhile emphasis on "heritage" and also the political pressures and interests involved, a point I will return to later in my discussion of politics in British Columbia:

> While the dominant Anglophone and Francophone groups generally are strongly in favor of learning the other official language, they see few benefits to promoting heritage languages for themselves, for Canadian society as a whole, or for children from ethnocultural backgrounds. The educational focus for such children should be on acquiring English and becoming Canadian rather than on erecting linguistic and cultural barriers between them and their Canadian peers. In short, whereas advocates of heritage language teaching stress the value of bilingual and multilingual skills for the individual and society as a whole, opponents see heritage languages as socially divisive, excessively costly, and educationally retrograde in view of minority children's need to succeed academically in the school language. (p. 285)

Other than this ideological controversy, tensions and threatened job action surrounding more practical matters of course/program scheduling, payment of teachers, length of the school day and week, and so on, were associated with HL programs in Ontario in the 1980s. These programs offered students an additional half an hour a day of instruction in their HL. Ashworth (1988) described this situation as follows:

> Heritage language teaching is both a political and an educational issue. Politically, the ethnic vote in large urban areas is important. Some politicians see the mounting of heritage language programs as likely to win them votes and therefore favour their immediate implementation. Educationally, heritage language teaching and bilingual education appear to be beneficial to children's academic achievement and social adjustment. The incorporation of heritage language classes into the already full school schedule is, however, causing organizational and administrative problems in some districts.... (pp. 200–201)

Heritage Language Education in British Columbia: Policies and Pedagogy

Benyon and Toohey (1991) and Reeder, Hasebe-Ludt, and Thomas (1997) describe the HL policy and programs context in British Columbia (BC). According to Benyon and Toohey (1991), there were approximately 17,000 students in community (after school or Saturday) HL programs for 31 different languages in 1988/89. At that time, federal funding was available to support HL schools but the funding was eliminated soon after. A small number of bilingual HL programs in public schools also existed as an alternative to French L2 programs. It was anticipated that by the year 2000, HL programs could be offered in BC schools and that there would be greater attention paid to HL teaching and the provision of credit-bearing HL courses.

However, in 1995 BC launched a new language education policy, as described in some detail by Reeder et al. (1997). This policy was problematic for several reasons: (1) it blurred and collapsed heritage and second (modern/international) language courses and programs; (2) it lowered the mandatory grade from which L2s were to be taught across BC public schools from Grade 8 to Grade 5, without having ensured that teachers would be properly trained to teach languages from that grade level or that there would be suitable materials for students and teachers; and (3) it left decisions regarding which language(s) would be offered at schools up to local school districts, with the proviso that all teachers be BC certified. This meant that decisions tended to be based on resources available within the district and on the linguistic interests of the community. In many school districts, French was selected as the default L2 course because it was easier to find staff and materials for French than for other languages.[6] However, certain aspects of the policy were also intriguing. For example, the new languages that were emphasized in the policy and that were the first to undergo curriculum review (besides French) were Punjabi, Mandarin, German, Japanese and Spanish. Of these, Punjabi and Mandarin were primarily HLs with large local ethnic constituencies. German, traditionally a HL in the interior of BC, is now offered in almost no Vancouver-area schools. Approved provincial curricula have more recently also been developed for American Sign Language and Korean. In fact, the local Korean community in Vancouver donated large sums of money to develop the curriculum and teachers' resource packages because of the perceived importance of maintaining Korean language proficiency in the next generation.

As a university representative on the BC Provincial International Languages Curriculum Overview Team during the 1990s and one of the people asked to examine and approve the new Korean curriculum in 2005, I learned first-hand how political factors entered into the decision-making process, often at the expense of good educational policy. One issue concerned the designation of courses as heritage or nonheritage.[7]

Of the new languages singled out for attention, Punjabi and Mandarin were actually HL courses, although in the language of the policy statements and curriculum guides (Integrated Resource Packages; see CASLT, 2005) these were designated as "international" L2s intended for non-HL learners. As one would expect, almost all the students in both the Punjabi and Mandarin courses are first generation speakers of those languages and non-HL learners quickly drop out of the courses because they cannot keep up with their typically much more proficient HL classmates.

As Ashworth's (1988) comment above suggests, there was pressure from the quickly growing Punjabi and Taiwanese-Chinese communities (the "ethnic vote") for those languages to be given priority. From an HL maintenance standpoint, they naturally had good educational reasons for doing so. But the timing was suspicious. Provincial elections were held soon after the new language policy was unveiled at press conferences in the provincial capital. It was perhaps not surprising that several of the provincial government ministers were from the Punjabi community and, indeed, that Punjabi was selected to be the first language to have new curriculum guides and materials developed. When the provincial curriculum was developed for Mandarin, the Ministry and its overview team (of which I was part) decided that simplified characters and not the more complicated traditional characters would be taught, following the example of Australian Mandarin education. However, before the curriculum could be printed and considered an official and therefore legal policy statement, the local Taiwanese community rose up and demanded that traditional characters also be taught. Therefore, the Mandarin curriculum (see CASLT, 2005) now requires that both simplified and traditional characters be taught.

As Reeder et al. (1997) point out, the new language policy was flawed and had relatively low expectations for target levels of L2 proficiency (and particularly for L2 literacy), emphasizing intercultural tolerance, understanding, positive attitudes toward L2 learning, and multiculturalism instead (e.g., with lessons on festivals, foods, and so on):

> the blurring of the distinction between social policy and language education policy raises important questions about the broad societal purposes of public education and its role in promoting particular ideologies, no matter how benign. (p. 375)

Furthermore, despite their emphasis on oral proficiency, developing L2s for purposes of creative expression and enjoyment, communication, information-seeking, and cultural awareness, the Grade 12 provincial final examinations are still traditional paper-and-pencil tests with no oral component.[8]

In addition to coursework for "international" L2 learners, the BC policy has provisions for its relatively small Francophone-minority community to be schooled through the medium of French if they so choose, though many opt instead for English-medium or French-immersion schools, and a new French school board was developed to coordinate Francophone minority programs in the late 1990s. In BC only 1.5% of the population speaks L1 French, whereas approximately 60% speak L1 English, and Francophones are assimilating very quickly into English-speaking society in BC. The next largest L1 group is Chinese (Cantonese, Mandarin, or other varieties), followed by Punjabi and German (Statistics Canada, 2005d). Although both Ontario and BC are the Anglophone Canadian provinces with the largest number of immigrants arriving each year, Ontario has a much larger proportion of Francophones, known as Franco-Ontarians, because of its geographical location in central-eastern Canada adjacent to Quebec. Reeder et al. (1997) also provide a summary of programs available historically and at present for aboriginal languages and for English as a second language or second dialect.

For the many hundreds of HL after-school or weekend teachers in BC, teacher education, methods, and materials have also been lacking—a common complaint from HL communities in other provinces as well. In the mid-1990s, the University of British Columbia's (UBC) Centre for Intercultural Language Studies and Continuing Studies (on whose advisory board I served) conducted a feasibility study and broad consultation with community HL groups. We also developed modules envisioned as part of a one-year program for local HL teachers desiring a noncredit pre-service or in-service certificate. However, most local HL teachers are volunteers, paid at most a small honorarium for their teaching, and HL schools have few financial resources. As a result, the HL/international language teachers would not be able to afford tuition fees for a cost-recovery program priced at several thousand dollars. The same teachers generally also lack the prerequisites to enter our B.Ed. program for modern language teachers because of their prior education in other countries. Unfortunately, teachers' HL and/or English proficiency, their language teaching methods, and the materials and curriculum they use are often inadequate as a result, despite their honorable intentions. For most of them, annual professional development and networking opportunities are therefore limited to activities offered by the BC Heritage Language Association, which serves about 150 HL groups representing 35,000 students.[9] Meanwhile, at the university, teacher education in heritage language pedagogy, which is subsumed under Modern (L2) Language Education, continues to present its own challenges as there are few qualified applicants who have all of the following: (1) proficiency in the languages and also experience studying grammatical analysis and composition in the language at a third- or fourth-year undergraduate level, (2) expertise in another teachable subject area since some languages are not yet widely enough taught to warrant full-time employment for teachers, and (3) requisite Canadian-content coursework at the undergraduate level as well as senior-level coursework in the target language.[10]

Finally, it is not sufficient to write about K–12 and extracurricular language policies in BC without also considering the effects of demographic and policy changes on higher education. UBC, for example, is currently witnessing a decline in enrollment of students in its language programs for French, German, and Russian (a problem commonly reported in other parts of North America). At the same time, it is experiencing a sharp increase in the number of students taking university-level Korean, Japanese, and Mandarin. However, this new population of students is different from the traditional Anglophone student body in that the vast majority of students in Korean and Mandarin (together totaling well over one thousand) are HL learners, while the vast majority in Japanese, though not HL learners, could be termed *untraditional* language learners: nearly 95% of them (1400 out of a total of 1500 students in Japanese) are first generation Chinese-Canadians who have some familiarity with Chinese orthography, which is used in writing Japanese characters.[11]

Since teacher education, materials, and curriculum at the post-secondary level were not designed for these populations, important areas for future research will be to examine more closely: (1) needs and aspirations of nontraditional or HL students in these language programs; (2) ways of also accommodating English-L1 learners; and (3) ways of improving instruction through pre-service and in-service activities.

Summary and Concluding Remarks

In this chapter, I have outlined some of the policies, programs, problems, and possibilities associated with HL education (and sometimes HL loss) in Canada over the past 30 years. In many respects, the Canadian experience has mirrored experiences in other countries. However, the level of political and financial support for HL education from the early 1970s through the early 1990s and the cluster of local constituencies connected with the separatist movement in Quebec, the need for constructive action regarding aboriginal groups' languages, and the extraordinary foment of research and program development associated with French immersion and official multiculturalism around the same time were likely unique. Despite the satisfaction expressed by many participants vis-à-vis bilingual HL programs and other community programs, commonly cited problems include the need for language programs that do more than simply pay lip service to a bland ideology of multiculturalism and, rather, really help students become highly proficient in the target language, develop nuanced intercultural understandings, and receive all the benefits associated with multilingualism, positive ethnic identification, and internationalism. Appropriate teacher education and suitable, engaging curriculum/materials development along with the incorporation of new media (whether in public schools, private schools, community HL, or higher education programs) is also desperately needed (Li & Duff, in press).

As policies and population demographics change, so too does the focus of research in applied linguistics as we more closely examine such issues as language and identity, language/multilingual socialization, language acquisition and loss, and teacher development (Duff, in press). Beyond what has already been learned from program evaluations involving language tests and satisfaction questionnaires, our understanding of HL education and its impact on learners and on society will no doubt be expanded by research methods drawing on phenomenology, narrative inquiry, ethnography, case studies, and other qualitative approaches as well as other quantitative (e.g., survey) methods. In addition, with an increasing focus on lifelong education, research needs to address new questions longitudinally, at different points in learners' lives, as they encounter multiple languages especially in urban areas, and not just a single official language plus their heritage language. Research can then examine to a greater extent individual educational and social-psychological experiences connected with multilingualism and with people's integration within different local and global ethnolinguistic communities even at later stages in their lives (Lie & Duff, in press). It can also consider the cumulative impact of such integration, multilingual engagement, and vitality on self, family, community, and society. Lastly, there can be an expansion in the HL research agenda from K–12 schooling to multilingualism in and well beyond postsecondary education.

Notes

1. This chapter is affectionately dedicated to the memory of Russell N. Campbell, a wonderful professor, international language program developer/evaluator, mentor, boss, and human being. Russ's career-long passion for innovating, designing, implementing, and researching effective models of language teaching and learning worldwide was legendary. I was privileged to have participated in one such research project, on dual-language education, in Hungary. I would also like to thank Donna Brinton, Olga Kagan, and Susan Bauckus for their editorial assistance and helpful feedback on an earlier version of this chapter.
2. Language retention in Montreal, especially, has been relatively successful.
3. Nationally, these accounted for 12% of the population in 1951, and 18% in 2001; and approximately 40% in Vancouver and Toronto in 2001, and 20% in Montreal (Statistics Canada, 2005b).
4. For example, in 2001, 5% of Canadians overall and 8% of British Columbians used a language other than English or French at work (Statistics Canada, 2005b).
5. Currently, Allophones constitute just over 10% of the Quebec population, according to Statistics Canada 2001 census data and now exceed the number of Anglophones in that province (Statistics Canada, 2005c).
6. Even then, there were far too few teachers trained to teach French from as early as fifth grade. The situation for the other languages was even worse. Punjabi, for example, had very few published materials available and almost no trained teachers for what was supposed to be a communicative-experiential approach to L2 teaching.
7. For example, German has historically enjoyed the status of being a HL in many parts of BC but is often studied by a mixture of HL and non-HL learners, depending on the region; and Spanish and Japanese are normally learned as additional languages by non-HL learners.
8. This can no doubt be traced to the fact that assessment is not part of the portfolio of the ministry branch that deals with curriculum for international languages.
9. See http://www.bchla.net/.
10. At UBC, the Modern Language Education Program has as yet no coursework in HL education specifically yet
11. In BC public schools, similarly, the majority of learners of Japanese are Chinese students lured by the cultural proximity, adolescent interests in Japanese pop culture, and perhaps also by the orthographic advantage that literate Chinese students have with Japanese.

References

Ashworth, M. (1998). *Blessed with bilingual brains: Education of immigrant children with English as a second language.* Vancouver: Pacific Educational Press.

Baker, C. (2001). *Foundations of bilingual education and bilingualism* (3rd ed.). Clevedon, England: Multilingual Matters.

Bannerji, H. (1995). *Thinking through: Essays on feminism, Marxism and anti-racism.* Toronto: Women's Press.

Benyon, J., & Toohey, K. (1991). Heritage language education in British Columbia: Policy and programs. *Canadian Modern Language Review, 47*, 606–616.

Bujea, E. (1989). *Heritage language schools in Regina: Yesterday, today and tomorrow.* Regina, Saskatchewan: Multilingual Association of Regina.

Canadian Heritage (2002). *Canadian multiculturalism: An inclusive citizenship.* Retrieved August 14, 2002, from http://www.pch.gc.ca/progs/multi/inclusive_e.cfm

Canadian Heritage (2005). *Official languages: History of bilingualism in Canada.* Retrieved February 20, 2005, from http://www.pch.gc.ca/progs/lo-ol/biling/hist_e.cfm

CASLT [Canadian Association of Second Language Teachers]. (2005). *Provincial second language curriculum guides and support documents.* Retrieved August 18, 2005, from http://caslt.org/research/curriculumguides3.htm#ns

Chow, H. P.H. (2001). Learning the Chinese language in a multicultural milieu: Factors affecting Chinese-Canadian adolescents' ethnic language school experience. *The Alberta Journal of Educational Research, 47,* 369–374.

Chumak-Horbatsch, R. (1999). Language change in the Ukrainian home: From transmission to maintenance to the beginnings of loss. *Canadian Ethnic Studies,* 31, 61–75.

Cummins, J. (Ed.). (1983). *Heritage language education: Issues and directions.* Ottawa: Minister of Supply and Services Canada.

Cummins, J. (1984). The minority language child. In S. Shapson & V. D'Oyley (Eds.), *Bilingual and multicultural education: Canadian perspectives* (pp. 71–92). Clevedon, England: Multilingual Matters.

Cummins, J. (1989). Heritage language teaching and the ESL student: Fact and friction. In J. Esling (Ed.), *Multicultural education and policy: ESL in the 1990s* (pp. 3–17). Toronto: Ontario Institute for Studies in Education Press.

Cummins, J. (Ed.). (1991). Heritage languages [Special issue]. *Canadian Modern Language Review,* 47(4).

Cummins, J. (1992). Heritage language teaching in Canadian schools. *Journal of Curriculum Studies,* 24, 287–296.

Cummins, J. (1993). The research basis for heritage language promotion. In M. Danesi, K. McLeod, & S. Morris (Eds.), *Heritage language and education: The Canadian experience* (pp. 1–21). Ontario: Mosaic Press.

Cummins, J., & Danesi, M. (1990). *Heritage languages: The development and denial of Canada's linguistic resources.* Montreal: Our Schools/Our Selves Education Foundation.

Cummins, J., & Swain, M. (1986). *Bilingualism in education.* London: Longman.

Dagenais, D., & Berron, C. (2001) Promoting multilingualism through French immersion and language maintenance in three immigrant families. *Language, Culture and Curriculum,* 14, 142–55.

Danesi, M. (1991). Revisiting the research findings on heritage language learning: Three interpretive frames. *Canadian Modern Language Review,* 47, 650–659.

Danesi, M., McLeod, K., & Morris, S. (Eds.). (1993*). Heritage languages and education: The Canadian experience.* Oakville, ON: Mosaic Press.

Dei, G. (1993). The challenges of anti-racist education in Canada. *Canadian Ethnic Studies,* 25(2), 36–51.

Duff, P. (in press). Multilingualism in Canadian schools: Myths, realities, and possiblities. *Canadian Journal of Applied Linguistics.*

Edwards, J. (1993). Identity and language in the Canadian educational context. In M. Danesi, K. McLeod, & S. Morris (Eds.), *Heritage languages and education: The Canadian experience* (pp. 123–139). Oakville, ON: Mosaic Press.

Feuerverger, G. (1991). University students' perceptions of heritage language learning and ethnic identity maintenance. *Canadian Modern Language Review,* 47, 660–677.

Feuerverger, G. (1997). "On the edges of the map": A study of heritage language teachers in Toronto. *Teaching and Teacher Education, 13*(1), 39–53.

Fillmore, L. W. (1991). When learning a second language means losing the first. *Early Childhood Research Quarterly, 6,* 323–346.

Goldstein, T. (1997). *Two languages at work: Bilingual life on the production floor.* New York/Berlin: Mouton de Gruyter.

Guardado, M. (2002). Loss and maintenance of first language skills: Case studies of Hispanic families in Vancouver. *Canadian Modern Language Review,* 58, 341–363.

Jedwab, J. (2000). *Ethnic identification and heritage languages in Canada.* Montreal: Université de Montréal and Les Éditions Images.

Kouritzin, S. G. (1999). *Face[t]s of first language loss.* Mahwah, NJ: Lawrence Erlbaum.

Lamarre, P. (2003). Growing up trilingual in Montreal: Perceptions of college students. In R. Bayley & S. Schecter (Eds.), *Language socialization in bilingual and multilingual communities* (pp. 62–80). Mahwah, NJ: Lawrence Erlbaum.

Lamarre, P. & Dagenais, D. (2004) Linguistic representations of trilingual youth in two Canadian cities. In C. Hoffman & J. Ytsma (Eds.), *Third language acquisition and trilingualism.* Clevedon, England: Multilingual Matters.

Li, D. (2005, July). *Attitudes, identities and motivations in learning Chinese as a heritage language.* Paper presented at the World Congress of Applied Linguistics, Madison, WI, July 26, 2005.

Li, D., & Duff, P. (in press). Issues in Chinese heritage language researche: In A. W. He & Y. Xiao (Eds.), *Chinese as a heritage language*. Honolulu: National Foreign Language Research Center.

Manitoba Education, Citizenship and Youth. (2005). Languages: International and heritage. Retrieved Aug. 24, 2005, from http://www.edu.gov.mb.ca/ks4/cur/languages/index.html.

Nakamura, E. (2005). *Language use in Japanese as a foreign language classrooms*. Unpublished MA Thesis. University of British Columbia.

Pendakur, R. (1990). *Speaking in tongues: Heritage language maintenance and transfer in Canada*. Ottawa: Multiculturalism and Citizenship Canada.

Reeder, K., Hasebe-Ludt, E., & Thomas, L. (1997). Taking the next steps: Toward a coherent language education policy for British Columbia. *Canadian Modern Language Review, 53*, 373–402.

Rincker, J. (1991). Community-sponsored heritage language programs. *Canadian Modern Language Review, 47*(4), 642–649.

Shapson, S., & D'Oyley, V. (Eds.). (1984). *Bilingual and multicultural education: Canadian perspectives*. Clevedon, England: Multilingual Matters.

Shinbo, Y. (2004). *Challenges, needs, and contributions of heritage language students in foreign language classrooms*. Unpublished M.A. Thesis, University of British Columbia.

Statistics Canada (2002). 1996 Census: Mother tongue, home language and knowledge of languages. *The Daily*, pp. 1–14. Retrieved August 14, 2002, from http://www.statcan.ca/Daily/English/971202/d971202.htm

Statistics Canada (2005a). 2001 summary tables. Retrieved Feb. 20, 2005, from http://www.statcan.ca/english/Pgdb/demo13a.htm

Statistics Canada (2005b). The non-official languages. Retrieved Feb. 20, 2005, from http://www.pch.gc.ca/progs/lo-ol/pubs/census2001/5_e.cfm

Statistics Canada (2005c). Tables by provinces or territories. Retrieved Aug. 24, 2005, from http://www40.StatCan.ca

Statistics Canada (2005d). Tables by subject: Population and demography. Retrieved Aug. 24, 2005, from http://www40.statcan.ca

Swain, M., & Lapkin, S. (1991). Heritage language children in an English-French bilingual program. *Canadian Modern Language Review, 47*, 635–641.

Swain, M., & Lapkin, S. (2005). The evolving sociopolitical context of immersion education in Canada: Some implications for program development. *International Journal of Applied Linguistics, 15*, 169–186.

Swidinsky, R., & Swidinsky, M. (1997). Determinants of heritage language continuity in Canada: Evidence from the 1981 and 1991 census. *Canadian Ethnic Studies, 29*, 81–92.

Yee, D., & Sodhi, S. (1991). Resource guide for heritage language instruction: An annotated listing of projects supported by multiculturalism and citizenship 1973–1990. *Canadian Modern Language Review, 47*, 712–785.

5

Chinese "Dialect" Speakers as Heritage Language Learners

A Case Study[1]

TERRENCE G. WILEY

Introduction

This chapter explores the fate of a Chinese "dialect" speaker in his mother tongue and his later attempts to develop and maintain Chinese as his heritage language. His story helps to illustrate some of the difficulties encountered by immigrant children in remaining connected with the language(s) of the home and source country. It also demonstrates why language program planners and instructors need to address fundamental questions such as: Who can be considered a legitimate HL (heritage language) learner? Which is more important in determining that status: language background, proficiency, ancestry, national origin, or ethnicity? How important is literacy instruction in the "standard" language? Which standard language should be the focus of instruction when there are, in fact, competing written standards? Before telling this story, some background information is necessary regarding heritage languages generally and Chinese specifically.

Heritage Language: The Problem of Definition

In the United States, the label HL is gaining considerable popularity. HL tends to be applied to both immigrant and indigenous languages. Foreign language (FL) programs are increasingly targeting HL learners in an effort to extend literacy and cultural knowledge. Many community-related programs are attempting to preserve or revitalize threatened languages (Fishman, 1991, 1999, 2001; Hinton & Hale, 2001). Some argue that HL learners provide an important resource for U.S. business, economic, and even security interests (Nunberg, 2001; Peyton & Ranard, 2001).

Nevertheless, as with any attempt to apply labels to a complex situation, defining heritage languages, learners, and programs is problematic (Wiley, 2001a). With regard to the languages themselves, outside of the United States, the HL label has less popularity. In Canada, for example, the term has been used, but "international" language is preferred (Baker & Jones, 1998).

Some eschew the HL label because it evokes association with ancient cultures and past traditions that "may fail to give the impression of a modern international language (IL) that is of value in a technological society" (Baker & Jones, 1998, p. 509). Community language (CL) is more commonly used in Europe (Horvath & Vaughan, 1991). Others (for example, Corson, 1999a) make a compelling case for community-based language education, especially in reference to programs for indigenous peoples, to emphasize that language education should begin with people and their immediate reality, noting that the goal of community-based language education is to allow people to become directly involved in shaping their own futures through school and other agencies in their communities (Wiley, 2001a). Thus, the labels applied to programs are important because they suggest goals and educational philosophies that may or may not correspond to those of the individuals and communities to be served.

Valdés (2000) has defined an HL student as one "who is raised in a home where a non-English language is spoken, who speaks or merely understands the heritage language, and who is to some degree bilingual in English and the heritage language" (p. 1). This definition assumes facility in the language; however, for some incipient learners, ethnic affiliation with a family or larger community in which the HL is widely used may give them sufficient reason for applying the HL learner label to themselves, whether or not they manifest any immediate competence in the target HL.

In HL programs, the variety of the home/community language may or may not correspond to the prestige variety taught in FL programs. Sometimes the home/community variety of the HL may be a socially stigmatized language variety. Similarly, some HLs may not be widely used as languages of literacy. In these cases, the constructive truism of the need to build on the home/community resources of the learner often confronts standardization and academic expectations that diverge from the practices of home/community. This divergence may require negotiation or mediation if programs are to be successful in meeting the goals and needs of learners. These are just a few of the issues that have implications for program planning and educational policy for HL learners. Promoting "Chinese" as an HL among Chinese "dialect" speakers involves confronting such issues even as efforts to advance Chinese as an HL gain popularity (see Chao, 1997).

What's in a Name? "Chinese" and Chinese "Dialects"

In the case of Chinese as an FL, IL, HL, or CL, the very term *Chinese* can be problematic. When Chinese is used to refer to ethnicity or national origin, it is necessary to note that ethnic Chinese may be speakers of any language. However, in discussions of Chinese language programs in the United States, the term *Chinese* is generally assumed to mean Mandarin. Mandarin is the official language of the People's Republic of China and the island of Taiwan. Thus, the use of Chinese to mean Mandarin seems quite natural. However, not all Chinese schools in the

United States promote Mandarin.[2] Some offer instruction in Cantonese in communities where larger numbers of immigrants originate from Hong Kong.

Essentially, there are seven major mutually unintelligible spoken varieties of the Chinese language. Customarily, these varieties are referred to as regional "dialects," or *Fangyan*, which may also be categorized on the basis of both geographical and linguistic-structural association (Li Wei, 1994). Despite their mutual unintelligibility, when viewed from a national perspective, "...the Chinese are loath to call them 'different languages'" (Taylor & Taylor, 1995, p. 28). National unity notwithstanding, the unintelligibility among the major *Fangyan* "...is often regarded by the Chinese as a social group boundary marker distinguishing people of different origins" (Li Wei, 1994, p. 40). The seven traditional *Fangyan* are[3]:

1. *Beifang* (northern, or Mandarin), the native language of more than 70% of the Chinese population.
2. *Yue* (5%), the majority of whose speakers are in Guangdong province, the southernmost Mainland province of China, with the capital city of Guangzhou (Canton) as its center. Large numbers can also be found among overseas Chinese diasporas.
3. *Kejia* (Hakka) (3.7%), whose speakers came from small agricultural areas and are now scattered throughout southeastern China.
4. *Min* (4.1%), spoken in Fujian (the Mainland province on the western side of the Taiwan Strait), Taiwan and the Hainan Islands. It is often further distinguished into Northern Min and Southern Min.
5. *Wu* (8.5%), spoken in the lower Changjiang (the Yangtze River) region, including urban, metropolitan centers such as Shanghai.
6. *Xiang* (4.8%), mainly spoken in south central region.
7. *Gan* (2.4%), spoken chiefly in the southeastern inland provinces (Li Wei, 1994, p. 40).

Distinctions can also be made within each *Fangyan* because there are sub-varieties. The variety known in the West as "Cantonese," for example, is a "dialect" of the *Yue* group (Li Wei, 1994). That which is popularly called "Taiwanese" among U.S. immigrant Chinese belongs to the *Min* group (Ramsey, 1987). Taiwanese is of particular interest in this study, because the principal informant can be considered a native speaker of Taiwanese and Mandarin. The *Min*-speaking region of China is largely in the southeastern province of *Fujian* where the sub-variety called "Amoy" is spoken. The island of Taiwan is only about 100 miles from *Fujian*, and historically, the majority of the island's population migrated from that region. According to Ramsey (1987):

> The dialect called "Taiwanese" is very close to that of Amoy, and the people who speak it still outnumber all other groups on the island, including the

Mainlanders who fled to Taiwan following the Nationalist [Kuomingtang] defeat at the hands of the Communists in 1950. (p. 107)

In addition to the regional varieties of Chinese, there is a spoken norm (popularly called Mandarin in the West) that is called *Guoyu* (national language). According the Li Wei (1994), it developed

> from Guanhua, a hybrid, standardised spoken form used during the Ch'ing (Qing) Dynasty (1644–1911), and which has been officially endorsed and promoted as the lingua franca in China since the 1920s. It is now widely used, in modified forms, in Mainland China, where it is known as Putonghua (or "common speech"), Taiwan, and Singapore (where it is known as Huayu), and is taught to non-native-Chinese speakers as the "standard" Chinese language. (p. 41)

As with other spoken standardized languages, regional differences in pronunciation can still be noted, and those whose pronunciation diverges from Beijing's are marked for their "accents." Moreover, because of the challenges posed by the mutual unintelligibility of the regional oral varieties, there have been a number of campaigns to popularize Mandarin. "One of the principal strategies used in the campaigns is to introduce a phonetic spelling system based on the Roman alphabet. This system is known as *"Pinyin"* (Li Wei, 1994, p. 42). As yet, however, there is no universally accepted system of Romanization.

Written "Standards" and Script Policies: The "Almost" Unifying Force

In discussing the Chinese language, it is also necessary to distinguish between the spoken and written forms of language. Li Wei (1994) notes that "only Mandarin has a corresponding written form, which is shared by all literate Chinese whatever Fangyan they may speak" (p. 41). Actually, other dialects can be adapted to Chinese characters, but the notion of a "common" language in China is based largely on the notion of a written standard of Mandarin. Ramsey (1987) notes,

> ...the speakers of all dialects look toward a common model. Just as a single European country such as France has established conventions for linguistic behavior, so China, too, has linguistic standards that are accepted throughout the country by all the Chinese people. These standards may be much farther removed from actual speech than is the case with French. It is also true that when most Chinese think of a language that unites them as a people, the "common language" they have in mind is still fundamentally their written language. (p. 17)

Ramsey (1987) optimistically concludes that "...we usually do not speak of Chinese in the plural..." largely because the written standard overrides the different oral varieties as a standard, adding "[t]he same factors that help divide

Romance into several languages serve to unite Chinese into a single language" (p. 18).

Script policies on the Mainland have received extensive attention since the Communist victory in 1949. There was considerable debate regarding whether Chinese characters should be simplified or replaced by a phonetic system. For some, simplification was seen as an intermediate step in reaching the ultimate goal of Romanization. *Pinyin* was developed to facilitate that purpose. The primary concern on the Mainland was how to promote mass literacy. According to Ramsey (1987), "Plans for both phonetic writing and character simplification thus began simultaneously" (p. 143). Initial simplification took place in 1955 (Hsia, 1956). Subsequent additions to the initial list of simplified characters have also been made (Dayle, 1983; Ramsey, 1987).

There has been considerable progress on the Chinese Mainland in promoting wider literacy, but it is not clear how much of this success is attributable to the simplified characters. Although simplified characters have been used with success in promoting a basic level of functional literacy, it is still necessary to learn the more complex traditional characters if one is to attain more advanced levels of education. As Ramsey (1987) notes, in Taiwan, the literacy rate is higher despite the fact that the traditional characters are used:

> [This] shows that the old system can be taught and taught well. To a very large degree, it has simply been assumed that the wider use of simplified characters has simplified the learning process. Very little evidence has been properly documented. (p. 150)

In addition to the emphasis on Mandarin, there has also been some effort to promote bilingual education among Chinese ethnic language minorities. According to Teng and Weng (2001), "fifty-six ethnic groups currently exist in China, of which Han is the dominant ethnic group" (p. 265). The non-Han groups constitute about 8% of the total population.

Relevance for Chinese HL Instruction in the United States

Given this background on Chinese language variation and script policy, the question may be raised: In what sense do the standardized oral and written varieties of Mandarin truly represent an HL for so-called dialect speakers of other Chinese languages? Because Mandarin is widely accepted as an HL for both Mandarin speakers and for those who speak other varieties of Chinese, its status generally precludes any debate regarding its technical status as an HL. In addition, differences in script policies pose dilemmas for a unified or common approach to Chinese literacy instruction in the United States. Many community-based programs are dependant on receiving materials from outside the United States. Programs attempting to cater to immigrants from Taiwan generally use materials that provide instruction in the more complex traditional characters.

Those serving immigrants from the Mainland tend to introduce the simplified characters. Given limited community resources and the local political orientations, community-based programs do not try to serve both Taiwanese and Mainlander populations by allowing for more choice between scripts used for primary literacy instruction.

Moreover, in the case of Taiwan specifically, even issues of a common oral language are not entirely resolved through the use of Mandarin as the official language. For example, since the end of martial law in 1986, and with the formation of oppositional political parties to the *Kuomingtang* or Nationalist Party (see Copper, 1999; Rubinstein, 1999), the ever increasing use of Taiwanese in public contexts such as political campaigns (see Tsao, 2000) (as well as its use as a medium of literature by a small number of writers) indicates that the status of Mandarin as a common "heritage" language for all ethnic Chinese is open to debate. Despite this fact, there is currently little attempt in the United States to promote HL instruction in other Chinese languages (with the exception of Cantonese) such as Taiwanese or Hakka. As these are languages of the home and local communities, they could also be considered HLs.

Beyond this, in the broader literature, there has been little theoretical and policy discussion regarding the notion of first language multilingualism and its possible implications for HL learners. Many so-called dialect speakers of Chinese are raised in multilingual families, which often code-mix Mandarin and a home/community variety of Chinese.[4] The following case will illustrate some of the difficulties encountered by Chinese dialect speakers in their efforts to develop Mandarin.

The Case of Devin

The principal informant in this case study is a thirty-one-year-old male lawyer, who is a naturalized U.S. citizen of Chinese/Taiwanese heritage named Devin Chen.[5] The data for this chapter were collected in a series of structured interviews with Devin and his mother during the spring and early summer of 2001. On numerous additional occasions, the author also had access to other members of Devin's extended family, including his aunts and uncles, cousins, grandfather, and friends, and has been able to observe Devin in this larger, multilingual social network.

Family Background

Like most Taiwanese families, Devin's can trace its ancestry back to *Fujian* Province on the Chinese Mainland, which stretches to the east just across the Straits of Taiwan. Devin's ancestors migrated to the island about two hundred years ago when Taiwan was a province of the Ch'ing Dynasty (1644–1911). Devin's great grandmother, who was still living in the household when he was born, spoke only Taiwanese and never had the opportunity to go to school, a plight not uncommon for women of her generation. Both of his grandparents were educated in Japanese under Japanese rule (which spanned 1895 to 1945 period) and were preparing to become schoolteachers as World War II ended.

However, when the Kuomingtang (Nationalists) fled to the island in 1949 after being defeated by the Communists on the Mainland, martial law was imposed.[6] The Kuomingtang's language policies included restrictions on Japanese, prohibitions against Taiwanese in school and other social domains, and a mandate for Mandarin as the sole language of instruction. Many Taiwanese of that generation who lived through that period regarded native speakers of Mandarin and other Mainlanders with great circumspection. With this background, Devin's grandparents gradually acquired a functional knowledge of Mandarin but never attained native-like proficiency in the language. Devin's grandfather continued to pride himself on his flawless command of Japanese.

Devin's family background prior to immigration from Taiwan was linguistically parallel to that of many Taiwanese households, which comprised the majority of the island's population. Economically, on the maternal side, his grandparents were upper-middle class business people whose fortunes had risen with the island's astounding commercial rise after World War II. His father's family was middle class. Devin's mother was linguistically atypical in that she attended a Jesuit college and majored in Spanish. This destiny was not based on any particular love of Spanish, but was the result of the college placement system of the time, which assigned major fields of study based on test scores. Candidly, she reports that had she scored fractionally higher, she would have been an English major. Nevertheless, her college-acquired Spanish would later prove to be an asset after she immigrated to Southern California, where she was

Table 5.1 Linguistic Profile of Devin's Mutlilingual Family in Taiwan

Relative	Native Language	Primary Language of Literacy	Additional Languages
Mother	Taiwanese (fluent native speaker)	Mandarin (fluent and literate)	English (middle school and secondary school) and Spanish (B.A.)
Father	Taiwanese (fluent native speaker)	Mandarin (fluent and literate)	English (middle school and secondary school)
Older Brother	Taiwanese (native speaker; semi-fluent)	Mandarin (two years in Taiwan, continued at Chinese community school in U.S.; became fluent in English after immigrating to the U.S.; graduated from two prominent U.S. universities with BA and MA degrees)	
Grandmother (maternal)	Taiwanese (fluent native speaker)	Japanese (fluent and literate)	Mandarin (functionally literate and semi-fluent)
Grandfather (maternal)	Taiwanese (fluent native speaker)	Japanese (fully fluent and literate)	Mandarin (functionally literate and semi-fluent)
Great-grandmother (maternal)	Taiwanese (fluent native speaker)		

able to negotiate in a multilingual work environment of a different mix than her native Taiwan. Table 5.1 summarizes the linguistic command of members of Devin's extended family.

Devin's Language Use Prior to Emigration

Devin was born in Taiwan in 1971 into the above-described multigenerational, multilingual household, where he lived until age five. He had one brother, who was two years and five months older. During the first five years of his life, three languages (Taiwanese, Mandarin, and Japanese) were used in his household. Table 5.2 summarizes for the language interaction profiles for all Devin's family members during this period.

By the time Devin was born in 1971, based on Devin's mother's best recollections, Taiwanese and Mandarin were used in his household and were frequently code-mixed by those who had facility in both. Thus, Devin's first languages were Taiwanese and Mandarin. Devin's family linguistic profile in Taiwan corresponded to that of other middle class Taiwanese but differed from Mandarin-dominant families, many of which fled the Mainland to Taiwan with the defeat of the Nationalists in the Chinese Civil War.[7]

Devin's Language Use Post-Immigration

When Devin was five, in 1976, his parents immigrated to the United States to establish an extended-family business and his family profile shifted from a multigenerational to a nuclear household. At home, Devin's family continued to use Taiwanese code-mixed with Mandarin. Devin had begun preschool in Taiwan, where Mandarin was used, but in Southern California he was enrolled in a preschool where only English was spoken.[8] Although there were other Taiwanese and Mandarin-speaking immigrants in his ethnically diverse middle-class community, all of the children he played with spoke English, a language that he rapidly acquired. Devin also attended a Chinese school on Saturdays, which focused on both spoken and written forms of Mandarin. For the first few years, however, the school was fairly loosely organized.

Table 5.2 Language Interaction Profile of Devin's Family in Taiwan

	Devin	Brother	Mother	Father	Grandmother	Grandfather	Great-Grandmother
Devin	—	T & M	T & M	T & M	T	T	T
Brother		—	T & M	T & M	T	T	T
Mother			—	M & T	T	T	T
Father				—	T	T	T
Grandmother					—	J & T	T
Grandfather						—	T

Key: T = Taiwanese; M = Mandarin; J = Japanese.

Around 1978, Devin's parents separated and subsequently divorced. He continued to live with his mother and older brother. His mother maintained her use of mostly Taiwanese code-mixed with Mandarin at home, and Devin continued with Chinese school on Saturdays. Despite being a recent immigrant, Devin excelled in his English-only public school and was skipped from the second grade to third.

By that time, his weekend Chinese school had become more formally organized as the Chinese immigrant community grew and resources became more available. Consequently, the school placed children into classes based on their oral and literate proficiencies in Mandarin, and Devin was assigned to a class with the youngest children. His experience with Mandarin from that point on, until he stopped attending Chinese school upon completing middle school, is recalled with painful memories. He hated being placed with younger children and resented having to give up his Saturdays. Devin frequently needed his mother's help and prodding to practice writing and memorizing the traditional Chinese characters still used in Taiwan.

In 1981, Devin's mother married again, this time to an American. Devin spoke only English with his Taiwan-born older brother and Anglo stepfather at home and with his peers at school. However, he continued to speak mostly Taiwanese in dyadic interactions with his mother. Devin continued to excel academically in middle school and high school, where he took four years of German and became one of the top students in that subject as well as in most of his other classes. Table 5.3 summarizes the language interaction profile of Devin's family post-immigration to the United States.

Graduating from high school at only 16 years of age, Devin received a partial scholarship to the University of California at Berkeley where he majored in economics. In both high school and college, Devin's peer group was ethnically diverse. He socialized with other "smart kids." Devin began casually dating in his senior year of high school. He went out with two young Taiwanese American women, also of immigrant background, who were fluent in English, but retained some Taiwanese and Mandarin. He also dated a Korean American immigrant who was bilingual in English and Korean, and another young immigrant who spoke English and Vietnamese.

In his junior year at Berkeley, Devin decided that it would be "useful" for his future career to improve his fluency in Chinese (Mandarin). He even thought

Table 5.3 Language Interaction Profile of Devin's Family in the United States

	Devin	Brother	Mother	Step-father	Public school	Chinese school	Peers / friends
Devin	—	E	T, M & E	E	E	M	E
Brother		—	T & M	T & M	E	M	E
Mother			—	E	NA	NA	T, M & E
Step-Father				—	NA	NA	E

Key: T = Taiwanese; M = Mandarin; E = English; NA = Not applicable.

about going to Taiwan or the Mainland and immersing himself in the language. He made inquiries with the Chinese program at Berkeley and was required to undergo an informal assessment prior to placement. He had not studied the language for about six years since quitting Chinese school. What he wanted most was to "start over" and take two years of intensive Mandarin. He had decided to conceal his prior Chinese school training during the assessment interview, but when the interviewer greeted him in Mandarin and commanded him to "sit," he obeyed and realized that his cover was blown. Based on the informal assessment interview, Devin was placed in a Chinese (Mandarin) reading and writing for native speakers class. Devin's classification as a native speaker was debatable because his oral Taiwanese was always stronger than his Mandarin. More accurately, his initial home language context in Taiwan was multilingual. Since early childhood, he had code-mixed Mandarin and Taiwanese, even as he rapidly acquired and became fluent in English. Devin retained marginal fluency in Taiwanese at home but had only a very rudimentary knowledge of school-taught spoken and written Mandarin by the time he completed middle school.

In his Chinese (Mandarin) reading and writing for native speakers class, there were about fifteen students, all of whom received an "A" but for two, Devin and a Cantonese HL speaker. Devin's professor was a Chinese Mainlander from Beijing who frequently corrected Devin's "Taiwanese" accent in Mandarin. Devin also was marked down when he reverted to writing the more complex traditional characters he still retained from Chinese school, when he could not produce the simplified characters he was being taught at Berkeley. After one semester, he felt stigmatized and overly self-conscious in the class. Devin concluded he was not up to the commitment required to improve his Mandarin and decided not to enroll for the second semester. Devin's performance and self-concept as an HL learner stood in complete contrast to his academic performance in all other subjects.

Devin's undergraduate grades were very good, and he scored in the ninety-ninth percentile on the LSAT. After graduating from Berkeley, he was admitted to Yale Law School, where he received his Juris Doctor. Following law school, Devin took a job with a prestigious firm in northern California, spent several years there and then moved to another prestigious firm. He now works as chief counsel for an upstart "dot com" in Silicon Valley. Since college, Devin rarely has any need to use Taiwanese or Mandarin, except when he is with his mother's relatives, or when he calls home to talk with his mother. When he does, they converse in Taiwanese code-mixed with both Mandarin and English.

Devin has kept up with a cadre of high school and college friends, some of whom are bilingual in English, Mandarin, and/or Taiwanese. However, all of his communication with them is in English. After law school, he had three prolonged relationships: one with a Taiwan-born, English-Mandarin-speaking bilingual lawyer, and another with a California Latina attorney who is bilingual in Spanish and English. Devin briefly considered studying Spanish, but the relationship ended and with it the motivation. He next became involved with a young Vietnamese American woman who is fluent in English and retains fluency in Vietnamese.

Devin's older brother married a Nisei (second generation) Okinawan-Japanese American. Devin's three little nieces speak English and household Japanese. His sixteen-year-younger half-bother speaks English, knows a few words of Taiwanese, and studies Spanish in secondary school. Such diversity in interethnic relationships is not uncommon in California, which is now a minority-majority state. It also helps to demonstrate why, apart from formal educational policies and practices, many young immigrants find it difficult to retain their home languages, as English becomes the mediator across other languages.

Will Devin ever study Chinese again? In my last interview with Devin, he concluded that the opportunity was probably lost. When asked whether he would like his children to attend Chinese school and learn Mandarin, Devin hesitated and said: "That's a tough one." He speculated that it would all depend upon whom he married and that if he did not marry a speaker of Chinese, he doubted that he would "push it." Subsequent to that interview, Devin married his Vietnamese American girlfriend.[9] The language in which Devin and his wife communicate is English. If the motivation and opportunity for Devin to study Chinese is slipping away, will he and his wife revisit the issue of a heritage language for their children? Will it be Vietnamese, Mandarin, and/or Taiwanese?

Implications for Policy and Practice

Devin's case as a Chinese HL learner, though complex, is not unique among the broader community of ethnic Chinese. His experience as an HL learner raises a number of questions. First, to what extent is he a heritage language learner of Chinese? Mandarin was one of the languages used in his family. However, it was used to a lesser extent than, and code-mixed with, Taiwanese, which more accurately implies that he was a native "multilingual." As he moved from his childhood home context to Saturday Chinese school, he moved from a multilingual environment to a monolingual Mandarin one. Years later, at the University of California at Berkeley, Devin's classification as a "Mandarin" HL speaker for the purposes of course placement was problematic. Had the course been designed to take into account the background and needs of dialect speakers, his regional Taiwanese accent in Mandarin might not have been treated in a stigmatizing way.

The status of Chinese dialect speakers within the overall conceptualization of Chinese HL programs remains an issue of considerable ambivalence. For example, in one of the more useful collections on Chinese HL instruction (X. Wang, 1996), Lee (1996) addresses "dialect" speakers but does so under the heading "Non-Chinese Heritage Language Learners." Lee estimates that approximately 15% of students enrolled in Chinese schools are from families where Chinese dialects other than Mandarin are spoken. Prescriptions for such students typically suggest immersing them in standard Mandarin (S. Hsieh, personal communication, July 2001).

Recall that Devin's problems in his college Chinese reading and writing for native speakers class also related to his use of the traditional characters used in Taiwan, which he had first learned. He found it easier to recall them over the simplified ones used in the People's Republic of China that he was being taught. Devin's problems with characters were not unique. Wang (1996) notes:

> The differences between the traditional and simplified forms of Chinese characters are significant. Many high schools and universities teach the simplified writing form of Chinese, whereas Chinese language schools with teachers from Taiwan still use the traditional forms. This difference creates problems for the students from Chinese language schools. (p. 24)[10]

A common rationale that teachers of Mandarin from Taiwan offer for continuing to teach traditional characters—apart from their use in Taiwan and extended range of vocabulary—is that they carry more semantic information than simplified ones, and that it is allegedly easier to learn simplified characters after traditional characters, rather than the reverse (S. Hsieh, personal communication, July 2001). Nevertheless, Devin's dilemma resulted from his college professor's lack of recognition, or outright rejection, of Devin's prior knowledge of traditional characters.

Issues involving the choice of traditional versus simplified characters fall under the heading of script policy as an aspect of language policies at school.[11] The more problematic issue facing program and curriculum planners for Chinese dialect speakers is how to take into consideration their multilingual backgrounds. Recall that in Devin's case Mandarin was code-mixed with Taiwanese. Clearly, any remedy for the lack of recognition of Chinese dialects reflects issues typically dealt with under the domain of status planning.

One possibility would be for teachers of Chinese dialect speaking students to be at least minimally trained in contrastive analysis and sociolinguistics of the major Chinese languages. Teachers so prepared could acknowledge, clarify, and accentuate the similarities and differences among Chinese dialects and Mandarin. Differences in regional accents could likewise be contrasted. Although the situation for dialect speakers of English is different because English dialects are mutually intelligible with standard English, contrastive approaches have been used with some degree of success, partly because they validate the "dialect" as being rule-governed just like the standard.

Additional recognition of the special needs of multilingual students might be gained by having teachers of Chinese for dialect speakers gain familiarity with the literatures for other language development programs for native speakers, such as Spanish for native speakers (SNS) (see Peyton, 1998, this volume; Valdés, 2001). Similar programs have been designed for speakers of non-standard varieties of English (Christian, 1997, 2000; Wolfram, Adger, & Christian, 1999).

Given the choice of traditional versus simplified characters in teaching Chinese, there is a need for more discussion regarding script policies and how instruction should be mediated between those programs that teach one form rather than the other. Language attitude surveys of Chinese language school administrators and teachers in community-based programs, as well as in colleges and universities, would be helpful in determining prevalent attitudes toward language diversity that might need to be addressed in teacher training or professional development. Additional study of the experiences of speakers of Chinese dialects and their individual circumstances in family, school, and community contexts is needed to inform program planning.

Notes

1. This chapter builds from a number of issues addressed at the Heritage Language Conference held in Long Beach California in fall 1999, where I chaired a panel on heritage language policy issues. Dr. Russell N. Campbell of UCLA was instrumental there, and later, in engaging scholars and language professionals. This case study focuses on research questions raised by a follow-up conference at UCLA in September of 2000 (see University of California, Los Angeles, 2001) in which Dr. Campbell was again most influential. A preliminary draft of this chapter was presented at the Bi-National Conference on Heritage Language Learning at the University of Victoria in Melbourne (July, 2001). Dr. Campbell was again influential in helping to organize that cross-national dialog and was a major inspiration in stimulating me to undertake this chapter and several other projects (Wiley & Valdés, 2000; Wiley, 2001a; 2001b).
2. Chinese schools, like other ethnic language schools in the U.S. and elsewhere, are community-based programs organized to promote heritage language development in children. They are typically offered during out-of-school hours (e.g., on Saturdays).
3. The seven regional *Fangyan* are recognized by custom. Using more strictly linguistic criteria based on phonological and grammatical criteria, Norman (1988) makes finer distinctions and identifies twelve major geographic dialects of Chinese that correspond roughly to a north-south distribution (pp. 182–183). Percentages of the Chinese populations speaking these languages are from Ramsey (1987, p. 87).
4. Code mixing and switching are common behaviors among bilinguals, particularly in areas of high language contact. Switching between languages occurs at the sentence or phrasal level (following grammatical constraints) and may be made for a variety of sociolinguistic reasons, e.g., to show distance, attention, or familiarity with another speaker. Switching and lexical borrowing also occur when one language is used more as a language of wider communication than another and has a richer vocabulary from which to draw.
5. Devin Chen is a pseudonym. Like many in his generation of Taiwanese immigrant children, Devin was given a western first name—because his parents thought it would be "easier" for him as an immigrant child in the United States—but retained a Chinese middle and last name.
6. Martial law, which lasted until 1986, was imposed when the *Kuomingtang* suppressed an ill-fated Taiwanese rebellion, which resulted in widespread loss of life among the Taiwanese elite in 1947 (see Rubinstein, 1999, pp. 292–296 for more information).
7. It also differs from native speakers of Hakka, who comprise a sizable minority of the Island's inhabitants, and from the indigenous peoples.
8. He recalls little from this period, except that he liked the animals, especially the pony at the pre-school.
9. Her story is perhaps even more interesting than his. She was orphaned during the Vietnam War, then adopted by a Vietnamese Catholic nun who left her station to assume responsibility for the child. Her mother later married, and with her Vietnamese husband, sought refuge in the United States.
10. Wang (1996) also notes that a similar problem exists concerning the phonetic notation systems that may be used to help students learn how to pronounce characters. "The majority of language programs in the formal education system teach the phonetic alphabet, whereas Chinese language schools use phonetic symbols" (p. 24).

104 • Terrence G. Wiley

11. Corson (1999b) provides a useful discussion of these issues generally, without reference to specific languages.

References

Baker, C., & Jones, S. P. (1998). *Encyclopedia of bilingual education and bilingualism.* Clevedon, England: Multilingual Matters.

Chao, T. H. (1997). *Chinese heritage community language schools in the United States.* Washington, DC: ERIC Clearinghouse on Languages and Linguistics. (ERIC Document Reproduction Service No. ED409744)

Christian, D. (1997). *Vernacular dialects and standard American English in the classroom* (Report No. EDO-FL-97-09). Washington, DC: ERIC Clearinghouse on Languages and Linguistics. (ERIC Document Reproduction Service No. ED406846)

Christian, D. (2000). Reflections of language heritage: Choice and chance in vernacular English dialects. In P. Griffin, J. Peyton, W. Wolfram, & R. W. Fasold (Eds.), *Language in action: New studies of language in society* (pp. 230–246). Cresskill, NJ: Hampton.

Copper, J. F. (1999). *Taiwan: Nation-state or province?* (3rd ed.). Boulder, CO: Westview Press.

Corson, D. (1999a). Community-based education for indigenous cultures. In S. May (Ed.), *Indigenous community-based education* (pp. 8–19). Clevedon, England: Multilingual Matters.

Corson, D. (1999b). *Language policies at school: A resource book for teachers and administrators.* Mahwah, NJ: Lawrence Erlbaum.

Dayle, B. (1983). The implementation of language planning in China. In J. Corbarribias & J. Fishman (Eds.), *Progress in language planning: International perspectives* (pp. 291–308). Berlin: Mouton Publishers.

Fishman, J. A. (1991). *Reversing language shift.* Clevedon, England: Multilingual Matters.

Fishman, J. A. (1999). *Handbook of language and ethnic identity.* Oxford: Oxford University Press.

Fishman, J. A. (Ed.). (2001). *Can threatened languages be saved?* Clevedon, England: Multilingual Matters.

Hinton, L., & Hale, K. (2001). *The green book of language revitalization.* London: Academic Press.

Horvath, B. M., & Vaughan, P. (1991). *Community languages: A handbook.* Clevedon, England: Multilingual Matters.

Hsia, T-T. (1956). *China's language reforms.* New Haven, CT: Far Eastern Publications, Yale University.

Lee, M. (1996). Non-Chinese heritage learners: Practices and implications. In X. Wang (Ed.), *A case study of Chinese heritage community language schools in the United States* (pp. 27–31). Washington, DC: National Foreign Language Center.

Li Wei (1994). *Three generations, two languages, one family: Language choice and language shift in a Chinese community in Britain.* Clevedon, England: Multilingual Matters.

Norman, J. (1998). *Chinese.* Cambridge: Cambridge University Press.

Nunberg, G. (Dec. 9, 2001). The answer is on the tip of our many tongues. *Washington Post.* Retrieved April 7, 2006, from http://people.ischool.berkeley.edu/~nunberg/tongues.html

Peyton, J. (1998, December). *Spanish for native speakers: Programs, curriculum, and materials* (*ERIC/CLL Minibib*). Washington, DC: Center for Applied Linguistics.

Peyton, K., & Ranard, D. A. (2001, November 5). We can't squander language skills. *Los Angeles Times.* Retrieved April 7, 2006, from http://www.cal.org/heritage/involved/list_archive.html

Ramsey, S. R. (1987). *The languages of China.* Princeton, NJ: Princeton University Press.

Rubinstein, M. A. (1999). *Taiwan: A new history.* Amonk, NY: Eastgate/M.E. Sharpe.

Taylor, I., & Taylor, M. M. (1995). *Chinese, Korean and Japanese.* Amsterdam: John Benjamins.

Teng, X., & Weng, Y. (2001). Bilingualism and bilingual education in China. In N. K. Shimahara, I. Z. Holowinsky, & S. Tomlinson-Clarke (Eds.), *Ethnicity, race, and nationality in education: A global perspective* (pp. 213–233). Mahwah, NJ: Lawrence Erlbaum.

Tsao, F. (2000). The language planning situation in Taiwan. In R. Kaplan (Ed.), *Language planning in Nepal, Taiwan, and Sweden* (pp. 60–106). Clevedon, England: Multilingual Matters.

University of California, Los Angeles. (2000). Heritage language research priorities conference report. *Bilingual Research Journal, 20*(4), 475–491.

Valdés, G. (2000). Introduction. In American Association of Teachers of Spanish and Portuguese (Ed.), *Professional development series handbook for teachers K-16: Vol. 1. Spanish for native speakers* (pp. 1–20). Fort Worth, TX: Harcourt College.

Valdés, G. (2001). Heritage language students: Profiles and possibilities. In J. K. Peyton, D. A. Ranard, & S. McGinnis (Eds.), *Heritage languages in America: Preserving a national resource* (pp. 37–77). Washington, DC/McHenry, IL: Center for Applied Linguistics/Delta Systems.

Wang, P.-F. S. (1996). Academic curriculum. In X. Wang (Ed.), *A view from within: A case study of Chinese heritage community language schools in the United States* (pp. 21–25). Washington, DC: National Foreign Language Center.

Wang, X. (1996). *A view from within: A case study of Chinese heritage community language schools in the United States.* Washington, DC: National Foreign Language Center.

Wiley, T. G. (2001a). On defining heritage languages and their speakers. In J. K. Peyton, D. A. Ranard, & S. McGinnis (Eds.), *Heritage languages in American: Preserving a national resource* (pp. 29–36). Washington, DC/McHenry, IL: Center for Applied Linguistics/Delta Systems.

Wiley, T. G. (2001b). Policy formation and implementation. In J. K. Peyton, D. A. Ranard, & S. McGinnis (Eds.), *Heritage languages in America: Preserving a national resource* (pp. 99–108). Washington, DC & McHenry, IL: Center for Applied Linguistics/Delta Systems.

Wiley, T. G., & Valdés, G. (Eds.) (2000). Special Issue. Heritage language instruction in the United States: A time for renewal. *Bilingual Research Journal, 24*(4).

Wolfram, W., Christian, D., & Adger, C. (1999). *Dialects in schools and communities.* Mahwah, NJ: Lawrence Erlbaum.

6

Heritage Languages and Ideologies of Language

Unexamined Challenges

GUADALUPE VALDÉS, SONIA V. GONZÁLEZ,
DANIA LÓPEZ GARCÍA, AND PATRICIO MÁRQUEZ

The challenges facing the field of heritage language teaching include determining the role that educational institutions should play in language maintenance. While these institutions are generally understood to be important to the work of heritage language maintenance,[1] we have barely begun to examine the role of educational institutions in reinforcing societal values about language in general. We call for such an examination and suggest that, as heritage language teachers and supporters who are charting the new course in heritage language education that Peyton, Ranard, and McGinnis (2001) outlined, we must reflect deeply on both our common societal context and the challenges we face in maintaining our languages through traditional educational institutions and programs. Arguing that hegemonic beliefs about monolingualism and bilingualism are deeply embedded in educational institutions in many complex ways, this chapter examines established institutional foreign language programs and suggests that—although involved in a non-hegemonic practice, the teaching of non-English languages—these departments are nevertheless working in concert with deeply held American ideologies and beliefs about language. By focusing on a single Spanish language department that is representative of many other well-established European language departments in colleges and universities in this country, we hope to contribute to an understanding of the ways in which educational institutions transmit what Phillips (1998) has termed *nation-imagining* beliefs and values that can often result in the alienation and marginalization of heritage students.

Language Ideology

Woolard (1998) defines language ideology as: "Representations, whether explicit or implicit, that construe the intersection of language and human beings in a social world" (p. 3). Arguing that ideologies of language are not about language alone, Woolard insists that they enact ties of language to identity and underpin "the very notion of person and the social group, as well as such fundamental social institutions as religious ritual, child socialization, gender relations, the nation-state, schooling, and law" (p. 3). On the other hand, Rumsey (1990) defines the concept as "shared bodies of commonsense notions about the nature of language in the world" (p. 346).

The relationship between language and nationalism has itself been a matter of controversy. As Stavenhagen (1990) points out, nations can be seen as objective facts, that is, as entities that bring together large numbers of people who share common objective traits such as language, religion, history, customs and values. In many cases, intellectual elites have been successful in creating a nationalistic consciousness by manipulating language as an instrument in the expression of a national essence.

According to Bourdieu, ([1982] 1991), the making of a nation also necessitates the creation of a "standard" language that is then legitimized as the normalized language and imposed upon its citizens. The educational system, therefore, plays an important role in both the legitimization of particular ways of speaking and the devaluing of popular or regional modes of expression. Interestingly, speakers of dominated languages or dialects collaborate in the destruction of what Bourdieu ([1982] 1991) called their "instruments of expression" because they believe that accepting the hierarchy of linguistic practices will increase their value on the educational market and lead to economic advantages (p. 49).

Departments of Foreign Languages in American Universities

Departments of foreign languages occupy a unique space in American universities. Faculty in these departments are engaged in carrying out intellectual work in "foreign" languages in a society that has been largely indifferent to and, at times, antagonistic toward the study and teaching of all non-English languages. In departments of foreign languages, in addition to the normal hierarchies of power based on subject matter specialization that are found in other academic departments, special power structures are developed that center around language. Faculty and students who are native speakers of the target language are often considered to be inherently superior to faculty and students who are non-native.

The Case of Spanish Language Departments

As is the case in other foreign language departments, within departments of Spanish, status and power reflect both native and non-native ability as well as other characteristics such as regional origin, ethnicity and class. In most departments, the faculty is made up primarily of individuals from two different backgrounds: (1) native speakers of Spanish raised in Spain or Latin America and (2) Americans who acquired Spanish as a foreign language. In some cases, for example, native speakers of peninsular Spanish may take the position that their own linguistic abilities are superior to those of Latin Americans who, they believe, speak a less pure and less authentic Spanish. They may recommend that their students travel to Spain to become immersed in the "best" Spanish and suggest that study in Latin America is less desirable. Latin Americans, on the other hand, may join their peninsular colleagues to sit in judgment of the language abilities of their American colleagues who acquired Spanish as a foreign language. In some departments, so-called near-native ability in the target language is not enough. The underlying belief is that only those persons who have grown up in the original culture and who have learned the language in the course of primary socialization can truly understand both the foreign literature and its culture.[2] The situation becomes even more complex when one considers the place of ethnic/heritage-language speakers in Spanish departments, that is, second-, third-, or even fourth-generation members of immigrant families who are American-born (e.g., Mexican Americans and Puerto Ricans) and who have developed their Spanish competencies in their homes and communities as well as in the American academy.[3]

More recently, the increased presence of U.S. Latinos in Spanish departments has led to the implementation of special courses for students who are currently referred to as *heritage speakers* of Spanish. While important efforts have been made in the last several years to provide instruction in Spanish to bilingual students in the United States,[4] there is no general consensus about how to work with students whose language, after many years of formal study, still appears to be seriously flawed. For some members of the profession, the issue is one of standardness versus nonstandardness.[5]

However, little debate has been held on the advantages or disadvantages of teaching language conventions, nor have there been discussions analogous to those represented within the field of English academic discourse by the positions of Delpit ([1993] 1998) and Gee (1990). Only a few individuals (Hidalgo, 1993; Valdés, 1995, 1998) have argued that, as Gee (1990) noted, the task for U.S. Latinos is not merely the acquisition of the standard superficialities or forms that are used as indicators of outsider or insider status, but the acquisition of the discourse used in the academy.

Spanish in the United States: The Case of Latino Heritage Speakers

The language experiences of Latinos who grow up in bilingual communities in the United States differ fundamentally from those of persons who are raised in Latin America or Spain. As is the case in monolingual Spanish-speaking countries, in bilingual communities in this country different registers are used in different situational contexts. However, "high" registers of English are used to carry out all formal/high exchanges, while Spanish, along with the informal registers of English, is used as the "low" variety appropriate primarily for casual/informal interactions.[6] In the United States, English is the prestige language.

In addition to being characterized by diglossia (the functional differentiation of languages) and bilingualism, bilingual communities also reflect the social class origins of their residents. In the case of groups of Latino immigrants, there is evidence to suggest that a large majority of immigrants to the United States are from relatively less-educated groups.[7] Latino immigrants are generally "ordinary" individuals from Spanish-speaking countries, that is, members of the non-elite strata.[8] We therefore conjecture that the linguistic repertoires of most ordinary Latinos (especially persons from Mexico) who emigrate to the United States are generally made up of mid to low registers of Spanish, and it is these registers that serve as models of language as bilinguals acquire Spanish in their families and communities. Moreover, the varieties of Spanish spoken in bilingual communities are at risk of undergoing change. Some researchers (e.g., de Bot & Weltens, 1991; Maher, 1991; Olshtain & Barzilay, 1991; Seliger & Vago, 1991) maintain that the language of immigrants attrites and undergoes structural loss. As a result of this attrition, immigrants transfer their tongue to the next generation in a "mutilated" form (de Bot & Weltens, 1991, p. 42) to the next generation. Work on tense-mood-aspect simplification by Silva-Corvalán (1994) among Mexican Americans in Los Angeles supports this position.

In sum, the Spanish spoken by Latino bilinguals in the United States is characterized by a narrower range of lexical and syntactic alternatives than the language of upper-middle-class speakers. In addition, because in bilingual communities the use of Spanish is often restricted to low-level functions and private sphere interactions, over time, as Huffines (1991) points out, "the immigrant language falls into disuse" (p. 125). As a result, many bilinguals do not acquire a full mastery of the registers and styles characteristic of even "ordinary" Latino monolinguals.

Support for Maintenance or Support for Shift? The Role of Spanish Departments

The question of whether and to what degree departments of foreign languages have a role in the language maintenance efforts of non-English languages in this country is one that according to Valdés (1992) is seldom examined or discussed within the profession. In undertaking our study of language ideologies in one Spanish language department, then, we hypothesized that within such departments, ideologies about language help justify the place of certain individuals within the social hierarchy in the department, their access to certain privileges, standing, and status. We also hypothesized that theories (i.e., generalizations and explanations) about how things work, about who learns and who does not learn language, about why some people learn quickly and others do not, and about how important the acquisition of academic discourse is for success in the study of literature, support wider social beliefs about the value and desirability of maintaining bilingual proficiencies among members of minority populations in this country.

The Study

We studied a Spanish department with 10 faculty members and 14 full-time lecturers. At the time we conducted the interviews, seven M.A. students and 26 Ph.D. students were in the department, and 19 of the latter group were in residence. The language backgrounds of faculty and students are representative of most Spanish departments (they include native speakers of Spanish, U.S. Latino speakers, and non-native speakers).

The research team was comprised of a senior faculty member, two Ph.D. students (González and López García), and one M.A. student (Márquez), all of whom identify themselves as U.S. Latinos. The faculty member is known for her work on bilingualism among U.S. Latinos. González and García have taught the department course series designed for heritage speakers of Spanish.

The study was conducted in the fall of the 1999/2000 academic year. All faculty, graduate students and lecturers were contacted by electronic mail, invited to participate in the study, and asked to schedule an interview with an author. We explained that the focus of the study was academic Spanish, defined as a variety of Spanish used to interact in academic settings. We stated that we believed that little is known about the acquisition of academic Spanish in a U.S. academic setting.

Table 6.1 lists the participants by language background. "Native speakers" includes those who identified themselves as peninsular or Latin American. "U.S. Latinos" includes students who were born in this country or who emigrated at an early age. (This group includes three students who returned to Mexico for several years and attended school there.)

Participants were offered a choice of speaking in English, Spanish, or a combination.[9] Interviews were conducted according to a protocol with suggested wording for discussing the following topics: a) general background; b) experience in acquiring or studying Spanish; c) self-evaluation of proficiency; d) definitions and examples of academic Spanish; e) experiences in acquiring academic Spanish; f) barriers to students' acquisition of academic Spanish; and g) recommendations for teaching. A total of 43 participants were interviewed.

The Department's Discourse on Academic Spanish

Our analysis of the interviews revealed a belief in the concept of the "educated native speaker." Originally drawn from the proficiency statements used by the

Table 6.1 Language Background of Study Participants

	Native Speakers	U.S. Latinos	Non-native Speakers
Faculty	3	0	4
Doctoral Students	6	8	2
Masters Students	1	5	1
Lecturers	5	1	7
Totals	**15**	**14**	**14**

Foreign Service (Clark & Clifford, 1988), the term is used in the profession especially in the area of measurement as a norm against which to compare foreign language speakers. Together, members of the department produced a coherent discourse that included strong doubts about the possibility of developing desired native-like proficiencies in both "uneducated" native speakers and foreign language learners.

Conceptualizations of Academic Spanish

All participants defined academic Spanish as a variety or type of language used for particular purposes in particular institutions and characterized by specific surface-level features.

Participants assigned three additional characteristics to academic Spanish: (1) as the intellectual practice of a specialized professional discourse; (2) as a specialized register characterized by particular surface-level features; and (3) as "standard," correct, or error-free language. The first theme occurred primarily in the definitions offered by faculty and doctoral students. It was less frequently found in the discussions of both lecturers and M.A. students. Definitions emphasizing this first theme viewed academic Spanish as a type of language used in the study of Spanish literature. These definitions tended to highlight the function of this specialized professional discourse, its approach to topic and audience, the intimate relationship between academic Spanish and the exposition of literary theory, and the conceptual complexity of textual genres used in writing about literature.

Both groups of participants using the first theme emphasized the context in which academic Spanish is used as in the following example:

Academic Spanish, I see it as a type of Spanish that is used for a specific audience or a specific reader, in the case of universities, students, professors or readers that share with me a certain interest in a given academic topic, in the sense that is not used in everyday talk (trans., Informant #9)[10]

With very few exceptions, the second theme occurred in all 43 descriptions produced by faculty, graduate students, and lecturers. Theme two tended to be used both by itself and in conjunction with the two other themes noted. Definitions using this theme generally attempted a characterization of a few representative surface-level features. Some individuals described academic Spanish, for example, as an oral code in which all traces of orality (regional and national features) are eliminated, as planned language, as a code characterized by the use of more elaborate syntax, connecting phrases, specialized lexicon, formality, and absence of colloquialisms. Others spoke of academic Spanish as a written discourse that required not only a codified language but also the use of certain stylistic and rhetorical strategies.

By comparison, the third theme, with its attention to error-free language, was used only by lecturers and by one third of all graduate students. No member of the faculty used this theme. Definitions giving prominence to theme three tended to make reference to the pedagogical context in American universities and offered definitions of academic Spanish that emphasized correctness and standardness such as the following:

> Academic Spanish is in a certain way, would also be called quote unquote "standard Spanish." It's not the Spanish that you would speak on the street or with family or friends. It is a Spanish to write essays or to make a speech. That kind of formal Spanish that is also grammatically, quote unquote, correct and has the accents in its place, and there are phrases that are pretty much only academic. (Informant #30)

In general, descriptions based on theme three tended to depict academic Spanish as a type of language that is free of grammatical errors—especially errors of mood—and that avoids Anglicisms and other contact features. It was not clear, however, to what degree individuals who focused on this theme in defining academic Spanish were making a distinction between standard Spanish and academic Spanish. Of the 13 doctoral students who were asked this question directly, only two attempted to make a distinction between the two terms, as in the following example:

> Academic Spanish in relation to standard Spanish has more prestige and is more, well at least it is viewed like this, standard Spanish. I am thinking of colloquial Spanish in (country), in relation to academic Spanish is a Spanish that is seen as defective, almost false, badly spoken, like a Spanish the mere existence of which is not recognized. It is spoken but people do not realize that they speak it. There would be people that would speak it and think that they are speaking academic Spanish. It has a relationship to academic Spanish as if it were the rich relative of standard Spanish. (trans., Informant #36)

> I would think that non-academic Spanish, it's a hard question to answer without getting into a lot of trouble with cultural studies people, or seem elitist in that way. But, I would think not speaking using slang. I wouldn't say it's the use of the slang, I am putting as an example…when you go to a conference or when you are presenting a paper or when you are talking to people after your paper, that you wouldn't tend to be sort of relaxed… hey… slang type of speaking…But, I don't know because that's a hard question to answer…a lot of people now feel that if that's the way you speak or that's the way that you communicate that that's ok. So it's not right to put Spanish in different levels. (Informant #34)

Acquisition of Academic Spanish

Participants identified three main contexts of academic Spanish acquisition: (1) experience in university settings, (2) books and reading, and (3) imitation. Interestingly, in describing contexts of acquisition, faculty, graduate students, and lecturers appeared not to differentiate between the acquisition of professional discourse as an identity kit, the acquisition of a specialized register, and the acquisition of the standard language.

Most participants spoke about the acquisition process as occurring naturally in an academic setting, as in the following example:

> In the first place, when you study at the university you latch on to or closely follow a professor as a paternal or maternal figure, that is to say, you admire someone and then in some way, even though you might not copy his/her language in its entirety, in some way you are imitating it. And then, I say that at the beginning, but it is gradually acquired; it is acquired in that way, and then, through books, lectures. (trans., Informant #3)

When asked about the acquisition of academic Spanish in Spanish-speaking contexts, all informants (with the exception of some M.A. students) appeared to be aware that not all persons who grow up in Spanish-speaking countries acquire academic Spanish. Several persons, for example, spoke of exclusion of the non-elite segments of society from educational contexts and consequently from opportunities for developing academic Spanish:

> … [its acquisition is] influenced by social class … it is a very specific register with very inflexible demands at times, spoken by an elite, it is managed by a certain sector of the elite, the academic sector of the elite. (Informant #23)

> … because of the given level of education and the social conditions in which they are born, those who have little access to education will not acquire it. (trans., Informant #16)

We found it interesting that formal education was given such an important place in the discussion of the acquisition of academic language in all of the definitions offered. We expected that, given the class structure of Latin American countries and the uneven distribution of a hierarchy of language styles that simultaneously expresses the hierarchy of corresponding social groups (Bourdieu, [1982] 1991), there would be an awareness of how position in the social structure might affect the acquisition of the higher levels of language at least by students native to Latin America. It is not clear to us why none of the Latin Americans interviewed made any reference to close ties between the development of linguistic repertoires and existing social hierarchies.

In comparison to discussions about the acquisition of Spanish in Spanish-speaking countries, there was much less discussion about whether and to what degree foreign-language learners of the language acquire academic Spanish. In general, comments relating to the acquisition of Spanish by English-language-background students were limited to comments such as the following: "If they study it they will learn it" (trans., Informant # 16) and "For those that continue taking classes, that is all they are getting" (Informant # 11). Interestingly, when referring to the acquisition of academic Spanish by foreign-language learners, the second definition of academic Spanish, that is, the view that it is a register characterized by particular surface-level features, was in evidence.

By comparison, discussions of the acquisition of academic Spanish by U.S. Latinos made reference almost exclusively to the third definition, which focused on standardness or correctness. Most individuals expressed strong feelings about the need for Chicano students, for example, to make an effort to learn Spanish: "If they are in college, if there is an effort to learn it, absolutely" (trans., Informant #16), and "If they study it with interest, they will acquire it" (trans., Informant #15).

Summarizing, discussions about the acquisition of academic Spanish by natives of Spanish-speaking countries, foreign language learners, and U.S. Latinos revealed a set of different beliefs about each of these three groups of learners. The most extensive discussions were focused around natives of Spanish-speaking countries. Most members of the department had some knowledge about the societal structure in Latin America and could comment intelligently about patterns of exclusion from educational institutions. Given this, it is interesting that Latin American natives place so much emphasis on the importance of education in the development of high levels of language. We conjecture that the profession-wide notion of the "educated" native speaker—with education defined narrowly—might have influenced these views.

By comparison with discussions about the acquisition of academic Spanish by native speakers, examinations of the same process by foreign language learners were limited. All comments focused on the study of language in classroom settings and implied that pedagogical Spanish is itself "academic." The discussion of the acquisition of academic Spanish by U.S. Latinos, on the other hand, while emphasizing its formal study, tended also to include strongly stated beliefs about the importance of personal effort, deep interest, and dedication.

Self-Evaluations of Linguistic Proficiency

Given existing views in departments of foreign languages about the notion of native and near-native ability as it is used in hiring decisions, we conjectured that our request for self-evaluation of proficiency might reveal important information about linguistic insecurities of various sorts that would reflect departmental and profession-wide ideologies about fluency, correctness, and proficiency. We thus asked all individuals to talk about their own academic Spanish and to share with us aspects of the use of this variety that they might want to change or improve.

In analyzing responses to these questions, we examined the comments themselves as well as team members' personal knowledge of given individuals' abilities and performance in numerous contexts over months and years. Not surprisingly, given problems with self-report data about language proficiency in general, we found that several students reported their abilities as much higher than we knew them to be, while others who have excellent skills in the language were very hesitant to say that they spoke or wrote it well. It is important to note that when we asked graduate students about their abilities in Spanish, some may have understood our question to be focused on their overall proficiency in the language and not on their particular strengths or limitations in the use of academic Spanish.

As expected, the notion of the educated native was very much in evidence in these self-evaluations. In one case, for example, when a native speaker of Spanish from Latin America was asked to talk about her proficiency in Spanish, the individual dismissed the question and responded simply that she was a native speaker. In another case, when asked what kinds of functions she could best carry out in Spanish with the greatest ease, an individual replied: "Everything; this is my native tongue" (trans., Informant #35).

Another Latin American native, when asked about her proficiency, also communicated the same belief about the unquestioned ability of native speakers, but made reference to other factors accounting for her proficiency, including study of the language and extensive reading:

> I am a native and moreover I have studied the language. Thus, I think that I am more than proficient, more than fluid. And furthermore I have read a lot. So, I am very proficient. (trans., Informant #25)

When the interviewer pursued the matter further and inquired of this same individual whether there was something in the language that she wanted to improve, the informant again replied with great confidence: "I have never asked myself that question. I don't know. Actually, I cannot think of anything. It comes very easy for me, honestly" (trans., Informant #25).

Interestingly, in carrying out these interviews, members of the team (often more senior to the persons interviewed) encountered native Latin Americans who felt free to correct their Spanish in ways that clearly indicated a belief system that viewed U.S. Latinos as inferior and in need of correction from their more able native-speaking peers.

Not all Latin American native speakers expressed the same degree of arrogance. For example, one individual was quite forthright in his evaluation of his limitations even as a native speaker. In the following example, he made direct reference to the first theme encountered in the definitions of academic language, that is, to a profession-specific set of practices and to his own limitations in developing the required specialized vocabulary.

Being a native speaker, ever since I came to the U.S., for me academic English comes out better when writing papers even when the class is...taught in Spanish and the texts are Spanish texts, it is, that is to say, the language for writing the paper, scholarly language, comes to me with all modalities and characteristics that are used in English. And I think that is either because I never learned how to do it well in Spanish, that is all the phrases that are used to write critical essays in Spanish, or because I have been reading more works in English, I have acquired it more and it is fresher in my mind. (trans., Informant #36)

In comparison with native Latin Americans, non-native-speaking students tended to self-evaluate their language fluency in broad terms, for example: "I feel pretty comfortable speaking in Spanish, but never as comfortable as I am speaking in English. And I feel that I talk like other people in Spanish" (trans., Informant #26). They said little about specific proficiencies or about their use of academic Spanish, although a number of individuals mentioned their limitations in writing.

U.S. Latinos, on the other hand, sometimes reported very strong abilities as in the following example:

I think I have always spoken well for the reason that I grew up in a (descriptor deleted) environment where Spanish is spoken extremely well. I think that perhaps in an informal context my Spanish is perhaps the best. (trans., Informant #40)

Most Latinos, however, communicated strong linguistic insecurities:

Spanish is the language in which I communicate the most, in which I feel more sure of myself. I feel that my Spanish is not at an academic level (demonstrating embarrassment) because I learned in (country) the basics with my family. (trans., Informant #38)

And:

I think it's very fluent. I can speak it well. I know how to write it well, but just colloquially at my house, with my friends and everything, I know how to carry myself well. But when I get to a higher level, let's say more academic, then it's like I'm missing words. At times I switch to English. I have learned more of those nice and handy academic words. (trans., Informant #39)

Others communicated a defensive posture about their Spanish in the light of sustained attacks and criticism.

[I want] to prove to them that I can speak Spanish as well as they can, in spite of the fact that I know linguistically there is no comparison between me being raised bilingually and them being raised monolingually Latin American. (Informant #23)

Given anxieties and linguistic insecurities present in the department, we were surprised at the number of individuals, including faculty, who spoke about their limitations and continued growth in the language. Some native speakers replied that they continue to strive to write more clearly, others replied that they wanted to read more incisively. Non-native speakers recalled their struggles to learn the language, the ways in which they were taught and not taught Spanish, and ways in which proficiencies acquired at one point slowly attrited over time. A number of participants reported struggling to prepare presentations for international conferences in Spanish.

Overall, we noted that responses—although they reflected the undergirding standards of the monolingual educated native—also revealed the reality of a profession within which the individual maintenance of second-language proficiency is a constant struggle. One individual best expressed this notion when she said:

There is a sense of adjusting the way I speak according to the environment. I don't have that facility in Spanish. I am not bilingual, alas. I wish I were. Even though it gets a little better every time I go to Spain, it will never be there. (Informant #6)

Barriers to the Acquisition of Academic Spanish

The discussion about barriers to the acquisition of academic Spanish by the three groups of students in the department—that is, native-speakers from Latin American countries, non-native speakers, and U.S. Latinos—was perhaps the most revealing of the beliefs and values centered around conceptualizations of the monolingual educated native speaker and the ways in which *educated* is also understood as a euphemism for membership in a particular social class. As we had hypothesized, most interviewees immediately identified our question asking which group of students faces more challenges and barriers as a politically delicate one that attempted to draw out their prejudices toward the Spanish of U.S. Latinos. Faculty members and the majority of the doctoral students and lecturers directly anticipated our position and answered carefully. Masters students, on the other hand, seemed unaware of the political implications of the topic. Most offered very direct, unedited or unmonitored views of U.S. Latinos and their Spanish.

In sum, most native speakers expressed a negative opinion of the Spanish spoken by U.S. Latinos and considered that they face almost insurmountable challenges. These opinions—while expressed with the use of much hedging—centered on the third definition of academic Spanish (i.e., the use of standard, correct, and error-free language). Several native speakers, however, stated that they were not familiar with the barriers faced by U.S. Latino speakers of Spanish. By comparison, the positions of U.S. Latinos toward the Spanish of Chicanos and Puerto Ricans were mixed. Many had strong personal feelings about the experience of trying to learn academic Spanish, while others had subscribed to the view that the acquisition of correct, if not academic, Spanish is essential. All agreed, however, that U.S. Latinos face the largest barriers in departments of Spanish.

In general, the majority of non-native-speaking lecturers and doctoral students taking part in this study had had little or no contact with U.S. Latinos and were, therefore, unaware of the challenges they face. Several lecturers, some faculty, and a number of graduate students were new to the area and had never been in an environment in the United States where Spanish was spoken in surrounding communities.

The following views emerged from the discussions of this topic: (1) Barriers are personal, and U.S. Latinos who have the desire to do so can acquire correct Spanish. (2) Barriers are contextual and societal and beyond the control of individuals. And (3) Barriers involve multifaceted issues of identity that go much beyond mere desire or opportunity to learn the language.

The following examples of comments reflect the views about the Spanish language "problems" of U.S. Latinos from the perspective of a native and a non-native speaker:

> Other students that have the problem in terms of writing or oral expression in Spanish, problems that I suppose stem from Spanish learned at home than learned at school. Then they obviously have certain deficits. (trans., Informant #3)

> When I would speak with advanced Chicano students and young Chicano professors, I asked them how would you handle this? How do you handle the question of Spanish? I was always impressed and here is, you know, tangentially gets to the question you asked earlier, was always impressed... with the answer—at a certain point they would tell me, and I am thinking of [name deleted]. I am thinking of [name and institution deleted]. They would say, you know, at a certain point I realized that in order to be effective in this system, I am going to have to learn Spanish well. One went to Mexico and learned Spanish beautifully. I mean fixed it. I mean they always knew Spanish. And then, the other one went to Madrid and learned Spanish beautifully without sacrificing the Latin American accent. They just looked upon that as a tool and even a weapon if you will in order to have the credentials to fight the system. (Informant #6)

Some native speakers were negative and dismissive of U.S. Latinos' existing proficiencies even when claiming to know little about them:

I am inclined to say that, although I don't have that much experience, that it might be Latinos who don't know that much Spanish. Like Latinos that might have heard it but never studied it. That would say "abuela" [grandmother] and spell it "ahuela," "auela" because they've learned it one way. If they learn it as "auela" it's going to be harder to unlearn. Whereas people who are coming in with a blank slate—it's the same to them, if it's this way or that way. (Informant #30)

Others were supportive but talked about the great leaps that students were forced to make in moving from colloquial speech to the use of academic language:

Bilingual students bring something very much in their favor, and this is that they can speak rather well, and it is a matter of giving them practical vocabulary in this context. They bring with them tools that those who learn Spanish as a foreign language don't possess. It is important to remind them that they have this advantage and they come with an array of information and knowledge, that it is just a matter of putting them into practice. But, they have the disadvantage that in many cases they have used Spanish to communicate with their relatives. And if they used academic language, I think that it was very limited. Therefore, they have to jump from colloquial to academic language, and this requires a change of circuits, rather self-conscious and meditated, which could be very hard for them since they are used to seeing Spanish as a language that is used to communicate with their relatives. (trans., Informant #9)

Most individuals from all three language backgrounds who had had experience as teachers and fellow students of U.S. Latinos were quick to offer examples of challenges faced by these students. They identified barriers as including: lack of access to models of academic (correct) language, negative attitudes toward Latinos by Spanish-teaching faculty, frustration with the seemingly impossible task of "fixing" their Spanish, embarrassment, low self-esteem, lack of desire to learn, and lack of academic preparation.

Many individuals—especially those who focused on correctness—tended to compare U.S. Latinos unfavorably with foreign language learners:

Latinos seem to have a real problem in acquiring academic Spanish, for what I think, one of the many reasons, because they grew up speaking it, which doesn't mean anything. It just means that they learned to speak in a different register, which is not the same as speaking academic Spanish. Just because they are fluent in the language doesn't mean they are capable of academic Spanish. It's more likely that foreign language learners acquire it [academic Spanish] than native Spanish speakers, only because foreign language learners are much more conscious of the language, because they learn structure, they learn grammar. (Informant #12)

Yes, I think that if they [foreign language learners] are exposed to it, they have more possibilities of learning it. (trans., Informant #16)

U.S. Latinos, on the other hand, spoke more directly about their experiences in using Spanish in Spanish departments. Some spoke of experiencing prejudice, fear, and pain.

Prejudice is a very big issue [as a U.S. Latino], not wanting to speak because of being afraid of what others are going to think when you speak. (Informant #23)

There's a lot of embarrassment and a lot of pain and emotion that comes from having learned Spanish or having your parents, for that manner, speak Spanish and you not so well, that the type of struggle is twofold in a way for Latino students. It's not only emotional, but it's also going to be academic too. So it's a way of finding your voice in a public sphere in academics, but also finding that voice too in a more private sphere and how do you try to negotiate those two spheres in your own personality. (Informant #34)

There's always pressure to clean up my Spanish, just like a lot of Latinos that I know; we're always making an effort to clean it up a little bit. And that means things like pronouncing our S's in certain places or, if we leave it out, make sure that the person understands what we're saying; use the right tenses despite our very natural tendencies to use the ones considered wrong. The criticism could be enough to traumatize anyone and make you shy away from even trying to set any goals for yourself, especially a goal of linguistic perfection, if there is such a thing. (Informant #29)

A few U.S. Latinos spoke about resisting the attitudes toward their own way of speaking that were being inculcated in the department and believed that dominant ideologies were the greatest barrier, not to their developing academic Spanish, but to being accepted professionally as equals by native Spanish speakers.

In sum, generalizations made about the barriers experienced by native speakers, foreign language learners, and U.S. Latinos revealed a different set of assumptions, expectations and beliefs about each group. With regard to U.S. Latinos, an ideology of correctness and standardness and a view of the existence of an agreed-upon standard (the monolingual educated native speaker) resulted in an especially negative evaluation of U.S. Latino Spanish and U.S. Latino bilingual speakers. Few responses communicated any sense of the department's role or responsibility in minimizing the barriers and challenges faced by these individuals. Rather, the problem was seen to reside at the level of the individual U.S. Latino who, when presented with available resources, would make a simple, uncomplicated choice about whether or not to take full advantage of these resources.

Recommendations to the Department about the Development of Academic Spanish

The same views concerning the need to "fix" the language of certain learners were abundantly present in responses to our request for recommendations about the development of academic Spanish. Various approaches to the topic were identified. Some understood the question as relating exclusively to U.S. Latinos and others understood the question more broadly. Three different perspectives were identified: (1) naysayers who claimed not to believe in the direct teaching of academic language, (2) classroom optimists who had many suggestions about how and what to teach, and (3) cautious cynics who questioned the entire enterprise of privileging academic Spanish.

In general, the few identified naysayers expressed little interest in classroom teaching and had no recommendations to make. Some viewed academic Spanish as acquired within the practice of the profession and not in language classrooms. Others considered the teaching of academic Spanish to be unimportant for undergraduates as well as for graduate students.

Classroom optimists, on the other hand, talked at length about strategies for teaching. It is interesting to note, however, that in speaking of students' abilities, references to a particular group of students (native speaking, foreign language learners, U.S. Latinos) were not made. However, it was evident, especially for those engaged in the teaching of language, that these recommendations were focused on the foreign language learner, the only type of learner with whom most members of the department were familiar.

Suggestions for teaching academic language, then, included: beginning the study of language early, using language models, giving intensive practice in imitation of models, and using genre analysis. Several individuals suggested the direct teaching of the concept of register as well as the use of texts on theory and literary criticism written in Spanish. One individual, for example, directly criticized the consistent use of English language texts in literature classes as follows:

> There are a lot of texts that could be read in Spanish. There are a lot of excellent texts in good Spanish. [I would recommend] to try to find, for majors and graduate students, texts in Spanish that handle an academic language, because, of course, we gravitate more towards English texts since they are easier. This is also why our capacity for developing in academic Spanish decreases. We become experts in the use of English terms because we use a lot of texts in English. (trans., Informant #25)

By comparison, responses from cautious cynics, among them both U.S. Latinos and native speakers, revealed a submerged, attenuated counter-discourse that viewed reality from a different perspective. These responses argued that departments should not privilege or prioritize academic Spanish.

One participant, for example, stated the obvious about the language of publication for members of American departments of language:

> The way things are now, that to publish or perish, it has to be to publish in English or perish, because if you publish in Spanish you are perishing anyway in this country. (trans., Informant #35)

Other individuals, while less direct, argued for a balanced view:

> I would also say that there should be an equilibrium, that academic language does not end up dominating nonacademic language, for me, it is *very important* [italics added] to be able to communicate with someone in a non-academic language. And even more important. (trans., Informant #9)

Both natives and U.S. Latinos shared this point of view and several made the recommendation that academic Spanish not be taught, as in the following comment:

> My recommendation would be that it should not be taught. I would even like for the notion that this Spanish works better than colloquial Spanish to be dismantled. What is more, there are themes within academia that would be better written or discussed in Standard Spanish, or in natural, colloquial, even dialectal Spanish because it has subtleties and words that academic Spanish doesn't have. (trans., Informant #36)

Others made reference to the place of U.S. Latinos in departments and pointed out the tensions underlying pedagogical decisions that directly support established hierarchies:

> To bilingual natives who grew up in the United States, I think that definitely, the whole thing about devaluing their Spanish, to say that this is the correct Spanish now and we are going to teach you the right way to say it. Careful. I think that any hierarchical language in terms of academic Spanish, that would worry me. I think that would be my recommendation, be careful with hierarchical order, of what is correct and good and what's bad. (Informant #30)

To summarize: our request for recommendations for developing academic language proficiencies in the department produced expected responses from the majority of participants. Most members of the department expressed strong beliefs in the teaching and learning process within the department and optimism about the possibility of teaching academic language, at least to foreign language learners. It is interesting to note that all such recommendations focused on the second definition of academic Spanish as a specialized register characterized by specific surface-level features and perhaps on the third definition with its emphasis on correctness. They did not address the development of professional-level language as "ways of behaving, interacting, thinking, believing, and speaking" described by Gee (1990, xix).

Recommendations also exposed the existence of a counter-discourse. As opposed to the dominant discourse centered on the conceptualization of the monolingual, educated native speaker, this counter-discourse questioned existing myths about the use of academic Spanish as a widespread professional language in the United States and concerned itself with the privileging of particular types of language.

Unexamined Challenges

Traditionally, the foreign language teaching profession in this country has been concerned with teaching foreign or non-English languages to monolingual speakers of English. As a field, the profession has been most active at the postsecondary and secondary levels. From a theoretical perspective, the foreign language teaching profession has been closely aligned with the field of second language acquisition. It has been concerned with understanding the mechanisms underlying the acquisition of languages other than the first.

By comparison, involvement in the maintenance of heritage languages in this country encompasses a very different set of concerns. As Valdés (1992) argued, were the foreign language teaching profession to play a role in maintaining non-English languages in this country, it would need to expand and broaden its scope far beyond what it has done in the past. Its areas of interest would need to extend to include a population of students who already have many language strengths and who now want to develop them further. The work of language-teaching professionals would therefore need to be informed, not by theories of second language acquisition, but by an understanding of societal bilingualism and language contact as well as by theories of second dialect learning. Instruction for heritage students would need to be informed by clear views about how immigrant bilinguals function, what role two languages play in an immigrant bilingual's life, what relationship contact varieties of language have to monolingual varieties of language, and how original languages now atrophied can best be retrieved.

Our interviews with 43 members of a Spanish language department suggest that, as we chart a new course for heritage language maintenance that involves the participation of traditional "foreign" language programs and departments, we must attend to a number of serious challenges. As we saw in a single, but typical university language department, the department's discourse with a capital D (Gee, 1990, xix), that is, the "ways of behaving, interacting, valuing, thinking, believing, speaking, and... reading and writing that are accepted as instantiations" (Gee, 1990, xix) of the roles of faculty and students within the department, revealed the existence of a set of beliefs constructed around the notion of the monolingual, educated native speaker. Ideologies concerning correct and appropriate language helped justify the place and status of members of the department. Native speakers of Spanish from Latin America and Spain were at the top of the hierarchy, followed by foreign language or non-native speakers. U.S. Latinos occupied the lowest levels of the power structure and, through numerous interactions with faculty and fellow students, were encouraged to accept the dominant definitions of appropriate and correct language.

The discourse surrounding the notion of the *monolingual* educated native speaker permeated all seemingly neutral departmental interactions. There was a fear of language transfer and contamination, of diminished strengths in one language if another was used well, and a sense of loss of native-speaker legitimacy if English was spoken too well. The term *bilingual*, moreover, was used narrowly to describe rare instances of equivalent proficiencies in two languages or employed as a dismissing euphemism for U.S. Latinos. Everyday interactions in the department transmitted consistent messages to students: Monolingual-like behavior in Spanish is the ideal, and few students not natively born to the language achieve this standard. U.S. Latinos, if they are to be valued in such departments, must be reconstituted as imitation monolingual native speakers of Spanish.

In sum, the Spanish department that we studied is a setting within which ideologies of language indirectly reproduce the ideological hegemony of the state. Although for different reasons, the department echoes the existing nation-imagining beliefs of U.S. society within which bilingualism—especially when developed in homes and communities by immigrant populations—is profoundly suspect. While engaged in the teaching of a literature written in Spanish and while preparing future faculty members for careers in American institutions, the department transmits views that support the idealization of the monolingual native, a view that, while focused on Spanish, nevertheless is complicit with the deep values and linguistic beliefs of American monolingualism.

Implications for the Teaching of Other Heritage Languages

The same ideologies that we have described in one Spanish language department are present in other established university language departments dedicated to the study of both commonly and uncommonly taught languages. We conjecture, moreover, that such ideologies will also be commonplace as new programs in the truly uncommonly taught languages are implemented, for a number of reasons. First, language departments are primarily made up of individuals who were raised in places where the language they teach is the dominant and/or national language. Besides this deep personal commitment to the languages and literatures they teach, they may have little knowledge or understanding of societal bilingualism. As a result, they give much attention to "protecting" the language from contamination from the English that surrounds them and to providing a model of a standard target language free of vulgar colloquialisms and popular jargon. Language practices, moreover, will be colored by a nationalist aesthetic (Thomas, 1991) that is concerned with the characteristic features of the original national language and culture. As Einar Haugen (1972a) pointed out when speaking of immigrant languages in America:

> Each language has parted from the strict purity of its native form and has taken elements from American English. Each language has been forced to adapt itself to new conditions, and thereby gives us a vivid picture of the immigrant's struggle for a position within the new nation and his gradual accommodation to its demands.

> The usual attitude to this phenomenon, among both lay and learned, has been one of scorn or amusement. The educated foreigner has regarded the lingo of his American compatriots as debased and vulgar, and has struggled against that "demoralizing" influence of his American environment as best he could. (p. 2)

A second reason for the continued presence of the ideologies of monolingualism in foreign language departments has to do with the idealized native speaker norm that is central to the activities of the foreign language profession as a whole, with job descriptions that advertise for "native and near-native proficiency," and with the persistent monolingualism of many foreign language faculty who themselves have not become bilingual in English and their home language. The native speaker norm interacts in important ways with notions of standardness and linguistic purism.

Finally, as Haugen (1972b) again tells us as he speaks of the pressures that all bilinguals experience in keeping their two codes separate:

> The pressure to maintain separate codes is greatest in the case of sophisticated circles using the highest prestige forms of a standard language. A French-English bilingual who is a writer or university professor is under great pressure to keep each of his languages pure, i.e., free from code convergence. (p. 9)

The foreign-language-teaching professional who is committed to the maintenance and teaching of her language may unfortunately become intolerant of the contact varieties of the language used by heritage speakers because she has little understanding of language contact and bilingualism. Fear of contamination and erosion in her own language may contribute to the scorn that she directs against American bilinguals who, unlike her, may be second or third generation speakers of the heritage language.

Beliefs about language held by members of non-English-language-teaching departments, especially among the less commonly-taught languages, have not yet been explored at great length. For many language groups, the experience of immigration is a new one, and little information is available about the characteristics of the language varieties of children raised in bilingual homes in this country. As the newly organized initiative on heritage languages moves forward, it will be important to examine not only practices and policies designed to support the revitalization and maintenance of indigenous and immigrant languages but also the shared common-sense notions about language correctness and purity held by language teaching professionals, as well as the role that institutional settings play in transmitting the kinds of dispositions that Bourdieu ([1982] 1991) argues will result in the abandonment of the original instruments of expression by speakers of minority languages. The teaching and study of heritage languages may not be successful if we are not able to address unexamined but central challenges to heritage language maintenance and development among second and third generation American bilinguals.

Notes

1. We note Fishman's (1991) reservations about educational institutions' contributions to the reversal of language shift.
2. Recently much attention has been given to the construct of native-speaking ability as it is used in departments of foreign languages in this country. The reader is referred to Eoyang (1999), Kramsch (1999), Maier (1999), Valdés (1998), and Tesser (1999).
3. Valdés (1991) offers an interesting description of the place of majorities and minorities in foreign language departments.
4. See for example Valdés (1995, 1998).
5. Examples of these discussions include: Colombi (1997); García & Otheguy (1997); Hidalgo (1987, 1993, 1997); Porras (1997); Torreblanca (1997); Valdés (1981); Valdés-Fallis (1976).
6. The terms high and low draw from discussions of diglossia (Ferguson, 1959; Fishman, 1967).
7. There are problems in generalizing about the class origins of both early and recent Mexican immigrants. According to Portes et al. (1978); Portes & Bach (1985); Jasso & Rosenzweig (1990); and Bean & Tienda (1987), Mexican-origin immigrants are poor and have low levels of educational attainment. However, Durand and Massey (1992) have argued that generalizations about Mexican migration to the United States are inconsistent and contradictory. They maintain that case studies (e.g., Cornelius, 1976a, 1976b, 1978; Mines, 1981, 1984; Dinerman, 1982; Mines & Massey, 1985; Massey, Alarcon, Durand, & Gonzalez, 1987; Reichert & Massey, 1979) of Mexican "sending" communities (communities from which large numbers of Mexican nationals have emigrated) have yielded very different views about a number of questions. Among other topics, these studies present contradictory evidence about the class composition of U.S. migration. Durand and Massey (1992) argue that a few community factors (including age of the migration stream, the geographic, political and economic position of the community within Mexico, and the distribution and quality of agricultural land) affect the class composition of migration. In short, the authors stress the difficulties surrounding attempts at generalization.
8. The term *ordinary* (following Selby, Murphy, & Lorenzen, 1990) excludes the "middle" and "upper sectors" that, in the case of many countries in Latin America, represent only 10 percent of the population. This term avoids the use of "working class" or "middle class" and the connotations these terms have for American and European readers.
9. Space limitations require us to present all participants' comments in English, even if they were made in Spanish. Comments that were translated from Spanish will be noted (trans.) following the quotation.
10. Transcriptions follow the conventions of written language. We have deleted all information that might reveal the identity of particular individuals including names of cities and countries. Such deletions are indicated in parentheses, e.g., (country).

References

Bean, F., & Tienda, M. (1987). *The Hispanic population of the United States (for the Committee for Research on the 1980 Census)*. New York: Russell Sage Foundation.

Bourdieu, P. (1991). *Language and symbolic power* (A. Raymond & M. Adamson, Trans.). Cambridge MA: Harvard University Press. (Original work published 1982)

Clark, J. L. D., & Clifford, R. T. (1988). The FSI/ILR/ACTFL proficiency scales and testing techniques: Development, current status, and needed research. *Studies in Second Language Acquisition, 10*, 129–147.

Colombi, M. C. (1997). Perfil del discurso escrito en textos de hispanohablantes: teoría y práctica [Profiles of Written Discourse in the Texts of Spanish Speakers: Theory and Practice]. In M. C. Colombi & F. X. Alarcón Eds.), *La enseñanza del español a hispanohablantes: praxis y teoría* [*Teaching Spanish to Spanish speakers: practice and theory*] (pp. 175–189). Boston: Houghton Mifflin.

Cornelius, W. A. (1976a). Mexican migration to the United States: The view from rural sending communities. *Migration and Development Monograph C/76-12*. Cambridge. MA: MIT Center for International Studies.

Cornelius, W. A. (1976b). Outmigration from rural Mexican communities. *Interdisciplinary Communication Program, Occasional Monograph Series*, 5(No. 2), pp. 1–39. Washington, DC: Smithsonian Institution.

Cornelius, W. A. (1978). Mexican migration to the United States: Causes, consequences, and U.S. responses. *Migration and Development Monograph C/78-9*, Center for International Studies, Massachusetts Institute of Technology, Cambridge.

de Bot, K., & Weltens, B. (1991). Recapitulation, regression, and language loss. In H. W. Seliger & R. M. Vago (Eds.), *First language attrition* (pp. 31–51). New York: Cambridge University Press.

Delpit, L. (1998). The politics of teaching literate discourse. In V. Zamel & R. Spack (Eds.), *Negotiating academic literacies across languages and cultures* (pp. 207–218.). Mahwah NJ: Erlbaum.

Dinerman, I. R. (1982). Migrants and stay-at-homes: A comparative study of rural migration from Michoacán, Mexico. *Monograph No. 5*. La Jolla: University of California Center for U.S.-Mexican Studies.

Durand, J., & Massey, D. (1992). Mexican migration to the United States: A critical review. *Latin American Research Review, 27*(2), 3–42.

Eoyang, E. (1999). The worldliness of the English language: A lingua franca past and future. *ADFL Bulletin, 31*(1), 26–32.

Fishman, J. A. (1967). Bilingualism with and without diglossia: diglossia with and without bilingualism. *Journal of Social Issues, 23*(2), 29–38.

Fishman, J. A. (1991). *Reversing language shift: Thoeretical and empirical foundations of assistance to threatened languages*. Clevedon, England: Multilingual Matters.

Furguson, C. (1959). Diglossia. *Word, 15*, 329–340.

García, O., & Otheguy, R. (1997). No sólo de estándar se vive el aula: lo que nos enseñó la educación bilingüe sobre el español de Nueva York [The Classroom does not live on Standard Spanish Alone: What Bilingual Education has Taught Us about the Spanish of New York]. In M. C. Colombi & F. X. Alarcón (Eds.), *La enseñanza del español a hispanohablantes: praxis y teoría* [*Teaching Spanish to Spanish speakers: Practice and Theory*] (pp. 156–174). Boston: Houghton Mifflin.

Gee, J. (1990). *Social linguistics and literacies: Ideology in discourses*. London: Falmer Press.

Haugen, E. (1972a). Language and immigration. In A. Dil (Ed.), *The ecology of language* (pp. 1–36). Stanford, CA: Stanford University Press.

Haugen, E. (1972b). Active methods and modern aids in the teaching of foreign languages. In R. Filipovic (Ed.), *Papers from the Tenth Congress of the Federation internationale des Professeurs de langues vivants* (pp. 1–14). London: Oxford University Press.

Hidalgo, M. (1987). On the question of "Standard" vs. "Dialect:" Implications for teaching Hispanic college students. *Hispanic Journal of the Behavioral Sciences, 9*(4), 375–395.

Hidalgo, M. (1993). The teaching of Spanish to bilingual Spanish-speakers: A problem of inequality. In B. J. Merino, H. T. Truega, & F. A. Samaniego (Eds.), *Language and culture in learning: Teaching Spanish to native speakers of Spanish* (pp. 82–93). London: Falmer Press.

Hidalgo, M. (1997). Criterios normativos e ideología lingüística: Aceptación y rechazo del español de los Estados Unidos. In M. C. Colombi & F. X. Alarcon (Eds.), *La enseñanza del español a hispanohablantes: Praxis y teoría* (pp. 109–120). Boston: Houghton Mifflin.

Huffines, M. L. (1991). Pennsylvania German: Convergence and change as strategies of discourse.

In H. W. Seliger & R. M. Vago (Eds.), *First language attrition* (pp. 127–137). New York: Cambridge University Press.

Jasso, G., & Rosenzweig, M. R. (1990). *The new chosen people.* New York: Russell Sage Foundation.

Kramsch, C. (1999). Response to Carmen Chaves Tesser and Eugene Eoyang. *ADFL Bulletin, 31*(1), 33–35.

Maher, J. (1991). A crosslinguistic study of language contact and language attrition. In H. W. Seliger & R. M. Vago (Eds.), *First language attrition* (pp. 67–84). New York: Cambridge University Press.

Maier, C. (1999). The nonnative speaker: Introduction. *ADFL Bulletin, 31*(1), 19.

Massey, D. S., Alarcon, R., Durand, J., & Gonzalez, H. (1987). *Return to Aztlan: The social process of international migration from western Mexico.* Berkeley: University of California Press.

Mines, R. (1981). *Developing a community tradition of migration: A field study in rural Zacatecas, Mexico and California settlement areas.* Monographs in U.S.-Mexican studies No. 3: La Jolla, Calif: Program in United States-Mexican studies. University of California at San Diego.

Mines, R. (1984). Network migration and Mexican rural development. In R. C. Jones (Ed.), *Patterns of undocumented migration: Mexico and the United States.* Totowa, NJ: Rowman and Allanheld.

Mines, R., & Massey, D. S. (1985). Patterns of migration to the United States from two Mexican communities. *Latin American Research Review, 20,*104–124.

Olshtain, E., & Barzilay, M. (1991). Lexical retrieval difficulties in adult language attrition. In H. W. Seliger & R. M. Vago (Eds.), *First language attrition* (pp. 139–150). New York: Cambridge University Press.

Peyton, J. K., Ranard, D. A., & McGinnis, S. (2001). Charting a new course: Heritage language education in the United States. In J. K. Peyton & D. A. Ranard & S. McGinnis (Eds.), *Heritage languages in America* (pp. 3–26). Washington, DC: Center for Applied Linguistics/Delta Systems.

Phillips, S. U. (1998). Language ideologies in institutions of power: A commentary. In B. B. Schieffelin, K. A. Woolard, & P. V. Kroskrity (Eds.), *Language ideologies: Practice and theory* (pp. 211–225). New York: Oxford University Press.

Porras, J. E. (1997). Uso local y uso estándar: un enfoque bidialectal a la enseñanza del español para nativos. In M. C. Colombi & F. X. Alarcón (Eds.), *La enseñanza del español a hispanohablantes: praxis y teoría* (pp. 190-197). Boston: Houghton Mifflin.

Portes, A. (1978). Illegal immigration and the international system. In *Undocumented Workers: Implications for U.S. Policy in the Western Hemisphere* (pp. 179–188). Hearings before the Sub-Committee on Inter-American Affairs, U.S. Congress, House Committee on International Relations. Washington, DC: Government Printing Office.

Portes, A., & Bach, R. L. (1985). *Latin journey: Cuban and Mexican immigrants in the United States.* Berkeley: University of California Press.

Portes, A., McLeod, S. A., & Parker, R. N. (1978). Immigrant aspirations. *Sociology of Education, 51*(October), 241–260.

Reichert, J. S., & Massey, D. S. (1979). Patterns of migration from a central Mexican town to the United States: A comparison of legal and illegal migrants. *International Migration Review, 14,* 475–491.

Rumsey, A. (1990). Wording, meaning and linguistic ideology. *American Anthropologist, 92,* 346–361.

Selby H. A., Murphy, A. D., & Lorenzen, S. A. (1990). *The Mexican urban household: Organizing for self-defense.* Austin: University of Texas Press.

Seliger, H. W., & Vago, R. M. (1991). The study of first language attrition. In H. W. Seliger & R. M. Vago (Eds.), *First language attrition* (pp. 3–15). New York: Cambridge University Press.

Silva-Corvalán, C. (1994). *Language contact and change: Spanish in Los Angeles.* New York: Oxford University Press.

Stavenhagen, R. (1990). *The Ethnic question: Conflicts, development, and human rights.* Tokyo: United Nations University Press.

Tesser, C. C. (1999). The nonnative speaker and literary studies instruction. *ADFL Bulletin, 31*(1), 20–25.

Thomas, G. (1991). *Linguistic purism.* London: Longman.

Torreblanca, M. (1997). El español hablado en el suroeste de los Estados Unidos y las normas lingüísticas españolas. In M. C. Colombi & F. X. Alarcón (Eds.), *La enseñanza del español a hispanohablantes: praxis y teoría* (pp. 133–139). Boston: Houghton Mifflin.

Valdés, G. (1981). Pedagogical implications of teaching Spanish to the Spanish-speaking in the United States. In G. Valdés, A. G. Lozano & R. García-Moya (Eds.), *Teaching Spanish to the hispanic bilingual: Issues, aims, and methods* (pp. 3–20). New York: Teachers College Press.

Valdés, G. (1989). Testing bilingual proficiency for specialized occupations: Issues and implications. In B. R. Gifford (Ed.), *Test policy and test performance: Education, language and culture* (pp. 207–229). Boston: Kluwer.

Valdés, G. (1991). Minority and majority group members in foreign language departments: Toward the examination of established attitudes and values. *ADFL Bulletin, 22*(2), 10–14.

Valdés, G. (1992). The role of the foreign language teaching profession in maintaining non-English languages in the United States. In H. Byrnes (Ed.), *Languages for a multicultural world in transition: Northeast Conference Reports* (pp. 29–71). Skokie, IL: National Textbook Company.

Valdés, G. (1995). The teaching of minority languages as 'foreign' languages: Pedagogical and theoretical vhallenges. *Modern Language Journal, 79*(3), 299–328.

Valdés, G. (1998). The construct of the near-native speaker in the foreign language profession: Perspectives on ideologies about language. *ADFL Bulletin, 29*(3), 4–8.

Valdés, G., González, S. V., García, D. L., & Márquez, P. (2003). Language ideology: The case of Spanish in departments of foreign languages. *Anthropology & Education Quarterly, 34*(1), 3–26.

Valdés, G., Lozano, A. G., & García-Moya, R. (Eds.). (1981). *Teaching Spanish to the Hispanic bilingual: Issues, aims, and methods.* New York: Teachers College Press.

Valdés-Fallis, G. (December, 1976). Language development versus the teaching of the standard language. *Lektos,* 20–32.

Woolard, K. A. (1998). Introduction: Language ideology as a field of inquiry. In B. B. Schieffelin, K. A. Woolard, & P. A. Kroskrity (Eds.), *Language ideologies: Practice and theory* (pp. 3–47). New York: Oxford University Press.

7

The Relevance of Bilingual Proficiency in U.S. Corporate Settings[1]

MARY MCGROARTY AND ALFREDO URZÚA

Conceptual Framework

Within the fields of applied linguistics and second language education, language study has often been justified based on its presumed relationship to national and individual occupational goals and changing international relationships (e.g., Tucker, 1993). Scholars interested in promoting advanced levels of second language proficiency for students in U.S. schools have also noted that variants of immersion instruction constitute one means of developing high level language skills; for students whose native language is not English, future occupational relevance is one factor motivating native language conservation and literacy development (Campbell & Schnell, 1987).

While language educators are concerned with individual skill development, other social scientists have investigated issues related to recruiting and managing the linguistically diverse workforce now typical of many large industrialized countries. Within the United States, social scientists have focused particularly on Spanish-speaking workers. Historians of the American Southwest and borderlands have documented the roles and labor market experiences of Spanish speakers, notably those from Mexico, in fields such as agriculture and mining over the last century (see, for example, Ríos Bustamante, 1998; Weber, 1998; Zamora, 1998). In the contemporary United States, Spanish speakers constitute a large and growing share of the workforce in areas of historic concentration—the southwest for Mexicans, the East Coast for Puerto Ricans, Miami and other parts of south Florida for Cubans—and other areas of the country to which they have moved more recently. Additionally, changing conditions along the U.S.-Mexico border that, particularly post-NAFTA, have led to establishment of twin plants, or *maquiladoras*, have favored both growth of a mainly Spanish-speaking work-force and the need for a certain number of bilingual supervisors and managers (Hidalgo, 1995; Teschner, 1995).

Most social science research focuses on relatively unskilled workers, often recent immigrants, hired by medium or large enterprises involved in construction, manufacturing, or the provision of various types of services (see, for example, Knouse, Rosenfeld, & Culbertson, 1992; Lamphere, Stepick, & Grenier, 1994; and Morales & Bonilla, 1993). Most policy discussions (e.g., Massey,

Durand, & Malone, 2002) and media reports (e.g., Barboza, 2001; Greenhouse, 2001) on immigrant workers have also discussed the experiences of unskilled or semi-skilled workers almost exclusively. With such workers, applied linguistics research is important in identifying the levels of proficiency needed to allow workers, supervisors, and managers to establish and maintain successful communication, defined as both exchange of job-related information and creation of a workplace environment where workers feel appropriately recognized and rewarded (Amason, Allen, & Holmes, 1999). Commentators examining the role of bilingual skills in U.S. corporations (Fixman, 1990) and in occupations ranging from restaurant work and operation of small business to nursing in a large U.S. metropolis (McGroarty, 1990) have found that several factors such as the nature of a company's product or services, as well as its geographic location, affect the relevance of bilingual skills to an individual's job performance.

However, a focus solely on the experience of unskilled workers or on individual experience alone leaves many critical questions related to language and work unexplored (Waldinger, Bozorghmehr, Lim, & Finkel, 1998). Much recent theoretical work in the social sciences emphasizes a community-wide rather than individualistic perspective on the receiving context and on the skills and abilities that immigrants bring to the world of work (Portes, 1995). It is, hence, essential to examine the relevance of bilingual skills in a variety of occupational settings and at different occupational levels, not only at the level of operatives or production workers. This case study of three Spanish-speaking professionals, all Mexican nationals holding at least bachelor's degrees, was designed as a contribution to an expanded framework for consideration of the interplay between bilingual skills and routine job activities of managers employed in U.S. corporations. Because "language is at the heart of management as a process and is directly linked to the exercise of power and control over the workforce" (McAll, 2003, p. 238), it is crucial to include the linguistic profiles of managers in a comprehensive account of any societal language environment. Although individualistic in exploring the experiences of three different well-educated bilingual workers, this small-scale study provides insights not only into the variety of individual factors shaping occupational language use but also into some of the dimensions of occupationally-relevant skills that suggest future directions for community-wide studies of the roles and utility of immigrant languages. Future research must include documentation of language use patterns of professional as well as blue-collar workers and the concurrent social evaluations of the relevant language varieties by the speakers and those with whom they interact.

Aims of the Study

In this chapter, we explore the extent to which three bilingual Mexican professionals employ their two languages, English and Spanish, in performing their jobs as managers in U.S. corporations. More specifically, we wanted to gather information about what role, if any, their native language, Spanish, fulfilled in their professional lives in comparison to their use of English, the socially dominant language. At the time data were collected (fall, 1998), our three informants worked in American-owned corporations in the United States, and their job descriptions did not include the use of a language other than English (LOTE). Hence, these professionals were involved in the mainstream or primary economy, rather than in ethnic enclave businesses that represent another possible employment venue for immigrant professionals (see Bohon, 2001). In light of the globalization trends characterizing today's corporate world, and given the increasing numbers of Hispanics in the American population, we considered that investigating the role that Spanish might play in the professional life of three immigrant professionals could contribute to our understanding of the many possible relationships that exist between bilingualism and occupational context.

Data Collection

To collect data, a questionnaire was designed and mailed to the informants. Subsequently, an in-depth interview with each person was conducted over the phone, in Spanish, by the second author, and tape-recorded with the informants' permission. General information about each person's current corporation was also collected, mainly through public-domain information posted on web pages or when offered by the informants.

The questionnaire elicited information about informants':

1. positions in their companies (e.g., type of contract, official title);
2. duties and responsibilities;
3. patterns of language use at and outside the workplace (e.g., frequency, purposes, interlocutors, functions);
4. English language learning experiences;
5. length of residence in the United States;
6. perceptions of and attitudes towards the use of Spanish on the job, and
7. self-selected ethnic/national identity categories.

We also collected information regarding the informants' job histories and work-related experiences (résumé writing, job-search strategies, participation in job interviews, and so forth). All three informants had worked for at least two U.S. companies at the time of the interviews; one of them had worked in Mexico for several years before moving to the United States.

The Informants

Two males (in their thirties, married) and a female (in her late twenties, single), born and raised in Mexico, participated in the study.[2] Spanish is their native language and English was learned as a foreign language, although it is now their dominant language. Members of middle-class families in Mexico, all three had

had contact with English from an early age in various ways: visits to the United States, the media, English classes, and so on. All completed elementary and secondary education (grades K–12) in monolingual Spanish schools in Mexico.

Daniel (all names used here are pseudonyms) obtained a degree in computer science from a private university in northern Mexico and, after graduation in 1983, worked for about six years as a systems manager in the computer science department of a public university in Mexico. Later, he started his own consultancy firm. After the Mexican peso devaluation of December 1994, and the subsequent economic crisis, he decided to seek employment in the United States and moved to California with his wife (a Spanish monolingual) and three children. Francisco also graduated from a private Mexican university with a bachelor's degree in biochemical engineering, but moved to the United States immediately after graduation in 1986. Married to an English monolingual, he has two children. Elizabeth, unlike the other two informants, first came to the United States as an undergraduate on an athletic scholarship and obtained a bachelor's degree in marketing and management at a midwestern university. After graduation in 1996, she decided to start her professional career in the United States and has been working in American corporations ever since, receiving an MBA degree in 2001.

At the time of initial data collection, our informants had been living in the United States for an average of more than seven years, and were working in management or mid-level positions in private, American-owned corporations, two located on the West Coast and one in the Midwest. They describe themselves as functionally bilingual, reporting that they used both Spanish and English regularly and with ease, with English being the language used most of the time. They consider themselves to have retained native proficiency in Spanish, despite their long residence in the United States, and they also feel comfortable using English, both at home and at work, even though they did not consider it to be native-like. Furthermore, Francisco and Elizabeth reported that they did not feel that their minor and infrequent language problems or traces of foreign accent in their speech constituted a disadvantage or liability in their respective positions. Daniel, however, expressed concern that his "strong" foreign accent may, at times, negatively influence the perceptions of some of the people with whom he communicates on the job. Although empirical research shows that moderately Spanish-accented English does not necessarily diminish comprehensibility when compared with English produced by native speakers—moreover, the listener's native language seems to play a role in relative ease of comprehension (Major, Fitzmaurice, Bunta, & Balasubramanian, 2002)—concerns about listener perceptions of and reactions to accented English have also been reported by members of other immigrant groups in the United States (Lippi-Green, 1997).

First Positions in the U.S.: Bilingualism Required

In contrast to their current jobs, all three informants reported that they had been previously hired for positions that explicitly required bilingual personnel.

These earlier jobs reflected many of the linguistic and cultural challenges that each informant has since encountered in the U.S. workplace.

Technical Support for Maquila Operations (Daniel)

Daniel's first job in the United States was as a systems administrator for a company that manufactured medical equipment within the *maquila* system, whereby a U. S. company locates factories across the Mexican border to produce goods to be sold in the United States. Daniel's job included communicating with employees working in the *maquiladora*, which often required the use of Spanish. He believes that his bilingual skills did not constitute the primary factor in the company's decision to hire him for this job, even though an important part of the company's operations was located in Mexico. He reported that his bilingual skills were not discussed much during the interview process. It could have been the case, he said, that "my accent and my obvious Latino appearance indicated to the interviewers that I was proficient in Spanish and thus, although probably taken into consideration, this was not further discussed since they were more interested in my technical abilities and experience." (The use of accented speech and appearance as indicators of likely Spanish language proficiency have been noted as strong social cues in U.S. border cities such as El Paso; see Teschner, 1995). Interestingly, Daniel later discovered that problems of miscommunication had not been uncommon between the U.S.-based computing services unit, staffed mostly by English monolinguals, and the staff at the *maquiladora* site in Mexico, staffed mostly by Spanish monolinguals or not-fully-bilingual personnel. He was, in fact, surprised to learn that his predecessor in the position did not speak Spanish at all, given the many occasions that Daniel had to use Spanish in his dealings with or at the *maquiladora*.

Three years later, Daniel moved to another job as a network administrator and computer programmer for a company that produced ornamental plants and flowers. At that time, the company relocated some operations to Central America, which required Daniel to communicate, mostly in Spanish, with those managing the new operation abroad. In addition, he traveled to the Central American site on several occasions and thus made extensive use of Spanish for business purposes. After about three years with this company, Daniel decided to look for another job and obtained a position as a Unix systems administrator in a company that manufactured medical equipment. This company also established its manufacturing operations within the *maquiladora* system.

Despite the usefulness of his bilingual skills on the job, ever since Daniel first started to apply for U.S. jobs, he has reported being somewhat worried about his level of English proficiency, particularly in relation to his pronunciation. He worries that some people might assume his accented English indicates poor comprehension or insufficient ability to perform well in an English-speaking job environment. This has been a continuing concern for him, both in terms of job interviews in the United States and job performance evaluations. Even if bilingual skills might be required for a position, he fears his accented English might negatively influence the interviewer's assessment of his overall knowledge and skills and thus the outcome of the interview.

Business Calls to Customers Abroad (Elizabeth)

After graduation in 1996, Elizabeth obtained a one-year contract as a customer service representative for a company that distributed auto parts and industrial equipment. Although she was not particularly looking for a position requiring bilingual skills, this first job required precisely such qualifications: a person to handle the company's Latin American accounts, which involved constant communication with distributors abroad, often using Spanish. These communications were mainly done on the phone and could take up to half of her daily routine. In these interactions, Elizabeth had to pay close attention to learning the equivalent of certain technical terms in various regional dialects of Spanish because many of her business contacts were located in Latin American countries with varieties of Spanish different from her own. She also had to familiarize herself with different pragmatic conventions and expectations when talking over the phone with interlocutors from many different Spanish-speaking countries. Although the job specified English-Spanish bilingual skills, she reported that no test of her Spanish abilities was required during the application process (a situation still not unusual in U.S. private industry, and also typical in Canada prior to efforts in the mid to late 1990s to standardize bilingual services; see Roy, 2000). After this temporary job, Elizabeth decided to seek a more permanent position in the United States. The rationale she gave for her decision was that, had she returned to Mexico, she would most likely have worked in the *maquiladora* industry, possibly in a supervisory position, and this option was not attractive to her. After sending out many applications, she was hired by a Fortune 500 company located in the Midwest, operating in the same sector as her previous company: the manufacture and distribution of heavy industrial equipment and related services. This large company had subsidiaries and operations in many countries; Elizabeth worked for three years as an account representative in the logistics department. Her job was conducted almost exclusively in English. However, during this period, she was also involved in establishing a new operation in northern Mexico, which occasionally involved the use of Spanish. She was then promoted to a management position that required relocation to the West Coast.

Supervision of a Spanish-Speaking Workforce in the U.S. (Francisco)

After moving to the United States, Francisco first tried unsuccessfully to get a job related to the scientific side of his field. He then found a job as a sales/customer service representative for an export company, where he handled accounts in Mexico and Puerto Rico. Duties at this job were similar to Elizabeth's in that he had to conduct business calls in Spanish on a daily basis. Soon after, Francisco decided to seek a job in the manufacturing industry. His first job was as a manufacturing line supervisor for an electronics company located on the West Coast where most of the workforce was Spanish-speaking. As a supervisor, he was the direct link between the workforce and company management. English, he remembers, was used only when talking to his superiors and at home. He reports using mainly Spanish (i.e., up to 90% of his communication) and often only Spanish since most of the workers in the factory were either Spanish mono-linguals or had limited English proficiency. Two years later, he obtained a job in a company that manufactured cosmetic products, also in the same geographi-cal area. In this position, he used English when talking with the administrative and management personnel, and Spanish when he needed to communicate directly with the workers. Francisco reported that he was able to obtain both of these initial jobs mainly because of his bilingual skills. Although his academic qualifications and technical skills also contributed to his positive assessment by potential employers, he feels that in both cases his bilingualism played a major role, even though his employers never evaluated it formally. His experience on these jobs confirmed the importance of fluent bilingualism in the manufactur-ing sector, on the one hand, and the lack of formal language assessments during hiring procedures, on the other.

After some years, the company moved all of its operations to the Midwest; Francisco and his family relocated along with the company. After almost ten years with the second manufacturing company, he decided to seek a better job and obtained a position as branch operations manager for a company that manufactures packaging devices, located in the region to which they had by then moved. In his new position, Francisco is the top authority in the plant, which is part of a conglomerate of twelve manufacturing plants, ten in the United States, one in Europe, and one in Mexico.

Current Positions: English Dominant, Spanish Useful though not Required

As noted, all three informants have sought and obtained better positions since beginning their occupational careers in the United States. Interestingly, none of them currently has a position in which bilingual skills are required in the cor-responding job description. However, in all three cases, the informants reported that they have used and continue to use their Spanish language skills at different times and for different purposes.

Spanish Used to Improve Communication and Socialize (Daniel and Francisco)

At present, Daniel seems to be using more Spanish than the other two informants. Although reading or writing in Spanish is rarely necessary, he reports that Spanish is used in his oral communication every day, i.e., approximately 20% of the time. In fact, Spanish has proven to be particularly useful in his communications with the *maquiladora* in Mexico. Using Spanish on the job, Daniel states, is sometimes unavoidable because some of the people he needs to contact regularly in the *maquiladora* do not speak English. At other times the use of Spanish is optional; for example, Daniel reports using Spanish often to socialize with Spanish-speaking colleagues in the United States. Reflecting on this, he considers that his bilingual skills definitely allow him to do a better job, even though these skills are not explicitly recognized or rewarded by the company.

Francisco also reports using Spanish every day on the job. He uses Spanish for business-related functions such as communicating with suppliers, customers, and carriers, or to communicate with his workforce orally or through written memos. He estimates that his oral communication in Spanish accounts for approximately 15% of his interactions, while communicating in Spanish in writing is necessary about 10% of the time. He also uses Spanish for socializing at work since he prides himself on making an effort to talk to employees about their personal lives and concerns, which he considers an important part of his managing style, an attribute thought to be more typical of Hispanic than Anglo management styles (Amason, Allen, & Holmes, 1999; Ferdman & Cortes, 1992). He states that with Spanish-speaking employees these interactions are almost always conducted in Spanish.

Spanish Used Occasionally but No Longer Relevant for the Job (Elizabeth)

Whereas Daniel and Francisco use Spanish for job-related purposes on a daily basis, mostly with co-workers and/or employees inside the company, Elizabeth feels the need to communicate in Spanish only rarely. For her, these occasions usually involve speaking to workers employed by service providers to do work in her company. Apart from these brief interactions, virtually all other communication in the company (with employees, colleagues, clients, workers, and supervisors) is conducted in English, including socializing interactions. Elizabeth thinks that her bilingualism has no real impact on her job performance, but believes that this skill is part of her personal and professional identities, an attitude shared by Daniel and Francisco. Despite using Spanish only occasionally, Elizabeth feels such minimal use is nevertheless important to her and to the way she presents herself to others.

Informants' Evaluations of the Worth of Bilingualism

We also wished to collect information on the informants' evaluation of bilingualism as part of the human capital they bring to workplace interactions and their sense of whether their superiors regard bilingualism positively. All three informants consider that being bilingual helps them perform their jobs more efficiently, even if Spanish is only occasionally useful. Although, at present, their bilingualism is not rewarded financially because it is not part of their official job descriptions, each of them articulated expectations for the future in which bilingualism could enhance their occupational progress. Daniel thinks that, in his present job, his use of Spanish as needed will lead to better performance evaluations and thus, eventually, to a better salary. Elizabeth, on the other hand, believes that her supervisors value her bilingual skills and her knowledge of Mexico and its economy because these traits distinguish her from monolingual English-speaking employees at the same level, and are consequently regarded positively, though not rewarded financially, by her superiors. Finally, Francisco believes that his bilingual skills are respected by others and have helped him arrive at his present position as top manager in the plant; he also perceives that his "Latino" management style is much appreciated by the workers in his company. He notes that, particularly in the manufacturing sector, being bilingual is a qualification very much in demand and predicts this demand will increase in the future.

All three thus think their bilingual skills are likely to help them progress in their careers, even if they do not speak or use Spanish on a daily basis. Furthermore, even in the face of U.S. contemporary political environment in which English-only legislation and referenda regularly appear, these professionals see no particular reason why it would be either necessary or advisable to avoid using Spanish on the job if doing so facilitated communication. All three said that, in the future, they would like to work in a multilingual environment. In terms of their current situations, all observe that coming to the United States to work was a good decision because their professional expectations have been fulfilled, for the most part. They thus expect to be working in the United States indefinitely. Although, in their present positions, their bilingualism is officially unrecognized—and thus, we might argue, institutionally invisible—it is, nonetheless, an aspect of their present occupational profiles, which they continue to value.

Despite their unanimous positive assessment of the occupational value of Spanish language skills, there were some issues on which the informants differed. One relates to the extent to which these managers encourage use of Spanish by others on the job. Both Daniel and Francisco are not only receptive and willing to use Spanish at work but also try to encourage other people to talk to them in Spanish. Elizabeth, in contrast, uses Spanish only in those instances when she feels it is necessary to improve communication. Furthermore, she comments that if she is in a job-related situation where her interlocutors are also English-Spanish bilinguals (e.g., on a business trip to Mexico or in dealing with a bilingual contractor), she prefers to use English. Daniel and Francisco, in contrast, say they choose to speak in Spanish in such situations.

Language and Occupational Identity: Dynamic and Idiosyncratic

We are also interested in the way occupational bilingualism interacts with other facets of personal identity such as one's self-identification. When our informants moved to American soil, they became not only Mexican immigrants but also members of a so-called minority group. These groups are identified and identify themselves in different ways, using terminology that commonly denotes immigrant status, national origin, linguistic background, race or ethnicity, political stance, or a combination thereof. To better discern possible links between linguistic behavior and cultural self-identification, we decided to obtain information regarding the way they describe themselves as U. S. immigrants. Self-descriptions can be telling of whether or not an individual feels comfortable with a bicultural or bilingual identity, and desires or hopes to maintain that part of their identity. Additionally, the possible links between occupational identity and language used on the job deserve study (Domino, 1992).

The informants were thus asked to select, from a number of choices, those they felt best described themselves in the context of their current social and cultural standing. Included among the choices were terms denoting linguistic and national background or origin, racial or ethnic identity, as well as immigrant status. Daniel selected only one term, "Mexican-American," among the many options available. Elizabeth, on the other hand, described herself using five different terms denoting national, cultural, and linguistic traits: "Mexican," "Latino," "Hispanic," "Spanish speaker," and "bilingual speaker." Similarly Francisco chose more than one term: opting for "Mexican," "Hispanic," and "bilingual." Moreover, he was also the only one of the three who also chose a term denoting a racial category, "white."

When asked to explain the rationale behind their selections, Daniel commented that his selection of the single descriptor Mexican-American relates to his recent acquisition of American citizenship, which in his mind provides him with an easily-definable identity: an American of Mexican origin. Elizabeth's U.S. status is that of a resident immigrant, which she said may have been the reason why she chose the terms "Hispanic" and "Latino," generic terms used in the United States by and for people of Latin American origin, including Mexicans, but without the political connotations of other terms, such as "Chicano." However, since the terms "Hispanic" and "Latino" apply to individuals of many different nationalities, she felt it necessary to add the term "Mexican." Francisco, who chose the term "white," reported doing so based simply on his physical appearance and the fact that race is a category often included in the bureaucratic forms he has had to fill out in the past, where "white" is the category he has always chosen. The multiplicity of labels selected by the informants attests to the variety of self-identification within the U.S. Hispanic population (Navarro, 2003).

In addition to being asked to select category labels for self-definitions, the informants were asked to place themselves on a continuum where one pole represented an individual considered "100% Mexican" (i.e., in terms of cultural identity, customs, way of thinking, behavior, etc.) and the opposite pole represented an individual considered "100% American."[3] Their choices on the continuum are shown in Figure 7.1 (initials used).

The informants' selections are particularly interesting given the lack of correspondence between length of residence in the United States and the tendency

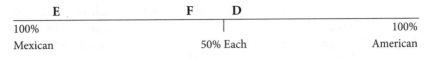

Figure 7.1 Infomants' choices on Mexican/American identity (initials used).

to develop an American identity, as might be expected. Daniel, who has been in the United States for eight years, is farther away from the Mexican pole than is Elizabeth, who has been in the United States for ten years; Francisco, who has been the longest in the country (16 years), still doesn't see himself as developing an American identity. The informants' choices suggest that occupational identity is very much an individual phenomenon and, in the contexts studied, is not closely tied to any kind of dichotomous national identification. All three of these professionals are clearly successful on the job, as indicated by continued employment and their ability to seek new positions of greater responsibility within U.S. corporations.

Implications and Research Directions

We cannot extract many generalizations from this very small-scale investigation. However, such an approach does provide us with a more detailed picture of the various factors that affect a manager's decision to use bilingual skills in the contemporary U.S. workplace. The qualitative data obtained show us the extent to which a LOTE, in this case Spanish, may be employed in the workplace even when not explicitly required for a position and even when the company involved is situated in the mainstream economy rather than an ethnic enclave. Additionally, we note that two of the three managers work in the western or southwestern U.S. where Spanish enjoys some passive legitimacy (Jaramillo, 1995), even though the language of all workplaces studied is clearly English.

Although each case is unique, some common features can be discerned. First, bilingual skills gave these managers a point of entry into U.S. corporate employment when they were first hired. However, even at initial hire, their bilingualism represented one type of human capital added to an already relatively high level of formal education and technical skill; simply being bilingual was not sufficient for them to obtain their first corporate positions. Second, the informants' descriptions of the role of Spanish in their current positions indicate something of a mismatch between the value they assign to their bilingual skills on the job and their perceptions of value their employers attach to it, a mismatch discussed previously in the literature on U.S. corporate culture. To wit, Lambert and Moore (1993) note that their data on foreign language use among international business graduates in the United States reveal that there is "some indication of corporate awareness of employees' foreign language competencies, but rewards for the possession of those skills are problematic" (p. 279), adding "in most cases, the company knows about the worker's competence and even enters it in the personnel file, although it is not sufficiently important to be formally certified by any kind of rating or testing procedure" (p. 280). They conclude that it is extremely difficult to identify any direct influence of language skills on promotion, salary, or any other conventional aspect of the corporate reward system.

Despite the lack of consistent monetary rewards for bilingualism, then, the experience of these informants may still suggest some subtle progress indicators. At least in the cases analyzed here, there do not seem to be any disincentives for the use of LOTEs at work, a situation that has been too often reported both in the media and in academic publications. Linguistic discrimination in the workplace, as identified by Macías (1997), Valdés (1997), and Zentella (1997), is a disturbing reality experienced by many Spanish-speaking workers. Because our informants are better educated and more highly qualified than most other Spanish-speaking immigrants, and because they have positions higher on the occupational ladder than most of their co-nationals, their attitudes and experiences with respect to bilingual behavior are probably not typical of the majority of Hispanic workers, but still worth documenting in the interests of representing the range of relationships between bilingualism and occupational progress in the contemporary United States. Bilingualism along with high levels of education clearly helped these three professionals land their first U.S. positions. Moreover, in their current professional positions, these managers receive varying degrees of positive recognition for their bilingual skills, although they are not additionally compensated for them. With respect to their future prospects, all perceive that bilingualism is likely to be a net plus. At the same time, some caution may be warranted. Along with the prospect of continuing occupational progress, we must note that future progress could be impeded by a "glass ceiling," a possibility identified in recent research using an econometric model to predict the career earnings of Asian-origin engineers working in the United States (Waldinger et al., 1998). Moreover, none of the informants, now mid-level managers, ever mentioned using Spanish to communicate upwards in the corporate hierarchies; when used, Spanish is a vehicle for lateral or downward communication, thus reflecting not only the present situation of the labor force but some of the past historical relations between speakers of Spanish and English in the United States. (For an insightful summary of the relevance of past social relationships to contemporary occupational communications in French and English in Canada, see McAll, 2003).

Will bilingualism become a more explicitly recognized and rewarded professional asset in American corporations in the future? Few predictions are warranted. Historically, bilingualism has often been met with suspicion in some locations and by some segments of American society. Furthermore, contemporary U.S. corporations demonstrate a variety of responses towards linguistic diversity in their public information (see Dicker, 1998), and, presumably, in their personnel policies, which are harder to assess directly. Current movements such as

English-Only and English-Plus have heightened the debate regarding the status of English in the United States and the treatment accorded other languages in educational settings, government offices, and the workplace (Zentella, 1997). These increasingly strident calls to emphasize English and denigrate or prohibit other languages in public domains such as work may, in future, restrict not only individual expression but opportunities for social harmony (Barker, Giles, Noels, Duck, Hecht, & Clément, 2001). On the other hand, concurrent international trends such as economic globalization, creation of special regional or inter-continental free-trade zones and specially-designated markets, and continuing patterns of migration all suggest that contact between speakers of different languages will only increase. English, as a language of international communica-tion, will likely play a significant role in fulfilling the companies' international needs, but competence in LOTEs relevant to the operations of different types of enterprises might very well become even more crucial, depending on business configurations of the future. Additionally, we also recognize that future business operations may simultaneously contribute to the redefinition of what counts as bilingualism and who counts as bilingual, as is occurring with French in some parts of Canada (see Roy, 2003).

The range of situations in which our informants engage in their professional lives points not only towards the wide variety of functions fulfilled by resorting to one or another language, but also to the demands imposed on these individu-als' linguistic and cultural repertoires. The diversity of interlocutors, types of discourse, activities, levels of formality, and degree of accuracy that character-izes their communicative interactions requires a sophisticated level of linguistic, sociolinguistic and pragmatic competence in their two languages. Such a level of proficiency is presumably the goal of many different types of language programs (e.g., immersion education, content-based instruction; and language for specific purposes, including workplace programs; see Duff, Wong, & Early, 2000), and it is also the ultimate goal of many language learners. Our informants reported having developed their considerable English proficiency through many differ-ent types of language-related experiences, such as attending intensive language programs in the United States, taking regular EFL classes in their home country, having frequent interactions with English-speaking people and with visual and printed material, as well as enrolling in specialized language and content courses at the university level. They report maintaining close contact with Spanish, also in a variety of situations and settings: visiting Mexico frequently, and speaking, reading and writing in Spanish with many different people on a regular basis. At present, all three informants agree that being bilingual allows them to perform their jobs more efficiently, even if their bilingual skills are used only occasionally. All are successful mid-level managers; their cultural self-identifications vary in ways that reflect individual orientations and experiences. The three informants seem to be comfortable interacting either in English or in Spanish according to the various demands of their job. They consider that being able to function in either language, as well as familiarity with the corresponding cultures, have been and continue to be a professional asset.

Although recent years have seen the arrival of Hispanic immigrants with relatively higher levels of educational attainment than was the case in the 1980s and 1990s, it is still true that only about 1 in 15 of Mexican-origin residents in the United States have college degrees (Weissert, 2006), making it unlikely that the majority of U.S. Spanish-speaking workers will soon be able to move into the professional class. Nevertheless, our small case study shows that, when the right conditions exist, bilingualism can indeed benefit all parties involved: the bilingual speakers themselves as well as their employers, employees, customers, and co-workers. The work environment can be enhanced by means of a LOTE if use of a language in addition to English relates to any aspect of work, whether in performing a particular job-related function, communicating more effectively, or simply improving the social relationships among workers and between workers and managers. Applied linguists, social scientists, policymakers, and language educators would benefit from additional studies of the occupational histories and language abilities of bilingual managers and professionals like our informants whose overall occupational profiles, including the bilingualism they may now use only occasionally, nonetheless contribute to the economic and social vitality of the entire enterprise.

Notes

1. We are grateful to Russ Campbell for his intellectual leadership in identifying the language of business as a significant area of scholarship and practical endeavor in applied linguistics.
2. We are deeply indebted to our informants, Daniel, Elizabeth, and Francisco, for their generosity in sharing their occupational histories with us. Their candid personal reports have allowed us to generate a more differentiated picture of job-related bilingualism in managerial positions than would have been possible without their first-hand insights.
3. We are aware that current thinking in the arts (e.g., Gómez-Peña, 2000) and social sciences (Cortés-Conde & Boxer, 2002) eschews such forced choices and emphasizes the fluid and situationally-specific aspects of bilingual identity. Nonetheless, similar classifications have been used to good advantage in recent research on groups in the process of cultural change (e.g., Suárez-Orozco & Suárez-Orozco, 1995), so it is not amiss to ask how our informants perceive and use these typical bureaucratic categories.

References

Amason, P., Allen, M. W., & Holmes, S. A. (1999). Social support and acculturative stress in the multicultural workplace. *Journal of Applied Communication Research, 27,* 310–334.

Barboza, D. (2001, December 21). Meatpackers' profits hinge on pool of immigrant labor. *New York Times,* p. A14.

Barker, V., Giles, H., Noels, K., Duck, J., Hecht, M., & Clément, R. (2001). The English-only movement: A communication analysis of changing perceptions of language vitality. *Journal of Communication, 51,* 3–37.

Bohon, S. (2001). *Latinos in ethnic enclaves: Immigrant workers and the competition for jobs.* New York: Garland.

Campbell, R. N., & Schnell, S. (1987). Language conservation. *Annals of the American Academy of Political and Social Science, 490,* 177–185.

Cortés-Conde, F., & Boxer, D. (2002). Bilingual word-play in literary discourse: The creation of relational identity. *Language and Literature, 11*(2), 137–151.

Dicker, S. (1998). Adaptation and assimilation: U.S. business responses to linguistic diversity in the workplace. *Journal of Multilingual and Multicultural Development, 19*, 282–302.

Domino, G. (1992). Acculturation of Hispanics. In S. Knouse, P. Rosenfeld, & A. Culbertson (Eds.), *Hispanics in the workplace* (pp. 56–74). Newbury Park, CA: Sage.

Duff, P., Wong, P., & Early, M. (2000). Learning language for work life: The linguistic socialization of immigrant Canadians seeking careers in health care. *The Canadian Modern Language Review/La Revue canadienne des langues vivantes, 57*, 9–57.

Ferdman, B., & Cortes, A. C. (1992). Culture and identity among Hispanic managers in an Anglo business. In S. Knouse, P. Rosenfeld, & A. Culbertson (Eds.), *Hispanics in the workplace* (pp. 246–277). Newbury Park, CA: Sage.

Fixman, C. (1990). The foreign language needs of U.S.-based corporations. *Annals of the American Academy of Political and Social Science, 511*, 25–6.

García, O., & Otheguy, R. (1994). The value of speaking a LOTE in a U.S. business. *Annals of the American Academy of Political and Social Science, 532*, 99–122.

Gómez-Peña, G. (2000). *Dangerous border crossers*. London: Routledge.

Greenhouse, S. (2001, April 9). Los Angeles warms to labor unions as immigrants look to escape poverty. *New York Times*, p. A14.

Hidalgo, M. (1995). Language and ethnicity in the "taboo" region: The US-Mexico border. *International Journal of the Sociology of Language, 114*, 29–45.

Jaramillo, J. A. (1995). The passive legitimization of Spanish: A macrosociolinguistic study of a quasi-border: Tucson, Arizona. *International Journal of the Sociology of Language, 114*, 67–91.

Knouse, S., Rosenfeld, P., & Culbertson, A. (Eds.). (1992). *Hispanics in the workplace*. Newbury Park, CA: Sage.

Lambert, R. D., & Moore, S. J. (1993). Foreign language use among international business graduates. In S. J. Moore & C. A. Morfit (Eds.), *Language and international studies: A Richard Lambert perspective* (pp. 274–285). Washington, DC: National Foreign Language Center.

Lamphere, L., Stepick, A., & Grenier, G. (Eds.). (1994). *Newcomers in the workplace: Immigrants and the restructuring of the U.S. economy*. Philadelphia: Temple University Press.

Lippi-Green, R. (1997). *English with an accent*. London: Routledge.

Macías, R. F. (1997). Bilingual workers and language use rules in the workplace: A case study of a nondiscriminatory language policy. *International Journal of the Sociology of Language, 127*, 53–70.

Major, R., Fitzmaurice, S., Bunta, F., & Balasubramanian, C. (2002). The effects of nonnative accents on listening comprehension: Implications for ESL assessment. *TESOL Quarterly, 36*, 173–190.

Massey, D., Durand, J., & Malone, J. (2002). *Beyond smoke and mirrors: Mexican immigration in an era of economic integration*. New York: Russell Sage Foundation.

McAll, C. (2003). Language dynamics in the bi- and multilingual workplace. In R. Bayley & S. Schecter (Eds.), *Language socialization in bilingual and multilingual societies* (pp. 235–250). Clevedon, UK: Multilingual Matters.

McGroarty, M. E. (1990). Bilingualism in the workplace. *Annals of the American Academy of Political and Social Science, 511*,159–179.

Morales, R., & Bonilla, F. (Eds.). (1993). *Latinos in a changing U.S. economy*. Newbury Park, CA: Sage.

Navarro, M. (2003, Nov. 9). Going beyond black and white, Hispanics in Census pick 'other.' *New York Times*, pp. A1, A21.

Portes, A. (Ed.) (1995). *The economic sociology of immigration*. New York: Russell Sage Foundation.

Ríos Bustamante, A. (1998). As guilty as hell: Mexican copper miners and their communities in Arizona, 1920-1950. In J. M. Hart (Ed.), *Border crossings: Mexican and Mexican-American workers* (pp. 163–183). Wilmington, DE: SR Books.

Roy, S. (2000). La normalisation linguistique dans une enterprise: Le mot d'ordre mondial. *Canadian Modern Language Review/La revue canadienne des langues vivantes, 57*, 118–143.

Roy, S. (2003). Bilingualism and standardization in a Canadian call center : Challenges for a linguistic minority community. In R. Bayley & S. Schecter (Eds.), *Language socialization in bilingual and multilingual societies* (pp. 269–285). Clevedon, UK : Multilingual Matters.

Suárez-Orozco, C., & Suárez-Orozco, M. (1995). *Transformations: Migration, family life, and achievement motivation among Latino adolescents*. Stanford, CA: Stanford University Press.

Teschner, R. (1995). Beachheads, islands, and conduits: Spanish monolingualism and bilingualism in El Paso, Texas. *International Journal of the Sociology of Language, 114*, 93–105.

Tucker, G. R. (1993). Language learning for the 21st century: Challenges of the North American

Free Trade Agreement. *Canadian Modern Language Review/La revue canadienne des langues vivantes, 50,* 165–172.

Valdés, G. (1997). Bilinguals and bilingualism: Language policy in an anti-immigrant age. *International Journal of the Sociology of Language, 127,* 25–52.

Waldinger, R., Bozorghmehr, M., Lim, N., & Finkel, L. (1998). In search of the glass ceiling: The career trajectories of immigrant and native-born engineers. [Working paper no. 28]. University of California, Los Angeles: Lewis Center for Regional Policy Studies, School of Public Policy and Social Research.

Weber, D. (1998). Historical perspectives on transnational Mexican workers in California. In J. M. Hart (Ed.), *Border crossings: Mexican and Mexican-American workers* (pp. 209–233). Wilmington, DE: SR Books.

Weissert, W. (2006, May 7). Educated Mexicans crossing border: Many immigrants from middle class. *The Arizona Republic,* pp. A1, A16.

Zamora, E. (1998). Labor formation, community, and politics: The Mexican working class in Texas, 1900–1945. In J. M. Hart (Ed.), *Border crossings: Mexican and Mexican-American workers* (pp. 139–162). Wilmington, DE: SR Books.

Zentella, A. C. (1997). The hispanophobia of the Official English movement in the U.S. *International Journal of the Sociology of Language, 127,* 71–86.

II
Heritage Speaker Profiles
and Needs Analysis

8

Heritage Language Narratives[1]

MARIA POLINSKY

This chapter is a preliminary exploration of the structure of heritage speakers' narratives. Although far from a full-fledged study, it aims to establish methodological foundations for an exploration of the structure of heritage speakers' narratives and will contribute to our understanding of the main properties of such narratives. Knowing what, if anything, makes heritage speakers' narratives different from those of fully competent speakers has implications for language acquisition studies and for the development of practical steps to improve the competency of heritage speakers.

Before moving to the discussion of the main issues addressed here, some terminological clarifications are in order. By *competent speaker* we understand a speaker who has full control of the grammar of their language as well as the ability to tailor their language to the particular audience this speaker has to address (control of styles and registers). *Narrative* is understood here very broadly, as an account of a story or past events, and does not presuppose a dialogical interaction. By *heritage language* I mean a language which was first for an individual with respect to the order of acquisition but has not been completely acquired because of the switch to another dominant language. An individual may use the heritage language under certain conditions and understand it, but his/her primary language is a different one (Valdés, 2000). The corresponding language that has been completely acquired (by a population of speakers other than heritage) and is spoken competently is referred to as the *full language*. If heritage language X is compared to a certain full language, the latter serves as the *baseline*; it is important to remember that the baseline does not have to correspond to a standard language. For instance, if dialect A of language L is the basis of the standard, but heritage speakers grow up surrounded by dialect B, which constitutes their main input, it is dialect B that serves as the baseline. In fact, correct identification of the baseline may assist people in understanding subjects' histories and sociolinguistic situation with respect to their heritage language.

The chapter is structured as follows. I first describe the research methods employed in this study. I then present the main results obtained in the study and identify characteristic features of heritage speakers' narratives compared with narratives elicited from fully competent speakers. Finally I discuss these findings from a more general perspective.

Research Methods

The design of this study followed the so-called frog story design successfully used for a cross-linguistic developmental study of narratives by a team of researchers (Berman & Slobin, 1994). The material for eliciting narratives was a picture book of 24 pictures showing a boy who loses his pet frog, goes through a series of adventures to find it, and reaches a happy ending (it is unclear from the picture if the boy finds his own frog or gets a replacement).

The task was also a replication of the original frog story study. Subjects were interviewed individually and given instructions very close to the ones used in Berman and Slobin: "Here is a set of pictures. They tell a story about a boy, his dog, and a frog. First please look at all the pictures. Pay attention to each picture and afterwards tell the story shown in these pictures" (Berman & Slobin, 1994, p. 22). The subjects were given five minutes to look at the pictures prior to the elicitation and then were able to see the pictures as they were telling the story. Since the study involved heritage speakers and controls, the heritage speakers were asked to tell the story in the heritage language and then in the dominant language (English). The controls, full speakers of the baseline language, were asked to tell the story only once.

Each session was digitally recorded and transcribed using standard transcribing techniques elaborated on in Berman and Slobin (1994, pp. 29–31 and 127–188). The basic unit of analysis here is a clause (as opposed to a sentence, utterance, or intonation unit), identified as a unit headed by an inflected or unified predicate.

The subjects for this study included two heritage speakers of Russian (both male) living in the United States. Following my earlier work (Polinsky 1995, 1997, 2000), I will refer to them as American Russian speakers. One of the American Russian speakers interviewed for this study was a child (M, age 9) representing the oldest age group considered by Berman and Slobin. He stopped using Russian actively around age 5 as he entered kindergarten. He lives in a Russian-speaking home and understands basic Russian but prefers to respond in English when addressed in Russian. The other subject was a college student (B, age 23) who was born in the United States and had a profile similar to the child's, having stopped using Russian actively upon entering kindergarten. Neither of these subjects can read Cyrillic.

The controls included S, a Russian-speaking child (age 8) and A, a Russian-speaking student (age 21).[2] English-speaking subjects were not interviewed; instead, I used the original frog story data for comparison (Berman & Slobin, 1994).

I compared the heritage speakers to fully competent speakers of Russian, within and outside of their age group, and to themselves as they told the story in English. In addition to the range and length of narrations (measures used by Berman and Slobin, 1994), I also measured the mean length of utterance (MLU) in words.[3]

Results and Preliminary Discussion

Quantitative Measures

The quantitative results obtained for the frog stories in question are summarized in Table 8.1 and Table 8.2. The numerical measures reflect the overall length of the narrative (number of clauses in the narrative) and the MLU in words. In addition, I counted the number of embedded clauses.

It is not unexpected that all the narratives are relatively similar in length; after all, they follow the same story plot, and the 9-year-olds are quite close to adults in terms of their ability to narrate the plot in general (for a discussion of narrative styles in 9-year- olds vs. adults, see Berman and Slobin, 1994). The three other measures, however, reveal significant differences between heritage speakers and full speakers, within and across languages. In Russian, the heritage speakers had much shorter utterances than the full speakers and also showed a significantly lower number of embedded clauses. The comparison of the heritage speakers with themselves when they speak English also shows significant differences. First of all, the English production shows that the heritage speakers are fully competent in the construction of English narratives. In fact, the child heritage speaker interviewed here is significantly more proficient than the children reported in Berman and Slobin (1994), and both heritage speakers are certainly on par with the adult speakers reported in their study. Second, given that the child speaker did very well in English, his relatively poor performance in Russian cannot be reduced to possible problems with his cognitive development. Likewise, the adult speaker's performance in English indicates that whatever problems arose for him in the construction of the Russian narrative were specific to the language used.

Table 8.1 Russian Narratives: Summary Data

	Heritage Speaker		Full Russian Speaker	
	child (M)	adult (B)	child (S)	adult (A)
# of clauses in the narrative	70	90	75	86
MLU (words)	5.1	4.6	8.5	9.8
# of embedded clauses	7	5	15	23

Table 8.2 English Narratives: Summary Data

	Heritage Speakers		Full English Speakers[a]	
	child (M)	adult (B)	children	adults
# of clauses in the narrative	71	85	45	84
MLU (words)	10.4	8.9	6.8	6.8
# of embedded clauses	12	15	6	19

Table 8.3 Average Speaking Rates (words per minute)

Heritage Speakers		Full Russian Speakers		English Speakers	
child (M)	adult (B)	child (S)	adult (A)	child (M)	adult (B)
68	59	100	105	163	145

Table 8.3 presents the statistics on speaking rate in the narratives. Since Berman and Slobin do not have similar statistics for their (presumably) monolingual English speakers, I will use the English narratives elicited from heritage speakers of Russian for the relevant measures. The speaking rate measures shown in Table 8.3 are particularly striking. Of course, cross-language comparisons have to take into account the average length of words in a given language; on average, Russian words are longer than English words. But even with that taken into account, the difference between the heritage speakers and the full speakers is remarkably strong: the adult heritage speaker's rate was almost half of the rate demonstrated by the full speaker control.

Problems with lexical retrieval represent the primary reason for this striking difference. Heritage speakers have serious problems with lexical access and retrieval (Polinsky, 1997; Andrews, 1998; Zemskaja, 2001), and this inability to access a relevant lexical item slows down their production significantly. As lexical retrieval problems arise, speakers also apply different strategies in coping with them. In the five-minute narrative, the child speaker did not resort to English at all, while the adult heritage speaker was much more liberal in code-switching and used English words and expressions 13 times over the same 5-minute narrative.

Structural Properties of Heritage Narrative

It is impossible to do justice to all the structural characteristics of heritage speakers' narratives here. One of the characteristic features of heritage language has become apparent from the quantitative measures presented earlier—namely, heritage speakers rarely utilize embedded structures.

In addition to the low incidence of embedding, I will discuss three other features: case marking, aspectual characteristics, and use of tenses. Before discussing these properties, it is important to note that many features of overt morphosyntax in American Russian cannot be characterized as categorical; rather, they are manifest as preferences or tendencies. This makes it tempting to associate the graded deviations from the Full Russian system as performance errors and problems with on-line production. While more work is needed to show conclusively that this is not the case, such a scenario is highly unlikely because of the rate at which the features are found. The differences between American and Full Russian discussed here fall under the category of syntactic errors. Such errors are extremely rare in heritage speakers (Berg, 1987; Deese, 1984; Fay, 1980; 1982;

Garnham et al., 1982; Poulisse, 1999, 2000; Stemberger, 1982).[4] Meanwhile, the features described below occur at the rate of 60–75%, which indicates that they cannot be reduced to errors. It is more plausible that these features represent a grammar competing with the elements of the Full Russian grammar.[5]

In what follows, I describe the relevant features without further reference to their status as tendencies (unless statistics are needed), so the reader is asked to bear this provision in mind. I use the following abbreviations: ACC—accusative, DAT—dative, IMPF—imperfective, PERF—perfective, RP—resumptive pronoun, UNM—unmarked case.

Case marking

A rather apparent and striking feature of American Russian is the simplification of its case system as compared to Full Russian. In short, the elaborate case system of Full Russian is replaced by a system where the citation form (the nominative) is used predominantly for both main arguments, subject and object. This means that the accusative case, used to mark most direct objects in Full Russian, is not regularly available for such marking in American Russian. Consider the following from the narrative:

(1) *i*   *mal´čik*   *idjot iskat´*   *ljaguška*
    and   boy.UNM   goes look for   frog.UNM
    'And the boy went looking for the frog.' (M)

Of the 25 direct objects in the child's narrative, almost half (12) still appeared in the accusative. The adult heritage speaker had accusative marking on 7 out 18 direct objects.

The accusative case as a morphological word form is not lost, however; it is reanalyzed as the case of the indirect object (goal) and is used quite consistently with pronominal goals (Polinsky, 1997), and variably with nominal ones. For example, in one of the narratives we find:

(2) *ètot mal´čik*   *on*   *skazal*   *sobaku*
    this boy   he   said   dog.DAT
    'This boy said to the dog...' (B)

The restructuring of case forms also has an effect on the cases used with prepositions. In Full Russian, the nominative case does not occur with prepositions; in American Russian, the unmarked nominative is the case associated with almost all prepositions. Some numerical data from the narratives illustrate this feature. The child heritage speaker had 30 prepositional phrases, of which 11 (36%) did not have the oblique case assigned by the relevant preposition. The adult heritage speaker had 26 prepositional phrases, of which 18 (69%) did not have the oblique case assigned by the relevant preposition.

Aspect

One of the advantages of the frog stories is that they present the relevant context for the expression of a number of aspectual distinctions used with all main types of verbs (accomplishments, achievements-letet, states, and activities). Russian aspect is notoriously difficult and its development in monolingual speakers is known to take quite a while (Gvozdev, 1961; Slobin, 1966; Stoll, 2001). The aspectual system of American Russian is quite different from that of the full language (Polinsky, 1994). To simplify things quite a bit, a number of verbs are not used in aspectual pairs (imperfective/perfective);[6] instead, only one member of the pair is typically used. When offered the lexical item they do not use themselves, heritage speakers recognize it, but on forced choice they cannot tell the difference between the members of the aspectual pairs.

With verbs of motion, the system of distinctions is further complicated by the contrast between unidirectional and multidirectional verbs of motion; each type has its own perfective and imperfective. Table 8.4 illustrates this for the verb 'fly.'

Usually, just one of the four cells is represented; for example, to conclude the narrative, the adult heritage speaker said the following:

(3) *mal´čik*   *i*   *ego*   *novyj* *ljaguška*   *budet idet*   *domoj*
     boy   and   his   new   frog   will   go.IMPF   home
     'The boy and the new frog were going home.' (B)

The corresponding Full Russian sentence should be something like this:

(4) *mal´čik*   *s*   *novoj* *ljaguškoj*   *pošli/pojdut*   *domoj*
     boy   with   new   frog   went.PERF/will go.PERF home

The child speaker chose only three lexical items incorrectly with respect to aspectual value; the adult heritage speaker made 11 such errors. In addition to the error shown in example (3), the following verbs were used incorrectly:

Table 8.4 Russian Verbs of Motion

	Unidirectional	**Multidirectional**
Imperfective	*letet´*	*letat´*
Perfective	PREFIX-*letet´* (e.g., *uletet´*)	PREFIX-*letat´* (e.g., *poletat´*)

(5)   'jump': *prygat'* (imperf.) instead of *prygnut'* (perf.)
      'sit': *sidet'* (imperf.) instead of *sest'* (perf.)
      'get up': *vstavat´* (imperf.) instead of *vstat´* (perf.)
      'call': *pozvat´* (perf.) instead of *zvat´* (imperf.)
      'go': *xodit'* (mulitidirectional) instead of *idti* (unidirectional)
      'run': *begat'* (mulitidirectional) instead of *bežat'* (unidirectional)

Two questions arise with respect to the use of aspect: Is it possible to predict which aspectual form is retained for each particular verbal concept, and assuming that the Full Russian system is no longer available to heritage speakers, what means of expressing aspect are used in Heritage Russian?

Let us address the first question: What explains the maintenance of the imperfective for some verbs and of the perfective for others in American Russian? It seems that if only one verb is maintained in American Russian, then it is the member of the aspectual pair that denotes a more common conceptualization associated with a given event. If an event has an inherent limit, it is conceptualized as telic (i.e., having an inherent limit). In this case, the perfective form of the verb is more likely to be maintained. If the event is more commonly conceptualized as atelic (i.e., lacking an inherent limit), then the imperfective form is maintained. If the more common conceptualization of a given verb is indeed the determining factor, then the frequency of the perfective and imperfective verbs in aspectual pairs of Full Russian (the input language) may serve as a fairly accurate predictor of what is going to be used in American Russian.

The use of verb forms in the heritage speaker narratives is summarized in Table 8.5 and Table 8.6. The frequencies in the input are taken from Brown (1996).

Table 8.5 Frequency of Imperfectives versus Perfectives in Full Russian and Retention of a Particular Form in American Russian

Event	Full Russian				American Russian Form
	Imperfective		Perfective		
	form	freq.	form	freq.	
cry, scream	kričat´	394	zakričat´	1741	imperfective
call	zvat´	428	pozvat´	1950	imperfective
give[a]	davat´	149	dat´	155	perfective
become	stanovit´ sja	622	stat´	59	perfective
stay, stand	stojat´	104	(v-)stat´	444	imperfective
sit	sidet´	143	sest´	343	imperfective
take	brat´	419	vzjat´	132	perfective
lie down	leč´	259	ležat´	1368	imperfective
search	iskat´	646	poiskat´	6641	imperfective
find	naxodit´	1197	najti	234	perfective
jump	prygat´	2994	prygnut´	7450	imperfective

[a]Frequency cannot distinguish between the two.

Table 8.6 Motion Verb Forms and Frequency: Full Russian and Retention in American Russian

Event	Full Russian Form				Form Retained in
	U, I	U, P	M, I	M, P	American Russian
go	idti	pojti	xodit′	prixodit′ or uxodit′	idti/ (u)xodit′
drive, move, travel	exat′	poexat′	ezdit′	s″ezdit′	pojti/exat′
run	bežat′	ubežat′	begat′	sbegat′	begat′
fly	letet′	uletet′	letat′	sletat′	letat′
Frequency					
go	64	79	247	348 186	
drive, move, travel	420	386	1662	6535	
run	370	1702	1844	5871	
fly	1523	7525	2707	< 10,000	

Note: U = Unidirectional; M = Multidirectional; I = Imperfective; P = Perfective.

The results summarized in these two tables confirm the generalization that the choice of the single aspectual form, lexicalized in American Russian, may be determined by the more frequent conceptualization of a given event as telic or atelic.[7] However, the lexicalizations of 'run' and 'fly' contradict this generalization; at this point, I have no explanation as to why this may be the case.

If this generalization is on the right track, it is important to bear in mind that heritage speakers of Russian do not perceive the verb they retain as imperfective or perfective. Since they no longer have the relevant morphosyntactic oppositions of Full Russian, for them the verb *dat′* 'give' or the verb *sidet′* 'sit' is just a lexical item without a specified aspectual value.

Assuming that the lexicalization of a single verb form, perfective or imperfective, is determined by the conceptual structure of the more frequent event, let us now turn to the second question: how does American Russian express aspect? American Russian means of expressing aspect are different from those used in Full Russian, but aspect is a conceptual, semantic characteristic, and it does not have to disappear even if the relevant morphosyntax used to express it is gone.

Instead of the fairly arcane system of affixes employed in Full Russian aspectual grammar, American Russian seems to use either the bare verb or the combination of a light verb (functioning similar to an auxiliary) and content-carrying verb (or another lexical category) to express aspectual distinctions. Roughly, the perfective for verbs of accomplishment and achievement is expressed using the light verbs *stat′* 'become' and *načat′* 'begin'; these same verbs are used in Full Russian, but in American Russian they become the major means of expressing perfectivity.

For example, in describing how the boy grabs the deer by the antlers, a speaker used the following:

(6) on načinaet deržit   olen´   roga
    he begins.impf holds.IMPF deer.nom horns.NOM/ACC
    'He grabbed the deer by the antlers.' (M)

The corresponding Full Russian sentence involves synthetic verb forms: a prefixal perfective or a suffixal imperfective:

(7) on sxvatil/xvataet   olenja   za   roga
    he seized.PERF/seizes.IMPF   deer.acc by   horns.ACC
    'He grabbed/grabs the deer by the antlers.'

The imperfective is either unmarked or is marked by the light verb *byt´* 'be', as in example (3). The same verb *byt´* is used as the auxiliary to express states if followed by a noun or adjective. This overall system of encoding aspect resembles aspect-marking strategies in creole languages (for an overview of the creole systems, see Singler, 1990). In American Russian, such a system may have arisen either under the influence of English or under the general creolization of the language. To determine which of these two possibilities is more likely, we need more data on heritage Russian in contact with languages other than English.[8]

Tense

In the use of tense, the two heritage speakers are quite different from each other. The child speaker consistently used past tense (forming it quite correctly in most cases), and this pattern of the past tense narrative is identical to the pattern he uses in English. The child speaker thus conforms to the overall tendency of English-speaking 9-year-olds to use the past tense in English (Berman & Slobin, 1994). The Full Russian counterpart also used past tense quite consistently, with the exception of a few episodes where he switched to historical present (the bees flying out of the beehive; the owl appearing in front of the boy; the boy finding a family of frogs).

The adult speaker (B), who used the past tense consistently in his English narrative, showed no consistency whatsoever in the use of tenses in the Russian narrative. He started out using the present tense, then switched to the past, then returned to the present. He also used a fair number of forms that correspond to future forms in Full Russian. Overall, B pays little or no attention to the use of tenses and their sequencing; it seems likely that the pragmatic sequencing, whereby he diligently follows the order of events in the pictures, is sufficient for his structuring of the narrative. Recall also that B has serious problems with lexical access, uses code switching, and shows an overall speaking rate even lower than that of the child heritage speaker. All this suggests that B simply has no time to construct the appropriate forms on-line; instead, he just uses the forms that most readily come to mind. While this is certainly a testable hypothesis, it would be rather hard to find a good way to test it in naturally occurring discourse. At this point, the conclusion is that the child heritage speaker uses the tenses appropriate to his age and to the narrative mode observed for both languages he controls (English and Russian). The adult speaker, meanwhile, shows significant deficiencies and inconsistencies in his temporal narrative mode.

General Discussion

The previous section reviewed some differences between baseline full speakers of Russian and heritage speakers; in this section, I will revisit these differences in a more general way. Heritage speakers clearly lag behind full speakers on every quantitative measure examined. They speak at a much slower rate, probably because of the encumbered lexical retrieval, and they use much shorter utterances. The heritage speakers also differ from the baseline in a number of structural characteristics. Here I examined the loss of cases, the restructuring of aspect, and the inconsistent use of tense by the adult speaker. With respect to case marking and aspect, the most important result is that the changes occurring in the language of heritage speakers are systematic in nature. American Russian essentially uses two cases: the unmarked case, which corresponds to the nominative in Full Russian, and the secondary object case, which corresponds to the accusative in Full Russian. One of the crucial changes in the case system of American Russian is the use of the unmarked case with prepositions, an impossible option in Full Russian. In addition to these two main cases, heritage speakers use some other case forms correctly; in the current sample, the child speaker utilizes more correct forms than the adult. The correct forms behave as 'chunks' that are retained outside the overall case system of a given noun. For example, the speakers correctly use *v dome* 'at home', *v lesu* 'in the forest', *utrom* 'in the morning', *v vode* 'in the water', *na zemle* 'on the ground'. It is noteworthy that most of these forms are scene-setting expressions, which establish the spatial or temporal coordinates of the proposition (Chafe, 1976). Such expressions constitute frequent input to heritage speakers. This frequency facilitates their retention as "chunks" but it is unclear whether these forms are actually related to the other case forms in the paradigm of Full Russian nouns.

The aspectual system of American Russian also supports the observation that the language of heritage speakers is structured in a principled way. The expression of aspect in American Russian is quite different from that in Full Russian. If one were to approach American Russian aspect from the standpoint of the preservation of Full Russian aspect, the conclusion would be that the American Russian system is much simplified and rather arbitrary. However, the American Russian aspectual system is actually quite principled. The encoding of aspectual distinctions is achieved by analytical means (the combination of an auxiliary type verb expressing inception, duration, or completion with a contentful predicative word). Full Russian has so-called aspectual pairs—perfective and imperfective verbs denoting similar events. Such verbs often have the same root. It is a striking feature of American Russian that usually just one of the members of such pairs is retained. At first glance, the choice of the lexical verb retained in American Russian seems somewhat arbitrary; however, the data examined suggest that the retention of particular lexical items is determined by their frequency in the input. If this hypothesis is correct, it opens up a more general question concerning the interaction between the frequency of linguistic elements and the rules and constraints that operate on them. Given the principled nature of structural properties observed in American Russian, it is clear that linguistic reanalysis takes place in that language. Whether frequency constitutes a primary motivation for the reanalysis or is concomitant with it remains an open question.

The distribution of tense forms in the two narratives is less conclusive. The child heritage speaker uses past tenses, with a few low-level morphophonemic errors (e.g., stress assignment). The overall use of tense is representative of narratives constructed by nine year olds. The adult heritage speaker uses tenses in a much more random manner, and it seems that the marking of tense appropriate to Full Russian is no longer valid in his system. Similar results were observed for other adult heritage speakers in other elicitation contexts (Polinsky 1997) suggesting that the Full Russian system of synthetic tense marking is supplanted by a new system where the tense operator is silent and needs to be recovered from the context. Given that the adult speaker interviewed here patterns with some other adult speakers in not overtly marking tense, it is certainly important to determine factors accounting for the differences between the child and adult speakers. I will return to this issue.

Ignoring the generational contrast for a moment, it is clear that the heritage speakers differ from the baseline in a number of ways. One might attribute the differences between the heritage speakers and the Russian baseline to cognitive impairment on the part of the former. However, the heritage speakers interviewed for this study clearly have no language deficiency in English, nor do they show any problems constructing narratives in English. The adult speaker's English narrative was comparable to the narrative elicited from monolingual English adults, as shown by the measures in Table 8.2 and Table 8.3. The child speaker is actually superior to his English-speaking cohort, at least as concerns the numerical measures, and he is consistent with his age cohort in the use of tense (all past) and the linear development of the narrative. The superior quantitative measures demonstrated by the child speaker in English motivate comparison to data from additional speakers.

Let us now examine the differences between the child and adult heritage speakers. One of the differences was already mentioned: The adult speaker uses grammatical tenses in a much more "scattered" manner than the child. An informal impression of the child narrative is that, although much more limited

Table 8.7 Structural Differences between Child and Adult Heritage Naratives

	Child	Adult
Correct use of case forms (non-nominatives) [a]	71% (n=46)	31.5% (n=38)
Correct agreement in gender	91% (n=71)	31.5% (n=19)
Resumptive pronouns : Full NPS	0:28	19:33
Embedded clauses : Total clauses	7:70	5:90
Code switching	0	13

[a]Four child and three adult narratives were excluded from the case form analysis because it was impossible to determine correctness.

lexically than the corresponding Full Russian narrative, it is fairly close to the Full Russian system. The adult narrative seems much more restricted both lexically and grammatically. This informal impression is confirmed by statistical data on the narratives, summarized in Table 8.7.

As the table shows, the adult speaker has a markedly low number of correct case forms, and the description of the American Russian case system is much more appropriate to his narrative than to the child narrative, where 71% of non-nominative case forms are still used correctly.

Let us now look at agreement. Full Russian has agreement in gender between the subject and the verb in past tense and between the head noun and modifying adjective; non-past tense verbs agree with their subjects in person and number. I will not discuss person agreement for two reasons: first, the narrative is mainly in the third person, so there is very little room for variation; second, the third person verb form often appears to be the default for American Russian (Polinsky, 1997), so its presence in the narratives is inconclusive. With respect to agreement in gender, the adult speaker shows a very low rate of correct agreement forms (31.5%), while the child speaker has 91% correct forms. The quantitative difference between the two speakers is thus similar to the one observed in the use of case forms.

The child and adult narratives show another striking difference in the use of resumptive pronouns. A resumptive pronoun is a copy of the full noun phrase appearing in the preverbal position; for example:

(8) *sobaka*   *on*   *ljubit ljaguška*   *tože*
     dog.UNM   RP   he   loves frog.UNM   also
     'The dog also likes the frog.' (B)

Resumptive pronouns are common in American Russian (Polinsky 1997, 2000), and the most obvious explanation for their emergence is that they serve as a compensatory mechanism replacing verbal agreement. The adult heritage speaker interviewed in this study, B, shows the same robust correlation between resumption and the decline in grammatical agreement frequently found in the baseline. Given that the use of resumptive pronouns in American Russian is otherwise well-attested, the child speaker's pattern, with fairly robust gender agreement and no resumption, is noteworthy. It not only suggests that the link between the decline of agreement and resumption is a correct one, but also shows that the child's grammar has not undergone the same reanalysis as the adult's.

What are the implications of the quantitative differences between the child's grammar and the adult's grammar? The most important one seems to be that the adult heritage speaker is not just "frozen" or "fossilized" at the stage of interrupted acquisition corresponding to age 5–6. If this were the case, then it would be impossible to explain such dramatic quantitative differences between M and B as shown in Table 8.7. If the adult speaker (B) has a grammar different from that of the child heritage speaker, then how did B acquire such a grammar? I hypothesize that this grammar develops as a result of a reanalysis of the mental representation rescued from the childhood years. The reanalysis is presumably shaped by interference from English and some universal principles governing language development with limited input; thus, it would be interesting to examine possible parallels between the emergence of American Russian grammar and the genesis of creoles (Bickerton, 1981; DeGraff, 1999, among many others) or Nicaraguan Sign Language.

At this point, any account of the differences observed here is entirely hypothetical: One needs far more quantitative data on both child and adult heritage speakers, and one also needs to rule out possible individual variation. Also needed is comparable data on heritage speakers, children and adults, whose primary language is not English. However, the realization that adult heritage speakers are not simply fossilized at some stage of incomplete acquisition is an important result that requires explanation.

An alternate hypothesis is that adult heritage speakers actually control a system fairly close to that of the baseline; the problems they experience occur in on-line performance only. At this juncture, I have no conclusive arguments against this hypothesis, but I will offer a few observations. First, as I mentioned earlier, on-line performance errors of the kind discussed here occur at a significantly lower rate than the "errors" found in adult heritage speakers. Second, if heritage speakers had no competence problems, then one would expect them to perform well on any tasks that involve choosing a correct grammatical form over an incorrect one (the so-called forced choice task); according to my own experimental observations, this is not the case (Polinsky, 1997). Third, if heritage speakers had problems only with performance, one would expect to see more variation across adult speakers; however, they show consistency in a number of grammatical properties both within one language and across languages. The use of resumptive pronouns to compensate for a decline in agreement is one such property (Polinsky, 1995); it is found in the speech of all heritage speakers of Russian as well as in several other heritage languages. Unless this feature can be explained by interference from English, it is unlikely to be a manifestation of on-line performance problems.

Conclusions

This chapter presents a preliminary investigation of the structure of narratives in heritage speakers, comparing those narratives to the ones elicited from competent speakers. The narrative used here is based on the well-known frog story elicitation used in a large-scale study by Berman and Slobin (1994). Using existing narrative elicitation techniques affords a distinct advantage because the heritage narratives elicited that way can be added to the existing body of frog stories and thus allow for broader cross-linguistic comparisons. One future goal is to collect more such narratives and use them as a basis to establish the continuum of heritage speakers.

Although the sample used here is quite small, it allows us to determine some characteristic features of heritage narratives: lack of embedding, short utterances, restructuring of the case system and aspect, and inconsistent use of tenses (the latter by the adult subject only).

An unexpected result obtained here is a significant difference between the grammars of the child and adult narratives. If this result is confirmed by more extensive studies, then heritage speakers' language is not simply "frozen" at the stage where acquisition stops. Instead, their limited mental representation of the heritage language may undergo reanalysis in concordance with universal linguistic rules and constraints.

Notes

1. I would like to thank Amalia Arvaniti, Elizabeth Bates, Ruth Berman, Hana Filip, Olga Kagan, and Robert Kluender for helpful comments on this project. All errors are my responsibility.
2. The session with S was recorded in Moscow, courtesy of Olga Sergeeva.
3. An obvious question here may be why morphemic MLU was not used. First, MLU is not effective for a cross-linguistic comparison, which was involved here. Second, as shown by several researchers, MLU is not effective in older children (Scarborough et al., 1991).
4. It is rather difficult to produce a numerical estimate of the range of syntactic and morpho-syntactic errors simply because the question of such estimates is hardly ever raised. In those studies where numerical assessment is possible, it is clear that the number of (morpho-) syntactic errors is extremely low. Fay (1982), for example, found 94 such errors in the corpus of 5,000 errors total; of the 191 errors discussed by Garnham et al. (1982), only 20 can be viewed as syntactic, and even that is based on a very generous interpretation of a syntactic error.
5. The statement about two co-existing grammars is certainly a loaded one—the issue of whether or not two grammars can co-exist in the mental representation of a single speaker is controversial. I am not prepared to take a definitive stand on it here.
6. The elimination of aspectual pairs is not an across-the-board process; some verbs are maintained in both perfective and imperfective form, as can be seen from the verb 'begin' below.
7. One could propose an alternative to this generalization, namely, that the retained form of the verb is the shorter one. While the correlation between phonetic weight (word length) and frequency is well established (Zipf, 1935; Bybee, 2001), even the small sample of verbs in Table 8.5 does not uphold this generalization; compare *sidet'* vs. *sest'* 'sit' where the longer word wins out, or the fairly equal in length *prygat'* and *prygnut'* 'jump'.
8. The rise of the analytical system of aspectual marking in Finnish Russian (heritage Russian as spoken in Finland), reported by Leisio (2001), suggests that the influence of English cannot be the sole factor determining the use of aspect.

References

Andrews, D. R. (1998). *Sociocultural perspectives on language change in diaspora: Soviet immigrants in the United States*. Philadelphia: John Benjamins.

Berg, T. (1987). *A cross-linguistic comparison of slips of the tongue*. Bloomington: Indiana University Linguistics Club.

Berman, R., & Slobin, D. I. (1994). *Relating events in narrative: A cross-linguistic developmental study*. Hillsdale, NJ: Lawrence Erlbaum.

Bickerton, D. (1981). *Roots of language*. Ann Arbor, MI: Karoma.

Brown, N. J. (1996). *Russian learners' dictionary: 10,000 words in frequency order*. New York: Routledge.

Bybee, J. (2001). *Phonology and language use*. Cambridge, UK: Cambridge University Press.

Chafe, W. (1976). Givenness, contrastiveness, definiteness, subjects, topics, and point of view. In C. N. Li (Ed.), *Subject and topic* (pp. 25–56). New York: Academic Press.

Deese, J. (1984). *Thought into speech: The psychology of a language*. Englewood Cliffs, NJ: Prentice-Hall.

DeGraff, M. (Ed.). (1999). *Language creation and language change: Creolization, diachrony, and development*. Cambridge: Massachusetts Institute of Technology Press.

Fay, D. (1980). Transformational errors. In V. Fromkin (Ed.), *Errors in linguistic performance: Slips of the tongue, ear, pen, and hand* (pp. 111–122). New York: Academic Press.

Fay, D. (1982). Substitutions and splices: A study of sentence blends. In A. Cutler (Ed.), *Slips of the tongue and language production* (pp. 163–196). Amsterdam: Mouton.

Garnham, A., Shillcock, R. C., Brown, G., Mill, A., & Cutler, A. (1982). Slips of the tongue in the London-Lund corpus of spontaneous conversation. In A. Cutler (Ed.), *Slips of the tongue and language production* (pp. 251–263). Amsterdam: Mouton.

Gvozdev, A. N. (1961). *Voprosy izučenija detskoj reči*. [Issues in child language acquisition] Moscow: Izd. Akad. ped. nauk.

Leisio, L. (2001). *Morphosyntactic convergence and integration in Finland Russian*. Unpublished doctoral dissertation, University of Tampere, Finland.

Polinsky, M. (1994, May). *Loss of aspectual features*. Paper presented at the Symposium on Aspect, UCLA, Los Angeles, CA.

Polinsky, M. (1995). Cross-linguistic parallels in language loss. *Southwest Journal of Linguistics, 14*, 87–124.

Polinsky, M. (1997). American Russian: Language loss meets language acquisition. In W. Browne, E. Dornisch, N. Kondrashova, and D. Zec (Eds.), *Annual workshop on formal approaches to Slavic linguistics: The Cornell meeting (1995)* (pp. 370–406). Ann Arbor, MI: Slavic Publishers.

Polinsky, M. (2000). A composite linguistic profile of a speaker of Russian in the USA. In O. Kagan & B. Rifkin (Eds.), *The learning and teaching of Slavic languages and cultures* (pp. 437–466). Bloomington, IN: Slavica.

Poulisse, N. (1999). *Slips of the tongue: Speech errors in first and second language production*. Philadelphia: John Benjamins.

Poulisse, N. (2000). Slips of the tongue in first and second language production. *Studia Linguistica, 5*, 136–149.

Scarborough, H., Rescorla, L., Tager-Flusberg, H., Fowler, A., & Sudhalter, V. (1991). The relation of utterance length to grammatical complexity in normal and language-disordered groups. *Applied Psycholinguistics, 12*, 23–45.

Singler, J. V. (Ed.). (1990). *Pidgin and creole tense-mood-aspect systems*. Philadelphia: John Benjamins.

Slobin, D. I. (1966). The acquisition of Russian as a native language. In F. Smith & G. A. Miller (Eds.), *The genesis of language: A psycholinguistic approach* (pp. 129–148). Cambridge: Massachusetts Institute of Technology Press.

Stemberger, J. P. (1982). Syntactic errors in speech. *Journal of Psycholinguistic Research, 11*, 313–345.

Stoll, S. (2001). *The acquisition of Russian aspect*. Unpublished doctoral dissertation, University of California, Berkeley.

Valdés, G. (2000). Introduction. In American Association of Teachers of Spanish and Portuguese (Ed.), *Professional development series handbook for teachers K-16: Vol. 1. Spanish for native speakers* (pp. 1–20). Fort Worth, TX: Harcourt College.

Zemskaja, E. A. (Ed.). (2001). *Jazyk russkogo zarubež´ja* [The Language of the Russian Diaspora]. Moscow/Vienna: Wiener Slawistischer Almanach.

Zipf, G. K. (1935). *The psycho-biology of language: An introduction to dynamic philology.* Boston: Houghton Mifflin.

9

Prior Language-Learning Experience and Variation in the Linguistic Profiles of Advanced English-Speaking Learners of Japanese

KAZUE KANNO, TOMOMI HASEGAWA, KEIKO IKEDA,
YASUKO ITO, AND MICHAEL H. LONG

Introduction

This chapter reports on a study of the relationship between type of language-learning experience and variation in the linguistic profiles of advanced English-speaking learners of Japanese. A typical advanced-level Japanese language class in the United States is a mix of learners with different learning backgrounds, including heritage learners, pure classroom-instructed learners, those who learned Japanese naturalistically, and those who have mixed learning experiences. It is important to ascertain whether all of these learners have similar instructional needs as they move toward a higher level of language proficiency and whether there is a set of identifiable characteristics in the interlanguages of each of these types of learners.

Very few studies (e.g., Nagasawa, 1995) have addressed this issue. The study reported here attempted to begin to remedy this situation by examining the linguistic profiles of heritage and non-heritage learners of similar second language (L2) proficiency, i.e., Advanced or Advanced Plus on the American Council on the Teaching of Foreign Languages (ACTFL) Proficiency Scale. As assessed by the Oral Proficiency Interview (OPI) (American Council on the Teaching of Foreign Languages, 1986), these levels are equivalent to Levels 2 and 2+ respectively on the Interagency Language Roundtable (ILR) scale (Interagency Language Roundtable, n.d.).

There were three research questions:

1. What are the common characteristics of, and differences among, the linguistic profiles of learners at the Advanced proficiency level?
2. How does prior language-learning experience affect those profiles? In other words, are profiles comparable for students (a) who have learned their L2 naturalistically, for the most part through in-country residence; (b) who have learned their L2 mostly through classroom foreign language

instruction; and (c) who grew up as heritage learners, hearing and sometimes speaking the L2 with one or more family members at home?

3. How many identifiably different learner groups or sub-groups are there
among students of this general proficiency range? Are the above three
categories "real," and are other ones relevant? In what areas are their linguistic profiles similar and different?

Participants

Fifteen English-speaking learners of Japanese at the University of Hawaii participated in the study in 2001. They were classified into four groups based on
type of previous language-learning experience. The first two groups consisted
of non-heritage learners, the second two of heritage learners.

Non-Heritage Groups

The non-heritage learners consisted of two types:

1. Group 1—Naturalistic Learners: three learners who had learned most of
their Japanese through lengthy periods of naturalistic in-country exposure
(3.2, 8, and 8 years, respectively, for a mean length of 6.4 years).
2. Group 2—Classroom Learners: four learners enrolled in 4th-year language
classes who had learned most of their Japanese through classroom foreign
language instruction. All four had been to Japan: two had gone there to
study the language as a second language for six months; the other two had
taught English there for 3 and 4 years, respectively but reported that their
use of Japanese had been limited.

Heritage Groups

Heritage learners also fall into two groups:

1. Group 3—Bilingual A (Bil. A): three heritage learners who once a week
had attended a *hoshuukoo*[1] (special auxiliary school) that followed the
academic curriculum employed in schools in Japan; they had comparable
abilities in all four language skills.
2. Group 4—Bilingual B (Bil. B): five heritage learners who had been exposed
to Japanese from birth but whose reading and writing skills were weaker
than their listening and speaking skills. This group was further divided
into subgroup 1 (n = 2) and subgroup 2 (n = 3) based on amount and
kind of prior exposure to Japanese. While the latter had been exposed
to the language only in the family context, the former had not only had
extensive exposure to Japanese but also more experience in a wider variety
of contexts.

Table 9.1 OPI Results for Four Groups of Language Learners

	Groups		OPI Result
Non-heritage	Naturalistic Learners (n=3)		Advanced Plus (2) Advanced (1)
	Classroom Learners (n=4)		Advanced Plus (2) Advanced (2)[a]
Heritage	Bilingual A (n=3)		Advanced Plus
	Bilingual B	Subgroup 1 (n=2)	Advanced Plus
		Subgroup 2 (n=3)	Advanced[a]

[a]One subject in Classroom Learners and one in Bilingual B (Subgroup 2) were placed at the Advanced Level although OPI testers noted that they were weak in vocabulary and on the borderline between Intermediate High and Advanced.

The proficiency levels of the 15 subjects—six Advanced, and nine Advanced Plus—were determined via the OPI. Their distribution across language experience types is shown in Table 9.1.

Instrumentation

Data were collected using three instruments: a written test, a guided narrative, and "free" conversation, i.e., the OPI. The written test consisted of five sections: four involved multiple-choice tasks, while the fifth (dealing with idiomatic expressions) utilized a fill-in-the-blank format. The first two parts tested learners' structural knowledge; the other three assessed their lexical knowledge. Since the OPI involves holistic assessment, and only general guidelines are provided, items in the written test were chosen from the lists of vocabulary and grammatical patterns of the Japanese Language Proficiency Test (JLPT) (The Japan Foundation, n.d.).[2] Two specific references used were the *Nihongo nooryoku-shiken shutsudai kijun* (The Japan Foundation, 1996) and *Ichiman-go goi bunruishuu* (Nihongo Gakuryoku Test Testing Committee, 1998).

Based on the guidelines and criteria for each level of the JLPT (the number of instructional hours, the size of vocabulary, etc.), JLPT Levels 1 and 2 roughly correspond to the ACTFL Superior and Advanced levels respectively on the OPI scale (American Council on the Teaching of Foreign Languages, 1986). JLPT Level 1 is typically the minimum requirement for acceptance into a regular college undergraduate/graduate program in Japan; hence, it is appropriate to assume that Level 1 corresponds to the ACTFL Superior level.

Structural Knowledge

Three key characteristics of the Advanced level used to assess learners' structural knowledge are: (1) control of frequent structural patterns, (2) partial control of honorific markings, and (3) paragraph-level discourse.[3] We examine these key characteristics.

Structural Patterns

There were twenty structural items, including:

1. Items involving persistent errors, such as anaphoric use of deictic demonstratives, and phrasal particles (e.g., 'topic marker' *wa* and 'subject marker' *ga*) (see Sakoda, 1993, 1997; Sakamoto, 1993; Yagi, 1993).
2. Items considered difficult to acquire: empathy/perspective-related patterns, giving/receiving verbs (see Tanaka, 1997, 1999).
3. Honorifics.
4. Other advanced structural patterns (modality and conditionals).

These are all JLPT Level 3 (or Level 4) test items, except those involving modality, which are Level 2 items.

Knowledge of Connectives/Functional Expressions

This section contained ten connectives/functional expressions from JLPT Level 2 (e.g., *...ni kanshite* 'regarding ...') essential for the paragraph-level discourse required for the Advanced level.

For each item in both sections, participants were asked to select one of four options.

Lexical and Collocational Knowledge

Three sections examined learners' lexical knowledge. A particular focus was knowledge of collocation, i.e., selectional properties of lexical items.

Collocations Involving Pairs of Elements

There were ten items from Level 2 in this section, e.g., *me-o tojiru* (for closing one's eyes, *tojiru* is the only verb that can be used; other 'closing' verbs, such as *shimeru*, are not appropriate).

Collocations Involving Frequently Used Fixed Idiomatic Expressions

Although the JLPT considers idioms as Level 1 items (and the OPI guidelines state that the use of idioms is one of the characteristics of the Superior level), there is no specific list. Eleven idioms were selected from among those introduced in teaching materials for intermediate/advanced level Japanese, and those that are frequent and colloquial involving body-part vocabulary, such as *hana-ga takai* ('the nose is high' = 'proud').

Collocations Involving Mimetics (i.e., ideophonic expressions, not onomatopoeic words)

Japanese makes quite extensive use of mimetics—far more than English does—and they are an integral part of the language. For instance, where English requires different words to make precise the nature of an action, such as *smile*, *giggle*, or *guffaw*, Japanese has only one verb *warau* 'laugh', which is accompanied by a mimetic expression, *nikoniko warau* 'grin', *kusukusu warau* 'giggle', and *geragera warau* 'laugh out loud.' These are considered to be Level 1 vocabulary items in the JLPT.

Guided Narrative

One of the characteristics of the Advanced level and above is the ability to narrate and describe in major time/aspect frames. Looking at a set of four photos depicting the September 11, 2001, attacks in New York City, the participants were asked to describe the events and express their thoughts. The September 11 topic was chosen for the following two reasons: (1) its high degree of familiarity to all, due to extensive media coverage, and (2) the need for use of more than everyday, basic vocabulary (i.e., high-level registers) including *kango* (Chinese origin words). (Note that the use of *kango* is one of the characteristics of the OPI Superior level.)

Free Conversation

Parts of the OPI data (i.e., excluding the role-play portions) were used for analysis. This interactive task involves daily and basic vocabulary and does not necessarily require use of high-level registers.

Written Test

As a validity assurance, ten native speakers also took the written test. They provided a uniform response (i.e., 100%) for every test item except one (anaphoric use of a deictic demonstrative, due to insufficient context having been given) in the grammar section. This item was excluded from the analysis. Table 9.2 presents overall accuracy rates for each section of the written test.

Results

The overall results indicated that the performance on the grammar section was the best among the sections, followed by sections involving pairs of elements, connectives, and mimetics. The performance on the section on idioms was the poorest. Although idioms and mimetics are both considered Level 1 items,

Table 9.2 Accuracy Rates on the Written Test

| | Structural Knowledge | | Lexical Knowledge | | |
	Grammar	Connectives	Pairs of Elements	Idiomatic Expressions	Mimetics
Naturalistic Learners (n=3)	66.7%	43.3%	56.7%	12.1%	40.0%
Classroom Learners (n=4)	67.5%	32.5%	62.5%	0.0%	30.0%
Bilingual A (n=3)	96.7%	93.3%	96.7%	36.4%	93.3%
Bil. B Subgroup 1 (n=2)	87.5%	75.0%	80.0%	36.4%	85.0%
Bil. B Subgroup 2 (n=3)	53.3%	36.7%	46.7%	6.1%	26.7%
Overall	**73.0%**	**53.3%**	**67.3%**	**15.8%**	**51.3%**

mimetics were found to be easier, perhaps because they occur frequently in the input and are an integral part of Japanese.

There were three key findings with respect to inter-group differences. First, the Bilingual A group not only outperformed the other groups in all sections, but was also very accurate, as indicated by their high scores on four out of five sections. They had difficulty only with the section on idiomatic expressions. Second, the two Bilingual B sub-groups exhibit quite different linguistic profiles: subgroup 1 scored very high in every section—almost as high as the Bilingual A group—whereas subgroup 2 scored the lowest on three of the five sections. Third, the classroom-instructed group did very poorly with connectives/functional expressions, although they were moderately accurate on the grammar items. All four subjects in this group scored zero for the section on idiomatic expressions.

Guided Narrative

Narrative data were also collected from three native speakers of Japanese for comparison (two graduate students and a business person). The narratives were transcribed, coded, and analyzed.[4] Data were examined for accuracy and complexity at both the structural and lexical levels. In this study, fluency was not included as an analytic criterion. To our knowledge, systematic and widely accepted methods of measurement pertaining to fluency in Japanese have yet to be determined. This is perhaps due to the specific linguistic nature of the Japanese language, particularly its agglutinative morphology. For instance, reaching consensus on an appropriate "unit" by which Japanese utterances are to be examined is not an easy task, with frequent occurrences of particle ellipsis and zero pronouns in the spoken mode complicating the process.

Structural Complexity

Structural complexity was measured using three ratios: (1) number of clauses per utterance,[5] (2) number of dependent clauses divided by the total number of

Table 9.3 Utterance and Clause Ratios

	Mean # of Clauses	Mean # of Utterances	C/U Ratio
Native Speakers	97.7	18.3	5.3
Learners	40.2	14.5	2.8

clauses, and (3) number of passives divided by the total number of clauses.[6] Table 9.3 presents the overall mean clause/utterance (C/U) ratio for the native speakers and learners of Japanese. These figures do not include inserted expressions, e.g., *nan-dakke* ('Gee, what was it?'). Native speakers produced 5.3 clauses per utterance, whereas learners produced only 2.8, approximately half the mean native-speaker ratio. There was considerable variation in the C/U ratio of individual learners (unlike the three native speakers), ranging from 1.722 to 6.285. Some learners' productions are structurally as complex as those of native speakers. There was no clear pattern to findings for the different learner groups.

Another measure, the dependent clause ratio, was used to examine the degree of embedding/subordination. It was calculated by dividing the number of dependent clauses (DC) by the total number of clauses (C). Table 9.4 presents the mean dependent clause ratio (DC/C) for native speakers and learners (sorted by learner type). In our data, we observed that most learner groups produced a particular clause-final pattern with a conjunction particle in Japanese, *kedo* (literally, 'although'). In spoken Japanese, the particle *kedo* is often used utterance-finally, leaving the whole utterance with an "uncompleted" nuance. *Kedo* is primarily used as a conjunction particle, attaching to a subordinate clause, as in *takakatta kedo kaimashita* "[it was] expensive but [I] bought [it]." However, utterance-final *kedo* is often used as a mere end marker, which cautions against counting all attested tokens of *kedo*-clauses the same way. Taking this into consideration, another DC/C ratio was calculated by dividing the number of dependent clauses without *kedo*-clauses by the total number of clauses.

As seen in Table 9.4, the bilingual groups uniformly exhibited a high dependent clause ratio (regardless of which DC/C ratio was used). The classroom instructed group had the lowest ratio, with naturalistic acquirers in the middle.

The passive ratio is another measure for calculating grammatical complexity (see, e.g., Kameen, 1979, cited in Wolfe-Quintero, Inagaki, & Kim, 1998) with a view to differentiating learners' developmental levels. This is consistent with the idea that passives are one of the essential linguistic devices for maintaining perspective within a sentence or paragraph. Tanaka's studies (1997, 1999) suggest that as proficiency improves, use of passives increases in the acquisition of Japanese as a second language. Table 9.5 shows the passive ratio for native speakers and learners.

Again, the two heritage groups, the Bilingual A group and Bilingual B, subgroup 1, exhibited a high passive ratio. However, the other heritage group, Bilingual B, subgroup 2, had a much lower ratio. As in the case of DC/C ratio,

Table 9.4 Mean Dependent Clause Rations

	Mean # Total Clauses	Mean # Dependent Clauses		DC / C Ratio	
		All Dependent Clauses	Clauses w/o kedo 'although'	All Dependent Clauses	Clauses w/o kedo 'although'
Native Speakers	97.6	61.3	50.0	.627	.511
Naturalistic Learners	39.6	14.0	9.6	.352	.243
Classroom Learners	50.0	13.5	9.8	.270	.195
Bilingual A	34.6	14.0	12.0	.403	.346
Bilingual B Subgroup 1	41.5	26.5	16.0	.638	.385
Bilingual B Subgroup 2	45.3	19.3	17.0	.426	.382

the classroom-instructed group had the lowest ratio. As the mean number of passives indicates, the four learners in the group (apart from a single token) simply did not use passives.

In summary, the dependent clause and passive ratios showed that with respect to structural complexity, the Bilingual A group and Bilingual B, subgroup 1 were the most advanced learners, and the classroom instructed group the least developed.

Accuracy

In this section, learner accuracy is examined via an error analysis of the narrative data. Two raters for each narrative identified all errors and classified them into four categories: particles, structure, discourse, and vocabulary. The last type was further broken down into three subcategories: use of English words, Japanized

Table 9.5 Passive Ratios

	Mean # of Passives	Mean # of Clauses	Passive Ratio
Native Speakers	8.6	97.6	.088
Naturalistic Learners	1.0	39.6	.025
Classroom Learners	0.33	50.0	.005
Bilingual A	2.6	34.6	.076
Bilingual B Subgroup 1	3.0	41.5	.072
Bilingual B Subgroup 2	1.0	45.3	.022

Table 9.6 Inter-Rater Reliability

Raters	Error Identification	Error Category
A—B	.936 (κ =.664)	.965 (κ = .952)
B—C	.909 (κ =.387)	.931 (κ = .906)
C—A	.926 (κ =.559)	1.00 (κ = 1.00)

English words (English words pronounced according to Japanese phonological rules), and others. Three pairs of raters participated. Inter-rater reliability coefficients for each pair of raters with respect to error identification and error categorization are shown in Table 9.6.

Two measures were used to assess learner accuracy: (1) the ratio of error-free clauses to total clauses, and (2) the error frequency rate. As shown in Table 9.7, all groups exhibited similar error-free clause ratios (around .60), except Bilingual B, subgroup 2, whose ratio was .41, showing subgroup 2 to have been the least accurate.

Given that some clauses contained more than one error, a second measure was used to assess the accuracy of each group. Table 9.8 presents the error frequency rate for each group (obtained by dividing the number of errors by the number of clauses): the lower the rate, the more accurate the learners were. Bilingual group A had the lowest rate of .30, making it the most accurate group. Bilingual B, subgroup 2 had the highest rate of .67, making it the least accurate. The other three groups fell between these two.

In summary, the error analysis of the narrative data showed the Bilingual group A to be the most accurate and the Bilingual group B, subgroup 2 to be the least accurate. This is parallel to what was found in the results of the written test. In

Table 9.7 Error-Free Clause Ratios

	Mean # of Clauses (C)	Mean # of Error-Free Clauses (EFC)	EFC Ratio (EFC/C)
Naturalistic Learners	41	26	.63
Classroom Learners	51	31	.60
Bilingual A	37	23	.62
Bilingual B Subgroup 1	43	26	.60
Bilingual B Subgroup 2	46	19	.41

Table 9.8 Error Rate per Clause

	Mean # of Clauses (C)	Mean # of Errors (E)	Error Rate (E/C)
Naturalistic Learners	41	19	0.48
Classroom Learners	51	27	0.53
Bilingual A	37	11	0.30
Bilingual B Subgroup 1	43	18.5	0.43
Bilingual B Subgroup 2	46	31	0.67

the next section, we examine the kinds of errors made, and explore the question of whether a particular type of error can be used to distinguish learner groups.

Error Types

As already noted, errors were classified as one of four types: (1) particles, (2) structure, (3) discourse (i.e., use of zero pronouns), and (4) vocabulary (including both English words and Japanized English words which have not become part of the Japanese language).[7]

In order to compare the groups, an error frequency rate (errors divided by total number of clauses) for each type was derived from the raw scores. Results of the comparison are shown in Table 9.9. A similar rank order for the four error types was observed for all groups. The most frequent error type in each case involved vocabulary, followed by particles, and then structure. The least frequent error type involved discourse. It is also worth noting that the Classroom Learners group made particle errors more frequently than other groups.

It is assumed that one of the characteristics of heritage learners is frequent borrowings from the dominant language, in this case English (see, e.g., Campbell & Rosenthal, 2000). In order to see if this tendency was present in our data, learners' vocabulary errors were divided into two categories: borrowings and others. The former includes the use of English words and of Japanized English words.[8] Table 9.10 shows mean error frequencies of these two types for each learner group.

As we can see here, all groups showed very few errors of this type. This is in accordance with the OPI data, which showed very similar results, i.e., that borrowing from English was not as frequent as is generally assumed.

Table 9.9 Error Types in Learner Narratives

	Vocabulary	Particles	Structure	Discourse
Naturalistic Learners	0.292	0.112	0.073	0
Classroom Learners	0.290	0.232	0.113	0.029
Bilingual A	0.150	0.122	0.027	0
Bilingual B Subgroup 1	0.178	0.131	0.043	0.053
Bilingual B Subgroup 2	0.326	0.123	0.181	0.035
Overall	0.247	0.144	0.087	0.023

Table 9.10 Vocabulary Errors by Type

	Vocabulary Errors		Mean # of Total Errors
	Borrowings	Others	
Naturalistic Learners	1.3	10.0	19.0
Classroom Learners	1.3	14.3	27.0
Bilingual A	1.0	4.7	11.0
Bilingual B Subgroup 1	1.5	8.0	18.5
Bilingual B Subgroup 2	4.3	9.7	31.0

Vocabulary in the Guided Narratives and OPI

The vocabularies used in the guided narratives and the OPI were first coded for syntactic category using the Janalyzer 'Japanese Morphology Analyzer' developed by Hidetoshi Shirai (n.d.), and then checked by a transcriber. Fifteen percent of the data was checked by a second rater independently. Inter-rater reliability for each of the same three pairs (mentioned earlier) was kappa .929, .928, and .917, respectively.

Lexical items used in the narratives and the OPI were categorized based on the syntactic coding, and types and tokens counted, but only items in lexical categories (i.e., nouns, verbs, adjectives, adjectival nouns, and adverbs) were used for analyses in this study. The vocabulary was also classified as "Basic," "Non-basic," and "Other" (i.e., English words and Japanized English words). Words in the non-basic category were further classified as *kango*, "sophisticated vocabulary," and non-*kango*. The list of 1,500 lexical items in *Nihongo nooryoku-shiken shutsudai kijun* (The Japan Foundation, 1996) was used to distinguish basic and non-basic vocabulary. *Kango* items were identified using *Nihon no kango* (Sato, 1979) and the *Iwanami shin-kango jiten* (Yamaguchi & Takeda, 1994).

The vocabulary in the narratives and OPI data were examined with respect to lexical variation and lexical sophistication. Lexical variation was measured by dividing the number of lexical word types (LWT) by the total number of lexical words (LW). Table 9.11 presents the LWT/LW ratios for both the narrative and OPI data. There was little difference in lexical variation among the learner groups in either case.

Ratios for all five groups hovered around 1.5/1.6 for the narratives and 2.0 for the OPI. (The difference between the two types of production data is to be expected given the much greater quantity of speech produced in the OPI.) The results show that the learners controlled sufficient lexical variation to avoid repeated 'recycling' of the same vocabulary items.

A measure of lexical sophistication was obtained by dividing the numbers of non-basic word types and of sophisticated *kango*-word types by the total number of lexical word types. Table 9.12 presents the lexical sophistication ratios, based on the non-basic word types and sophisticated *kango*-word types, for both the narrative and OPI data. Overall, learners were not using non-basic and sophisticated *kango* as much as native speakers, relying on basic vocabulary instead to

Table 9.11 Lexical Word Type/Token Ratios

| | Mean Ratio | |
	Narratives	OPI
Native Speakers	1.817	No data
Naturalistic Learners	1.549	1.882
Classroom Learners	1.557	2.101
Bilingual A	1.512	1.955
Bilingual B Subgroup 1	1.640	2.069
Bilingual B Subgroup 2	1.666	2.040

Table 9.12 Lexical Sophistication Ratios

		Narrative	OPI
Native Speakers	Non-basic	47.0%	No data
	Sophisticated Kango	25.5%	
Naturalistic Learners	Non-basic	22.4%	20.3%
	Sophisticated Kango	05.0%	08.5%
Classroom Learners	Non-basic	21.1%	28.3%
	Sophisticated Kango	10.1%	13.0%
Bilingual A	Non-basic	36.3%	24.0%
	Sophisticated Kango	13.0%	08.4%
Bilingual B Subgroup 1	Non-basic	37.4%	24.1%
	Sophisticated Kango	05.3%	09.4%
Bilingual B Subgroup 2	Non-basic	21.5%	13.2%
	Sophisticated Kango	06.7%	06.3%

Note: Ratio calculated as number of lexical word types divided by the total number of lexical words.

a higher degree. This can be seen more clearly in Figure 9.1, which shows the proportions of basic, non-basic other than *kango*, and *kango* vocabulary in the narrative data. Recall that because of the nature of the topic, the use of *kango*, or sophisticated words, was required in the narratives. Native speakers employed roughly the same proportions of basic and non-basic words (53% and 47%, respectively), and half of their non-basic words were *kango*.

In the case of the learner groups, the highest proportion of non-basic words was Bilingual B, subgroup 1's 37.4%, followed by Bilingual A's 36.3%; the remaining three groups had proportions lower than 25%. This suggests that, even at this advanced level, learners still lack lexical sophistication, a conclusion further supported by their very low use (a mean of 8%) of *kango*. These findings suggest a need for future research to investigate the nature of learners' lexicon. In

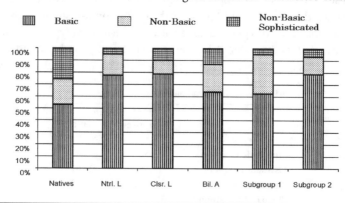

Figure 9.1 Lexical Sophistication Ratio for Narrative Data.

the case of Japanese, the multiple layers of complexity within the category of *kango*, which vary according to register, context, and topic, must be carefully taken into consideration. To our knowledge, a systematic coding system is yet to be created.

Discussion and Conclusion

This study sought to identify relationships between types of language-learning experience and variation in the linguistic profiles of advanced English-speaking learners of Japanese. In particular, an attempt was made to identify common characteristics of, and differences among, the linguistic profiles of five groups of learners: naturalistic learners, classroom learners, bilingual learners (Group A) with comparable abilities in all four language skills, and two additional types of bilingual learners (Group B, subgroups 1 and 2) with weaker reading and writing skills, sub-group 1 having experienced Japanese both inside the home and outside, sub-group 2 only within the family context.

Three types of data were collected: performance on a written test, a guided narrative, and the OPI. There were three major findings:

1. The Bilingual A Group outperformed all other groups with respect to accuracy and complexity. This was evident in all three data sets.
2. The two subgroups in the Bilingual B group exhibited different linguistic profiles: subgroup 1 performed quite well (placed second in the ranking) in most areas, whereas subgroup 2 did very poorly, particularly with respect to accuracy.
3. The results of the written test and the lexical analyses of the narrative and OPI data suggested that learners' weakest area (the area where improvement was most needed) is vocabulary and collocation. In particular, learners used sophisticated lexical items much less frequently than native speakers of Japanese.

It would be premature to draw more than the most tentative conclusions about effects of various types of language-learning experience on subsequent foreign language abilities. This was a small-scale descriptive study, after all, not an experiment. It would also be unjustified to make strong recommendations for curriculum design on the basis of the results from such a small-scale study, and one, moreover, that did not compare the effects of different curriculum designs on achievement. A larger replication is clearly called for, and is justified, in light of the initial findings. If the sizeable differences observed in the groups' linguistic profiles were sustained, firmer inferences would be warranted concerning relationships between type of language-learning experience and instructional needs of such learners entering advanced classes (ILR 2, ACTFL Advanced, or above). As it is, we simply note the following:

- The potential need to make distinctions within the traditional heritage and non-heritage categories when grouping students for research or instructional purposes even at these advanced proficiency levels, and so almost certainly earlier.
- What is likely to be the proportionately greater importance of a systematic instructional emphasis on lexis (especially non-basic *kango*) and collocation, and to a lesser degree on particles, at these proficiency levels, and so probably earlier as well.
- The support found for the often reported finding that the "classic" heritage experience (hearing the ancestral language in the home as a child, perhaps speaking it there sparingly, especially with older family members, but little or no contact with the language outside the family setting) needs extensive and targeted supplementing, and not just with regard to literacy, if heritage students are serious about obtaining advanced, functional ability in the language.
- The possibility that Bilingual A group's *hoshuukoo* experience accounted for the markedly superior accuracy and complexity of their Japanese (while recognizing the possible contribution of several confounded variables, such as child and parental motivation), and the corresponding need for classroom research into the nature of that experience, with a view to incorporating elements of it, modified for adults if need be, in the tertiary foreign language curriculum.
- The potential value for the grouping of students and curriculum design of a new diagnostic test based in part upon the tasks and items employed here for the purpose of data collection.

Finally, it should be noted that, even if corroborated, the results obtained in this study were for native speakers of English learning Japanese. Replications are in order with English-speaking learners of other languages, possibly those of heritage groups (e.g., Koreans) with somewhat differing recent immigration patterns from the Japanese in Hawaii and California.

Notes

1. A *hoshuukoo* serves the children of Japanese nationals who reside in a foreign country for an extended period of time, and follows the academic curriculum in Japan.
2. JLPT (The Japan Foundation, n.d.) is a standardized test used for the admission to undergraduate/graduate programs in Japan.
3. See Makino (1991) for detailed descriptions of each OPI level for Japanese as well as for details on ACTFL's Proficiency Guidelines.
4. For the units of analysis (utterance, T-unit, clause, etc.) and specifically for the treatment of insertions, repetitions, fillers, and corrections, we followed Tamaru & Yoshioka (1994): (1) insertion: treat inserted phrase or clause as a separate unit; (2) repetition: count the last one; (3) filler: ignore fillers; and (4) correction: count the last one.
5. Utterances are defined as a stream of speech with at least one of the following characteristics (Crookes 1990; Crookes & Rulon 1985): (1) under one intonation contour; (2) bounded by pauses; and (3) constituting a single semantic unit. However, because pauses appear in the data

even where there is no syntactic or semantic unit (e.g., between a noun and a case particle) it was difficult to code (1) and (2) reliably. We therefore relied more on (3)—especially in the case of the non-heritage learners.
6. See Wolfe-Quintero, Inagaki, and Kim (1998) for other potential measures.
7. The Japanese dictionary *Koojien* (Shinmura, 1998) was used to determine this.
8. Note that English loan words that are already part of the Japanese language and proper nouns such as "Twin Towers" were not included.

References

American Council on the Teaching of Foreign Languages. (1986). *ACTFL proficiency guidelines.* Hastings on Hudson, NY: Author.
Campbell, R. N., & Rosenthal, J. W. (2000). Heritage languages. In J. W. Rosenthal (Ed.), *Handbook of undergraduate second language education* (pp. 165–184). Mahwah, NJ: Lawrence Erlbaum.
Crookes, G., & Rulon, K. (1985). *Incorporation of corrective feedback in native speaker/non-native speaker conversation* (Tech. Rep. No. 3). Honolulu: Center for Second Language Classroom Research, Social Science Research Institute, University of Hawaii.
Crookes, G. (1990). The utterance, and other basic units for second language discourse analysis. *Applied Linguistics, 11,* 183–199.
Interagency Language Roundtable. (n.d.). *Interagency Language Roundtable language skill level descriptors.* Available at: http://govtilr.org
Hidetoshi, S. (n.d.) Janalyzer [Japanese morphology analyzer]. Available at: http://cyber.sist.chukyo-u.ac.jp/jchat/run-run/run2.html
The Japan Foundation. (n.d.). *Japanese language proficiency test.* Tokyo: Bonjinsha. Retrieved May 3, 2006, from http://www.jflalc.org/?act=tpt&id=8
The Japan Foundation. (1996). *Nihongo nooryoku-shiken shutsudai kijun* [Japanese language proficiency test: Test content specifications]. Tokyo: Bonjinsha.
Kameen, P. T. (1979). Syntactic skill and ESL writing quality. In C. Yorio, K. Perkins, & J. Schachter (Eds.), *On TESOL '79: The learner in focus* (pp. 343–364). Washington, DC: Teachers of English to Speakers of Other Languages.
Makino, S. (1991). ACTFL no gaikokugo nooryokukijun oyobi soreni motoduku kaiwanooryoku tesuto no rinen to mondai [Issues in ACTFL proficiency guidelines and oral proficiency interview]. *Sekai no Nihongo Kyooiku, 1,* 15–32.
Nagasawa, H. (1995). L1, L2, bairingaru no Nihongo-bunpoo-nooryoku [Differences in Japanese grammatical proficiency among L1, L2, and bilingual learners]. *Nihongo Kyoiku, 86,* 173–189.
Nihongo Gakuryoku Test Testing Committee. (1998). *Ichimango-go goi bunruishuu* [The classification of 10,000 words]. Tokyo: Senmon Kyooiku Shuppan.
Sakamoto, T. (1993). On acquisition order: Japanese particles *wa* and *ga.* In K. Yoshioka, B. Murdoch, J. Smith, & Y. Kato (Eds.), *Proceedings of the 4th Conference on Second Language Research in Japan* (pp. 105–122). Niigata, Japan: International University of Japan.
Sakoda, K. (1993). Hanashikotoba ni okeru ko-, so-, a- no chuukangengo kenkyuu [A study of the interlanguage of demonstratives in spoken Japanese]. *Nihongo Kyooiku, 81,* 67–79.
Sakoda, K. (1997). Nihongo gakushuusha ni okeru shijishi so-, a- no tsukaiwake ni kansuru kenkyuu [The role of semi-formulaic patterns in the interlanguage variation of the Japanese demonstratives *so-* and *a-*]. *Daini Gengo to shite no Nihongo no Shuutoku Kenkyuu, 1,* 57–70.
Sato, K. (1979). *Nihon no kango* [Sino-Japanese words in Japan]. Tokyo: Kadokawa Shoten.
Shinmura, I. (1998). *Koojien* (5th ed.) [Dictionary (5th ed.)]. Tokyo: Iwanami Shoten.
Tamaru, Y., & Yoshioka, K. (1994). Nihongo hatsuwa-shiryoo bunseki no tani o meguru mondai [Some problems surrounding the units of analysis for spoken data of Japanese as a second language]. In S. Kimura & M. Leong (Eds.), *The language programs of the International University of Japan working papers: Volume 5* (pp. 84–100). Niigata, Japan: The Language Programs of the International University of Japan.
Tanaka, M. (1997). Shiten, voice, hukubun no shuutoku yooin [Factors affecting the acquisition of point of view, voice, and complex sentences]. *Nihongo Kyooiku, 92,* 107–118.
Tanaka, M. (1999). Dainigengo shuutoku ni okeru Nihongo voice no shuutoku junjo [The acquisition order of the Japanese voice system]. In P. Robinson (Ed.), *Representation and process: Proceedings of the 3rd Pacific Second Language Research Forum, Volume 1* (pp. 117–127). Tokyo: PacSLRF.

Wolfe-Quintero, K., Inagaki, S., & Kim, H-Y. (1998). *Second language development in writing: Measures of fluency, accuracy and complexity*. Honolulu: University of Hawaii Press.

Yagi, K. (1993). Shokyuu gakushuusha no sakubun ni mirareru Nihongo no joshi no seiyoojunjo [The accuracy order of Japanese particles in elementary level compositions: An analysis of particles, particle functions, and functional groups]. *Sekai no Nihongo Kyooiku, 6*, 65–81.

Yamaguchi, A., & Takeda, A. (1994). *Iwanami shin-kango jiten*. Tokyo: Iwanami Shoten.

10
Academic Writing Proficiency of Russian Heritage Speakers
A Comparative Study

DEBRA FRIEDMAN AND OLGA KAGAN

The presence of heritage learners of Russian in the Russian language classroom is a relatively new but rapidly increasing phenomenon. The majority of the heritage students currently studying Russian in the United States belong to what are termed the Third and Forth Waves of emigration from Russian-speaking countries in the 20th century.[1] The Third Wave dates from the early 1970s to late 1980s, when the Soviet Union eased restrictions on Jewish emigration to Israel (although many of these émigrés eventually settled in the United States), and the Fourth Wave commenced in the late 1980s during perestroika and post-perestroika. While close chronologically, these two groups display differences in attitudes and motivations that may affect the degree of their language loss and maintenance. A major difference is each group's relationship with the home country: whereas the political situation limited the possibility for Third Wave émigrés to return to their home country or to maintain ties with relatives or friends in Russia, post-Soviet émigrés fully expect to maintain ties and may travel freely between Russia and their country of residence.

These latest two waves of immigration from Russia to the United States are substantial. In 2002, there were over 700,000 Russian speakers living in the U.S., up from 245,000 in 1990 (Shin & Bruno, 2003). The majority of these immigrants are urban, middle-class people with high expectations regarding educational and professional attainments. Andrews (1998) notes that these fairly recent (and still arriving) Russian émigrés display a strong desire to adapt to life in the United States, and he describes them as "a sophisticated and cosmopolitan group ... appreciative of their rich cultural heritage and aware of their unique background" (p. 55). As a result, especially in metropolitan areas such as New York and Los Angeles, large (especially public) universities have seen a significant enrollment of students from Russian-speaking families.

According to their initial proficiencies, heritage learners of Russian can be divided into the following three groups (Kagan & Dillon, 2003). Group 1, the most proficient group, comprises students who graduated from high school in Russia or Russian-speaking countries and, consequently, have not been away from the full Russian-speaking community for long. These students can be considered educated native speakers because they have a fully developed grammatical system, a native range of vocabulary, and inside familiarity with Russian culture and sociocultural norms. Based on the ACTFL *Standards for Foreign Language Learning* (American Council on the Teaching of Foreign Languages, 1996), these students display competence in the *interpersonal mode* (dealing with face-to-face communication and personal written communication), but are often unfamiliar with the demands of the *presentational mode*, defined as "spoken or written communication for an audience" (p. 33), as manifested in Russian.

Group 2 consists of students who attended school in a Russian-speaking country for five to seven years (the approximate equivalent of an American junior high school education) and therefore experienced an interruption in their language development during early adolescence. These students have a fairly complete knowledge of the grammatical system but do not have the complete range of vocabulary and register available to educated native speakers. They are also unfamiliar with many sociolinguistic, sociocultural, and cultural conventions because they have not interacted in Russian with the adult world on adult terms.

Group 3 can be characterized as 'incomplete acquirers' and 'forgetters' (Polinsky, 2000). There are two subgroups in Group 3: (a) students who attended elementary school in a Russian-speaking country and (b) students who emigrated as preschoolers or were born in the United States to Russian-speaking parents, that is, those students whose education has been entirely in English. Although Group 3b students could be considered a separate group, for programmatic purposes they can be placed together with 3a students.

Like other heritage language learners, Russian heritage learners' initial oral/aural proficiency distinguishes them from students of Russian as a foreign language. At the same time, however, because heritage speakers have had little or no exposure to formal registers of Russian or to Russian language literacy, they differ from educated native speakers. Previous studies of the spoken language of Russian heritage learners in the United States have noted both grammatical and pragmatic deviations from standard Russian, including heavy lexical borrowing from English (Andrews, 1998; Pavlenko & Jarvis, 2002; Polinsky, 2000; Zemskaja, 2001), loss of certain Russian phonological features and incorporation of English intonational patterns (Andrews, 1998; Polinsky, 2000; Zemskaja, 2001), semantic extension and syntactic translation from English (Andrews, 1998; Pavlenko & Jarvis, 2002), reduction of cases (Polinsky, 2000), and overuse of informal terms of address (Polinsky, 2000).

However, we know of no previous study that analyzes the written academic discourse of these heritage speakers. As Zemskaja (2001) notes, Russian émigrés use Russian mostly for oral communication, and limit their use of written Russian to personal correspondence. We therefore hypothesize that in terms of their proficiency in the written academic language, heritage writers would share some characteristics with those whom English composition teachers refer to as *basic* or *developmental writers*. These writers, who are often native or near-native speakers of English, come from a home culture that differs greatly from the academic culture in which they find themselves upon entering college. While fluent in the spoken language, they have little to no experience with the academic register and evidence a range of problems in their writing, such as numerous errors in grammar and spelling, a limited grasp of appropriate academic vocabulary, and difficulty in forming complex sentences (see, e.g., Shaughnessy, 1977; Sternglass, 1997).

The Study

This study seeks to answer the following research questions:

1. How does the written Russian of heritage learners compare to that of college-educated Russians?
2. How does the written Russian of heritage language learners compare to that of advanced learners who have learned Russian as a foreign language?
3. To what extent can the learner's competence in written Russian be correlated with his/her age of departure from a Russian-speaking country?
4. To what extent can the learner's competence in written Russian be correlated with his/her competence in written English?
5. Which pedagogical strategies would facilitate the development of Russian-language writing proficiency for Russian heritage learners?

To determine which features of written Russian discourse were most problematic for heritage language learners, we began with a small pilot study in the summer of 2001 in which we compared final exam essays written by heritage language students enrolled in a Russian literacy course to expository essays written on a variety of topics by Russian high school seniors (Basovskaja, 1997). We analyzed these essays for features such as sentence length, variety of sentence types (simple, compound, and complex), formation of compound and complex sentences, and the use of linguistic devices for establishing textual cohesion.

Based on the results of that pilot study, in the current study we have focused on two areas that distinguished the writing of heritage learners of Russian from that of native speakers: (a) the formation of complex sentences through relative clause constructions and (b) the use of temporal cohesive devices (such as logical connectors and adverb clauses). These two strategies and the resources available for realizing them in Russian are briefly outlined below.

Relative Clauses in Russian

Relative clauses consist of a type of embedding in which one sentence is combined with another. For example, the sentences *The woman is my professor* and

The woman is reading the newspaper can be combined through use of the relative pronoun *who* to form a single complex sentence: *The woman who is reading the newspaper is my professor.* It is possible to form similar complex sentences in Russian through the use of relative pronouns such as *kotoryj* ('who, which, that') and *gde* ('where'), as follows:

(1) *Ženščina,* **kotoraja** *čitaet*   *gazetu*   mоj *professor.*
     woman   who   read(3rdSingPres) newspaper   my   professor
     'The woman who is reading the newspaper is my professor.'

Alternatively, a relative clause in Russian can be formed with the use of a participle (*pričastie* in Russian). The Russian *pričastie* is similar to the English participle in that it is a verb form that functions as an adjective. However, unlike the English participle, which has only two forms, present (-ing) and past (-ed), the Russian *pričastie* has four: present active, past active, present passive, and past passive. In most constructions, these forms may be used instead of a clause with a relative pronoun; for example, sentence (1) could also be expressed as follows:

(2) *Ženščina,* *čitajuščaja*   *gazetu,*   *moj* *professor*
     woman   read (PresActPart) newspaper   my   professor
     'The woman reading the newspaper is my professor.'

Like other adjectival forms in Russian, participles are marked for gender, number, and case, which adds to the complexity and makes this linguistic form a difficult one for foreign-language learners of Russian to master. Moreover, while the use of participles is common in formal written Russian, only short forms of the past passive participle are typically used in the colloquial spoken language. We would therefore expect that educated native speakers would use this linguistic device in their essays whereas heritage learners (whose primary Russian language input has been oral) and foreign-language learners (who are challenged by the complexity of the form) would not.

Temporal Cohesive Devices in Russian

Temporal relationships, that is, the order in which various events in a narrative take place relative to each other, can be marked in many different ways. One simple and frequently used means of expressing such temporal relationships is by use of logical connectors of time, such as *then, after that,* or *next.* Russian also has words and phrases that serve as logical connectors of time, such as *potom* ('then'), *v to že vremja* ('at the same time'), and *posle ètogo* ('after that') which function in the same way as their English counterparts, as in the following example:

(3) *On čital* *gazetu.* **Potom** *on pil* *čaj.*
He read(3rdSingPst) newspaper then he drink(3rdSingPst) tea
'He read the newspaper. **Then** he drank tea.'

Since this strategy involves simply inserting a word or phrase between the sentences and requires no further syntactic alterations, it can be viewed as the simplest and least linguistically problematic means for expressing temporal relationships.

Another slightly more syntactically complex means of expressing temporal relationships is through use of adverbial clauses of time; that is, clauses that begin with an adverb of time (such as *before, after, while,* etc.), as follows:

(4) **Posle togo kak** *on pročital gazetu, on*
after that as he read(3rdSingPst) newspaper he
pil čaj.
drink(3rdSingPst) tea.
'**After** he read the newspaper, he drank tea.'

Finally, a third means of expressing temporal relationships is through the use of what in English are termed adverbial participles or verbal adverbs (in Russian, *deepričastie*). Just as the *pričastie* ('participle') is a verb form that functions as an adjective, the *deepričastie* is a verb form that functions as an adverb. There are two types of *deepričastie* in Russian. One, formed from imperfective verbs, indicates an action that takes place simultaneously with that of the sentence's main verb; the other, formed from perfective verbs, indicates an action that takes place prior to that of the main verb. For example, the actions described in sentences (3) and (4) could also be rendered using a perfective adverbial participle:

(5) **Pročitav** *gazetu, on pil čaj.*
read(PerfAdvPart) newspaper he drink(3rdSingPst) tea.
'**Having read** the newspaper, he drank tea.'

Like the *pričastie*, the Russian *deepričastie* is more common in the written language than in speech. We would therefore expect that this form would also be relatively rare in the writing of heritage learners.

Subjects and Data Collection

Our subjects for this study were 11 students who were enrolled in a course entitled "Russian for Native and Near Native Speakers: Literature and Film" at the University of California, Los Angeles. Seven of these students were classified as heritage learners of Russian, whose age at emigration ranged from 5 months to 16 years, thus representing all three of the proficiency groups identified by Kagan

& Dillon (2003). The remaining four students were foreign-language learners of Russian, all of whom were born in the United States. Three of these students came from English-speaking families and one from an Armenian-speaking family. As summarized in Table 10.1, the biographical questionnaires completed by the students provided information on native language, individual emigration history, and prior and current experience with Russian language literacy.

The data were obtained through an elicitation technique in which the students were shown a short excerpt from a Russian film, *Princessa na bobax* (*A Princess on the Beans*), without the sound and were then asked to write a brief description of the excerpt in Russian. To provide a basis for comparison, three native speakers of Russian who had completed their education through the university level in Russia also viewed the film excerpt and wrote a description in Russian.

In the excerpt, a poorly dressed woman is seen cleaning a staircase. A group of workmen come up the stairs, rudely push past her, and take over her cleaning job. She then notices a man dressed in a tuxedo standing on the landing below. The two have a brief conversation. In the next scene, an expensive sports car is seen driving through the streets. It stops outside of an expensive looking women's clothing shop, and the man and woman from the first scene emerge from the car and go into the shop. The man goes outside to answer his cell phone. He is sitting in his car and talking on the phone when he notices an attractive woman dressed in a white suit come out of the shop. It is the woman from the first scene, now transformed. He gazes at her intently as she gets into the car. After a brief conversation, the man starts the car and the two drive off.

Subsequently, another excerpt from the same film (in which the woman receives a makeover at a salon) was shown, and students were asked to write a description of the scene in English.[2] The Russian native speakers were not asked to perform this task.

We then analyzed the Russian essays for the following linguistic features:

Table 10.1 Biographical Information

Participant	Age	Place of Birth	Home Language	Age at Emigration
HL-1	21	Russia	Russian	16
HL-2	22	Russia	Russian/English	16
HL-3	22	Armenia	Armenian	15
HL-4	18	Russia	Russian	14
HL-5	26	Ukraine	Russian/English	11
HL-6	19	Belarus	English/Russian	9
HL-7	20	Ukraine	English/Russian	5 mo.
FL-1	21	U.S.	Armenian	n/a
FL-2	26	U.S.	English	n/a
FL-3	22	U.S.	English	n/a
FL-4	32	U.S.	English	n/a

Table 10.2 Method of Expressing Relative Clauses

	Native Speakers	Heritage Learners	Foreign-Language Learners
Participles	12	4	0
Relative Pronouns	3	19	4

1. Formation of relative clause constructions through the use of relative pronouns and participles, and
2. Establishment of temporal cohesion through the use of logical connectors, adverb clauses, and adverbial participles.

Results

Relative Clauses

The results of the frequency count of the subjects' construction of relative clauses are summarized in Table 10.2.

Because of the different numbers of subjects in each group, it is not possible to compare uses of these linguistic devices across the three groups. However, an examination of their use within each group reveals that the Russian native speakers displayed a strong tendency to use participles rather than relative clauses (12 tokens of participles vs. 3 tokens of relative pronouns). It should be noted, however, that one native speaker used no participles and only one relative pronoun, and she also used an informal conversational style, employing slang and idiomatic expressions. The absence of participles from this essay is thereby consistent with the observation that these forms are characteristic of the formal written register and less frequent in the spoken register.

In contrast to the native speakers, the heritage learners tended to use relative pronouns rather than participles (19 tokens of relative pronouns vs. 4 tokens of participles). In fact, the distinction is even more pronounced than implied by the total numbers, as all four of the tokens of participles that appeared in the heritage learners' essays came from a single essay; the remaining six heritage writers did not use participles at all.

In order to determine the reason for this asymmetry in the use of participles versus relative pronouns, we examined specific instances of these forms in our data. Our analysis reveals that heritage learners often used clauses with relative pronouns to express the same ideas that native speakers expressed through use of participles. These two different strategies can be seen in the following examples that describe the opening scene from the film excerpt.

Example 1 (NS-3)[3]

Dama,	***drajaščaja***	*pol*	*lestničnogo prolëta,*	*udivlena*
woman	scrub(PresActPrt)	floor	stairwell	surprised

pojavleniem	*gruppy*	*mužčin,*	**podnimajuščixsja**	*vverx*
Appearance	group	men	rise(PresActPrt)	up

po	*lestnice.*
along	stairs.

'A woman, **scrubbing** the floor of a stairwell, is surprised by the appearance of a group of men **coming up** the stairs.'

In Example 1, the writer, a native speaker of Russian, uses the present active participial forms *drajaščaja* (from *drait'* 'to scrub') and *podnimajuščixsja* (from *podnimat'sja* 'to rise' or 'to go up') to construct relative clauses describing the activities of both the woman and the men who intrude upon her cleaning. In contrast, two of the heritage learners described the same scene using relative pronouns:

Example 2 (HL-3)

V	*otryvke*	*ètogo fil'ma*	*my*	*vidim*		*moloduju*	*ženščinu,*
in	scene	this film	we	see(1stPlPres)		young	woman
kotoraja	*byla*		*zanjata*	*uborkoj*	*doma.*		
who	be (3rdSingPst)		occupied	tidying up	house		

'In the scene of this film, we see a young woman who was occupied with tidying up a house.'

Example 3 (HL-6)

V	*načale*	*otryvka,*	*pokazana*	*ženščina*	**kotoraja**
At	beginning	scene	shown	woman	**who**
moet			*pol.*		
clean(3rdSingPres)			floor		

'At the beginning of the scene, a woman **who** is cleaning the floor is shown.'

In the previous two examples, the two heritage learners use relative clauses with the relative pronoun *kotoraja* ('who' in the feminine) to describe the woman rather than using a participial form as the native speaker did in Example (1), although in both cases a participle could have been used to express the same idea.

Meanwhile, as indicated in Table 10.2, the foreign-language learners in this study rarely formed complex sentences through embedding, with only four tokens of relative pronouns and no tokens of participles. Furthermore, as was the case with the heritage learners, three of the four tokens of relative pronouns found in the foreign-language learners' essays came from a single essay; another foreign-language learner used one token of a relative pronoun, and the remaining two did not use any. Instead, the foreign-language learners tended to write sequences of simple, subject-verb-object sentences rather than combining these sentences using relative clauses, as seen in the following description of the same scene by a foreign-language learner:

Example 4 (FL-2)

V   načale   ètogo otryvka,   odna ženščina   ubiraet.
at   beginning this   scene   one   woman   tidy up (3rdSingPres)
Drugie   liudi   vyxodjat   i   proxodjat mimo neë.
other   people   come out(3rdSingPres) and   pass   by   her.
'At the beginning of this scene, a woman is tidying up. Other people come out and go past her.'

Like the native speaker in Example (1), the foreign-language learner in Example (4) describes both the woman cleaning and the men who come up the stairs. However, unlike the native speaker, who uses participial constructions and combines these events into one complex sentence, the foreign-language learner uses verbs in the present tense in two separate sentences.

The following examples further illustrate these different strategies as employed by native speakers, heritage learners, and foreign-language learners in their descriptions of the scene in which the man in the tuxedo first makes his appearance.

Example 5 (NS-1)

*Pojavljaetsja   geroj, **odetyj**   v   šikarnyj*
Appear(3rdSingPres)   hero   dressed(PstPassPrt)   in   expensive
vyxodnoj   kostjum   s   babočkoj.
going out   suit   with   bowtie
'The hero appears, **dressed** in an expensive dressy suit with a bow tie.'

Example 6 (HL-6)

V   tot-že moment,   v   pod"ezd   zaxodit   mužčina,
At   same moment   in   entry   appear(3rdSingPres)   man
kotoryj   odet   v   *kostjume.*
who   dressed   in   suit
'At the same moment, in the entry there appears a man **who is dressed** in a suit.'

Example 7 (FL-2)

Ona   vidit   mužčinu   na   drugom   etaže.
She   see(3rdSingPres)   man   on   another   floor

On   v   čornom   kostjume.
he   in   black   suit
'She sees a man on another floor. He is in a black suit.'

Examples (5) and (6) are particularly interesting in that both the native speaker in Example (5) and the heritage learner in Example (6) use the past passive participle *odetyj* (short form *odet*) formed from *odet'* 'to dress'; however, the native speaker uses it in a participial construction, while the heritage learner uses the form as a predicate adjective in a construction with a relative pronoun. The heritage learner's usage of the short form of the participle rather than the long form reflects everyday conversational use. Meanwhile, the foreign-language learner in Example (7) avoids a relative clause construction altogether and instead expresses the same idea in two separate sentences.

In summary, the analysis of relative clause constructions reveals a hierarchy, from least to most linguistically complex, which correlates to whether the writer is a native speaker, a heritage learner, or a foreign-language learner. The foreign-language learners rarely attempted relative clause constructions of any kind, preferring to express ideas in a series of simple sentences. Heritage learners, on the other hand, did use relatively simple relative clauses constructions with relative pronouns such as *kotoryj*. Finally, the native speakers freely employed the linguistically complex, yet expressively rich resource of the Russian *pričastie*.

Temporal Cohesion

We found a similar hierarchy when examining how temporal cohesion was established in these essays, as evident in Table 10.3.

As was the case with the *pričastie*, the *deepričastie* (adverbial participle) was a well-exploited resource in the native speakers' essays, with a total of 11 tokens. All the native speakers used adverbial participles to express the temporal order of different events within the same sentence. The following example, describing the woman's return to the car after her visit to the clothing store, offers a typical example of native speakers' use of these participles:

Example 8 (NS-2)

*Ona saditsja   v   mašinu   (slegka   **spotknuvšis',***
she   get in(3rdSingPres)   in   car   slightly   trip(PerfAdvPart)

Table 10.3 Methods of Expressing Temporal Relationships

	Native Speakers	Heritage Learners	Foreign-Language Learners
Adverbial Participles	11	3	0
Adverb Clauses	1	6	4
Logical Connectors	3	7	7

Note: Number of tokens.

no	*ne*	***poterjav***			*elegantnosti)...*
but	not	lose(PerfAdvPart)			elegance

'She gets in the car (**having** slightly **tripped**, but not **having lost** her elegance) ...'

In Example 8, the writer expresses three separate events (getting in the car, tripping, and "not losing her elegance") within one sentence by expressing the main event with a verb in simple present tense (*saditsja* 'gets in') and the two secondary events with perfective adverbial participles (*spotknuvšis'* from *spotknut'sja* 'to trip' and *poterjav* from *poterjat'* 'to lose'). At the same time, the use of the perfective participle forms, which express action occurring prior to the action of the main verb, enables the writer to place the clauses containing these forms after the main clause while still indicating that the "tripping" and "not losing" actions took place before the "getting in" action.

In contrast, in the heritage learners' essays, there are only three total tokens of adverbial participles used by three different writers (that is, one token each). Consider the following example from a heritage learner's essay:

Example 9 (HL-6)

Mužčina	*ostavljaet*		*ženščinu*	*v*	*ètom*	*magazine*	*i*
man	leave(3rdSingPres)		woman	in	this	store	and
razgovarivaja		*po*	*telefonu*	*saditsja*		*obratno*	
converse(ImpAdvPart)		on	telephone	get in(3rdSingPres)		back	
v	*mašinu.*						
in	car						

The man leaves the woman in the store and, **conversing** on the telephone, gets back in the car.'

In this example, the writer uses an imperfective adverbial participle (*razgovarivaja*, from *razgovarivat'* 'to converse') to express an action that takes place simultaneously with that of the main clause (*saditsja* 'gets in').

A far more common strategy among heritage learners, however, was to express temporal relationships through use of adverb clauses (six tokens) or logical connectors of time (seven tokens). As with the relative clauses discussed above, in many instances the heritage learners used these forms in situations in which the native speakers used adverbial participles. The following examples illustrate different strategies for depicting the man's reaction after the woman returns to the car in her new outfit:

Example 10 (NS-2)

Mužik	*s*	*mobiloj*	*proiznosit*		*(možno*	*pročitat'*	*po*
guy	with	mobile	say(3rdSingPres)		able	read(Inf)	by

gubam):	"Ja	tebe	potom	pozvonju",	**ne**	**otryvaja**
lips:	I	you	later	call(1stSingFut)	not	tear away

ot	neë	vzgljada.
from	her	glance

'The guy with the mobile phone says (you can read his lips), "I'll call you later," **not tearing** his glance from her.'

Example 11 (HL-5)

Kogda	ona	sela	v	mašinu,	on	glaz	s	neë
when	she	sat(3rdSingPst)	in	car	he	eye	from	her

snjat'	ne	mog.
take off(Inf)	not	able(3rdSingPst)

'**When** she sat in the car, he could not take his eyes off her.'

In Examples 10 and 11, both writers express the temporal relationship of simultaneity, but the native speaker in Example 10 does so by using an imperfective adverbial participle (*otryvaja*, from *otryvat'* 'to tear away'), while the heritage learner in Example 11 uses an adverb clause with the adverb of time *kogda* ('when').

Once again, the foreign-language learners avoided usage of the more grammatically complex adverbial participle in favor of adverb clauses (a total of four tokens) and logical connectors of time (seven tokens). It should be noted, however, that three of the four tokens of adverb clauses came from a single essay; two of the foreign-language learners did not use any adverb clauses of time. Further, one of these writers accounted for five out of the total seven tokens of logical connectors of time found in the foreign-language learners' essays. Unlike the heritage learner's essays, which contained a variety of logical connectors (including *tem vremenem* 'at that time', *posle čego* 'after that', and *so vremenem* 'with time') in the foreign-language learners' essays six out of the seven total tokens of temporal logical connectors were of a single form: *potom* 'then'. The following example, describing the same scene as the previous examples, illustrates the usage of logical connectors in the foreign-language learners' essays:

Example 12 (FL-2)

Mne	kažetsja,		čto	on	tože	dumaet,
me	seem(3rdSingPres)		that	he	also	think(3rdSingPres)

čto	ona	xorošo	vygljadit.		**Potom,**	ženščina
that	she	good	look(3rdSingPres).		then	woman

podxodit		k	mašine,	otkryvaet		dver'	i
walk(3rdSingPres)		to	car	open(3rdSingPres)		door	and

saditsja		v	mašinu.
get in(3rdSingPres)		in	car

'It seems to me that the man also thinks that she looks good. **Then**, the woman walks to the car, opens the door, and gets in the car.'

Example 12 also illustrates another strategy commonly employed by foreign-language learners to express the temporal relationship between events: placing the clauses in the order of the occurrence of the actions that they are describing, often connecting them with the conjunction *i* ('and'). For instance, the second sentence of Example 12 lists three actions taken by the woman: walking to the car (*podxodit k mašine*), opening the door (*otkryvaet dver'*), and getting into the car (*saditsja v mašinu*). Rather than using adverbial participles or adverb clauses, either of which would be possible here, the writer chooses to indicate this sequence of events by describing the actions with verbs in the simple present tense that are then placed in the appropriate sequential order. Of course, the native speakers and heritage learners also used this means for expressing temporal relationships between clauses, but both groups varied this usage with other strategies, such as adverbial participles or adverb clauses, while the foreign-language learners rarely did so.

Once again, the analysis reveals a connection between the grammatical complexity of the linguistic device, with adverbial participles (*deepričastie*) being the most complex and logical connectors and clause ordering the least complex, reflected in the use of these devices by the three groups. The native speakers used all of these strategies, but most frequently used adverbial participles to express time relationships. Heritage learners, on the other hand, only occasionally used adverbial participles, and instead favored adverb clauses and logical connectors. Finally, the foreign-language learners never used adverbial participles and only rarely used adverb clauses. Instead, they tended to express temporal relationships with the simplest devices: logical connectors such as *potom* ('then') and clause ordering.

Proficiency in Written Russian and Age at Emigration

Previous research (Kagan & Dillon, 2003) as well as our own pilot study have posited a correlation between the Russian language proficiency of heritage learners and the age of emigration and amount of schooling in a Russian-speaking country. To determine whether our current study could support this correlation, we evaluated the heritage learners' essays based on the criteria outlined above (construction of relative clauses and expression of temporal cohesion) as well as other salient features of literary Russian, such as the use of suitable vocabulary and, where appropriate, of non-SVO (subject-verb-object) word order (Kagan & Dillon, 2006). We then classified the essays as evidencing "high", "medium" or "low" Russian written language proficiency and matched these classifications against information regarding the heritage students' emigration history. The results are shown in Table 10.4.

Table 10.4 Written Language Proficiency

	Age at Emigration	Russian	English Rater 1	English Rater 2
HL-1	16	Medium	5	5.5
HL-2	16	Medium	5.5	6
HL-3	15	Low	4	5
HL-4	14	High	6	5.5
HL-5	11	High	5.5	6
HL-6	9	Medium	5	6
HL-7	5 months	Low	6	6

As seen in Table 10.4, our results are somewhat inconclusive. In support of the correlation between language proficiency and age at emigration, we found that the two essays rated "high" (H-4 and H-5) were written by heritage learners who emigrated in early adolescence; one of these writers (H-4), who emigrated at the age of 14, was the only heritage learner in our data to use participle forms. In addition, one essay rated "medium" was written by a learner who emigrated at age 9 (H-6) and one rated "low" (H-7) was written by a learner who emigrated at age 5 months. On the other hand, two other heritage learners who emigrated in their mid-teens (H-1 and H-2) were rated as demonstrating only "medium" proficiency, while a third, who emigrated at age 15, was rated "low." This latter case, however, can be explained by the fact that for this writer Russian is actually a second language (the writer comes from an Armenian-speaking family); indeed, the writer rated his/her own proficiency in written Russian as "low" on our biographical questionnaire.

The ambiguity of these results in addition to the small sample size leaves us unable to make any strong claims regarding a correlation between proficiency and age at emigration. However, the results suggest that although age at emigration may be a factor in oral proficiency, it does not necessarily equate with equivalent levels of proficiency in the written academic language.

Proficiency in Written Russian and in Written English

A related question that we wished to explore in this study was whether there exists any correlation between heritage learners' proficiency in written Russian and their proficiency in written English. In our pilot study we found some evidence for a negative correlation, with heritage speakers rated "low" in Russian proficiency coming closest to native speaker norms in their English language essays. To examine this question in the current study, the English-language essays written by the heritage language students were evaluated by two raters, both of whom are experienced instructors of university-level English as a Second Language (ESL) composition courses. The raters were asked to rate the essays based on a 6-point scale, with a score of "1" corresponding to "pre-university" (i.e., an English proficiency level below the minimum required for university study) and a score of "6" corresponding to "native proficiency." The ratings were based on factors such as the number and type of grammatical errors, variety of sentence types, appropriate use of academic vocabulary, and ability to form complex sentences.

As seen in Table 10.4, there was a high degree of inter-rater reliability, with no more than a point difference between the scores given by the two raters. In contrast to our earlier findings, in this study we did not find a negative correlation between proficiency in written Russian and written English, with the exception of one heritage learner (HL-7), who emigrated at the age of 5 months. This writer, whose Russian essay was rated among the lowest of the heritage learner essays, received a score of "6" from both raters on his English essay, indicating that English is his/her dominant language. In some cases, the scores on the English essays mirrored the scores received by those writers on their Russian essays: The two writers who received ratings of "high" on their Russian essays (HL-4 and HL-5) received ratings of 5.5 or 6 on their English essays, while one who received a rating of "low" on the Russian essay (HL-3, the Armenian speaker) also received the lowest score given by each rater (4 from one rater, 5 from the other) for the English essay.[4] The situation with those writers whose Russian essays were rated "medium" is more mixed: One (HL-1) received scores of 5 and 5.5, another (HL-6) received scores of 5 and 6, and a third (HL-2) received scores of 5.5 and 6. However, with the exceptions of HL-2 and HL-7 (both of whom were rated higher on their English essays than on their Russian essays), the relative ranking of these writers in terms of their proficiency in written English is similar to that of their proficiency in written Russian.

Clearly, these results preclude us from making any claims regarding the dominance of one language (English or Russian) over the other for most of these learners. What they do suggest, however, is that assuming a certain minimum level of language proficiency (as would be the case for all of these learners in English and for all but HL-7 in Russian), it may be possible to transfer writing proficiency from one language into another.

Summary of the Results

This study sought to measure the written Russian language proficiency of heritage learners of Russian with that of native speakers of Russian and advanced learners of Russian as a foreign language. Our data set is not large enough to generalize our results to the Russian heritage language learner population as a whole, but we believe the study has located some intriguing patterns and trends that can form a basis for further research.

First, it is clear that there are substantial differences between the Russian writing of university-level heritage learners and their native-speaker counterparts. While Russian heritage speakers were able to form complex sentences with relative clauses and to achieve temporal textual cohesion in their Russian essays, they used a relatively limited range of linguistic devices in comparison to those employed by native speakers. At the same time, the heritage learners also differed from foreign-language learners of Russian in their command of a wider range of linguistic resources, such as adverb clauses of time and a greater variety of temporal logical connectors.

We also noted a tendency in the heritage learners' essays to rely on forms and structures, such as relative clauses with *kotoryj*, that have equivalent forms in English and to avoid unique Russian discourse features, such as the Russian *pričastie*. While it was not the focus of this study to examine the issue of "transfer" from English into written Russian, these results are consistent with the findings of researchers who report the strong influence of English on the lexicon, phonology, and syntax of the spoken Russian of heritage learners (see, e.g., Andrews, 1998; Pavlenko & Jarvis, 2002; Polinsky, 2000, Zemskaja, 2001).

Furthermore, we also found some evidence to support prior findings of a correlation between language proficiency and age at emigration, with heritage learners who emigrated in adolescence receiving higher ratings on their Russian essays than those who emigrated as children. However, the fact that two of the heritage learners who emigrated in their mid-teens received only "medium" ratings on their Russian essays implies that this correlation is by no means a straightforward one. Rather, these results seem to support the observation made earlier that Group 1 learners (those who attended high school in a Russian-speaking country) may lack proficiency in the presentational mode in Russian despite their facility in the interpersonal mode.

Finally, the results of this study posit a positive correlation between these heritage learners' ability to write in Russian and their ability to write in English. While these results contradicted our expectations of a negative correlation that would parallel the findings of our pilot study, they raise intriguing questions regarding the nature of "writing ability" and its connection to overall linguistic competence. While answers to these questions are beyond the scope of this study, we believe that they are well worth exploring in future research.

Pedagogical Implications

Heritage learners of Russian are relative newcomers on American campuses; consequently, not enough is known about how to provide these learners with a coherent program. However, the results of this study support our hypothesis that heritage language learners are similar to basic or developmental writers described in literature of English or ESL composition studies and therefore might benefit from the methodology used in teaching academic writing in English. While the linguistic structures involved differ across languages, both groups have similar deficiencies. Such common assignments as combining sentences, rewriting a paragraph to emphasize a different point, embedding parenthetical expressions, writing a premise and a conclusion, summarizing a plot or formulating a problem in a limited number of sentences, and employing specific cohesive devices to create particular text relationships (e.g., comparison, cause and effect) are similar to the ones used by teachers of English composition or ESL writing and may also be used to good effect in teaching heritage language writing.

Textual analysis is another technique used in English composition instruction that can be successfully applied in heritage language composition courses. It should also be noted that by analyzing syntactical structures of a text, students develop both interpretational and presentational skills as well as hone their reading skills. By paying close attention to style in their own writing, they not only gain an understanding of the text structure but also the social and cultural implications of the language.

A question that arises repeatedly is whether a program for heritage learners should be the same as one for traditional foreign-language students. Russian instructors are also trying to find ways to teach both groups together because of lack of resources to provide two distinct curricula.

Our data provide a partial answer to some of the pedagogical questions. As has been shown, neither group of students is able to use the wide range of syntactical devices that are an integral part of the linguistic repertoire for educated native speakers. That commonality may be used as a starting point in designing a curriculum that would serve both groups well. If a mixed group of students were to be offered a class that focuses on a narrowly defined goal, such as learning to use academic level syntax in their writing, they may be able to work together.

The class whose work we have analyzed in this chapter was in fact a mixed class. Our experience in teaching the class proves that after the non-heritage students recovered from their initial shock of being in a class with "fluent" speakers, both groups were capable of carrying out the assigned tasks and improved their written performance by the end of the course. They were also capable of cooperating in class while analyzing texts and written assignments, working on text structure, and so on. Precisely because the focal point of the class was not conversation, non-heritage students were not threatened by their Russian-speaking peers and did not feel at a disadvantage. It also helped that the students were told explicitly that grades would be based solely on their individual progress and no comparison among students would be attempted.

There were some unexpected benefits to this approach as well. Although the focus of the class was not conversation (i.e., students were not graded on their speaking skills), the class was conducted entirely in Russian. This provided many opportunities for the foreign-language learners to interact in Russian with fluent speakers, and one of the non-heritage students observed at the end of the course that both her listening comprehension and speaking had improved.

In summary, our data indicate that heritage learners do not have a ready-made repertoire of complex syntactical devices merely because they were raised speaking Russian. Even those who attended high school in a Russian-speaking country did not display the writing skills characteristic of the educated native speakers in our study. Without these skills, heritage learners of Russian cannot function at the professional (Superior or higher) level of proficiency. By teaching them the requisite skills we can help them reach, or at least approach, high-level proficiency. The distinct needs of the Russian heritage language learner present a challenge to the language teacher to devise curricula conducive to developing the heritage learners' existing oral language proficiency into a full command of the literary language.

Notes

1. The First Wave followed the Communist Revolution of 1917, and the Second Wave came after World War II.
2. Our goal was to compare students' proficiencies in written English and written Russian to explore whether there is a correlation between these proficiencies. We hypothesized that there might be a negative correlation and that students who immigrated at a later age would be more proficient in writing in Russian than in English.
3. Examples from the essays appear here exactly as written in the original text; no attempt has been made to correct errors in spelling, grammar, or word choice.
4. It must be remembered that for this writer neither Russian nor English is a primary language.

References

American Council on the Teaching of Foreign Languages. (1996). *Standards for foreign language learning: Preparing for the 21st century.* Yonkers, NY: Author.

Andrews, D. R. (1998). *Sociocultural perspectives on language change in diaspora: Soviet immigrants in the United States.* Philadelphia: John Benjamins.

Basovskaja, E. N. (Ed.). (1997). *100 lučšix sočinenij na svobodnuju temu [100 best essays on a free theme].* Moscow: Olimp.

Kagan, O., & Dillon, K. (2003). A new perspective on teaching Russian: Focus on the heritage learner. *Heritage Language Journal 1*(1). Retrieved June 15, 2006, from http://www.heritagelanguages. org. (Reprinted from *Slavic and East European Journal 45*(3), 507–518, 2001).

Kagan, O., & Dillon, K. (2006). So what happens now? *Slavic and East European Journal, 50*(1), 83–96.

Pavlenko, A., & Jarvis, S. (2002). Bidirectional transfer. *Applied Linguistics, 23*, 190–214.

Polinsky, M. (2000). A composite linguistic profile of a speaker of Russian in the USA. In O. Kagan & B. Rifkin (Eds.), *The learning and teaching of Slavic languages and cultures* (pp. 437–466). Bloomington, IN: Slavica.

Shaughnessy, M. (1977). *Errors and expectations: A guide for the teacher of basic writing.* New York: Oxford University Press.

Shin, H. B., & Bruno, R. (2003, October). *Language use and English-speaking ability: 2000.* United States Census 2000. U.S. Department of Commerce. Retrieved June 15, 2006, from http://www. census.gov/prod/2003pubs/c2kbr-29.pdf

Sternglass, M. (1997). *A time to know them: A longitudinal study of writing and learning at the college level.* Mahwah, NJ: Lawrence Erlbaum.

Zemskaja, E. A. (Ed.). (2001). *Jazyk russkogo zarubež'ja [The language of the Russian diaspora].* Moscow/Vienna: Wiener Slawistischer Almanach.

11
Stigmatized Spanish Inside the Classroom and Out
A Model of Language Teaching to Heritage Speakers

CLAUDIA PARODI

This chapter deals with the California Spanish vernacular (SV) as spoken in the Los Angeles area. The information presented is based on a study involving 120 heritage speakers in several advanced Spanish classes at Long Beach City College (LBCC) during the years 1999 to 2002. In the first part of the chapter, I deal with the formation and main characteristics of SV using data from my research. In the second part, I discuss the stigma attached to SV, both in the classroom and out, elaborating on the problems SV speakers face while learning standard Spanish in the classroom and while attempting to communicate with monolingual speakers of Spanish. Finally, I propose a model of language teaching to SV speakers that aims to alleviate some of these problems.

Introduction

Some time ago a student of mine, Carolina, a Chicana[1] from Los Angeles, went to Mexico to meet her relatives who lived in Tlaquepaque, a small town of artisans near Guadalajara. When she arrived at the airport, she hailed a taxi and asked the driver to take her to Tlaquepaque. She was excited about being in Mexico and began chatting with the driver. After she had uttered a few sentences, she realized that she had encountered a narrow-minded interlocutor. Not only did he comment negatively on her choice of vocabulary, slow pace of speaking, and grammatical mistakes, he also commented that he could not understand why a Mexican-looking person was not fluent in Spanish. Similar situations occurred several times while Carolina was in Mexico. Her relatives made jokes about her speech, and Mexican store clerks were puzzled by her Spanish. Carolina also had problems adapting to Mexican culture—often feeling that people asked questions that were too personal and/or inappropriate.

The experience just described is relatively common to Spanish-speaking heritage speakers who visit Latin American countries. Some who experience negative attitudes of this sort decide as a result to cut their ties with Mexico and other Latin American countries. Fortunately, many Chicanos seek to overcome these obstacles by choosing to study their heritage language and culture in college.

They want to master these subjects in depth to clarify their own identity and receive better job opportunities.

One of the biggest barriers these bilingual heritage students must overcome in their Spanish classes at American universities is the attitude of their Spanish instructors (see chapter 6, this volume). Frequently, they encounter instructors with the same negative attitudes as monolingual speakers of Spanish towards the way they speak Spanish. These instructors stigmatize SV because it is different from standard Spanish. Moreover, they may not be aware that bilingual heritage speakers process Spanish differently than English monolingual second language (L2) learners of Spanish. This difference in processing results from the fact that heritage speakers have been exposed since early childhood to Spanish, acquiring it outside the classroom during the critical period (cf. Chomsky, 1972). Thus, they have acquired the core of the language, with a higher or lower degree of proficiency, in a naturalistic environment. Most importantly, they have developed an intuition or subconscious knowledge of the language that L2 learners of Spanish lack, as I will show below.

Who Speaks Stigmatized Spanish in Southern California?

In this first section of the chapter, I discuss why SV is stigmatized among monolingual speakers of Spanish, and what heritage speakers of Spanish know when they arrive in the classroom. The stigma attached to a certain language or dialect is directly related to the prestige of the people who speak it; as noted above, the SV spoken in Southern California is highly stigmatized (cf. Luján & Parodi, 2001). To understand the stigma it carries, it is therefore important to learn what constitutes Chicano Spanish in California and who speaks it.

In the 21st century, Spanish is widely spoken in Southern California, one of the most heavily populated Hispanic areas in the United States, the majority of these Hispanics being Mexican or Mexican-American. Historically, Mexicans have been in the area since the 18th century, when Spaniards came from Mexico to conquer California and christianize Indians through their mission system. During the 19th century, Mexican immigration into California was sparse. However, since the Mexican revolution of 1910, Mexicans have immigrated to Southern California continuously. During the 1970s and 1980s, due to political and economic hardships, Central Americans (mostly Salvadorans and Guatemalans) arrived in Southern California as well. In addition, some Puerto Ricans and Cubans moved from the East Coast to California. The 2000 Census (U.S. Census 2000, Total Population) registered over 6 million Hispanics, which constituted 40.7% of the total population of Southern California.[2] It should be noted that these figures are official and do not include illegal immigrants, of which there are large numbers in Southern California. Table 11.1 presents the official figures of the Hispanic population in 1990, broken down by country of origin (cf. Allen & Turner, 1997, pp. 100–107).

Table 11.1 Hispanic Population in the Los Angeles Area

Country of Origin	Population	%
Mexican	3,752,000	83%
Salvadoran	275,000	6%
Guatemalan	140,000	3%
South American	123,000	3%
Other Central American	86,000	2%
Puerto Rican	62,000	1%
Cuban	58,000	1%

Dialect Contact in Southern California

Mexicans in Southern California generally come from several small towns, where different variants of rural Spanish are spoken. When speakers of various dialects of a language are in contact, the situation usually gives rise to a *koine*, a linguistic variant that comprises features of several regional varieties (cf. Parodi, 1999). As noted by Siegel (1985), a koine is usually based on one dominant dialect, but it is frequently a reduced and simplified variant in comparison to the dialect that it originated from, due to accommodation (cf. Giles & Smith, 1979) and dialect leveling (cf. Siegel, 1985). Historically, a koine is a lingua franca that, through time, becomes a regional standard. Immigrant speakers of a language often develop a koine in an amalgamated immigrant community. This is the case of Hindustani of Fiji, the Japanese of Hawaii, and the SV of Southern California, which is the result of the contact of speakers of different rural dialects of Mexican Spanish. The SV of Southern California (also known as Chicano Spanish), together with English, are the primary languages of most Hispanics born in the Los Angeles area. The SV of Los Angeles is the result of leveling different Mexican rural dialects spoken by people who originally lived in small towns of Mexico and now reside in urban areas in the counties of Los Angeles, Ventura, and San Bernardino (Parodi, 1999). Through this situation a *rururban* variant emerged, similar to what Bortoni-Ricardo (1985) and Hidalgo (1987) have found in the middle and lower social classes in cities of Brazil and Mexico. Although, as Table 11.1 indicates, the Hispanic population includes a significant number of Salvadorans and Guatemalans, a process of *rekoineization* of the SV of Los Angeles has not occurred. That is, the children of Central American immigrants speak the SV of Los Angeles, despite the fact that their parents speak Salvadoran, Guatemalan, or Honduran Spanish. The SV of Los Angeles is therefore a well-established linguistic variant in Los Angeles, even though Spanish is a minority language in this English-speaking society (Parodi, 2003).

Main Features of the SV of Los Angeles

The SV of Los Angeles is a rururban variant of Mexican Spanish that shares several features characteristic of rural Spanish. It is considered "incorrect" and "uneducated" among monolingual speakers of standard Spanish. However, the features that these native speakers stigmatize are usually Old Spanish forms that were common in the Spanish American koine spoken in colonial times in Latin America, during the 16th to 18th centuries. These features have been lost or changed in Modern Spanish, but they are preserved and alive in the speech of small towns throughout Latin America (Lapesa, 1981; Parodi, 1995). Thus in reality, the negative attitude of urban speakers (which is generalized among almost all monolingual speakers of Spanish) reflects a lack of understanding of Latin American history. Table 11.2 compares some features of standard Spanish with typically stigmatized features found in the SV of Los Angeles that existed in the Old Spanish koine.

The languages of immigrants in the United States are affected by contact with English. In Los Angeles, speakers of Spanish become bilingual, to a greater or lesser extent, and they incorporate new loan words from English into their Spanish vocabulary. Moreover, limited exposure to their heritage language, coupled with no academic instruction in Spanish, causes their Spanish to have the characteristics of a language that has been acquired only orally.

Monolingual speakers of Spanish can also strongly stigmatize speakers that code switch from Spanish to English and incorporate loan words from English into Spanish. Monolingual speakers of Spanish often feel that the introduction of foreign words to their language corrodes the overall integrity and preservation of the Spanish language. In the Latin American world and in Spain, there are several

Table 11.2 Stigmatized Features of the SV of Los Angeles

The SV of Los Angeles	Monolingual Standard Spanish
Generalization of the 2nd person morpheme -s: *vinistes, hicistes, comistes* 'you came,' 'you did,' 'you ate'	Absence of -s in the 2nd person preterit: *viniste, hiciste, comiste*
Presence of morphene -nos in the 2nd person imperfect preterit of *ar* verbs: *andábanos, caminábanos, tomábanos* 'we used to go, walk, take'	Morpheme ending in –mos: *andábamos, caminábamos, tomábamos*
Analogical stress in the verb root in 1st person: *véngamos/vénganos, téngamos/ténganos, hágamos/háganos* 'we come, have, do'	Stress in the thematic vowel plural, present subjunctive: *vengamos, tengamos, hagamos*
Contraction of the article before a vowel: *l'água, l'águila, l'arena, l'espada* 'the water,' 'the eagle,' 'the sand,' 'the sword'	No contraction: *el água, el águila, la arena, la espada*
Diphthongization of hiatus: /pjor/ '*peor*', /kwete/ '*cohete*', /tjatro/ '*teatro*', /twaya/ '*toalla*' 'worse,' 'fireworks,' 'theater,' 'towel'	No diphthongization: /peor/ '*peor*', /koete/ '*cohete*, /teatro/ '*teatro*', /toaya/ '*toalla*
Pronunciation of the phoneme /f/ as /h/ before the diphthong ue: /hwera/, *fuera*, /hwersa/ *fuerza*, /hwente/ *fuente*. 'outside,' 'strength,' 'fountain'	/f/ is pronounced: /fwera/ *fuera*, /fwersa/, *fuerza*, /fwente/*fuente*
Lexical archaisms: mesmo, haiga, ansina/asina 'same,' 'have,' 'this way'	Modernized forms: mismo, haya, así

Table 11.3 English Loan Words/Anglicisms in the SV of Los Angeles

SV of Los Angeles	Monolingual Standard Spanish
yarda (<yard)	*patio, jardín*
marqueta (<market)	*mercado*
taipear (<to type)	*mecanografiar, escribir a máquina*
troca (<truck)	*camión, autobús*
cora (<quarter)	*25 centavos, tostón*
carpeta (<carpet)	*alfombra, tapete*

official institutions devoted to formulating language policy. These institutions are called *academias de la lengua*, 'language academies.' Since the 18th century, they have been dedicated to preserving the integrity of the Spanish language. The Royal Academy has engraved in its emblem, which is reproduced in all its publications, the motto "*limpia, fija y da espeledor,*" 'it cleans [the language], selects [the best forms] and makes it shine' (see Real Academia Española, 2001). In the 20th century, *academias* have directed some of their language policies to "protect" Spanish from English in their countries. The loan words or "Anglicisms" included in Table 11.3 form part of everyday Chicano Spanish vocabulary, but they are highly stigmatized by the *academias de la lengua* and most monolingual speakers of standard Spanish.

Contact with English, in addition to affecting the vocabulary, has triggered grammatical and sociolinguistic changes in the Spanish spoken in the United States. Some of these changes, such as the reduction of contexts in which the subjunctive is used, the redundant use of the subject pronoun, and the restructuring of the aspectual verbs *ser* and *estar* (to be) have been addressed by Silva Corvalán (1994). Different levels of proficiency of Spanish can also be found among bilinguals (see Valdés, 2000). Few bilingual speakers have acquired full grammatical, textual, illocutionary, and sociolinguistic competence. However, it is important to stress that this educated proficiency in Spanish is also rare among monolingual speakers. In fact, in any society, only highly educated monolingual speakers control all sociolinguistic registers, write different types of texts, and are able to understand sophisticated readings. In England, for example, this issue is depicted by George Bernard Shaw in his play *Pygmalion* (1916/1994).

Language instructors should be aware of these facts, since it is not uncommon for Spanish teachers to expect bilingual speakers to know all registers of standard Spanish at almost all levels of competence. Thus, when they find out that most of their heritage students of Spanish know a variant other than standard Spanish, they stigmatize these students by showing intolerance towards the linguistic variant they speak. Most instructors try to force their bilingual students to speak standard Spanish only. Such stigmatization of the SV causes problems for heritage students inside the classroom and out. The heritage students may feel ashamed of their vernacular variant of Spanish and tend to criticize the variant of Spanish spoken by their family members.

The role of the language instructor is therefore crucial in helping students achieve the following: (1) to value the heritage language and (2) to realize that there are two different variants of Spanish, the vernacular and the standard. The instructor can teach the student to use the vernacular in certain contexts (such as the family and the community) and to use the standard in other contexts (including the classroom and monolingual environments). That is, in addition to teaching language, culture, and literature, teachers must also deal with issues of sociolinguistics in the classroom. Thus the role and attitude of Spanish instructors is crucial to preserving the SV of Los Angeles which, likewise, is threatened by English only policies, such as California Proposition 227 (English Language Education for Immigrant Children, 1999) and anti-Hispanic attitudes among the population. Nonetheless, many Spanish speakers of Los Angeles preserve their linguistic heritage by using Spanish at home and with their friends and families. They learn English at school and become bilinguals. It is therefore not unrealistic to talk about stable bilingualism in Los Angeles (Hidalgo, 1987). In the following section, I will address some issues related to what heritage speakers of Spanish know when they arrive in the classroom.

What Heritage Speakers of Spanish Know when They Arrive in the Classroom

In this part of the chapter, I will provide data and make some generalizations on heritage speakers' knowledge of Spanish. This information is based on my findings and on the observations of others who have worked with heritage speakers of Spanish. Because there are as yet few experiments, analyses, or publications that deal with proficiency among bilinguals of Spanish to support my claims, they should be considered tentative. Moreover, I will incorporate the findings of my research on advanced bilingual Spanish speakers, such as Carolina (the adult bilingual speaker whose story I summarized at the beginning of this chapter) and other students at her level. These students live in a Mexican-populated area of Los Angeles County and have been exposed to SV at home and in the community. Most of them did not speak English until they went to an English speaking school at age five. Overall, their proficiency in Spanish corresponds to the ACTFL Advanced level (American Council of the Teaching of Foreign Languages, 1989).

Oral/Aural Proficiency

Carolina and the other students at LBCC, like most bilingual speakers of Spanish, have learned Spanish orally. As a result, their oral/aural proficiency is very high; they have internalized the Spanish phonological system completely, as is common with most bilinguals (Valdés, 2000). The fact that they pronounce some words as in the examples below is due to their exposure to the vernacular variety of Spanish or Chicano Spanish, which preserves some Old Spanish pronunciations that monolinguals stigmatize:

/medesina/ 'medicina', medicine
/dotor/ 'doctor'
/peksi/ 'pepsi'
/asina/ 'así'

Advanced heritage students have mastered the stress and intonation patterns of Spanish. Moreover, their listening skills are advanced. They have little trouble adjusting to the pronunciation of other dialects of Spanish, such as Peninsular or Caribbean Spanish. When I tested their aural skills by showing them videos spoken in Peninsular and Caribbean Spanish, all 120 students tested understood the content completely. Their high level of oral and aural proficiency is related to their exposure to spoken Spanish at a young age.

Grammar

Carolina and the other students, having been exposed to the language at an early age, have internalized the core grammar of Spanish. However, they have difficulty using complex grammatical structures when they speak about topics that are not commonly discussed at home, and discuss these topics at a slower pace than they do familiar topics. Hypothetical situations and abstract concepts are the most difficult for them. As is the case with many bilingual Spanish speakers, they have mastered the pronominal and the prepositional systems. Occasionally they produce clitic-doubling utterances such as:

"*lo vi el libro*" 'I saw it the book'

These utterances reflect their exposure to Los Angeles SV (see Luján & Parodi, 2001). In general, advanced heritage speakers have internalized most tenses, except for the subjunctive in some complex contexts. They have developed a quasi-native grammatical intuition of Spanish. Like most native speakers of any language, they cannot explain why they use one or another tense, pronoun or preposition since most of them do not possess a metalinguistic knowledge of Spanish to explain the rules of grammar. They answer grammatical exercises by applying their intuition to the context rather than by applying consciously learned grammatical rules.

This characteristic, typical of most bilingual speakers of Spanish at all levels, was confirmed by an experiment I conducted with six groups of advanced heritage speakers of Spanish (120 students) at LBCC during the years 1999 and 2001. After I had taught the subjunctive, I tested the students. In the test I asked them to fill in the blanks of an exercise with fifteen sentences that required the subjunctive.

The majority of the students (90%) answered correctly by using the context. In another part of the test, I asked the students to explain the terms *mood* and *subjunctive*. I also asked them to identify the tense used in each sentence. The results were completely different from the cloze exercise, with very few students (15%) answering correctly. Most of them guessed the answers, revealing that they did not know the grammatical concepts. The polarization in the results shows that most heritage speakers learn and expand their knowledge of their heritage language intuitively, without consciously using the rules of grammar, even if they are in an academic environment. Future studies could expand on heritage speakers' intuition by pursuing this line of inquiry.

Vocabulary

Carolina and the other advanced students have a good grasp of Spanish vocabulary. They understand and can speak on a variety of topics such as family, personal issues, school, work, religion, and current events. However, they have lexical gaps in all semantic fields. They solve this problem by paraphrasing, using body language, using English loan words, code switching, or changing topics. Their knowledge of passive vocabulary allows them to understand any monolingual statement or monolingual discourse, even if they cannot reply using vocabulary in the same sociolinguistic register. Like most heritage speakers, these students learn words very quickly and are able to grasp lexical subtleties while reading.

Reading Comprehension

Reading comprehension is a skill that bilinguals develop quickly because Spanish texts are written in the same alphabet as English, and because Spanish spelling is relatively easy for English speakers. In addition, Spanish and English share many cognates whose meaning can be easily grasped by bilinguals. Tests of reading comprehension that I conducted on the 120 bilingual students mentioned above showed that 90% of them understood 100% of what they read. These tests consisted of five questions on writings by monolingual Spanish writers, such as Cervantes, Martí, Carlos Fuentes, Elena Poniatowska, and Guillermo Samperio. The only time that these students had problems with reading comprehension was, as expected, when the texts addressed topics about which they had no world knowledge. Their reading comprehension is usually as sophisticated as that of monolingual speakers of Spanish.

Writing

Writing is the most difficult part of language for heritage speakers to acquire because, on the one hand, their knowledge of Spanish is oral and, on the other hand, they became literate in English only. These two factors show up consistently in their writing. As I pointed out before, they understand Spanish spelling very easily at the reading level. However, it is difficult for them to write in Spanish without misspellings due to the lack of exposure to written Spanish in the first years of schooling. The most difficult part for them to master is spelling when a sound has several written variants, as in the following instances:

<s,c,z> /s/, <b,v> /b/, <g,j> /x/ , < c,qu> /k/, <ll,y> /y/, <h, o> /o/

It is thus hard for them to internalize the difference between <s,c,z> or to know when they should use <h> For example, the word /aser/ is spelled <hacer> in standard Spanish, with mute <h> and <c>. Thus, it is not unusual to find misspellings such as the following:

<ise > instead of <hice> or <haci> instead of <así>
<caye> instead of <calle>
<lla> instead of <ya>
<bino> instead of <vino>

Very few bilinguals are able to write the stress marks correctly, even after they have learned the accent spelling rules (see *mas* instead of *más* in the next example). Students at the advanced level know the irregular verb forms, but many bilinguals regularize the verb paradigms in examples such as *piensamos*, instead of *pensamos* or *puedemos* instead of *podemos*. In addition, their lack of exposure to academic Spanish is shown in the use of colloquial Spanish in written texts, such as the use of the verb *mirar* instead of *considerar* or *pensar* in the following example written by Georgina, an advanced student of Spanish:

"*La mentalidad de Don Quijote la* **mirarian** *muchos como no muy* **sana,** *pero creo mas bien que es un personaje muy imaginativo y original* " 'Don Quijote's mind could be seen by many as insane, but I believe instead he is very imaginative and original'

The influence of English is evident in spelling, the selection of words and, to a lesser extent, in the syntax of the written texts by bilinguals. Common misspelling examples such as the following show their knowledge of English spelling:

característica for *característica*
philosophia for *filosofía*
effecto for *efecto*

In the example from Georgina, a semantic extension of the word *sano* based on English 'sane' was created instead of using the standard Spanish adjective *cuerdo*. (*Sano* in standard Spanish means 'physically healthy'.) Semantic extensions are very common in the written language of bilinguals, due to their lack of exposure to Spanish academic vocabulary. In the written samples I have gathered from the LBCC students, semantic extensions are the most salient feature of their Spanish

Table 11.4 Use of Semantic Extensions in Writing

Semantic Extension	Context
misinterpretación (<misrepresentation) instead of *malentendido*	La sátira consiste en *misinterpretaciones* 'The satire consists of misinterpretations'
proyecto (<project) instead of *trabajo*	Nunca terminó el *proyecto* que hacía en el sueño 'He never finished the project he was doing in his dream'
experimentar (<experiment) instead of *vivir*	Una amiga mía, la cual sí *experimentó* ese suceso 'A friend of mine who experienced that event'

writing. Other examples of semantic extensions I found in several bilingual students, along with the contexts in which they appeared, are in Table 11.4.

The use of redundant subject pronouns is also a feature common in Chicano Spanish of Los Angeles (Silva Corvalán, 1994; Luján & Parodi, 2001):

Yo creo que yo voy a estudiar historia "I think I will study history " instead of monolingual Spanish: *Creo que voy a estudiar historia.*

Sociolinguistic Competence

Most advanced heritage students are able to take turns in a conversation, interrupt, and argue. They use formal and informal pronouns *usted* and *tú* with the corresponding verbal forms at home and in the neighborhood following the Spanish rules of politeness. However, their vocabulary selection is sociolinguistically awkward in monolingual and standard Spanish environments. For example, they may choose to say "*Qué padre falda!*" 'what a cool skirt!' to an older lady that they have just met, or to the principal of the school, when they should have said "*Qué bonita falda!*" 'what a pretty skirt!,' which is the appropriate form in that context.

As previously mentioned, heritage speakers of Spanish use the vernacular in monolingual and in formal environments. For example, they may use the following stigmatized words in monolingual environments: *mesmo* 'same,' *haiga* 'present subjunctive of to have,' *ansina* 'this way.' These stigmatized words cause a strong negative reaction from their interlocutors in monolingual countries, such as Mexico, or in the classroom. This reaction surprises bilingual speakers because they are unaware of the dialectal difference between the vernacular *mesmo, haiga* and *ansina* and standard Spanish *mismo, haya* and *así*. In order to avoid a difficult situation for bilinguals, the Spanish instructor may teach heritage speakers the differences between the vernacular and standard Spanish as a sociolinguistic topic in a classroom environment.

Finally, when bilingual speakers are together, they code switch, which is a normal way of communicating for bilingual speakers (see for example Zentella,

1997; Urciuoli, 1998). Thus, a sentence like the following is common among Chicano speakers: "Hola bato, mi vieja se enojó conmigo because I got home at 3 am" (Hi buddy, my mother was upset with me because I got home at 3 am.")

Culture

Chicano culture has features in common with Mexican civilization, but it has characteristics of its own as well. It is customary that in the classroom, Mexican culture is considered paradigmatic by instructors who teach language and culture to heritage speakers in Los Angeles. The cultural differences between Mexicans and Chicanos are usually ignored. However, on the few occasions that Chicano culture is discussed, there are reactions of bewilderment and criticism among non-Chicano students and Spanish instructors. Outside the classroom, Mexican middle-class monolinguals have the same negative response to Chicano culture. They often react as if Chicano culture were a misconception of Mexican culture.

Through my research, I have found four main differences between the two cultures: extensions, omissions, syncretism, and creations.

Extensions

Several Chicano cultural idiosyncrasies are extensions of Mexican manners applied to new contexts. For instance, religious events such as first communion are sometimes celebrated with a big party where *tamales* are served. As an extension of this custom, California Chicanos usually celebrate Christmas by serving *tamales*, whereas in Mexico Christmas is typically commemorated with a turkey dinner. Another extension of Mexican culture is the great importance given to *5 de mayo* in Chicano culture, which commemorates the triumph of the Mexicans over the French invaders in Puebla. In Mexico, however, this is a minor holiday. The most important non-religious holiday in Mexico is *16 de septiembre*, which celebrates the independence of Mexico from Spain. This holiday is not typically celebrated in Chicano culture.

Omissions

Traditional Mexican *posadas,* parties in which the guests sing and reenact the birth of Christ, do not take place in California, and *mole*, a special sauce that is eaten with turkey or chicken to solemnize important events, is not as popular in Chicano culture as it is in Mexico.

Syncretism

Some new practices reflect syncretism of Chicano culture with other cultures in the United States or certain regions of Mexico. For example, funerals may have

mariachis, who sing non-religious music, to honor the deceased in Chicano culture, as it is done sometimes in the northern but not in the central part of Mexico.
Black communities in Los Angeles frequently have non-religious music in their
funerals. Thus, the use of music in Chicano funerals can be seen as an example
of syncretism with the African-American population of Los Angeles.

Creations

Finally, there are original creations exclusive to the Southwest, such as the myth
of *Aztlán,* in which the Southwest is portrayed as the place of origin of the Aztecs.
The *pocho* and the *pachuco*, Mexican American male characters that code switch
while speaking and dress in an oversized suit respectively, are also Chicano creations (see Hernández, 1990, for details). Finally, low riders, old cars colorfully
decorated on the outside, are Chicano inventions as well.

When Carolina talked about these Chicano cultural practices during her trip
in Mexico, people looked at her in a puzzled way and made her feel uncomfortable by telling her that these were strange customs. In the United States, most
students of Spanish as a second language are also unfamiliar with the Chicano
culture, since in the classroom and in textbooks the culture of monolingual
Hispanic countries is emphasized.[3]

A Model of Language Teaching for Heritage Speakers

In what follows I will propose a model of Spanish language teaching for Chicano
bilingual speakers. This model is designed to help heritage speakers of Spanish
learn to write and use standard Spanish in formal contexts. At the same time, it
aims to help them maintain their vernacular speech in some contexts and use
standard Spanish in others. In addition to addressing linguistic and sociolinguistic issues, the proposed model also addresses the psychological issues that
most heritage speakers face.

According to this model, the linguistic aspect of the Spanish class for heritage
speakers should include grammar, vocabulary, writing, reading, speaking, and
listening. In addition, it should include sociolinguistics and cultural studies.
In the area of sociolinguistics, heritage speakers should be made aware of the
main features of bilingualism, such as code switching, lexical borrowing, and
semantic extensions, which are typical among bilinguals. The ideal curriculum
should include areas of emphasis discussed below.

Psychological and Attitudinal Issues

As I have discussed at length at the beginning of this chapter, these issues must
be addressed in the classroom to help heritage speakers overcome the awkward-
ness they often feel when speaking Spanish. Here I include the two most salient
issues, but there could be more:

1. *Insecurity.* Most heritage speakers need help overcoming the insecurity they feel in Spanish academic environments because their exposure to Spanish is mostly oral. They need to receive positive reinforcement in the classroom from their instructors. Instructors will explain to them how languages are acquired by natives, the advantages of being bilingual, and the notion of linguistic intuition. Learning about the origins of the Spanish language in Latin America and its strong relation to their vernacular is crucial in this model.

2. *Stigma.* Heritage speakers need guidance to deal with the psychological effects of the stigma attached to their vernacular speech, which is quite strong among Spanish monolinguals and Spanish instructors. This can be done through discussion and debate.

Main Features of Bilingualism

Code switching, lexical borrowing, and semantic extensions are typical of bilingual speech, and students should be aware that monolingual speakers tend to stigmatize these features. Heritage students need to know when it is appropriate use these features and how to deal with the stigma attached to them.

Linguistic aspects

1. *Grammar.* Bilinguals have internalized the blueprint of Spanish grammar through exposure during childhood. This internalized grammar is demonstrated in their ability to fill in blanks in exercises on topics they did not study in a Spanish class. To help bilingual students structure their existing knowledge of Spanish and acquire academic Spanish, the instructor should present grammar as a metalinguistic and analytical subject. The process of learning grammar is different for students of Spanish as L2 than it is for heritage speakers. While foreign language students employ grammar to have access to the language, heritage speakers use the language to have access to the grammar. In other words, the learning process is the opposite in second language students and heritage speakers. Heritage students can acquire explicit knowledge of grammar when they are able to draw on their already existing knowledge of the language. For example, in classes for heritage students, the subjunctive can be elicited by using key words such as *ojalá* ("I wish") or *quizás* ("I wish" or "maybe"), terms that usually require subjunctive forms. Then, after learning the subject pronoun paradigms and the tenses of the subjunctive, these students will be able to organize, analyze and use all the paradigms of the subjunctive, as presented in grammars, very easily.

2. *Vocabulary.* Exercises devoted to the subtleties of the meaning of words, as well as exposure to topics that are not usually addressed in Spanish

spoken contexts in the U.S., will enable heritage speakers to expand their vocabulary.

3. *Writing*. This aspect should be stressed more than others, since heritage speakers' exposure to Spanish is mostly oral. Writing practice must include accents, spelling, punctuation, and writing styles.

4. *Reading*. Heritage speakers should be exposed to a variety of texts that will expand their knowledge of Spanish culture, vocabulary, and written structures. Summarizing short readings will help students learn these three aspects of written Spanish.

5. *Speaking*. Heritage speakers must practice speaking in the classroom to debate and express themselves using academic and formal speech in standard Spanish, as well as informal speech in monolingual and bilingual contexts, using colloquial Spanish and Chicano Spanish.

6. *Listening*. To familiarize students with the different registers of Spanish, listening exercises should include samples of a range of situations using various styles of speech.

Sociolinguistics

The curriculum should include basic principles of regional and social variation, language change, diglossia, standardization, the use of registers, language attitudes, code switching, borrowing, and semantic extensions. All these aspects should be dealt with in their social context. The correlation between language use and society should be made clear.

Cultural Studies

Habits shape the identity of the people who practice them. Learning both the local Hispanic culture in the United States and other Hispanic cultures outside the country deepens heritage speakers' self-knowledge and broadens their perspective of the Hispanic world. Such knowledge empowers them, makes them proud of their roots, and helps them overcome their insecurities. Their curriculum must address the main features of the culture of Spanish speaking countries, including Spain and all Latin American countries. Chicano culture and the Caribbean culture of the United States should be taught in detail. Students should learn literature, history, and art, as well as popular culture, lifestyle, and customs of the Hispanic world both inside and outside the United States, including Christmas celebrations, burials, fashion, national holidays, and other cultural aspects mentioned above.

Summary and Conclusions

In this chapter, I have addressed several issues related to Chicano Spanish or the SV spoken in the Los Angeles area, including its origins, its features, and who

Table 11.5 Relative Language Proficiency of Spanish Speakers

	Educated Native Speaker	Superior	Advanced	Intermediate			Novice
				High	Mid.	Low	
Oral Proficiency	*	+			<		
Grammatical Usage	*		+	<			
Metalinguistic Knowledge	*		<				+
Grammatical Intuition	*		+	<			
Informal Vocabulary	*		+	<			
Academic Vocabulary	*		<		+		
Reading	*	+	<				
Writing	*			<		+	
Socio-linguistics	*		+	<			
Chicano Culture	N/A	+				<	
Mexican Culture	*		+	<			

Key: * Mexican educated native speakers
+ Chicano advanced heritage speakers
< Advanced L2 speakers

speaks it. I have also proposed that heritage speakers should be taught Spanish in a manner different from that used for L2 students since there are clear differences among native speakers of Spanish, heritage speakers, and L2 learners at the advanced level. Table 11.5, modeled on Campbell and Rosenthal (2000), summarizes the knowledge of Spanish that these three types of speakers possess.

I have shown contexts in which heritage speakers' non-standard variant of Spanish is stigmatized. I have also indicated the psychological outcome of the stigma and the main issues that heritage speakers have to deal with when learning Spanish in an academic environment. Finally, I have presented a model of language teaching for heritage speakers that takes these issues into consideration and includes both standard Spanish and the SV. In my proposal, I suggest that both linguistic variants must be used in complementary distribution, depending on the circumstances and the interlocutors. The model I propose aims to alleviate some of the issues Chicano bilinguals have to deal with both inside the classroom and out.

Notes

1. A Chicano (female, Chicana) refers to a person born in the United States of Mexican ancestry.
2. This figure is based on the population in the counties of Los Angeles, San Bernardino, Orange, and Ventura. The percentage of Hispanics to the total population differs in each county.
3. There are some exceptions, such as Samaniego, Alarcón, Ohara, & Rojas (2001), which includes substantial coverage of Hispanics in the United States.

References

Allen, J. P., & Turner, E. (1997). *The ethnic quilt: Population diversity in Southern California*. Northridge: California State University.

American Council on the Teaching of Foreign Languages. (1989). *ACTFL proficiency guidelines.* Hastings on Hudson, NY: Author.

Bortoni-Ricardo, S. M. (1985). *The urbanization of rural dialect speakers: A sociolinguistic study in Brazil.* Cambridge, UK: Cambridge University Press.

Campbell, R. N., & Rosenthal, J. W. (2000). Heritage languages. In J. W. Rosenthal (Ed.), *Handbook of undergraduate second language education* (pp. 165–184). Mahwah, NJ: Lawrence Erlbaum.

Chomsky, N. (1972). *Language and mind.* New York: Harcourt Brace Jovanovich.

English Language Education for Immigrant Children. (1999). 1.3 California Education Code §§ 300–340 (1999).

Giles, H., & Smith, P. (1979). Accommodation theory: Optimal levels of convergence. In H. Giles & R. Saint Clair (Eds.), *Language and social psychology* (pp. 45–65). London: Blackwell.

Hernández, G. (1990). *Chicano satire.* Austin: Texas University Press.

Hidalgo, M. (1987). Español mexicano y español chicano: Problemas y propuestas fundamentales. *Language Problems and Language Planning, 11,* 166–193.

Lapesa, R. (1981). *Historia de la lengua española.* Madrid: Gredos.

Luján, M., & Parodi, C. (2001). Clitic-doubling and the acquisition of agreement, Spanish. In J. Gutierrez-Rexach & L. Silva-Villar (Eds.), *Current issues in Spanish syntax and semantics* (pp. 193–220). New York: Mouton de Gruyter.

Parodi, C. (1995). *Orígenes del español americano.* Mexico City: Universidad Nacional Autónoma de México, Instituto de Investigaciones Filológicas.

Parodi, C. (1999). Koinización e historia: la sincronía, ventana de la diacronía. *Boletín de Filología, 37,* 915–931.

Parodi, C. (2003). Contacto de dialectos del español en Los Ángeles. In G. Perissinotto ed. *Ensayos de lengua y pedagogía.* Santa Barbara: University of California Linguistic Minority Research Institute, 23–38.

Real Academia Española (2001). *Diccionario de la lengua española.* Madrid: Real Academia Española.

Samaniego, F., Alarcón, F. X., Ohara, M., & Rojas, N. (2001). *Mundo 21* (edición alternativa). Boston: Houghton Mifflin.

Shaw, G. B. (1916/1994). *Pygmalion.* New York: Dover Publications.

Siegel, J. (1985). Koines and koinezation. *Language and Society, 14,* 357–378.

Silva Corvalán, C. (1994). *Language contact and change: Spanish in Los Angeles.* New York: Oxford University Press.

U.S. Census 2000. (n.d.). *Summary File 3 – Sample Data.* [Total Population: Total and Total Population: Hispanic and Latino, Los Angeles, Orange, San Bernardino, and Ventura Counties, California.] Available at: http://www.census.gov.

Urciuoli, B. (1998). *Exposing prejudice.* Boulder, CO: Westview Press.

Valdés, G. (2000). Bilingualism and language use among Mexican Americans. In S. L. McKay & S-L. C. Wong (Eds.), *New immigrants in the United States* (pp. 99–136). Cambridge: Cambridge University Press.

Zentella, A. C. (1997). *Growing up bilingual: Puerto Rican children in New York.* Malden, MA: Blackwell.

12

A Profile of Japanese Heritage Learners and Individualized Curriculum

MASAKO O. DOUGLAS

The Heritage Language Research Priorities Conference Report (University of California, Los Angeles, 2001) addresses a pressing need for a research agenda for heritage languages. The report identifies seven areas as essential to heritage language education: the heritage speaker, the family, the community, a language-specific focus, policies, programs, and assessment.

This case study focuses on two of those research areas, the heritage speaker and the program, and presents a profile of the students enrolled in an intermediate course in Japanese for heritage speakers (JHL) offered at the University of California, Los Angeles in 2000 and 2001. This chapter includes (1) the results of language background and linguistic ability surveys of these learners, (2) a description of an individualized curriculum designed for these learners, and (3) an assessment of the curriculum's effectiveness.

Student Profiles

Language Background

At the beginning of the spring term of 2000 and 2001, students in Intermediate Japanese for heritage speakers (six students for 2000, eight students for 2001) completed a survey on language background, consisting of 21 questions organized into five categories: (1) home languages and language shift; (2) self-assessment of language proficiency in four skills; (3) students' and their parents' place of birth, age of entry and length of stay in the United States; (4) history of formal instruction in the Japanese language; and (5) reasons for studying Japanese. Table 12.1 shows the learners' home languages before and after beginning school.

These students generally used Japanese exclusively before starting school and shifted to using Japanese and English once they began school. Students commonly reported that they used English with their siblings and Japanese with one or both parents.

Table 12.2 shows the results of students' self-assessment of their skills in Japanese and English.

Table 12.1 Home Languages

	Japanese only	Japanese and other languages[a]	English only	English and other languages
2000 (n=6)				
Home languages before schooling	3	3	0	0
Home languages after schooling	1	5	0	0
2001 (n=8)				
Home languages before schooling	2	5	1	0
Home languages after schooling [a]	0	6	1	1

[a]The question of home languages for the class of 2001 is complicated: two learners spoke Korean or Chinese at home before schooling, and one learner started speaking Spanish in addition to Japanese and English after schooling started. One learner stopped using Japanese after entering elementary school and spearation from his Japanese father.

The results indicate that the learners have underdeveloped literacy skills in Japanese. The learners ranked their Japanese oral skills higher than their literacy skills, and all rated themselves highly for all skills in English. Five learners in the class of 2000 reported that they first learned literacy skills in English, and one reported that he first learned to read and write in Japanese. In the class of 2001, five out of eight students learned to read and write in English before Japanese. The other three learners reported that they first learned to read and write in Japanese, Spanish, or Japanese and English simultaneously.

Table 12.2 Self-Assessment of Language Skills

Class of Spring 2000 (n=6)

	very good - - - | - - - - | - - - not good at all			
Japanese				
Listening	1	5	0	0
Speaking	0	4	2	0
Reading	0	2	3	1
Writing	0	2	3	1
English				
Listening	6	0	0	0
Speaking	5	1	0	0
Reading	5	1	0	0
Writing	5	1	0	0

Class of Spring 2001 (n=8)

	very good - - - | - - - - | - - - not good at all			
Japanese				
Listening	4	4	0	0
Speaking	1	6	1	0
Reading	0	3	5	0
Writing	0	1	6	1
English				
Listening	6	2	0	0
Speaking	6	2	0	0
Reading	6	2	0	0
Writing	6	2	0	0

Table 12.3 Formal Instruction on Japanese

Class	JHL School	School for Returnees	High School	College	Tutor	None
2000	2	2	1	2	0	0
2001	2	2	1	2	1	2

Note: The number represents the students who studied at JHL schools, Japanese schools for returnees, high schools, community colleges, and four-year colleges.

Responses to the questionnaire also reveal that at least one parent of each student was born and grew up in Japan. A majority of the learners was U.S. born; three were born outside the United States but entered the country before formal schooling (two learners) or at third grade (one learner). Most students had some formal education in Japanese, either at heritage language schools (HS), at schools for returnees to Japan, and/or in Japanese courses in high school or college (see Table 12.3). Some students went to more than one type of school.

The last question in the survey asks the learners to indicate all their reasons for studying Japanese. Some learners chose multiple answers. Table 12.4 shows that their reasons were evenly distributed between integrative motivation (e.g., an interest in the Japanese language, in Japanese culture, and in speaking Japanese with friends and relatives) and instrumental motivation (to learn Japanese for their career). Only one learner took the course as a requirement. These results can be interpreted as an indicator of learners' high motivation to learn Japanese.

The data show that after entering school, 11 out of 14 learners (78.6%) began speaking two (Japanese and English) or three languages (Japanese, English, and another language). While they have confidence in their knowledge of English as an academic language and as a tool for communication with siblings, they are not as confident of their knowledge of Japanese, which they speak with their parents. They feel especially deficient in literacy skills, despite having studied Japanese since early childhood.

One reason for the underdevelopment of Japanese literacy skills is likely to be the limited exposure to Japanese as an academic language, particularly for those who attended Japanese heritage schools or studied Japanese as a foreign language (JFL) at the college level. Although the children at the schools for returnees to Japan are educated in an immersion setting, they attend Japanese school for only six hours every Saturday. Moreover, due to the intensive curriculum, many children drop out of these schools by grade three or four. During the past four years, only three students in heritage Japanese courses at UCLA had studied up to the high school level at these schools. Students who attended weekend

Table 12.4 Reasons for Studying Japanese

Class	Interested in Language	Interested in Culture	Speak with Friends/ Relatives	Required	Career	Speak with Mother	Live in Japan	Other
2000	5	4	5	1	4	1	0	0
2001	5	6	5	3	6	0	1	2

Table 12.5 Language Proficiency Test Results[a]

	Range	Mean	SD
Grammar	81– 96	89	11
Listening	88 – 100	94	6
Reading	45 – 82	65	4
Kanji Writing	0 – 65	18	20
Kanji Reading	0 – 96	47	38

[a]2000 and 2001 heritage learners, combined.

Japanese schools for returnees to Japan had more highly developed literacy skills than students who attended other schools, because the curriculum of returnees' schools is content-based and intended for native speakers of Japanese.

Language Proficiency

The test scores of the 12 heritage learners who were placed in a heritage course in 1999 show a range of competencies and proficiencies (Table 12.5). This variation presents a challenge for curriculum design, which must accommodate the needs of all learners. The scores distribute in a narrow range for grammar and listening, but across a wide range for writing and reading kanji.[1] Learners are deficient in their knowledge of kanji.

A comparison of the scores shows that they distribute widely in both groups from zero to 77 out of 100 ($M = 37.5$, SD 38) in the class of 2000, and from zero to 100 ($M = 39$, SD 33.25 in the class of 2001. The average scores of these two groups were lower than that of the Intermediate JFL (51.5), which means that the reading ability of JHL students is lower that that of JFL students.

The ACTFL Oral Proficiency Interview (OPI) was administered to all JHL students in Spring 2001 by a certified tester. The results are shown in Table 12.6.

The OPI results indicate that the heritage learners in this group had highly developed oral skills. Their oral proficiency was higher by far than that of the Intermediate level students who learned Japanese as a foreign language; even the lowest score (Intermediate High) was higher than the JFL students' scores.

However, in contrast with their oral proficiency results, the heritage learners' cloze test scores were lower than the JFL learners' scores, 39 and 51.5, respectively. A cloze test requires linguistic manipulation and assesses language proficiency closely related to the development of literacy skills (Cummins, 1980). A

Table 12.6 Oral Proficiency Interview Results

Levels	Number of Learners
Superior	5
Advanced High	1
Advanced	1
Intermediate High	1

comparison of the oral proficiency level and cloze scores of the heritage learners with the Intermediate-level JFL learners showed that the heritage learners had a highly developed natural communicative proficiency and underdeveloped cognitive/academic language proficiency (CALP) (Cummins, 1980).

In summary, the emerging profile of these heritage learners is that their competence in basic interpersonal communication skills is remarkably higher than that of students who studied Japanese as a foreign language for several years. As the test results show, competence varied greatly, especially in literacy skills (basic kanji knowledge, sophisticated use of kango, and reading and writing).

It has been suggested that heritage learners of other languages exhibit characteristics similar to Japanese heritage learners (for example, for the characteristics of Spanish heritage learners, see Valdés, 1995; Valdés & Geoffrion-Vinci, 1998). Curricula for heritage learners should be designed with these characteristics kept in mind, and should accommodate the different needs of individual learners. Such a curriculum is described in the following section.

An Individualized Curriculum

Rationale for Curriculum Development

The rationale for developing a course for learners of Japanese as a heritage language is as follows:

1. As the test results show, HL learners have a different type of language competence than JFL learners: HL students have greater interpersonal communication skills and underdeveloped CALP.
2. HL learners' needs differ individually according to differences in their knowledge of Chinese characters and vocabulary, literacy skills, formal register, and stylistic variations in oral and written language.
3. Instructional time for this course is limited to one quarter (ten weeks), which is not enough to improve underdeveloped language skills. Students need to continue their language study by themselves after completing the course, and the curriculum therefore must include strategies for autonomous learning.

Goals of the Course

The curricular goals are for heritage learners to:

1. Strengthen their underdeveloped language competence, including kanji knowledge and written and oral knowledge of formal registers.
2. Acquire procedural knowledge (i.e., how to learn) and factual knowledge (i.e., what to learn), and use that knowledge to continue learning Japanese by themselves after completion of the course.

Course Overview

For individualized learning, the course used the Internet for material selection, a computer program called JWPce for kanji and vocabulary learning, and a portfolio for assessment. This chapter briefly describes the course, but for a more detailed course description and rationale for using portfolio assessment, please refer to Douglas (1999, 2002).

The course was offered in the spring quarter. It met for two 1.5-hour sessions a week over ten weeks. All sessions were conducted in Japanese. One session per week was used for lectures and practice, with a focus on strategies for learning kanji and recognition and production of a formal register in oral and written language. Sessions were held to provide learners with effective strategies for kanji learning, and to reduce their anxiety about learning kanji. Moreover, the course incorporated learning strategies into instruction. Specifically, the students were assigned to read a book (Douglas, 2001) designed for self-instruction in kanji, which also teaches learning strategies. Students were also required to keep a check list of the strategies they used when learning kanji in reading assignments. They were also taught about registers, and classroom activities were designed to call on the use of various registers.

One session per week was conducted in a computer lab. For that session each learner chose reading materials from the Internet and selected kanji to learn. Learners studied their target kanji using a computer program called JWPce, which provides a number of learning tools, including an on-line dictionary, kanji information and a kanji frequency counter. Kanji quizzes and oral interview tests were created for each learner.

Assessment of Learner Progress

Learner progress was assessed over the ten-week term with the Kanji Diagnosis Test Strategy Inventory of Kanji Learning (Douglas, 1998), and cloze tests. The results of the pre-tests also provided diagnostic information about learners' language competence upon enrollment in the course. The results of these assessments are presented in the following sections.

Kanji Diagnosis Pre-/Post-Tests

To measure learners' knowledge of kanji, the Kanji Diagnosis Test (Kano Shimizu, Takanaka, Ishii, & Akutsu,1993) was administered at the beginning and end of the course. The test assesses 13 aspects of kanji knowledge: meaning, internal structure, shape (radicals), writing single kanji, writing compound kanji, making choice from context, parts of speech, conjugation, reading from context, reading single kanji (Japanese reading), reading compound kanji (Chinese reading), homophones and phonetics, and word boundaries.[2] The results are shown in Table 12.7.

Table 12.7 Kanji Diagnosis Tests

	Pre-test Mean	Post-test Mean
Spring 2000 (n = 6)	64.4	74.9
Spring 2001 (n = 8)	45.0	52.5

Table 12.8 Strategy Inventory of Kanji Learning

	Pre-test		Post-test	
	Mean	SD	Mean	SD
Spring 2000 (n = 6)	46.2	37.0	53.3	33.1
Spring 2001 (n = 8)	50.6	23.4	54.8	20.9

Note: Total score is 100.

All students scored better in the post-test, and the difference between the pre-test and post-test results is statistically significant in the class of 2000 ($t = 1.94$, $df = 5$, $p = .002$). The test results of the year 2001 are not statistically significant at the level of .001, but the post-test scores are higher than the pre-test scores ($t = -3.440$, $df = 7$, $p = .011$). The learners significantly improved their kanji ability over ten weeks.

Kanji Learning Strategies Pre-/Post-Tests

The Strategy Inventory of Kanji Learning (Douglas, 1998) was administered at the beginning and end of the quarter. Average scores of the post-tests are higher than the pre-test scores for both groups (see Table 12.8). Although the statistical analysis sign test for nonparametric repeated measure is not significant ($p = .219$ and $p = .07$, respectively), the learners nonetheless improved their strategies for learning kanji over the course.

Cloze Pre-/Post-Tests

Pre- and post-cloze tests were administered in the spring of 2000 and 2001. The post-test scores in Table 12.9 are significantly higher than the pre-test scores ($p = 0.12$) in 2000. The post-test scores are higher than the pre-test scores in 2001 as well, although the difference is not statistically significant ($p = .213$).

As a basis for comparison, cloze tests were administered to 27 students who completed Intermediate Japanese as a foreign language in Spring 2000 and

Table 12.9 Cloze Tests

	Pre-test Mean	Post-test Mean
Spring 2000 (n = 5)[a]	37.5	45.5
Spring 2001 (n = 8)	39.06	45.83

[a]One of the learners did not take the test.
[b]Total score is 100.

2001. To increase the validity of the test, morpheme-level rational deletion and acceptable scoring were used (Douglas, 1994). Their average score was 51.5 out of 100.

Awareness Training in Strategy Use and Kanji Knowledge

This study examines the relationship between awareness training in strategy use and the development of kanji knowledge. The curriculum aimed at increasing learners' awareness of their own learning characteristics and improving their knowledge of Japanese.

During the course, the learners were instructed to focus on some strategies from their checklist every time they learned kanji and vocabulary. The frequency of strategy use for learning kanji was counted for each learner, and areas of kanji knowledge that showed an increase in post-test scores in the kanji diagnostic test were selected. Rank orders of the frequency of the strategies used and items in the kanji test were then compared. The correspondence between kanji learning strategies and kanji knowledge in the diagnostic test is shown in Appendix 12.1. The strategies and corresponding kanji knowledge found in the kanji test were assigned the same number for rank order comparison.

Spearman's *rho* correlation between these two variables is not significant, except in the case of one learner (learner #1, $r = 0.66$, $p = 0.02$). However, the strategies learned over the course are associated with an increase of the scores of items in the kanji diagnosis test related to the given strategies (Table 12.10).

Table 12.10 Correlation between Kanji Learning Strategies and Knowledge

Learner #	Strategies Used	Aspects of Kanji Knowledge
Spring 2000		
1	4, 7, 8, 9	2, 7, 8, 9
2	4, 3, 8, 9	2, 3, 5, 8
3	2, 3, 4, 8, 9	3, 4, 6, 9
4	8, 9	2, 3, 4, 5, 7, 8
5	3, 7, 8, 9	4, 7, 8
6	2, 3, 7, 8, 9	2, 4, 5, 6, 8, 9
Spring 2001		
1	8, 9, 4, 7, 6	1, 8, 7
2	8, 4, 6, 7, 9, 3	5, 1, 4, 8, 3
3	4, 9, 8	4, 5, 8
4	8, 4, 9, 3	2, 8, 1, 4
5	8	7, 2, 8
6	8, 4, 6	8, 2, 3, 6, 9, 1
7	8, 4, 9, 3, 7	6, 9
8	8, 9, 6	2, 1, 4, 8

Note: Strategies are listed by number in Appendix 12.1; Aspects of kanji knowledge are listed by number in Appendix 12.2. Strategies and aspects for each learner are reported in frequency order (greatest to least).

Among the strategies, strategy #8 *Learn On yomi (Chinese reading)* and *Learn Kun yomi (Japanese reading)* is ranked highly in five out of six learners' check lists in the class of 2000 and all eight check lists in the class of 2001.

Further analysis reveals that learners' use of Strategy Number 8 contributed to an increase in the post-diagnosis test scores in the items reading single kanji (Japanese reading), reading compound kanji (Chinese reading), homophone and phonetic knowledge. All items involve sound-related knowledge.

Effectiveness of the Curriculum

Kanji knowledge, which is crucial to the development of literacy skills in Japanese, is difficult to acquire. The purpose of this study was to examine the effectiveness of instruction in kanji and supporting learning strategies, and whether the curriculum goals were achieved. In spite of the small sample size, the encouraging results of direct measurements of kanji knowledge and self-reports on strategic knowledge suggest that the curriculum achieved its intended goal. It appears that the learners strengthened their language competence through individualized learning using effective strategies. The cloze test scores revealed that 8 out of 14 learners improved their reading ability by the end of the course. The learners reported that they learned formal vocabulary, which is related to kanji knowledge.

Theory on second and foreign language acquisition views strategic competence as a major component of language ability (Bachman, 1990; Bachman & Palmer, 1996); Canale & Swain, 1980; Celce-Murcia, Dörnyei, & Thurrell, 1995). Research has been conducted in second language learning strategies and categorization of strategies, the effect of training in language learning strategies on second and foreign language acquisition, and variables that affect the use of language learning strategies (Bialystock, 1981; O'Malley & Chamot, 1990; Oxford, 1989, 1990; Oxford & Crookall, 1989; Oxford & Nyikos, 1989; Politzer & McGroarty, 1985; Rubin, 1975). Studies report that training language students to use learning strategies is effective (Bourke, 1997; Carrell, Pharis, & Liberto, 1989; O'Malley, Chamot, Stewner-Manzanares, Russo, & Kupper, 1985).

The curriculum presented in this study was created to raise learners' awareness of their learning characteristics (i.e., training of procedural knowledge) as they learned Japanese. The frequency analysis of the strategies used and of items in the kanji diagnosis test, which showed an increase in the post-test scores, suggests some correlation, although statistical significance is not found. Learners reported, however, that they found effective ways of learning kanji and planned to continue using them.

The results of this study suggest that if instruction is individualized so that the learners can focus on areas needing improvement, then learning occurs effectively but differently for each student. The examined areas in this case study are limited to the development of kanji knowledge, kanji learning strategies, and reading ability. Future studies need to measure learners' reading ability with a large sample by a cloze test and other assessments, such as analysis of learners' recall of a reading passage, measurement of writing ability and development of formal register and stylistic differences in oral and written language.

Notes

1. In the reading test, in order to prevent kanji knowledge from influencing students' reading scores, all kanji were presented in yomigana syllabary, which represents the sounds of kanji.
2. Appendices 12.1 and 12.2 summarize the test's dimensions of and correspondence between test results and learning strategies.

Appendix 12.1 Kanji Learning Strategies

1   Learn meaning of each kanji, utilizing mnemonic association and other methods

2   Break kanji into small parts and pay attention to familiar parts of kanji

3   Learn radicals of kanji

4   Write the kanji a few times, paying attention to stroke orders

5   Make a sentence using the target kanji words

6   Pay attention to grammatical usage of the kanji 勉強する (verb) 勉強 (noun)

7   Pay attention to Okurigana (conjugating parts written in hiragana) 買う

8   Pay attention to sound (yomigana) of each kanji

8   Learn On-yomi (Chinese reading) and Kun-yomi (Japanese reading)

8   Learn yomigana of kanji words (words consisting of two or three kanji)

9   Group kanji that have the same On-reading, e.g. 校、講

9   Pay attention to components that have the same sound. 校、交、効

10 Utilize suffixes and prefixes, e.g., kanji related to buildings (館, 室) that appear in movie-theater (映画館) and classroom (教室)

n.a. Associate a new kanji with those you know

n.a. Pay attention to similar looking kanji that share a common component

n.a. Focus on learning synonyms. Paraphrase a target word with other expressions

n.a. Review compound kanji words that have the same kanji, e.g., 便利、利用

Note: Numbers correspond to those in the table of Kanji Diagnosis Test, "na" means corresponding items were not tested in Kanji Diagnosis Test.

Appendix 12.2   Aspects of Kanji Knowledge

1   Meaning of single kanji

2   Internal structure

3   Radical knowledge

4   Writing single kanji

4   Writing compound kanji

5   Making choice from context

6   Part of speech

7   Conjugating parts

8   Sound of kanji (yomigana) in context

8   Sound of single kanji

8   Sound of compound kanji

9   Homophone and phonetic compound

10   Word boundary

Note: Some categories are assigned the same number due to the similarity of construct of kanji knowledge.

References

Bachman, L. (1990). *Fundamental consideration in language testing*. Oxford: Oxford University Press.

Bachman, L., & Palmer, A. (1996). *Language testing in practice*. Oxford: Oxford University Press.

Bialystock, E. (1981). The role of conscious strategies in second language proficiency. *Modern Language Journal, 65*, 24–35.

Bourke, B. (1997) *Maximizing efficiency in the kanji learning task*. Unpublished doctoral dissertation. Department of Asian Languages and Studies, University of Queensland, Australia.

Canale, M., & Swain, M. (1980). Theoretical bases of communicative approaches to second language teaching and testing. *Applied Linguistics, 1*, 1–47.

Carrell, P., Pharis, B. G., & Liberto, J. C. (1989). Meta-cognitive strategy training for ESL reading. *TESOL Quarterly, 23*, 647–678.

Celce-Murcia, M., Dörnyei, Z., & Thurrell, S. (1995). Communicative competence: A pedagogically motivated model in content specification. *Issues in Applied Linguistics, 6*, 5–35.

Cummins, J. (1980). The cross-lingual dimensions of language proficiency: Implications for bilingual education and the optimal age issues. *TESOL Quarterly, 14*, 175–187.

Douglas, M. (2002). Teaching heritage language: Individualized learning. In K. Nakajima (Ed.) *Learning Japanese in the Network* (pp. 145–172). Society. Alberta, Canada: University of Calgary Press.

Douglas, M. (2001). *A practical guide to learning kanji: For learners from an alphabetic background* (2nd ed.). San Francisco: McGraw-Hill.

Douglas, M. O. (1999). Individualized learning utilizing the Internet and JWPce computer program: A case study of heritage Japanese language learners. *Proceedings of the Second International Conference on Computer Assisted System for Teaching and Learning Japanese* (pp.46–51). Toronto: University of Toronto.

Douglas, M. O. (1998). *Strategy inventory of kanji learning*. Unpublished survey form.

Douglas, M. O. (1994). Japanese cloze test: Toward their construction. *Japanese language education around the globe, 4*, 117–131.

Kano, C., Shimizu, Y., Takanaka, H., Ishii, R., & Akutsu, T. (1993). *Intermediate kanji Book: Kanji 1000 plus*. Tokyo: Bonjin-sha Co.

O'Malley, J. M., & Chamot, A. U. (1990). *Learning strategies in second language acquisition*. Cambridge: Cambridge University Press.

O'Malley, J. M., Chamot, A. U., Stewner-Manzanares, G., Russo, R. P., & Kupper, L. (1985). Learning strategy application with students of English as a second language. *TESOL Quarterly, 19,* 557–584.

Oxford, R. L. (1990). *Language Learning Strategies*. New York: Newbury House Publishers.

Oxford, R. L. (1989). Variables affecting choice of language learning strategies by university students. *Modern Language Journal, 73,* 291–300.

Oxford, R. L., & Crookall, D. (1989). Research on language learning strategies: Methods, findings, and instructional issues. *Modern Language Journal, 73,* 404–418.

Oxford, R. L., & Nyikos, M. (1989). Variables affecting choice of language learning strategies by university students. *Modern Language Journal, 73,* 291–300.

Politzer, R. L., & McGroarty, M. (1985). An exploratory study of learning behaviors and their relationship to gain in linguistic and communicative competence. *TESOL Quarterly, 19,* 103–123.

Rubin, J. (1975). What the good language learner can teach us. *TESOL Quarterly, 9,* 41–51.

University of California, Los Angeles. (2001). *Heritage language research priorities conference report*. Los Angeles, CA. Retrieved January 24, 2006, from http://www.cal.org/heritage/involved/hl-prioritiesconf00.pdf

Valdés, G., & Geoffrion-Vinci, M. (1998). Chicano Spanish: The role of the "underdeveloped" code in bilingual repertoires. *Modern Language Journal, 82,* 473–501.

Valdés, G. (1995). The teaching of minority languages as academic subjects: Pedagogical and theoretical challenges. *Modern Language Journal, 79,* 299–328.

III
Program Development and Evaluation

13
From Mirror to Compass
The Chinese Heritage Language Education
Sector in the United States

SCOTT MCGINNIS

Introduction

A review of the last thirty years of U.S. foreign and second language instruction reveals a relatively clear decade-by-decade delineation of the major issues that have shaped curricular, methodological and assessment models. During the 1980s, the focus was on proficiency, both as an organizational principle for program design and, as its more precise and proper use, for student skill assessment. During the 1990s, it was initially national, language-generic, and ultimately state and local language-specific standards that came to serve as the driving force for both the "how" of teaching methodology and the "what" of learning content.

As for the new millennium, it may still be somewhat premature to state absolutely its major issues.[1] Nonetheless, a tremendous amount of energy is being invested in the development of national teacher standards for pre-service training through the National Council for the Accreditation of Teacher Education (NCATE), initial teacher certification through the Interstate New Teacher and Assessment Support Consortium (INTASC), and advanced professional qualification through the National Board for Professional Teaching Standards (NPBTS). It therefore appears that professional development will certainly prove to be one of the critical themes, if not *the* critical theme, for at least the first decade of the 21st century.

One cannot deny the crucial importance of proficiency guidelines, level-by-level standards, and professional development for all foreign and second language instruction, Chinese included. However, even while justifiably focusing our energies and talents on these issues, we have not even begun to efficiently and effectively address the one issue that has had an even more fundamental effect on the ways in which we teach and our students learn Chinese. This is the heritage issue, arising from the growing number of heritage learners in the Chinese classroom and the resulting need to find appropriate methods to address this unique learner population.

Indeed it may be argued that for many of us teaching Chinese in colleges and universities, all of the aforementioned issues—proficiency, standards, and professional development—had at best only a very indirect effect on our instructional lives. For us, the more fundamental issue is Chinese as a heritage language. This issue is clearly evident in the presence of heritage learners in all formal language instructional settings as well as in the so-called heritage "sector" (i.e., Chinese community schools, often referred to as Saturday schools or weekend schools), explicitly recognized by Richard Brecht and the late A. Ronald Walton as one of the language "national capacity sectors" within the United States (1994, p.195). The products of such heritage schools constitute an increasing percentage of American tertiary, secondary and even primary Chinese language programs.

To be sure, there are examples of programmatic innovations within a handful of higher educational institutions that have at once enhanced their ability to meet American national and international language needs while at the same time responding to the unique skills of their resident heritage learner population. A potential model for such a learner-responsive, university-level Chinese language program (McGinnis, 1996) was first proposed in the mid 1990s. More recent, and even more flexible and innovative approaches include the "Penless Chinese Language Learning" approach to developing literacy skills among heritage learners currently underway at the City University of New York-Baruch College ("Penless Chinese," 2004). In these, as well as in other cases, attention has been focused upon heritage language learner populations that, as Brecht and Walton (1994) suggest, are unique in their "potential to supply language capacity without instruction" (p. 195–96).

However, this chapter will not focus on what has traditionally served as the "mainstream" setting for Chinese language education in the United States, i.e., colleges and universities. Instead, it will focus on the heritage language educational sector, which over the past several decades has replaced both the college/university and K–12 sectors as the majority provider for American Chinese language instruction. Consider the following data from the close of the previous and beginning of the current centuries:

- As reported by Brod and Welles (2000), the 1998 survey of foreign language enrollments at institutions of higher education conducted by the Modern Language Association (MLA) charted Chinese (Mandarin) enrollments in American colleges and universities at 28,456 students, up 7.5% since 1995 (p. 21). Comparable trends seen since the late 1980s have continued and in fact accelerated at the beginning of the 21st century, with tertiary institutional enrollments in Chinese language courses in the fall of 2002 at 34,153—up 20% in four years (Welles, 2004).
- Also in 1998, the annual count of K–12 enrollments, as documented by the Geraldine R. Dodge-funded Secondary School Chinese Language Center (SSCLC) at Princeton University was 19,852—up a staggering 130% since 1995 (2002, p. 5). Unlike the MLA, the SSCLC conducted its enrollment survey on an annual basis until its unfortunate cessation of operation in

the fall of 2002. Thus, we do have even more recent solid numbers for the fall of 2001, at which time total K–12 Chinese language course enrollment was stated to be 23,900—almost three times greater than the pre-collegiate enrollment figures from a mere six years earlier (p. 5).

- Arguably the least firmly documented, but nonetheless overwhelmingly compelling, are the heritage school numbers. According to Hai-Yu Bien, Vice-President of the Taiwan-immigrant-predominant National Council of Associations of Chinese Language Schools (NCACLS), the most recent survey data from the summer of 2007 confirmed an approximate enrollment of over 80,000 students from pre-school to pre-collegiate levels (personal communication, 2007). As reported by both former and current leaders of the Mainland-oriented Chinese Schools Association in the United States (CSAUS), reliable estimates from the beginning of the 2007–2008 academic year suggest a count of between 60,000 and 70,000 students (personal communication, 2007). Once again, given these prior figures and clearly observable national trends with regard to the development of heritage schools, there is every reason to safely assert an estimate of a combined total (from NCACLS and CSAUS programs) of at least 140,000, and more likely closer to 150,000 students in the year 2007.

So, even on the most conservative projected basis, pre-collegiate Chinese language enrollment accounts for at least 80% of the Chinese language course enrollment in the United States. Well over 70% of that instruction is provided in the Chinese heritage sector. Put in other more historical terms, over the course of the past three decades, the Chinese heritage language sector has moved from a largely insular or peripheral status in American second/foreign language education to being the largest provider of Chinese language teaching in the United States. While comparable patterns have been observed for a number of Less Commonly Taught Languages (LCTLs), most notably Korean, none of them can claim the degree of educational infrastructure development within their respective heritage sectors that serves to support such a national transformation as has been the case for Chinese.

This chapter will provide an overview of the current state of affairs for Chinese heritage language education in the United States, with particular attention paid to the unique demographic and systemic conditions both supporting and hindering development of that sector. It will be proposed here that the Chinese heritage language education sector has not merely quantitatively but also qualitatively taken on a role as a more significant pedagogical trendsetter than either its K–12 or collegiate counterparts. It has done so by shifting its outlook from being derivative, modeling itself first after home country and then later the American K–12 systems, to being innovative—in short, changing from a "mirror" of overseas educational models (i.e., either Taiwan or Mainland China) to being a "compass" that increasingly helps guide the course for Chinese language education in the United States.

The Mirror Phase

A Mirror of the Home Country

In its earliest days, the Chinese heritage language educational system was quite separate from the American academic sector. Chao (1996) noted that "[s]ince the early 1900s, Chinese language schools have operated successfully *outside* [italics added] the United States education system" (p. 11). Additionally, beyond their mission of providing Chinese language and cultural education to young people, it may well be argued that the heritage schools were as important as family centers as they were for any formal instructional role—a feature that persists to this day, not only for the individual schools but also for some of the multiple-school organizations. They were and to a great degree still are, as Chao terms it, "Family-Oriented Chinese Language Schools" (1996, p. 7).

One principal feature of the Chinese heritage school system that served to support that earlier insular condition is the relationship between these schools and the home country of the school's organizers—primarily Taiwan (the Republic of China) through the early 1990s, but with an increasing proportion of Mainland Chinese connections since then. This relationship manifests itself in the form of both materials and methodologies. Concerning the former, Chao (1996) noted at the time of her article that in American community schools, "the primary and secondary school textbooks used most frequently are published in Taiwan or the People's Republic of China" (p.10).

The presence of such a textual set of resources minimized the need for teachers to create their own materials, or to draw on what had been published or produced in the United States. For that latter textual option, it must be conceded that of the textbooks produced in America, the vast majority were and still are designed primarily for college and university students. These textbooks are thus pedagogically inappropriate for those teachers working with primary and secondary school students, Chinese community schools included. However, distinctly but equally problematic for those texts produced in Mainland China or Taiwan, as Pey-Fen Wang observed, is the fact that "[t]he theme or subject matter of some lessons is not well suited to the cultural background of heritage students in the United States. Many lessons . . . reflect the cultural perspective of Taiwan, which is very different from the students' perspectives and daily experiences" (Wang, P-F., 1996, p. 22). Compounding this problem of the textual "mirroring" of the home country is the experiential basis of the majority of the heritage school teachers— generally speaking, more reflective of those who have learned Chinese as a native language somewhere in greater China. Shuhan Wang comments that "most of the teachers in Chinese language schools are native Chinese, with no experience with the American education system . . . it is vital that they understand how the American education system works. This knowledge is indispensable because the teaching and promotion of the Chinese language and culture are occurring in the social and political contexts of the United States" (Wang, S-H. C., 1996, p. 65).

A Mirror of American K–12 Education

Shuhan Wang's comment (1996) on the need for the Chinese heritage educational sector to comprehend the American academic sector is particularly insightful given what transpired during the latter half of the 1990s. The watershed point for pre-collegiate Chinese language instruction in the United States is quite clearly the year 1994, when the SAT II Chinese Test with Listening (The College Board & Educational Testing Service, n.d.) was first administered through the Educational Testing Service (ETS). It is striking to note that the two national-level Chinese heritage language school associations—the NCACLS and the CSAUS—were also established in 1994, although that timing is purely coincidental. From that time forward, there has been an ever-accelerating trend for Chinese heritage language teacher organizations to focus their efforts less on mirroring the pedagogical features of home country educational systems and more on the K–12 infrastructure in the United States. Since that time, both the NCACLS and the CSAUS have embarked upon a series of major projects in areas including standards formulation, text and curriculum creation, professional development, and student skills assessment. These have been either consistent with or identical to emerging trends in the compulsory schools.

No clearer evidence of the evolving enhanced interrelationship between K–12 and heritage schools can be seen than in what has developed with regard to the SAT II Chinese Test with Listening (College Board & ETS, n.d.). Both NCACLS and CSAUS have developed their own "Mock SAT Chinese Test." These tests are identical in format to the official version produced by the ETS and are designed to help prepare students for the actual test, not unlike other college and graduate program entrance test preparation programs offered by Kaplan and the Princeton Review.[2] The rate of student participation in these Mock SATs is nothing short of astounding. In April of 2001, the NCACLS version of the Mock SAT attracted over 5,000 participants (Tao-chung Yao, personal communication, 2001)—a staggering statistic given that the annual administration in November, 2001 recorded a total of 5,129 test takers (College Board & ETS, 2002) of the official SAT II Chinese Test with Listening (College Board & ETS, n.d.). What is ironic about the development of this test preparation "industry" is the fact that the vast majority of the heritage school students that take the Mock SAT II tests, as well as the "real" SAT II, are in fact not the ETS- and College Board-described "target audience" for the SAT II foreign language tests. According to official statements from both ETS and The College Board (College Board, 2000, p. 41), the prototypical SAT II foreign language test taker for any of the languages offered is presumed to be a student with from two to four years of classroom-based experience learning the language in question as a foreign language in a formal instructional setting, most typically beginning no earlier than the upper middle school level and continuing through senior high school, and who self-describes his or her language skills as "English as best language."

In the administration of the SAT II Chinese Test with Listening in November 2001, based upon the self-reported demographic data provided by that year's Chinese SAT II test takers, the "target population" accounted for only 27% of the total test taking population (College Board & Educational Testing Service, 2002). There are striking cultural implications regarding the value that has been placed by the Chinese heritage community upon their students' success in the SAT II test-taking process, which are all the more striking given the general lack of attention paid to these test results by virtually all American colleges and universities—the results of a student's SAT II Chinese test are rarely used in any aspect of his or her college career, from Chinese language course placement to satisfaction of a college or university foreign language requirement.

What at least partly underlies the development of an SAT II Chinese test preparation industry is the indigenous Chinese educational system's tradition of an examination process whereby successful examinees ultimately achieve a degree of certainty with regard to their future career prospects. Prior to the end of the final (Qing) Chinese imperial dynasty in 1911, the Chinese national examination system enabled successful test takers to achieve a position within the civil service hierarchy—the better the score, the higher the position. While that type of examination model no longer exists either in Taiwan or the Mainland, there are very strong echoes of its lingering status and societal influence in the national examination system for entrance into public universities in both places. In these modern times, the better one's score, the better one's undergraduate institution—and, as is seen in a number of other countries, both within Asia (e.g., Japan) and beyond, the prestige of one's higher educational institution has a high degree of correlation to one's vocational placement and overall career success.

We thus see that while the Chinese heritage community has moved more to mirror the American educational system than the systems of their homelands, there is at the least an implicit continuing maintenance of the traditional value placed upon a national examination. However, unlike the indigenous Chinese models both in Taiwan and on the Mainland, this national examination provides little to no guarantee of any success, either for the short term (i.e., for admission to a prestigious college or university) or the long term (i.e., for a privileged status within the working world on the basis of the college or university from which one graduated).

The "Compass" Phase

A Compass for Curriculum: Towards a Chinese Advanced Placement Curriculum and Test

Even while arguably embracing the SAT II Chinese Test since its introduction, the Chinese heritage sector has begun to move beyond merely reflecting and accepting the status quo of the official United States education system. In other words, as noted previously, it has begun to be less of a mirror and more of a compass. As with the SAT II experience, one will note that the initial impetus for and focus of innovation by the Chinese heritage community has at least indirectly arisen from the traditional Chinese values that equate national test performance with personal career success. That focus comes in the form of a multi-year public awareness and advocacy campaign for the establishment of a Chinese Advanced Placement (AP) curriculum and test that continues to gain momentum within both the Mainland and Taiwan Chinese heritage language communities.

To be sure, this movement is in large part a reflection of the inadequacy of the SAT II Chinese to fully address the needs and assess the skills of either its minority target audience (the "true" foreign or second language learner of Chinese) or its majority non-target audience (the often near-bilingual heritage language learner of Chinese). But it is at the same time a positive response to the skills of the non-target audience, as well as a desire to provide some degree of validation, in the form of college credits, for the significant levels of linguistic, communicative, and cultural competence possessed by many Chinese heritage learners. However much their motivational and instructional profiles may differ from their foreign language learner counterparts, they are every bit as critical a part of the American pre-collegiate Chinese language instructional scene as are their foreign language learner counterparts.

Initially, the "grassroots" for a campaign to heighten The College Board's awareness of the need for an additional test above and beyond what could be tested by the SAT II came from academic sector-based organizations rather than from the Chinese heritage community. It began in early 1998 in the form of a letter from the SAT II Chinese Test Development Committee strongly expressing support for the creation of a Chinese AP curriculum and examination. At the time, I was serving as a member of that committee as well as President of the Chinese Language Teachers Association[3] (CLTA), and brought the issue of promoting a broader-based letter-writing campaign to the CLTA Board of Directors. With the Board's approval, an announcement providing information regarding to whom and what to write was published in the March 1998 *CLTA Newsletter*. In a series of responses to me from Wade Curry, Director of Advanced Placement at The College Board, the promise was made to "continue to study the feasibility of offering an Advanced Placement course in Chinese language" (personal communication, March 4, 1998).

Since 1998, however, the major source of advocacy for the establishment of an AP curriculum and examination has shifted from the academic sector to the heritage one. While in Houston, Texas for the 1999 meeting of the SAT II Chinese Test Development Committee, I had a conversation with Grace Li, who was then CSAUS President, and suggested that CSAUS might undertake a letter-writing campaign similar to the one that had been proposed to the CLTA membership during the previous year. While there were reports of activity by CSAUS in the form of letters written to The College Board and/or ETS between 1999 and 2001, it was Ms. Li's successor as CSAUS President, Lianggen (Jeff) Zheng, who took to the pages of his organization's newsletter to set forth the rationale for why and how they should advocate for a Chinese AP (CSAUS, 2001, pp. 17–18). In August of 2001, during the initial meeting of the National Chinese Language Commission for the Chinese Language Field Initiative,[4] which included representatives from CLTA, the Chinese Language Association of Secondary-Elementary Schools (CLASS), NCACLS and CSAUS, it was primarily due to the urging of Mr. Zheng that a letter was drafted on behalf of the Commission to The College Board to advocate once again for the establishment of an AP curriculum and test. Since that time, a working group within CSAUS has continued to mobilize support through a variety of means, in a letter of petition with 75 signatures from CSAUS-affiliated school leaders from throughout the United States (Zheng, personal communication, 2003).

The challenge that lies ahead is to convince College Board officials that, rather than limiting their sales and distribution to the K–12 sector, they need to recognize that Chinese community schools can and should be part of the potential market for both the AP Chinese curriculum and test.[5] However much Board officials believe that they are "not in the business of testing heritage learners," they need only look at the previously-cited demographics regarding target test-taker percentages (never more than 28%) (Unpublished data, 2002) among the total annual SAT II Chinese Test-taking population to know that while perhaps not by explicit design, they are in fact very much "in the business" of Chinese heritage language learner assessment.[6] And even while allowing that there is a considerable amount of audience overlap, particularly in the eastern and western United States, of K–12 and heritage school Chinese language learners, to eliminate a potential additional "buying public" of tens of thousands of students (cf. the previously mentioned 23,900 total enrolled in K–12 Chinese programs and the projected 140,000 students in all heritage school settings) is at the least very bad business. There is as well an even greater potential positive effect of bringing in the heritage educational community to the AP course and examination "market," namely the potential for enhanced program articulation. This includes the possibility of enhanced horizontal articulation between K–12 and heritage language programs, where there is so much overlap already in many geographical settings, as well as the eventuality of enhanced vertical articulation between pre-collegiate and collegiate programs.

Indeed, towards that end of making a persuasive case with The College Board, the Chinese heritage communities now have a role model to look at in the form of another LCTL, Italian. In what may frankly be termed a primarily pragmatically economic approach to encouraging a more diverse AP program, in 2002 The College Board presented an offer to representatives of the Italian heritage language community in the United States and the official in charge of the School Office of the Embassy of Italy in Washington, DC: Quantify an enrollment in pre-collegiate Italian language courses sufficient to justify an AP Italian curriculum and test, and raise a seed fund of $500,000, and The College Board will agree to develop an AP Italian curriculum and test. Within six months of that initial meeting, the Embassy of Italy had coordinated a successful response to the conditions set by the Board, with the financial seed fund raised primarily not through government sources, but through private, benevolent and fraternal organizations such as the Sons of Italy and the National Italian American Foundation (Graziana Morini, personal communication, 2002).

To be sure, there is no way that the Chinese heritage community will be able to make an AP Chinese program a reality without the cooperation of the academic sector, both at the pre-collegiate and collegiate levels, and vice versa. In addition, there may also be additional potential sources of collaborative support outside of the Chinese field alone. Over the course of the past several years, I have been in regular communication with Dan Davidson, President of the American Councils for International Education: ACTR/ACCELS. A leader in Russian and East European language pedagogy for over thirty years, the Councils have been working with The College Board in the development of a prototype Web-based AP curriculum for Russian, including modules for professional development and computer-based student assessment. In a meeting with representatives of the Councils at The College Board in the fall of 2002, the Board expressed not only continuing interest in developing the model, but in expanding it to other LCTLs, including Chinese (Richard Brecht, personal communication, 2002).

In sum, the ultimate success of the Chinese heritage community in promoting the establishment of a Chinese AP curriculum and examination will depend on its ability to learn from the experience and expertise of others, including the Italian and Russian constituencies. It will also depend on its employment of collaborative approaches and financial strategies.[7] The fact of the matter is that like any business enterprise, ETS and The College Board are as much motivated by financial pressures as by academic standards, as has been reported with regularity in the media (see, for example, Associated Press, 2001). For many years, the conversations that I had with representatives of both The College Board and ETS regarding the establishment of an AP Chinese program always returned to their perception that a Chinese AP would simply never be a money-maker. Given this perception, the Chinese heritage sector will undoubtedly need to adopt the Italian approach, locating support from Chinese business and community leaders who are both institutionally and personally involved in Chinese heritage language education. In pursuing the AP initiative, the Chinese heritage sector has a major opportunity to lead rather than merely respond to prevailing trends and methodologies in the K–12 educational system.

A Compass for Professional Development: The Penn Summer Chinese Institute

If establishing successful (or even survivable) Chinese language programs in K–12 settings has been a challenge, it has in no small part been due to the paucity, bordering on a near-total lack, of pre-service academic programs for teachers of Chinese as a foreign or second language (to say nothing of as a heritage language) with the opportunity for public school certification. While a number of Chinese language teacher training programs have been established and have expanded in the last several years (most notably those at the University of Iowa and New York University), an almost equal number of potential programs set for establishment in the early 1990s (e.g., the University of Oregon and University of Maryland) died in their infancies. This can be traced to a number of factors, some controllable, some not. They included the nationwide decline in levels of state-provided support for higher education in general, a lack of intra-institutional inter-departmental and college cooperation, and a general lack of strategic vision and commitment that translated into program financial support by college leaders.

More immediately problematic for heritage school teachers, however, has been the issue of access to professional development opportunities, either pre-service or in-service. Certainly the various national, regional, and metropolitan community school organizations have done a laudable job of providing frequent opportunities for sharing expertise, both from within and outside of the organizations. But the occasional half-day workshops and annual conferences—the latter as much social events as they are true professional development experiences—are not enough to sustain any continuing program of teaching quality enhancement. Moreover, for those heritage school teachers that might aspire to enter the American academic sector and teach in one of many emerging K–12 Chinese language programs in the United States, the lack of either a foreign language teaching certificate or the time sufficient to earn that certificate, if such a certification program is even available in the area, serves as a major disincentive for an otherwise highly motivated heritage school instructor.

Responding to such needs of heritage sector teachers in the greater Philadelphia area, and working collaboratively with what would later become the Taoli Chinese Teachers Association (TCTA),[8] the University of Pennsylvania established the Penn Chinese Language Teachers Institute in the summer of 1998. Originally composed of a single course offering, the Institute has now grown to include at least two and sometimes three courses each summer. Certain courses have been offered on an annual or biannual basis, including Second Language Acquisition (SLA) and Chinese applied linguistics. Other courses have taken on a "selected topics" approach with the focus changing each year, including the teaching of language and culture, managing learner diversity, and national standards-based instructional methodology. Each course is taught as a stand-alone course over a series of five days with seven hours of classroom instruction each day. The instructors are not regular University of Pennsylvania faculty, but rather come from a variety of pre-collegiate and collegiate academic institutions. All instructors have earned their doctorates or are doctoral candidates. Students receive one continuing education credit per course, which generally equates to three credit units from most other universities or colleges.

What is particularly noteworthy about the Institute is that while its initial target audience was the Greater Philadelphia area, it has attracted students from throughout the United States and even from Taiwan. Equally impressive is that while the perceived core audience was presumed to be heritage school teachers seeking to work toward gaining certification as primary or secondary school teachers, practicing certified K–12 teachers and even instructors from prestigious colleges and universities such as Williams have also taken one or more courses. As such, the Institute has served as a setting, albeit a short-term one, for teachers in all instructional settings to address issues of articulation among K–12, colleges and universities, and heritage schools in a pedagogically practical manner. Perhaps most importantly, at least two of the Institute's "graduates" have been able to apply the credits earned through the Penn program to obtain certification for and positions in public school systems. In all these ways, the Institute has served as a model for how an initiative from within the heritage sector, with the support of an academic sector institution, can tailor professional development to the unique conditions of Chinese heritage language educators while at the same time providing a model for professional development that is of value to all teachers regardless of institutional setting.

A Compass for Societal Improvement: Outreach to Families with Children from China

A final aspect of the development of the Chinese heritage education sector's shift from a reflective to a guiding role can be seen in the rise of programs specially tailored to a growing societal phenomenon, referred to in the 1990s as programs for "students of non-Chinese speaking parents" and more recently termed as outreach to "Families with Children from China" (FCC). The change in terminology is particularly significant in that it represents a growth in the target constituency to include not just the adoptive children but their generally non-Chinese speaking adoptive parents. In helping these children maintain their cultural/linguistic traditions and in assisting their adopted parents to facilitate the maintenance process (while at the same time enhancing their knowledge of their children's ethnic and cultural roots), the FCC programs are serving a role that transcends purely educational enrichment (Families with Children from China, n.d.).

There are a number of exemplary FCC programs throughout the United States, for both NCACLS- and CSAUS-connected Chinese heritage schools. In the mid-Atlantic area, one of the oldest and best developed programs is the *Dinghao* Chinese program at the Main Line Chinese School in metropolitan Philadelphia, established in 1996. A more recently established institution (in May of 2002) is the *YingHua* Language School near Princeton, New Jersey. The principal of that school, Bonnie Liao, reports that there may be as many as 3,000 children, most often girls, adopted from China in New Jersey alone (personal communication, 2002). In addressing the challenge of establishing an essentially dual-track curriculum, Dr. Liao makes the following observations:

Our potential adult [Chinese as a Second Language] students will have two hours per week in school, and most of them would be the parents of our students . . . I'd say the majority of them are motivated by the desire to be "part of the girl's world," as one parent put it. . . . I need to think through what the goal of such a course should be. Adults learn differently from children. Should I teach them so that they would be able to help with their children's homework? Should I teach them the adult-appropriate materials that would be independent of what their kids learn? (personal communication, 2002)

Programs such as those at *Dinghao* and *YingHua* may over time ultimately provide the academic sector with experience-based lessons and models for teaching both the true second or foreign language learner of Chinese, and the wide range of iterations of Chinese heritage language learners. Albeit in a more integrative (versus instrumental) motivational setting, these programs' applications to more traditional classroom-based models at the primary, secondary and tertiary levels could be considerable.

Conclusion

Chinese heritage language education in the United States is no longer purely a heritage sector issue. As has been detailed in the preceding discussion regarding the emerging "compass" role of the heritage sector, it is not merely the American educational system, but society as a whole that is benefiting from the sense of responsibility that is being fostered by the Chinese heritage sector. As the heritage community once did on a very insular basis for the Chinese immigrant population in the United States, so it now also provides a means of sustaining, expanding, and enhancing understanding of Chinese language and culture. Even though we have entered the 21st century still woefully impoverished in undertaking such a teaching task within our compulsory school settings, we can take heart that those generally perceived as being outside of the mainstream are contributing so much to Chinese language education. Our failure to integrate heritage learners into the American educational system is a squandering of a precious natural resource that may only serve to leave us in an isolationist position of no small potential peril, for ourselves and the world.

Notes

1. Recall that in the early part of the 1990s before the ACTFL national standards project (American Council on the Teaching of Foreign Languages, 1989) gained momentum, it was arguable that the theme of inter-level articulation, particularly between K–12 and college programs, was even more central to the national dialogue.
2. Information on NCACLS and CSAUS's Mock SAT tests is available at their respective web sites (National Council of Associations of Chinese Language Schools [n.d.]; Chinese School Association in the United States, [n.d.].

3. Established in 1962, the Chinese Language Teachers Association (CLTA) is the oldest professional organization devoted exclusively to the study of Chinese language, culture and pedagogy. Approximately half of its membership is composed of specialists in Chinese language, literature, linguistics, and culture teaching at colleges and universities throughout the world, with the other half composed of a mix of primary, secondary, and Chinese community school teachers, students of the language, and other interested parties. Given these demographics, as well as CLTA's purported mission to "act as an advocate for and facilitator of enhanced articulation among all Chinese language learning settings" (Chinese Language Teachers Association, n.d.), it seems somewhat surprising that CLTA did not take a continuing active role in promoting the establishment of an AP curriculum and examination.

4. The Chinese Language Field Initiative (CLFI) is a program of field-wide discussion and study to strengthen Chinese language instruction in the United States. The Initiative is being led by CLTA and CLASS, with administrative support from the National Council of Organizations of Less Commonly Taught Languages (NCOLCTL) and consultative expertise by the NFLC. In addition, both NCACLS and CSAUS have an official representative serving on the oversight body for the Initiative, the National Chinese Language Commission.

5. This potential has been the topic of an ongoing series of personal communications between me and selected College Board officials. With the official announcement on December 5, 2003 that an AP Chinese Curriculum and Test will be established, there is at least implicit evidence that this particular case has been made successfully.

6. These demographics became a particular bone of contention when, in the spring of 2001, The College Board conducted a web-based feasibility study of offering a new AP course and exam in Chinese language. The problem was that in focusing only on K–12 programs for potential clients, the Board could not accurately gauge where in fact the majority of interest in an AP Chinese program really lies, namely in the heritage sector.

7. In October of 2002, at the Second National Conference on Heritage Languages in America in Tysons Corner, Virginia, I had a conversation with Lenore Blank, formerly of the San Francisco Unified School District and one of the leaders in the development of the SAT II Korean Test with Listening, and Ailee Moon, a professor of sociology at UCLA and President of the Foundation for SAT II Korean, regarding collaboration with the Chinese heritage sector to work for the development of Chinese and Korean AP programs. No further developments can be reported at this time.

8. Quoting from the promotional brochure for the 2002 Penn Chinese Language Teachers Institute, "In order to provide year-round service to prospective and practicing Chinese language teachers, TCTA was established soon after the 1998 Penn Chinese Teachers Summer Institute. Its membership is open to all Chinese language teachers nationwide, Chinese heritage community schools included."

References

American Council on the Teaching of Foreign Languages. (1989). *ACTFL proficiency guidelines.* Hastings on Hudson, NY: Author.

Associated Press. (2001, February 18). *ETS trying new ventures, focusing on bottom line.* Retrieved February 10, 2003, from MSNBC data base, http://www.msnbc.com/local/wnbc/1220780.asp

Brecht, R., & Walton, A. R. (1994). National strategic planning in the less commonly taught languages. *The Annals of the American Academy of Political and Social Science, 532,* 190–212.

Brod, R., & Welles, E. (2000). Foreign language enrollments in United States institutions of higher education. *ADFL Bulletin, 31*(2), 20–29.

Chao, T. H. (1996). Overview. In X. Wang (Ed.), *A view from within: A case study of Chinese heritage community language schools in the United States* (pp. 7–13). Washington, DC: National Foreign Language Center.

Chinese Schools Association in the United States. (2001). A discussion of the proposal for an "AP Chinese Examination" (in Chinese). *CSAUS Newsletter, 24,* 17–18.

Chinese Schools Association in the United States. (2002). Association membership statistics: A brief report (in Chinese). *CSAUS Newsletter, 30,* 17.

Chinese Schools Association in the United States. (n.d.). [SAT materials.] Available from http://clta.osu.edu

The College Board. (2000). *Real SAT II: Subject tests—Japanese/Chinese/Korean*. New York: The College Board.

The College Board & Educational Testing Service. (n.d.). *SAT II: Chinese test with listening*. New York: The College Board.

The College Board & Educational Testing Service. (2002). *Unpublished data—The SAT II Chinese Test with Listening*. New York: The College Board.

Families with Children from China. (n.d.). Retrieved April 10, 2006, from http://www.fwcc.org

McGinnis, S. (1996). Teaching Chinese to the Chinese: The development of an assessment and instructional model. In J. E. Liskin-Gasparro (Ed.), *Patterns and policies: The changing demographics of foreign language instruction* (pp. 107–121). Boston: Heinle & Heinle.

National Council of Associations of Chinese Language Schools. (n.d.). [SAT materials]. Available from National Council of Association of Chinese Language schools web site, http://www.csaus.org/about.asp

Penless Chinese Language Learning: A Computer-Assisted Approach. (n.d.). Retrieved April 10, 2006, from http://www.penlesschinese.org

Secondary School Chinese Language Center. (2002). A report on 2001–2002 Chinese enrollments at the pre-collegiate level. *Secondary School Chinese Language Center Newsletter, 13*, 4–13.

Wang, P-F. S. (1996). Academic curriculum. In X. Wang (Ed.), *A view from within: A case study of Chinese heritage community language schools in the United States* (pp. 21–25). Washington, DC: National Foreign Language Center.

Wang, S-H. C. (1996). Improving Chinese language schools: Issues and recommendations. In X. Wang (Ed.), *A view from within: A case study of Chinese heritage community language schools in the United States* (pp. 63–67). Washington, DC: National Foreign Language Center.

Welles, E. (2004). Foreign language enrollments in United States institutions of higher education. *ADFL Bulletin, 35*(2), 7–26.

14

Spanish for Native Speakers Education

The State of the Field

JOY KREEFT PEYTON

Teachers working in schools have limited opportunities to work with colleagues to define their field or to articulate their visions for its future and often must make do with the definitions and aspirations supplied by others.

One opportunity for teachers to participate in directed discussions on the state of their field was held at UCLA in the summer of 1999 at a National Endowment for the Humanities (NEH) institute for teachers of Spanish to Spanish speakers.[1] The institute was designed and carried out in collaboration with the Center for Applied Linguistics (CAL) under the leadership of Dr. Russell N. Campbell.[2] Thirty secondary school teachers from across the United States convened at UCLA for six weeks to consider linguistic and cultural issues related to the education of their students and to develop curricula and instructional strategies for use in their classes.

The participants wrote and revised drafts under Dr. Campbell's inspiration and direction, to articulate their knowledge and understanding of current conditions in SNS education in America's schools.[3] This chapter is the result of that work. It is also a tribute to Dr. Campbell's dedication to helping practitioners reflect on and articulate the critical issues in their fields.

Introduction

Our future success or failure in international endeavors will rely almost entirely on the global competence of our people. Global competence is a broad term that ranges from the in-depth knowledge required for interpreting information affecting national security, to the skills and understanding that foster improved relations with all regions of the world. It involves, among other things, foreign language proficiency and an ability to function effectively in other cultural environments and value systems, whether conducting business, implementing international development projects, or carrying out diplomatic missions. (American Council on Education, 2002, p. 7)

As the ACE report points out, proficiency in languages other than English and knowledge of other cultures are critical to our success as a nation in the areas of national defense, international diplomacy and business, and cross-cultural understanding. In addition to improving foreign language programs to achieve these purposes, we need to build on the linguistic abilities and cultural knowledge of our heritage speakers, who already have a foundation on which to build.

The following sections summarize the NEH participants' discussions on the state of the field of teaching Spanish for heritage speakers—often called Spanish for native speakers (SNS)—in six key areas: benefits and challenges, characteristics of students, teacher qualifications and training, programs and instruction, assessment, and policy.[4] At the end of each section, actions to be taken are recommended.

Benefits and Challenges of SNS Education

Providing opportunities for students to develop proficiency in at least two languages can benefit students, schools, communities, and the nation.

Benefits

Heritage language speakers can benefit from instruction in their home language. In addition to the benefits of being literate in two languages, literacy skills in English can, in some cases, be developed more effectively when taught first in a student's native language (Thomas & Collier, 1997). In addition, children, whose personal sense of identity and worth develop in the formative years, generally strive to be accepted and valued by those around them. Children who enter school speaking a language other than English can maintain their sense of identity if they are given the opportunity to retain and develop their first language and culture through heritage language instruction while they are learning English. Finally, increased business and professional opportunities may be available to individuals who are proficient in languages in addition to English (Carreira & Armengol, 2001).

In schools with a multicultural student population, students who are comfortable in more than one language and culture can promote cross-cultural understanding and tolerance. Furthermore, the experience of summer institute participants indicates that Spanish speakers in SNS programs are more successful than other students in passing exams such as the Advanced Placement (AP) Spanish Language Exam (The College Board, n.d.) and the Spanish Language Golden State Exam (California Department of Education, 1987) and in qualifying for the language requirements of the International Baccalaureate degree (International Baccalaureate Organization, n.d.).

On the other hand, when Spanish-speaking students are placed in middle and high school foreign language Spanish classes and the language skills that they already have are not recognized or developed, they may become bored or frustrated and lose their motivation to continue their Spanish studies. When this happens, important language skills and cultural knowledge are lost.

When speakers of languages other than English have opportunities to develop those languages, their communities can benefit. For example, community members who have a sense of social connection may engage in more community building and social activism than those who do not (Compton, 2001). A community that supports multilingualism and multiculturalism promotes pride and a positive sense of identity among its members, which can contribute to community solidarity and cultural maintenance.

Professionals are needed in the United States who can carry out business and international diplomacy in languages other than English; these are part of the "expanded international knowledge and skills" called for in the report by the American Council on Education (2002, p.7).

As economic borders open, bilingual executives and professionals with technical skills are needed in business. As Brecht and Rivers (2000) note,

> International trade, specifically exports, which constituted a small fraction of the gross domestic product of the United States in the early 1960s, now represents a major driving force in this country's economy. The North American Free Trade Agreement (NAFTA) and World Trade Organization (WTO) are now in place, and American participation is growing through other agreements touching the Western Hemisphere (such as the Free Trade Area of the Americas) and the Pacific Rim (Asia Pacific Economic Cooperation). Language is a major consideration in all these free trade agreements, where even a seemingly obvious issue such as the languages used in product labeling must be negotiated and prescribed. (p. 10)

In international diplomacy and security, the General Accounting Office has pointed out that staff shortages at several federal agencies have adversely affected agency operations and hindered U.S. military, law enforcement, intelligence, counter terrorism, and diplomatic efforts (General Accounting Office, 2002).

In spite of these needs, little attention has been given to developing and coordinating well-designed and carefully articulated foreign language programs for heritage language students (Campbell & Peyton, 1998). If our schools nurture the heritage languages of students who already speak languages other than English, we may be able to address this challenge. Instruction of Spanish-speaking students should be undertaken with the goal that these students should be able to pursue both professions and personal enrichment that call on high-level language skills.

Recommendations

- Teachers and school and district administrators should be aware of the language needs in the United States, the importance of heritage language maintenance and development, and the actions needed to bring this about.

- The education of bilingual and bicultural students should be based on an "additive" approach, building on the language and social skills they already have (Cummins, 1986), rather than a "subtractive" model, in which one language or dialect replaces another.

Characteristics of Heritage Speakers of Spanish

A native or heritage speaker of a language other than English is an individual who has acquired that language early in life, often in the home or the community. Guadalupe Valdés (2000) characterizes these speakers as follows:

> Within the foreign language teaching profession in the United States, the term "heritage speaker" is used to refer to a student of language who is raised in a home where a non-English language is spoken, who speaks or merely understands the heritage language, and who is to some degree bilingual in English and the heritage language. . . . For the most part, the experiences of these heritage speakers have been similar. They speak or hear the heritage language spoken at home, but they receive all of their education in the official or majority language of the countries in which they live. What this means is that, in general, such students receive no instruction in the heritage language. They thus become literate only in the majority language. (p.1)

In addition, heritage language speakers include those who speak only their heritage language (e.g., Spanish monolinguals who have recently begun schooling in U.S. schools), those who speak their heritage language and English but are more proficient in one or the other (e.g., Spanish- or English-dominant bilinguals), and those who know their heritage language to some extent but for social or political reasons do not speak it (Aparicio, 1983; Valdés, 2001).

Among Hispanics in the United States in 2000, 66 percent were from Mexico; 14 percent were from Central and South America; 9 percent from Puerto Rico; and 4 percent from Cuba (Therrien & Ramirez, 2001). Nearly half lived in central cities of metropolitan areas (compared with around one-fifth of non-Hispanic Whites), but Hispanics are also moving to smaller cities (A. Roca, personal communication, May 30, 2002).

Many Spanish-speaking students in the United States come from low-income families (Ruiz de Velasco & Fix, 2000; Therrien & Ramirez, 2001). Parents often work two jobs, which prevents them from being fully involved in their children's education. The jobs of many parents involve hard labor or agricultural work in which they must move seasonally from region to region. As a result, their children's education may be scattered and incomplete. Although parents may value and encourage education, students may need to work to help the family economically and therefore find it difficult to participate in activities and organizations that could lead to more academic options.

Spanish-speaking students are often placed in remedial track programs in school, preventing them from receiving a college-preparatory education (Ruiz-de-Velasco & Fix, 2000). These programs are not always staffed with practitioners who understand or meet students' social, psychological, and linguistic needs. The results may be lack of motivation and social problems at school, low academic achievement, absenteeism, and dropping out of school.

In order to break this trend of academic failure among Spanish-speaking students, the following actions are recommended:

Recommendations

- Tests should be developed by schools or school districts to assess Spanish speakers' language proficiency, so that they can be placed in Spanish classes at appropriate levels.
- Interdisciplinary Spanish for Spanish speakers curricula should be developed so that Spanish-speaking students may expand their proficiency in Spanish, transfer those skills to English and academic subjects, and become fully bilingual and biliterate.
- Students and parents should be informed about students' Spanish language proficiency and academic progress and about educational opportunities that can lead to a college education.
- Language programs should be developed within school systems that will foster and strengthen the language skills of all students, including heritage Spanish speakers. Where appropriate, Spanish-speaking students can play key roles in these programs (e.g., as classroom aides or peer tutors).

SNS Teacher Qualifications and Training

Teachers of heritage Spanish speakers differ widely in terms of qualifications, training, and language proficiency (Schwartz, 2001). Because teaching Spanish to heritage Spanish speakers is a new field, universities and school districts have generally not yet established standards for teacher preparation. School district requirements range from none to required bilingual certification. In an informal survey of the SNS teachers attending the NEH summer institute, only one state represented was identified as having certification requirements for SNS teachers, and no state was identified as having standards for SNS teacher language proficiency. The state of Washington plans to require a Spanish proficiency test for all K–12 Spanish teachers. As a result, however, the language teacher shortage in Washington may increase, making it even more difficult to sustain SNS classes there. California and a few other states represented require high school Spanish teachers to demonstrate Spanish language proficiency and knowledge of pedagogy through the Spanish Praxis Exams (Educational Testing Service, n.d.), but those exams do not address SNS teacher proficiencies.

Pre-Service Training

Methodology courses focusing on teaching Spanish as a foreign language are not sufficient for preparing teachers to work with heritage Spanish speakers. However, even in states with large heritage Spanish student populations, there are limited pre-service training opportunities focused specifically on these students' needs.

In-Service Training

SNS teachers often learn to teach on the job, and teachers who are motivated to learn more must be resourceful and determined in their search for in-service workshops and institutes. Some training opportunities are available at state and national conferences held by the American Association of Teachers of Spanish and Portuguese (AATSP), the American Council on the Teaching of Foreign Languages (ACTFL), the National Association for Bilingual Education (NABE), and some state affiliates of these organizations. NEH and New Mexico State University offer summer institutes for teachers. State-based programs such as the California Foreign Language Project are designed to reach teachers who work with students from beginning to advanced language proficiency.

In addition, ACTFL and the Department of Curriculum and Teaching at Hunter College in New York City collaborated on a 3-year project, funded by a grant from the U.S. Department of Education's Fund for the Improvement of Postsecondary Education (FIPSE), to establish a program to prepare teachers to work more effectively with heritage language speakers (Webb & Miller, 2000). The project provided a forum for SNS teachers to share their practical expertise and provide insight into how teachers should be trained to work in the SNS classroom. The teachers were an integral part of the team that implemented the resulting SNS teacher training program, which will be part of the undergraduate and graduate certification programs at Hunter College.

Resources for Teachers

Information for SNS teachers is becoming increasingly available and includes online resources in addition to books and journal articles. A list of recommended resources is in Appendix 14.2 of this chapter.

Recommendations

- State and district policy makers and university departments of education should understand the differences between first and second language development.
- Every language teacher preparation program should have at least one course that focuses on methodologies for working with heritage language speakers.

- Courses that lead to a teaching endorsement or certificate for teaching SNS classes should include Chicano studies, Latino culture, and language arts methods.
- States should establish a credential program for SNS teachers.
- SNS teachers should have ongoing training in teaching Spanish to Spanish speakers, provided by district programs and professional organizations such as AATSP and ACTFL.

SNS Programs and Instruction

While program models, curricula, and instructional materials for SNS education are emerging, in the experience of the teachers attending the summer institute, many schools rely on teachers to design and develop their own SNS courses and to find a place for those courses in the larger foreign language program.[5]

Recommendations

- States and school districts should set standards for SNS curricula and instructional materials based on high academic goals and excellent classroom practices. Standards should be developed with input from SNS teachers and field-tested in SNS classrooms.
- School and district language program staff should be familiar with SNS curricula and materials and make them available for SNS classes where needed.
- SNS teachers should visit other schools with active SNS programs, establish and maintain relationships with other SNS teachers, and advocate for SNS programs in their schools and districts.
- SNS programs should be articulated so that students move smoothly from elementary through high school courses and so that Spanish language learning is integrated across subject areas.
- Policies should be established so that students receive appropriate academic recognition or credit for SNS courses.
- Language learning should take place within a meaningful context that prepares students to succeed at home, in the workplace, and in society. SNS teachers and school district staff should develop curricula that meet the needs of SNS students, foster their self-esteem, and prepare them for the demands of our multicultural and global society.
- Spanish language instruction should be combined with other fields of study, including literature, history, political science, art, music, philosophy, economics, the sciences, technology, international business and diplomacy, and religion, to create a more interdisciplinary approach to teaching.
- SNS courses should include instruction in listening, speaking, reading,

and writing (including vocabulary and grammar) as well as in the literature, cultures, and history of the people who speak the language being taught.

- Listening comprehension should reflect the language varieties and cultures of heritage Spanish speakers in the United States.
- The teaching of oral language skills should include such activities as peer interviews, oral book reports, and student discussions of current events and issues, which draw on various discourse registers.
- Reading instruction should include reading of published literature, provide a model of standard Spanish, and give students familiarity with literary terms and genres, and provide information about the cultures and history of Spanish-speaking groups.
- Writing instruction should include a variety of writing types and formats, such as basic paragraph development, essay writing, guided compositions (with prompts), and journal writing.

Assessment of SNS Students

Assessment includes diagnostic, placement, and achievement testing, all of which can contribute to effective instruction and program evaluation.[6]

Diagnostic Testing

Most tests that SNS teachers use to assess the Spanish language skills of Spanish speakers were developed either for English speakers learning Spanish or for English-dominant Spanish speakers (Otheguy & Toro, 2000). One test that K–12 SNS teachers use is the Woodcock Language Proficiency Battery-Revised in Spanish (WLPB-R, Riverside Publishing, 1991b). It has listening, grammar, and reading portions, rates students at five different levels, and identifies students by language dominance and proficiency. It is used primarily to identify students who need instruction in English but can also gauge students' Spanish proficiency. Another test used regularly is the Language Assessment Scales-Oral (LAS-O) (CTB/McGraw Hill, 1990). Students are classified as Fluent, Limited, or Non-Spanish Speaker.

Placement Testing

Placement procedures for SNS courses are not uniform. Many schools place students in classes on the basis of an oral interview or student self-selection. One assessment used for placement in SNS classes is La Prueba de Ubicación Para Hispanohablantes (Riverside Publishing, 1991a). Some schools and districts use a locally adapted version of the Advanced Placement (AP) Spanish Language Exam (The College Board, n.d.).

Achievement Testing

Some SNS programs use the AP Spanish Language Exam (The College Board, n.d.) for achievement testing. This exam measures students' mastery of listening, speaking, reading, writing, and grammar. Students with high scores can receive college credit for Spanish study. Some SNS programs also prepare students for the AP Spanish Literature Exam (The College Board, n.d.). Two versions of the Scholastic Assessment Test II (SAT II) are available for Spanish: multiple-choice and multiple-choice with listening (The College Board, n.d.). The International Baccalaureate Exam (International Baccalaureate Organization, n.d.), for which high school Spanish language credit is given, is also used. According to summer institute participants, California's Spanish Language Golden State Exam (California Department of Education, 1987) was given for the first time to intermediate Spanish students in the spring 2000.

Program Evaluation

Outcomes on assessments may be required when schools or programs receive federal funding. In the experience of the summer institute participants, few schools have implemented a rigorous system to document student progress and SNS program success. Often the only records kept are of the number of students who take and pass the major Spanish exams (such as the AP Spanish and SAT II).

The AP Spanish Exams (The College Board, n.d.) allow comparison of scores across the nation, and distinguish between English speakers studying Spanish and SNS students in their reports.

Recommendations

- SNS program staff should be knowledgeable about assessments for Spanish-speaking students and involved in the development of and decisions about use of these assessments.
- Achievement tests in Spanish should be developed so that SNS programs can demonstrate what students are learning.
- Guidelines for SNS student assessment and program evaluation should be developed by national professional organizations such as AATSP and ACTFL and distributed for consideration by professionals in the field.

Language Policies

Although educational policy in the United States does not directly address instruction of heritage languages, indirect policies do help shape SNS instruction. Among these are federal guidelines that shape instruction in ESL, bilingual education, and language immersion programs and corresponding funds that assist school districts to comply with federal legislation. National organizations such as Fulbright-Hays and NEH also make funds available for specialized programs that include SNS instruction.

Among the private organizations that attempt to influence national policy for both heritage and foreign language instruction are AATSP, ACTFL, CAL, the Joint National Committee on Languages (JNCL), and NABE. As a result of their work, there is increased awareness among practitioners of language policies and practices.

State and district requirements for foreign language or SNS instruction vary in areas such as language preparedness, focusing either on the completion of a sequence of language courses or proficiency testing, and in the existence of policy that encourages the development of ESL, bilingual education, and two-way immersion classes.

Many schools do not offer SNS courses, even when the need is evident. Other schools adapt district policies to meet their own needs. The size and demographics of the school are important variables that influence whether a school provides special classes for heritage language speakers. Clearly, there is a need to define SNS policy even at the school level.

Recommendations

- National language policies should recognize the value of language resources, encourage the study of second languages, provide resources for developing bilingual or multilingual language proficiency, and guide state and local policies.
- Organizations such as AATSP, ACTFL, and NABE should collaborate to promote SNS instruction, disseminate information about SNS education, and carry out projects such as: a) determining the status of SNS instruction state-by-state; b) working with organizations such as CAL and the National Clearinghouse for English Language Acquisition (NCELA) to publish, through their Web sites, program and course profiles used at all levels of SNS instruction; c) disseminating information about funding available to develop SNS programs; and d) maintaining electronic discussion forums for SNS teachers and researchers.
- Study of languages other than English should be required at both the elementary and secondary school levels.
- Separate language classes should be offered for heritage Spanish speakers, especially at the secondary school level, when the need for them can be demonstrated. In areas with low numbers of SNS students, school districts should provide alternatives to full classes, such as independent study or tutoring.

Conclusion

As Brecht and Rivers (2000) point out, this nation faces unprecedented challenges in meeting its language needs. At the same time, heritage language speakers comprise a large and growing segment of the U.S. population. We need to put into place policies, programs, curricula, assessments, and instructional strategies to develop the heritage language proficiencies of heritage Spanish speakers and to prepare and empower teachers to work with them.

Appendix 14.1 1999 NEH SNS Summer Institute Participants

Jeanette Arnhart, Oakdale Junior High School, Rogers, Arkansas
Sandra Arnold, Palisades Charter High School, Pacific Palisades, California
Graciela Bravo-Black, Sunnyside High School, Sunnyside, Washington
Yolanda Cortez, Sholes Middle School, Milwaukee, Wisconsin
Sharla R. Dobson, Portsmouth High School, Portsmouth, Rhode Island
Maria del Carmen García, Woodrow Wilson High School, Long Beach, California
Virginia Haase, Plainfield School, Des Plaines, Illinois
David Philip Hanes, Los Angeles High School, Los Angeles, California
Christy Hargesheimer, Lincoln High School, Lincoln, Nebraska
Marilyn Hernández, Julius West Middle School, Rockville, Maryland
Roberto Jiménez, Holy Cross School, New Orleans, Louisiana
Michael Kraus, Western Oaks Middle School, Bethany, Oklahoma
Louis Lillard, Clewiston High School, Clewiston, Florida
Aurora Martínez, John C. Fremont High School, Los Angeles, California
Enrique Nárez, Rialto High School, Rialto, California
Nancy Neel, Jefferson Middle School, Oceanside, California
Lori Nelson, USC/MaST High School, Los Angeles, California
Rossnilda Oliveras, Boone High School, Orlando, Florida
Claudia Ossorio, Thomas Jefferson High School, Los Angeles, California
Maria Pérez-Tapia, James Monroe High School, North Hills, California
Cynthia Azucena Quintero, Mira Costa High School, Manhattan Beach, California
Analuz Ramirez-Palomo, Torrey Pines High School, Encinitas, California
Heriberto Ríos, Woodrow Wilson Classical High School, Long Beach, California
Adán Rodriguez, Pasco High School, Pasco, Washington
Norma Cervantes Sharpe, Mabton Junior-Senior High School, Mabton, Washington
Sheryl Singh, Hall Elementary School, Grand Rapids, Michigan
Pamela Snyman, Okanogan School District, Okanogan, Washington
Ed Stering, Mercy High School, San Francisco, California
Judi B. Turner, John Marshall High School, Los Angeles, California
Isabel Vázquez-Gil, Silver Spring International Middle School, Silver Spring, Maryland

Appendix 14.2 Professional Organizations, Journals, Institutes, and Discussion Lists Dedicated to Providing Support for the Teaching of SNS

Professional Organizations

- American Association of Teachers of Spanish and Portuguese (AATSP). Available at: http://www.aatsp.org/
- American Council on the Teaching of Foreign Languages (ACTFL). Available at: http://www.actfl.org/
- National Association for Bilingual Education (NABE). Available at: http://www.nabe.org/

Online Teaching Resources

- University of Maryland. (2001). REACH. A site for Spanish teachers, Spanish-speaking students in the US, and the general public. College Park, MD: University of Maryland. A joint project of the National Foreign Language Center, University of Maryland and the American Association of Teachers of Spanish and Portuguese (AATSP). Available at: http://www.nflc.org/REACH/
- Winke, P. & Stafford, C. (2002). Selecting materials for SNS instruction. Washington, DC: Center for Applied Linguistics. A guide to selecting SNS materials, on the CAL web site. Available at: http://www.cal.org/resources/Digest/0203winke.html
- Kreeft Peyton, J., Lewelling, V., & Winke, P. (2001). Spanish for native speakers: Developing dual language proficiency. Washington, DC: Center for Applied Linguistics (EDO-FL-01-09). Available at: http://www.cal.org/resources-ces/digest/spanish_native.html
- Roca, A. (1992). Spanish for U. S. Hispanic bilinguals in higher education. Washington, DC: ERIC Clearinghouse on Languages and Linguistics. (ERIC Document Reproduction Service No. ED350881). Retrieved June 7, 2003, from http://www.ericdigests.org/1992-1/spanish.htm.
- Roca, A., Marcos, K., & Winke, P. Teaching Spanish to Spanish speakers (n.d.). Washington, DC: Center for Applied Linguistics. A comprehensive collection of resources for SNS teachers, including an extensive bibliography. Available at: http://www.cal.org/resources/archives/rgos/sns.html

Books (for full references for books see the Reference section).

- La ensenanza del español a hispanohablantes: Praxis y teoria, (Colombi & Alarcon 1997).
- Spanish for native speakers: Professional development handbook for teachers K–12 (American Association of Teachers of Spanish and Portuguese, 2000).
- Spanish for U. S. Hispanic bilinguals in higher education, (Roca, 1992).
- Mi Lengua: Spanish as a Heritage Language in the United States (Roca & Colombi, 2003).

Journals

- *Bilingual Research Journal* (National Association for Bilingual Education & Arizona State University). Available at: http://brj.asu.edu/
- *Foreign Language Annals* (ACTFL). Available to members. Information available at: http://www.actfl.org/i4a/pages/index.cfm?pageid=3320
- *Heritage Language Journal* (UCLA Center for World Languages & UC Consortium for Language Learning and Teaching). Available at: www.heritagelanguages. org
- *Hispania*. Published by the American Association of Teachers of Spanish and Portuguese. Available to AATSP members at: http://www.hipaniajournal.org.

Institutes and Discussion Lists

- American Council on the Teaching of Foreign Languages (ACTFL) special interest group for Spanish for Native Speakers (SNS-SIG). Available at http://www.actfl.org/i4a/pages/index.cfm?pageid=3428
- Foreign Language Teaching Forum (FLTEACH). Available at http://www.cortland.edu/flteach/

Acknowledgments

The summer institute for SNS teachers was made possible by a grant from the National Endowment for the Humanities (NEH). I am grateful for their support, and particularly to Tom Adams, our NEH project officer, for providing valuable insights and guidance throughout the project.

Notes

1. This institute, Building the Knowledge and Expertise of Teachers of Spanish to Heritage Spanish Speakers, is referred to throughout this chapter as the 1999 NEH Summer Institute.
2. One of Dr. Campbell's professional goals was to give teachers opportunities to articulate their views of their field, and he used every venue possible to make this happen.
3. See Appendix 14.1 for a list of teachers who participated in the 1999 NEH Summer Institute.
4. The "SNS" designation also may refer to Spanish classes for heritage speakers or "fluent" speakers.
5. For an excellent overview of all aspects of SNS program development see Samaniego and Pino (2000).
6. For a list of tests used in SNS programs and more information about them, see Otheguy and Toro (2000).

References

American Association of Teachers of Spanish and Portuguese (2000). *Professional development series handbook for teachers K–16: Vol. 1. Spanish for native speakers.* Fort Worth, TX: Harcourt College.

American Council on Education. (2002). *Beyond September 11: A comprehensive national policy on international education.* Washington, DC: Author.

Aparicio, F. R. (1983). Teaching Spanish to the native speaker at the college level. *Hispania, 66,* 232-238.

Brecht, R. D., & Rivers, W. P. (2000). *Language and national security in the 21st century: The role of Title VI/Fulbright-Hays in supporting national language capacity.* Dubuque, IA: Kendall/Hunt.

California Department of Education. (1987). *Golden state exam* (Spanish language). Sacramento, CA: Author.

Campbell, R., & Peyton, J. K. (1998, Fall). Heritage language students: A valuable language resource. *ERIC Review, 6*(1), 38–39.

Carreira, M., & Armengol, R. (2001). Professional opportunities for heritage language speakers. In J. K. Peyton, D. A. Ranard, & S. McGinnis (Eds.), *Heritage languages in America: Preserving a national resource* (pp. 109–42). Washington, DC/McHenry, IL: Center for Applied Linguistics/Delta Systems.

The College Board. (n.d.). *Advanced Placement (AP) Spanish Language Exam.* New York: Author.

The College Board. (n.d.). *Advanced Placement (AP) Spanish Literature Exam.* New York: Author.

The College Board. (n.d.). *Scholastic Assessment Test II (SAT) in Spanish.* New York: Author.

The College Board. (n.d.). *Spanish Language Golden State Exam.* New York: Author.

Colombi, M. C., & Alarcón, F. X. (1997). *La enseñanza del español a hispanohablantes: Praxis y teoría.* Boston: Houghton Mifflin.

Compton, C. J. (2001). Heritage language communities and schools: Challenges and recommendations. In J. K. Peyton, D. A. Ranard, & S. McGinnis (Eds.), *Heritage languages in America: Preserving a national resource* (pp. 145–165). Washington, DC/McHenry, IL: Center for Applied Linguistics/Delta Systems.

CTB/McGraw-Hill. (1990). Language assessment scales-0 (LAS-0). New York: Author.

Cummins, J. (1986). Empowering minority students: A framework for intervention. *Harvard Educational Review, 56,* 18-36.

Educational Testing Service. (n.d.). *Spanish Praxis Exams.* Princeton, NJ: Author.

General Accounting Office. (2002). *Foreign languages: Human capital approach needed to correct staffing and proficiency shortfalls.* Washington, DC: Author. Retrieved on June 7, 2006, from http://www.gao.gov/new.items/d02375.pdf

International Baccalaureate Organization. (n.d.). International Baccalaureate (IB) Exam (Spanish). New York: Author.

Kraul, C. (2000, June 25). Latino talent pinch hobbling U.S. firms' expansion plans. *Los Angeles Times,* p. B1.

Otheguy, R., & Toro, J. (2000). Tests for Spanish-for-native-speaker classes. In American Association of Teachers of Spanish and Portuguese (Ed.), *Professional development series handbook for teachers K–16: Vol. 1. Spanish for native speakers* (pp. 91–98). Fort Worth, TX: Harcourt College.

Riverside Publishing. (1991a). *La prueba de ubicación para hispanohablantes.* Itasca, IL: Author.

Riverside Publishing. (1991b). *Woodcock language proficiency battery—revised* (WLPB-R). Itasca, IL: Author.

Ruiz-de-Velasco, J., & Fix, M. (2000). *Overlooked & underserved: Immigrant students in U.S. secondary schools.* Washington, DC: The Urban Institute.

Samaniego, F., & Pino, C. (2000). Frequently asked questions about SNS programs. In American Association of Teachers of Spanish and Portuguese (Ed.), *Professional development series handbook for teachers K–16: Vol. 1. Spanish for native speakers* (pp. 29–64). Fort Worth, TX: Harcourt College.

Schwartz, A. M. (2001). Preparing teachers to work with heritage language learners. In J. K. Peyton, D. A. Ranard, & S. McGinnis (Eds.), *Heritage languages in America: Preserving a national resource* (pp. 229–252). Washington, DC/McHenry, IL: Center for Applied Linguistics/Delta Systems.

Therrien, M., & Ramirez, R. R. (2001). The Hispanic population in the United States: March 2000. *Current Population Reports,* P20–535. Washington, DC: U.S. Census Bureau. Retrieved June 7, 2006, from http://www.census.gov/population/socdemo/hispanic/p20-535/p20-535.pdf

Thomas, W. P., & Collier, V. (1997). *School effectiveness for language minority students* (NCBE Resource Collection Series, No. 9). Washington, DC: National Clearinghouse for Bilingual Education. Retrieved June 7, 2006, from http://www.ncela.gwu.edu/pubs/resource/effectiveness/thomas-collier97.pdf

Valdés, G. (2000). Introduction. In American Association of Teachers of Spanish and Portuguese (Ed.), *Professional development series handbook for teachers K-16: Vol. 1. Spanish for native speakers* (pp. 1–20). Fort Worth, TX: Harcourt College.

Valdés, G. (2001). Heritage language students: Profiles and possibilities. In J. K. Peyton, D. A. Ranard, & S. McGinnis (Eds.), *Heritage languages in America: Preserving a national resource* (pp. 37–77). Washington, DC/McHenry, IL: Center for Applied Linguistics/Delta Systems.

Webb, J. B., & Miller, B. L. (Eds.) (2000). *Teaching heritage language learners: Voices from the classroom.* Yonkers, NY: American Council on the Teaching of Foreign Languages.

15

School-Based Programs for Heritage Language Learners

Two-Way Immersion

DONNA CHRISTIAN

Introduction[1]

Support in the nation's public and private schools for the preservation of heritage languages is not a new concept, though it may seem innovative in the context of current-day school policy and practice. Fishman (2001) points to the numbers of schools in the late 19th and early 20th centuries that incorporated instruction through heritage languages into the curriculum, inspired by the vitality of immigrant communities. A notable example is found in the German heritage schools, which numbered nearly 4,000 at the turn of the 20th century (Fishman, 2001). Some states even had explicit policies supporting such schools, such as the Nebraska law that allowed bilingual public schools (English plus another language) if parents of 50 students asked for such a program (Fishman, 2001). The extent of these policies and schools declined dramatically as a result of World War I, and support for heritage language maintenance and development in elementary and secondary schools has been low since then. As a result, most heritage language education, where it exists, is found in community-based schools, which often have no relationship to the local school system.

Lack of support for heritage language development has consequences for both individuals and our society. For individuals, loss of the ancestral language can lead to weaker connections with their community and culture and even with their immediate family. For our society, heritage languages represent the potential source of high levels of proficiency in hundreds of languages needed for trade, diplomacy, security, and defense (Brecht & Ingold, 2002). Failure to preserve and develop this resource wastes that potential. The years that students spend in elementary and secondary schools are key to the preservation of heritage languages.

In this chapter, I will discuss the educational and linguistic aspects of programs that may facilitate the maintenance and development of heritage languages from kindergarten through grade 12 in public and private schools in the United States. In this discussion, heritage language (in the U.S. context) will refer to a language other than English that has "a particular family relevance to the learners" (Fishman, 2001, p. 81). In other words, in a school setting, students whose families express a connection with a non-English language, either historically or currently, may be considered heritage language students.

In the following sections, I will begin with a brief overview of program types that may serve the purpose of maintaining and developing heritage languages in contemporary schools and then focus on dual language programs, in particular, two-way immersion education. For two-way immersion, I will discuss the approach, some ongoing research, and some issues that remain in need of attention.

School-Based Programs for Heritage Language Speakers

In designing school-based programs, important factors to consider include the vitality of the heritage language in the home and local community and the language proficiency profile of the students in both English and the heritage language. Communities vary widely in the extent to which the ancestral language is in everyday use, as well as in the attitudes of members toward the use of the language. As Wang and Green (2001) point out, heritage language community members, particularly those of school age, may be anxious to appear as "American" as possible, so that the use of English becomes an important symbol for them.

Valdés calls our attention to the range of proficiency levels a heritage language student may possess:

> Many immigrant students who come to this country as young children enter American schools with little knowledge of English and are classified as limited English proficient (LEP). By the time they arrive in high school and college, however, most will have acquired some English. Some will continue to be heritage language dominant; that is, their overall abilities in the heritage language will be much greater than their English language abilities. Second-, third-, and fourth-generation students, however, will be clearly English-dominant. Their strengths in English will very strongly overshadow their abilities in the heritage language. (Valdés, 2001, pp. 43–44)

Successful programs will take both the community context and the proficiency of students into account. When students begin school already proficient in English, instruction in other languages is usually seen as enrichment (and called "foreign language education"). Such English-dominant or English monolingual students may have a connection to the language of instruction (such as a second generation Chinese American with a limited familiarity with Chinese from the home community). On the other hand, when students have proficiency *only* in languages other than English, a major purpose of schooling in the United States is to add English skills to their repertoire, whether the heritage language is supported or not. This difference in students' language profiles (e.g., whether or not they are proficient in English) has enormous impact on the way programs in schools are viewed, and this fact cannot be ignored when looking at school-based programs. From the viewpoint of the resources represented by heritage languages, of course, all of these students bring valuable skills and knowledge with them (in terms of cultural knowledge and linguistic foundations), even if their proficiency levels are not very high.

Students in both language groups (English-dominant and heritage-language-dominant) may be heritage language speakers whose families desire to maintain those languages, or they may not. We cannot tell without considering family and community factors, including their attitudes toward various languages. In other words, school-based programs may need to be geared towards English-speaking students looking to reclaim their heritage language, or towards heritage-language-speaking students looking to learn English and develop their home language as well.

For English-proficient students, a range of language programs can be offered to help preserve and extend whatever proficiency in the heritage language they bring with them to school. These programs vary greatly in intensity–from weekly foreign language classes to full immersion, and they may or may not be tailored to the talents of heritage language speakers. For example, some schools are offering separate sections of foreign language courses designed to meet the needs of heritage language students, such as "Spanish for Native Speakers" (Roca, Marcos, & Winke, 2001). Such courses, currently found most often at the secondary level, build on the oral fluency that students may already possess, and focus on literacy and standard dialect issues.

One form of language immersion seeks to revitalize a language that is declining in use in a community by making it the medium of instruction in the classroom. This approach demonstrates a strong commitment to heritage language education on the part of the community and the school. Good examples are found in indigenous communities, exemplified by programs for Hawaiian (Yamauchi & Wilhelm, 2001), Mohawk (Jacobs & Cross, 2001), and Mäori (Benton, 2001). In these cases, students come to school speaking a majority language and the immersion program gives them an opportunity to acquire their heritage language, a critical link to their cultural heritage. The Hawaiian Language Immersion Program, *Papahana Kaiapuni*, for example, is implemented in kindergarten through grade 12 at a number of public schools in Hawaii. The program started in 1987, after parents and Hawaiian language activists who wanted to preserve the Hawaiian language vigorously promoted it. Students who speak either English or Hawaiian Creole English are immersed in Hawaiian in kindergarten through grade 4, with English introduced in grade 5. Curriculum development also aims at greater cultural relevance than evidenced in the traditional curriculum. Program evaluations indicate that students in the program are learning both Hawaiian and English and are achieving as well as their peers in other programs (Slaughter, 1997).

For heritage-language dominant students, other factors come into play. A major concern for educators is the need for these students to learn English, and this often overrides any consideration of the home language.[2] When bilingual programs are offered, they are generally transitional, with the primary goal to move into all-English programs, and they thus tend to be subtractive as a result. That is, the native language is used only as a bridge to all-English instruction, and no attention is focused on preserving or expanding knowledge of that language. As a result, use of the native language often declines, as students use English for more and more purposes, in and out of school. Naturally, the message conveyed by the school and community about the relative value of English and other languages plays an important role in this outcome.

Some programs do, however, aim to maintain and develop the heritage language while English is added. In these schools, programs lasting at least four to six years foster the goals of bilingualism and biliteracy. They have been called "maintenance bilingual programs," "developmental bilingual programs," and, recently, "dual language education." They are typically offered to classes that are only, or primarily, made up of English language learners. With academic instruction in the heritage language and in English, they represent an enriched, additive approach, where development of students' native language, along with English, is a desirable outcome. Developmental bilingual programs are found primarily in elementary schools, but they may articulate with specially designed language and content courses for heritage language students at the secondary level, so that language development can continue.

Two-way immersion education is one form of developmental bilingual or dual language education. In this approach, English-dominant and heritage-language-dominant students are integrated for all or most of the instructional day and are given content instruction and literacy instruction in both languages. In a sense, these programs are built on the foundations of both the foreign language immersion programs and developmental bilingual education. Goals of these programs include: (a) high levels of proficiency in the first and additional languages for all students, (b) academic performance at or above grade level (comparable to or better than other programs), and (c) positive cross-cultural attitudes and behaviors. Thus, two-way immersion is by definition a heritage language program, since students are expected to progress in their native language.

This approach can provide an effective means for heritage language learners to develop high levels of proficiency in the heritage language. Fluent speakers of a heritage language have the opportunity to develop that language for use in a wide range of contexts while also learning English. English-dominant students from the same cultural background may reclaim their heritage language and become bilingual. Thus, the two groups of students who come together may both include heritage language learners. Non-heritage language students (those English-dominant students who have no personal connection to the other language of instruction) also gain a second language.

Two-Way Immersion Education

Two-way immersion is increasingly popular in schools in the United States. A directory (Center for Applied Linguistics, n.d.), compiled as part of our research[3] at the Center for Applied Linguistics and updated regularly, gives an overview of programs in 338 schools as of 2007. Summarizing information across the entries in the 2001 directory, we find:

1. There has been a rapid growth in such programs since 1987, when 30 two-way programs were found.
2. Most two-way programs operate in Spanish and English (316 out of 338), but others pair English with Cantonese, French, Korean, and Navajo.
3. Most programs operate at elementary grade levels, kindergarten through grade 6, with 59 extending into the secondary level.
4. Programs vary in their design, language allocations, and student integration, as well as on a number of other characteristics.

While there are certain core characteristics shared by two-way programs, there is a great deal of variation in the conditions and manner of implementation. For example, design variations abound. The two major model variations are termed "90/10" (comparable to total immersion language programs) and "50/50" (comparable to partial immersion), based on the proportion of time spent in each language of instruction at the beginning of the program. In the "90/10" model, a large part of the instruction in the early grades is given in Spanish (or other target language). The amount of English instruction is increased at each grade level until the balance of the two languages is about equal. The allocation of languages of instruction by grade level in a 90/10 Spanish/English program might look as follows:

Grades K–1:	90% Spanish, 10% English
Grades 2–3:	80% Spanish, 20% English
Grades 4–5:	60% Spanish, 40% English
Grade 6:	50% Spanish, 50% English

In the "50/50" model, approximately half the instruction is provided in each language at every grade level, and the proportions of use of the two languages of instruction remain relatively constant over time.

Two-Way Immersion as Heritage Language Program

While all two-way immersion programs provide support for heritage language maintenance and development for at least half of the students, some place a special emphasis on that goal. A good example is L'Acadien du Haut St-Jean in the St. John Valley of Maine, a community near the Canadian border (The Education

Alliance, 2003). In the past, the community functioned as a bilingual French-English society, but in recent years, the school-age students are primarily English-dominant, and French speakers are in the minority.[4] In the early 1990s, a study of the local community documented the decline of the French language and the loss of Acadian identity, and community members reacted with concern. A Club Français was formed to encourage French in the schools (by donating French materials and sponsoring contests) and in the church, and the Maine Acadian Cultural Preservation Commission was established with federal funding.

A major development occurred in 1995, when a consortium of two school districts received federal funding to establish a two-way immersion program for French speakers and English speakers, mostly of Acadian heritage. In 2000, there were 200 students in the program, equally divided by language background, in grades kindergarten through 5. They are instructed in French 50% of the time in kindergarten, 70% of the time in grades 1–3, and 30% of the time in grades 4–5. Content areas are taught in both languages at all grade levels. According to school district reports, students in the program achieve excellent results in terms of both language learning and academic achievement progress. They consistently outperform other students on standardized assessments given in English in grades 1–5. The district does not report outcomes for assessments in French, but they note that "students ... develop fluency and literacy in two languages" (The Education Alliance, 2003). During the summer, a French immersion camp is offered. Parents are actively involved, volunteering in school activities and promoting language development outside school.

While it is too soon to assess the impact of this school-based program on French language vitality in the community, it is clear from reports that community enthusiasm is high, the profile of the language in local settings has been raised, and at least 200 students are much more proficient in French than they would have been without the program.

Ongoing Research on Two-Way Immersion

Programs like L'Acadien du Haut are increasing in popularity in the United States, but many questions remain, including issues related to how well such programs function for heritage language education in a society so dominated by English. In addition to documenting the range and features of programs around the country, our research[5] is addressing language learning and academic achievement in two-way immersion. Our sample includes programs at 11 schools in 8 states, all Spanish-English, spanning kindergarten through grade 5. Data on oral language proficiency, literacy, and academic achievement have been collected at regular intervals from a cohort beginning in grade 3 and followed through grade 5. In some of the schools, the students who entered the program as English-dominant speakers include members of Latino communities. At the end of three years, over 300 students remained in the sample.

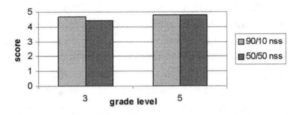

Figure 15.1 Oral Spanish Proficiency of Native Spanish Speakers (nes) in 90/10 vs. 50/50.

Of particular relevance to the present discussion are the results for Spanish language development, since this represents the heritage language in these programs. Analyses are ongoing, but preliminary findings indicate that the native Spanish speakers are orally fluent by grade 3 with little room for improvement on the measure used through grade 5 (see Figure 15.1), based on oral interview ratings. As might be expected, the levels are slightly higher in the 90/10 program where Spanish is used for more of the instructional day in the early grades. The native English speakers lag behind a bit, but are reasonably fluent in oral language by grade 5 (Figure 15.2).[6] It is worth noting that both groups of students were near the top of the scale in English as well. In Spanish writing, assessed on the basis of narrative writing samples collected three times per year, both sets of students show growth in mechanics, grammar, and composition over three years, with native Spanish speakers consistently rated higher than native English speakers, but with a great deal of variation in pace and path in both groups.

Our findings so far support the general observation that two-way immersion programs contribute to the maintenance and development of heritage languages for participating students. We do not have data disaggregated yet among English speakers to determine those who are of Latino heritage (i.e., in order to factor in heritage language affinity for that group), but our general results would indicate that they become fluent in Spanish along with all the others. Lindholm-Leary (2001), in a study of 16 elementary two-way immersion schools, also found that Spanish speakers were highly proficient in their native language through sixth grade, and consistently higher than Spanish speakers in transitional bilingual programs. For the purposes of heritage language preservation, the significance of these results lies in the fact that native Spanish speakers are gaining, rather than losing, language proficiency as a result of schooling.

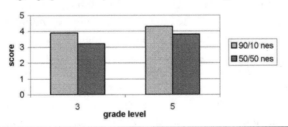

Figure 15.2 Oral Spanish Proficiency of Native English Speakers (nes) in 90/10 vs. 50/50.

In a related study, Lindholm-Leary and Borsato (2001) investigated the effect on high school students of participation in a two-way immersion program in elementary school. The study compared responses from Hispanic students who were native Spanish speakers, Hispanic students who were native English speakers, and non-Hispanic students. From a sample of over 100 two-way immersion graduates, the researchers found that Hispanic students, whether they entered school as Spanish speakers or English speakers, continued to use Spanish often in high school (nearly daily), especially with parents and other family members. They used the language significantly more often than non-Hispanic students and also felt more "comfortable" using Spanish. These results indicate further that two-way immersion programs support maintenance of heritage language use through high school, at least.

Issues and Research Needs

The efficacy of two-way immersion for heritage language education seems clear under many, but not all circumstances. The situations where two-way immersion works well need to be better understood and specific research questions need to be posed (e.g., What role do community attitudes play? What resources are critical? How important is stability of the student population?) Furthermore, the details of implementation also need further investigation, in order to make wise decisions about curriculum and instruction. In addition, a number of issues are particularly relevant to heritage language education, as I detail below.

Status, Power, and Heritage Languages

Very often, there is a socioeconomic differential between heritage language speakers and English speakers in two-way immersion. In addition, the power structures in the school and classroom usually reflect the broader society and the general dominance of the English-speaking community, resulting in, among other things, a clear status difference between the two languages. As Valdés (1997) cautions, this differential may cause the needs and perspectives of the heritage language students in two-way programs to be overlooked in favor of a middle-class, English-speaking population. There are several possible consequences of this situation for heritage students. The first is that they may lose interest in developing their heritage language given its low status. Another is that they may not be challenged and/or pushed to succeed given the program's focus on the perceived needs of the English speakers (with their lower proficiency levels in the heritage language).

Societal pressures promote assimilation to English, even when students are in programs like two-way immersion, so the preservation of other languages in schools requires focused attention. This issue relates closely to the challenge of creating a truly additive bilingual environment (one where another language is equally valued alongside English). Some question whether this is feasible or possible. If two-way immersion is to be effective for heritage language education, the issue merits serious attention (Christian, Howard, & Loeb, 2000).

Academic Achievement

Very often, heritage language speakers in two-way immersion have characteristics that may put them at risk academically, beyond their low level of English proficiency at school entry.[7] Emerging results suggest that these students perform better than their counterparts in other types of classrooms, but that there remains a gap between the performance of native English speakers and heritage language speakers within two-way immersion (Lindholm-Leary, 2001). The questions are far too great to go into here, but academic achievement issues must remain prominent in the discussion of school-based approaches to heritage language education in order to ensure that achievement is optimized along with language learning. For example, we need to understand much more about how literacy skills are acquired and flourish in first and second languages. When biliteracy is a goal, the various paths that may be followed in achieving it need further investigation, particularly in relation to different contexts, students, and languages.

Articulation

As we have seen, the majority of two-way immersion programs are in elementary schools. While it is generally agreed that well-articulated kindergarten through grade 12 programs are desirable, they are far from the norm. We do not yet have a good picture of the language, cognitive, and attitudinal effects of different lengths of participation in two-way immersion. In particular, we need to investigate if, for heritage language education, there are threshold levels and minimum amounts of instructional support that will promote continued growth in language skills for heritage language speakers. In other words, what is the minimum, and perhaps the optimum, follow-on to six years of two-way immersion to preserve and extend heritage language skills after elementary school? A number of secondary schools are now implementing programs designed to support ongoing language development for graduates of elementary two-way immersion schools (Montone & Loeb, 2000). Building on their experience to conduct further research, we may be able to begin to address these questions.

Heritage Languages Other than Spanish

As noted above, the vast majority of two-way programs pair Spanish with English. This is partially attributable to demographic characteristics and sheer numbers in the population. However, large communities of speakers of other languages, such as Chinese, Arabic, and Korean, make it feasible to offer two-way immersion in those languages in some communities (see chapter 16, this volume). Constraints that work against the creation of programs in languages other than Spanish include societal attitudes and the availability of resources (including prepared teachers who are proficient in the languages). We need to understand better what conditions foster the establishment of two-way immersion in languages other than Spanish/English and what can be done to bring those conditions about.

Another line of inquiry derives from the relationship between the particular languages paired in two-way immersion. For example, what differences come with pairing non-cognate languages, particularly when they do not share a writing system? A foundational premise of two-way immersion is the notion of transfer of skills across languages. However, as we examine transfer more closely, we find it to be a complex process, and differences emerge related to the languages involved in the case of literacy (Bialystok, 2001). Various pedagogical strategies might be more and less effective, depending on the languages. In sum, we should be careful not to overgeneralize results obtained from Spanish-English programs. Heritage languages other than Spanish in the United States may call for different paths through two-way immersion or in any school-based program.

Conclusion

The preservation of heritage languages in the United States is a deserving, but not widely held, goal of public and private education. At the moment, communities seeking to pass their language on to their younger members usually must rely on family and community-based efforts. However, as discussed here, a number of educational models integrate heritage language development with challenging academic curricula. They range from foreign language programs (for English-dominant students) to bilingual programs (for English language learners). Two-way immersion, a combination of the two, serves heritage language students across the continuum of proficiency.

Research on two-way immersion education supports its use for heritage language preservation, at least through elementary school. Many issues remain to be addressed, but they should not discourage schools from implementing two-way immersion when the demographic, attitudinal, and academic factors support such an approach.

The years devoted to elementary and secondary education are critical for language development. During these years, students come to understand the importance of English in our society. If they bring with them to school a connection with a heritage language, they can also learn, and learn to appreciate, that language. While it is not impossible to regain or acquire skills in a language at a later age, it is much less likely for most individuals who, as adults, find it hard to devote the time and effort required. The elementary and secondary school years are ideal for laying the foundation of language proficiency, and public/private school programs can incorporate that goal into their curricula. Two-way immersion and other school-based heritage language programs belong in the portfolio of offerings in our schools, to complement family and community efforts, so that families have this choice available to them for their children.

Notes

1. Preparation of this chapter was supported under the Education Research and Development Program, PR/Award No. R306A6001, the Center for Research on Education, Diversity & Excellence (CREDE), as administered by the Office of Educational Research and Improvement (OERI), National Institute on the Education of At-Risk Students (NIEARS), U.S. Department of Education (USED). The contents, findings, and options expressed here are those of the author and do not necessarily represent the positions or policies of OERI, NIEARS, or the USED.
2. See Genesee (1999) for an overview of programs for English language learners.
3. Within the research program on two-way immersion at the Center for Applied Linguistics, this project is part of the Center for Research on Education, Diversity & Excellence (CREDE), being conducted by a team led by Elizabeth Howard. Compilation of the online directory of two-way immersion programs is part of the CREDE project.
4. This is partly due to English-only policies in the schools that were enforced beginning in the 1950s.
5. These data are from the study of two-way immersion conducted by CREDE. For a summary of this project, see Howard, Christian, and Genesee (2004).
6. The scores are based on an oral interview where general conversational ability and grammatical sophistication and accuracy are rated on a 5-point scale, with a "5" indicating that a student always comprehends speech at a normal rate of speed, consistently uses varied and descriptive language when communicating about social and academic topics, uses grammatical forms usually or always correctly, and so on.
7. These characteristics often include ethnicity and socioeconomic status.

References

Benton, R. A. (2001). Balancing tradition and modernity: A natural approach to Mäori language revitalization in a New Zealand secondary school. In D. Christian & F. Genesee (Eds.), *Bilingual education* (pp. 95–108). Alexandria, VA: Teachers of English to Speakers of Other Languages.

Bialystok, E. (2001). Literacy: The extension of languages through other means. In R. L. Cooper, E. Shohamy, & J. Walters (Eds.), *New perspectives and issues in educational language policy* (pp.19–34). Amsterdam: John Benjamins.

Brecht, R. D., & Ingold, C. W. (2002). *Tapping a national resource: Heritage languages in the United States* (Report No. EDO-FL-02-02). Washington, DC: ERIC Clearinghouse on Languages and Linguistics, Center for Applied Linguistics. (ERIC Document Reproduction Service No. ED464515)

Center for Applied Linguistics. (n.d.). *Directory of two-way bilingual immersion programs in the U.S.* Washington, DC: Author. Retrieved August 15, 2007, from http://www.cal.org/twi/directory

Christian, D., Howard, E. R., & Loeb, M. I. (2000). Bilingualism for all: Two-way immersion education in the United States. *Theory into Practice, 39*(4), 258–266.

The Education Alliance, Brown University. (2003). Madawaska Elementary School and Gateway Elementary School, L'Acadien du Haut St. Jean. *Portraits of Success: National Association for Bilingual Education.* Providence, RI: Brown University. Retrieved retrieved April 2, 2006, from http://www.alliance.brown.edu/pubs/pos/madawaska.html

Fishman, J. A. (2001). 300-plus years of heritage language education in the United States. In J. K. Peyton, D. A. Ranard, & S. McGinnis (Eds.), *Heritage languages in America: Preserving a national resource* (pp. 81–97). Washington, DC/McHenry, IL: Center for Applied Linguistics/Delta Systems.

Genesee, F. (Ed.). (1999). *Program alternatives for linguistically diverse students* (Education Practice Report 1). Santa Cruz, CA: Center for Research on Education, Diversity & Excellence.

Howard, E., Christian, D., & Genesee, F. (2004). *The development of bilingualism and biliteracy from grades 3 to 5: A summary of findings from the CAL/CREDE study of two-way immersion education.* Santa Cruz, CA: Center for Research on Education, Diversity and Excellence.

Jacobs, K. A., & Cross, A. E. J. (2001). The seventh generation of Kahnawà:ke: Phoenix or dinosaur? In D. Christian & F. Genesee (Eds.), *Bilingual education* (pp. 109–121). Alexandria, VA: Teachers of English to Speakers of Other Languages.

Lindholm-Leary, K. J. (2001). *Dual language education.* Clevedon, England: Multilingual Matters.

Lindholm-Leary, K. J., & Borsato, G. (2001). *Impact of two-way bilingual elementary programs on students' attitudes toward school and college* (Research Report No. 10). Santa Cruz, CA: Center for Research on Diversity, Education and Excellence.

Montone, C., & Loeb, M. (2000). *Implementing two-way immersion programs in secondary schools* (Educational Practice Report 5). Santa Cruz, CA: Center for Research on Education, Diversity & Excellence.

Roca, A., Marcos, K., & Winke, P. (2001). *Teaching Spanish to Spanish speakers* (ERIC/CLL Resource Guide Online). Washington, DC: Center for Applied Linguistics. Available at: http://www.cal.org

Slaughter, H. (1997). *An evaluation study of the ninth year of the Hawaiian language immersion program, school year 1995–1996* (Report to the Hawaiian Language Immersion Program and to the Planning and Evaluation Branch of the Department of Education). Honolulu: Department of Education.

Valdés, G. (1997). Dual language immersion programs: A cautionary note concerning the education of language-minority students. *Harvard Educational Review, 67,* 391–429.

Valdés, G. (2001). Heritage language students: Profiles and possibilities. In J. K. Peyton, D. A. Ranard, & S. McGinnis (Eds.), *Heritage languages in America: Preserving a national resource* (pp. 37–77). McHenry, IL and Washington, DC: Delta Systems, Inc. and Center for Applied Linguistics.

Wang, S-H. C., & Green, N. (2001). Heritage language students in the K–12 education system. In J. K. Peyton, D. A. Ranard, & S. McGinnis (Eds.), *Heritage languages in America: Preserving a national resource* (pp. 167–196). Washington, DC/McHenry, IL: Center for Applied Linguistics/Delta Systems.

Yamauchi, L. A., & Wilhelm, P. (2001). *E Ola Ka Hawaii I Kona 'Ōlelo*: Hawaiians live in their language. In D. Christian & F. Genesee (Eds.), *Bilingual education* (pp. 83–94). Alexandria, VA: Teachers of English to Speakers of Other Languages.

16

The Korean/English Dual Language Program in the Los Angeles Unified School District

SUNG-OCK S. SOHN AND CRAIG C. MERRILL

Like all immigrant groups, Korean-born and second generation Korean-Americans lose competency in their heritage language through successive generations. The attrition of Korean language skills in children is often exacerbated by parental preferences and schooling practices. For example, in Los Angeles, Korean-speaking parents often prefer to enroll their children in all-English programs. This chapter describes the documented success of a program that helps children maintain and develop knowledge of their heritage language while acquiring high levels of English and academic skills.

Background

The Los Angeles Unified School District (LAUSD) has approximately 4,000 Korean English language learners (ELLs), whose proficiency in English upon entering school is limited. These students attend one of three programs—an English only (EO) program, a modified bilingual (MB) program, and a Korean/English dual language program (KDLP). The EO program delivers all instruction in English. In the MB program, Korean-speaking ELLs are instructed in English, are provided minimal primary language support, and are not taught literacy in Korean.[1]

While the EO and MB programs aim toward mainstreaming ELLs, LAUSD's Korean/English dual language program is a two-way immersion program (Cloud, Genesee, & Hamayan, 2000), with Korean-speaking ELLs and English-speaking students in the same classroom. All subjects are taught in English and Korean at all grade levels. Literacy is taught in both languages beginning in kindergarten. The program's goal is for all students to become bilingual and biliterate in Korean and English.

The KDLP began in 1992 in a kindergarten class of 30 students. Today, it is the only Korean/English dual language program in the nation offering instruction from kindergarten through Grade 12, and it serves more than 600 students in seven schools throughout the district. Over half of the program's students are Korean/Americans. Student achievement in the KDLP has surpassed that of students in other programs, and the program is considered one of the most successful dual language programs in the country.[2]

Theoretical Underpinnings

The KDLP program was proposed by Russell N. Campbell. Its design was informed substantially by his immersion work (Campbell, Snow, Rhodes, & Gray, 1984; Galvan & Campbell, 1979; Snow, Galvan, & Campbell, 1983), the second language acquisition theories of Krashen and Cummins, and the construct of sheltered language instruction.[3]

Central to the program is Krashen's (1981, 1982, 1984, 1985) notion that students are best able to acquire a second language through comprehensible input (i.e., language aimed at a level slightly above students' current level of language proficiency) and when the students' affective filter (or level of anxiety when encountering the second language) is reduced.

Also of critical importance is Cummins' (1981, 1984) distinction between Basic Interpersonal Communication Skills (BICS) and Cognitive Academic Language Proficiency Skills (CALP). Cummins proposes that the language used at home, in the neighborhood, and on the playground (BICS) and the language used in academic settings (CALP) differ both in nature and in the length of time needed to acquire proficiency. Cummins demonstrates the difference between BICS and CALP through analysis of the vocabularies used for each. In English, BICS favors the use of monosyllabic words of Anglo-Saxon origin, while CALP draws on vocabulary of French, Latin, or Greek origin. In Korean, on the other hand, BICS makes use of native Korean words, whereas CALP is composed of words primarily of Chinese origin. According to Cummins, acquiring BICS can occur in as few as one to two years, while acquiring proficiency in CALP is more demanding, requiring five to seven years of formal study.

Cummins also distinguishes between Common Underlying Proficiencies (CUPs) and Separate Underlying Proficiencies (SUPs) (Cummins, 1984; Cummins & Swain, 1986). CUPs refer to skills, knowledge, and concepts in the first language that will transfer across languages. For example, students who are literate in their first language will more readily acquire literacy in the second language due to their existing concept of a sound/symbol correspondence. SUPs, on the other hand, refer to skills that require no underlying proficiency and that are entirely language dependent. For example, knowing how to conjugate verbs in Spanish will not enable a student to conjugate verbs in Korean since conjugation in these two languages shares no commonalities.[4] Despite clear evidence that learning in the primary language facilitates SLA, there has been much debate concerning the value of teaching second language learners in their native language (Carrasquillo & Rodríguez, 2002). Cummins' advancement of CUPs and SUPs supports the notion that bilingual programs can be positive for ELLs, since instruction in both languages maximizes students' opportunities to both transfer existing concepts from the L1 and acquire new, non-transferable concepts in the L2.

Finally, the KDLP is grounded in the principles of sheltered content instruction (Brinton, Snow, & Wesche, 2003; Echevarria & Graves, 2003). This approach advocates the simultaneous learning of language and content with "sheltering" of the instructional delivery to allow learners to access challenging content. Such sheltering involves techniques such as a slower rate of speech, careful enunciation, gestures, realia, pictures, modeling, and scaffolding[5] to help students understand instruction in the second language. Sheltering not only enables learners to internalize new content knowledge; it also leads to increased language proficiency via comprehensible input.

KDLP students receive content instruction in both languages, allowing them to develop CALP. Exposure to concepts in the students' primary language increases the amount of CUPs available when students make a similar application in the second language. The common knowledge base afforded through CUPs allows students to capitalize on prior learning to make sense of what would otherwise be incomprehensible. Being able to connect concepts already understood with new language patterns allows the student to acquire language.

Research Findings

The KDLP at Cahuenga Elementary School received the California Association for Bilingual Education Seal of Excellence Award in 1998 and Exemplary Status from the California Department of Education in 1999. The process of applying for these awards and the attendant program evaluation led to the identification of features deemed critical for program success. Data presented in conjunction with the application process for Exemplary Status are presented in this chapter.

The chapter reports on two studies that document the academic success of the KDLP. Study One presents data collected at Cahuenga Elementary School from 1992 to 1996, the KDLP site offering the most comprehensive longitudinal data. This study represents the most extensive one to date on the effects of the KDLP and conclusively demonstrates its success. Study Two is a follow up begun in 2000 under the auspices of the Language Minority Research Institute at the University of California, Santa Barbara (Sohn & Merrill, 2000). It is a cross-sectional study of fourth and fifth-grade Korean/American students in the Oral Primary Language Development Program, the EO Program, and the KDLP. The data from both studies show that KDLP students outscore EO students on standardized tests of English and Korean and document the KDLP's positive influence on maintaining Korean language proficiency.

Study One: Cahuenga Elementary School

Methodology

Cahuenga Elementary School was chosen as a site for the KDLP because of its large Korean-speaking limited English proficient (LEP)[6] population and sufficient

272 • Sung-Ock S. Sohn and Craig C. Merrill

numbers of English-speaking participants. All students had access to bilingual credentialed teachers[7] and bilingual paraeducators.

The evaluation team that reviewed the program for the application for Exemplary Status identified the following program features as critical to program success:

1. Services provided: KDLP students receive instruction in both Korean and English according to a matrix that outlines the use of language, Specially Designed Academic Instruction in English or Korean,[8] and grouping strategies used in all content areas. The articulated curriculum and language arts program combines text, thematic instruction, and reflective writing.
2. Service providers: The service providers are administrators, teachers, and paraprofessionals who have received extensive training in the implementation of dual language programs. All teachers have either A-level proficiency in Korean (as determined by a LAUDS-administered exam in which proficiency is rated as A–C with A being the highest degree) or the BCLAD/BCC (California bilingual) credential to teach in Korean. All paraprofessionals are proficient in Korean as well.
3. Service recipients: The service recipients are English- and Korean-speaking students, at a ratio of approximately 30:70. English-speaking students may enter the program in kindergarten and first grade only. Korean-speaking students may enter the program at any grade level beyond first grade provided they are literate in Korean.

Our study considered four groups of students:

(1) Korean (Project) students who entered the KDLP in kindergarten and had no program changes thereafter.[9]
(2) English (Project) students who entered the KDLP as EO in kindergarten or first grade and had no program changes thereafter.[10]
(3) Korean (District) students who entered any program other than KDLP in kindergarten and had no program changes thereafter.
(4) District students who entered mainstream programs as English proficient in kindergarten and had no program changes thereafter.

Table 16.1 presents the relevant population statistics.

Within groups (1) and (2) above, two cohorts exist: those who entered kindergarten in 1992 (the Grade 4 cohort) and those who entered kindergarten in 1993 (the Grade 3 cohort.)[11] Group (3), the comparison group, consists of Korean-speaking students at the same grade level as the KDLP project students tested in the same or different years who did not participate in a dual language or full bilingual program. Finally, group (4) consists of all other students in the district; statistics on this group provide baseline data.

Table 16.1 Cahuenga Elementary School (1998)

	Number of Students	Percentage of Total
Total Enrollment	1158	100%
Total LEP Enrollment	950	82%
Korean LEP Enrollment	257	27%
Low Income Enrollment	989	85%

The Comprehensive Test of Basic Skills (CTBS) and the SAT 9 were used to test general academic achievement.[12] These tests are used by over 90% of California school districts and are considered reliable assessments of LEP and EO student progress.[13] To test Korean proficiency, a UCLA-developed Korean language test was designed (Bae, 2000; Bae, 2001; Bae & Bachman, 1998).[14]

Both project and comparison groups in this study consisted of longitudinal cohorts. The length of instructional exposure for all students was kindergarten through Grade 4. Project students in the Grade 3 and Grade 4 cohorts with fewer than two years of program participation and any students who did not have a continuous length of treatment, were not included.

Findings

To support the application for Exemplary Status from the California Department of Education, four claims were made that KDLP students outperformed students in monolingual programs and demonstrated an accelerated rate of improvement in the areas of English language development and student academic achievement (see Summary of Claims below).

Claim 1: Redisignation (English Language Development)

Redesignation is the process whereby students initially classified as LEPs are reclassified as English proficient based on test results.[15] Table 16.2 displays the English proficiency of Korean (Project) and Korean (District) students in the Grade 3 and 4 cohorts upon entry at kindergarten.[16] It is important to note that none of the Korean (Project) students were designated as functional or proficient upon program entry, whereas 21.7% of the Korean (District) students fell into these categories. In fact, 94% of the Grade 3 and 78.3% of the Grade 4 Korean (Project) cohort were designated non-proficient, as compared to the corresponding Korean (District) comparison groups (67.5% and 74.3%, respectively).

As shown in Table 16.3, Korean (Project) students in the Grade 3 cohort redesignated at a rate 40% higher than Korean (District) Students in EO or MB programs,[17] while Korean (Project) students in the Grade 4 cohort redesignated at a rate 25% higher than their Korean (District) peers in EO and MB program.[18] Note that both the Korean (Project) and Korean (District) students redesignate at a far higher rate than students in the district and statewide.

Claim	Target Group	Level of Achievement	Instrument
Claim #1: Redesignation (English Language Development)	Korean (Project) Students: Grade 3 & 4 Cohorts	On average, 40% and 25% higher than comparison group	District redesignation criteria
Claim #2: English Reading (Student Academic Achievement)	Korean (Project) Students: Grade 3 & 4 Cohorts	On average, 15 and 18 normal curve equivalents (NCEs) higher growth than comparison group	CTBS and SAT 9 English Reading components
Claim #3: English Reading (Student Academic Achievement)	English (Project) Students: Grade 3 & 4 Cohorts	On average, 12 and 14 NCEs higher growth than comparison group	CTBS and SAT 9 English Reading components
Claim #4: Korean Language (Student Academic Achievement)	Korean (Project) Students: Grade 3 & 4 Cohorts	On average, 14% and 41% more correct answers than comparison group	UCLA-developed Korean language test
Claim A: Mathematics (Supporting Evidence of Academic Achievement)	Korean (Project) Students: Grade 3 & 4 Cohorts	On average, 13 and 20 NCEs higher growth than comparison group	CTBS and SAT 9 Math components
Claim B: Mathematics (Supporting Evidence of Academic Achievement)	English (Project) Students: Grade 3 & 4 Cohorts	On average, 23 to 24 NCEs higher growth than comparison group	CTBS and SAT 9 Math components

Summary of Claims Claims made in the application for Exemplary Status. Note: *The Comprehensive Test of Basic Skills* (CTBS; CTB/McGraw Hill, n.d.) and the *Stanford Achievement Test, Ninth Edition* (SAT 9; The College Board, n.d.) are nationally-normed tests of English and math skills for grades 1 through 12.

This higher rate of redesignation may well be due to KDLP students having a strong knowledge base in their primary language, which is accessible when instruction is conducted in English. LEP students in non-dual language programs, on the other hand, receive content area instruction only in English, a language they do not understand, and therefore their knowledge base is inadequately developed. Also, because KDLP students are mixed with native speakers of English in all content areas and receive less formal instruction in English than they would in MB or EO programs, their exposure to authentic models and usage of English is greater.

Table 16.2 Pre-LAS and LAS English Proficiency Levels

	N	Non	Limited	Functional	Proficient
Grade 3 Cohort					
Korean (Project)	24	94.4%	5.6%	0.0%	0.0%
Korean (District)	360	67.5%	10.8%	13.1%	8.6%
Grade 4 Cohort					
Korean (Project)	17	78.3%	13.0%	8.7%	0.0%
Korean (District)	311	74.3%	5.6%	11.8%	7.3%

Note: For description of Pre-LAS and LAS test intruments, see CTB/McGraw Hill (n.d.). Pre-LAS: Language Assessment Scales for Kintergarten. LAS: Language Assessment Scales.

Table 16.3 Percent of LEP Students Redesignated

Cohort	Korean (Project)	Korean (District)	District	State
Grade 3	86%	46%	31%	28%
Grade 4	76%	51%	39%	36%

Claims 2 and 3: Student Academic Achievement (English Reading)

As shown in Table 16.4, Grade 3 cohort Korean (Project) students scored 7 Normal Curve Equivalents (NCE) higher than their Korean (District) peers in English reading during year 3. Although Korean (District) students were not tested in year one, the downward trend in this group's scores over the three-year period contrasts with the general upward trend in the Korean and English (Project) students' scores. Similarly, by the end of year three, Grade 3 cohort English (Project) students scored 28 NCEs higher than their English-speaking peers in the district's monolingual programs. It is likely that even though the English (Project) students received nearly 60% of their total instructional time in Korean, they outperformed their peers in the monolingual program because their literacy skills in Korean transferred to English and because they received reinforcement of their literacy skills across the curriculum in both languages.

During year one, Grade 4 cohort Korean (Project) students scored an average of 10 NCEs below their Korean (District) counterparts in English reading (Table 16.4). This trend is continued in year two, with KDLP students actually showing slightly lower scores.[19] However, by year three, program students showed an improvement of nearly 5 NCEs, while their Korean (District) counterparts dropped nearly 10 NCEs. Korean (Project) students continued their upward trend in year four while Korean (District) and District students appeared to stagnate around the 50th NCE. Displaying a slightly different pattern, Grade 4 cohort English (Project) students had a 12 NCE point lead in reading skills

Table 16.4 English Reading Scores

Grade 3 Cohort			
Group	# of Students	Year One (1994-95)	Year Two (1995-96)	Year Three (1996-97)
---	---	---	---	---
Korean (Project)	24	61.0	60.4	65.8
English (Project)	8	58.1	62.3	70.7
Korean (District)	345	a	67.4	58.7
District	15,500	41.3	36.5	42.0

Grade 4 Cohort				
Group	# of Students	Year One (1993-94)	Year Two (1994-95)	Year Three (1995-96)	Year Four (1996-97)
---	---	---	---	---	---
Korean (Project)	17	50.0	46.3	51.6	61.0
English (Project)	9	53.2	67.0	68.5	67.7
Korean (District)	303	61.1	61.3	51.6	53.9
District	15,500	41.3	42.5	42.5	42.5

Note: Scores expressed in Normal Curve Equivalents (NCEs)
[a] Not tested during this periods.

over peers in the district's monolingual programs in year one. While District students hovered around the 40th percentile, English (Project) students gained an additional 14 NCE points in year two, maintaining a nearly 25 point lead over their monolingual peers.

The test scores of the Grade 3 project cohort were taken from 8 students whose home language was English and 24 students whose home language was Korean. The test scores of the Grade 4 cohort were taken from 9 students whose home language was English and 17 students whose home language was Korean. Both groups of students had been in the KDLP for two or more years.

For the Grade 3 cohort, the differences in English reading between the Korean (Project) students and the Korean (District) comparison group and the District baseline comparison group were significantly in favor of project students, with standard deviation differences of .86 and .23, respectively (Table 16.5).[20] The difference in reading between English (Project) and English (District) students was also statistically significant, with a standard deviation difference of .60. For the Grade 4 cohort, the differences in English reading between the Korean (Project) students and the Korean (District) comparison group and the District baseline comparison group were significant in favor of project students, with standard deviation differences of .63 and .47, respectively. The difference in reading between English (Project) and English students in the District was also statistically significant, with a standard deviation difference of .70.

In both cohorts, the difference in reading between the English (Project) and District students was also statistically significant, with a standard deviation difference of .60 (Grade 3 cohort) and .70 (Grade 4 cohort) respectively (see Table 16.5). Both the English- and Korean-speaking students in the Korean/English Dual Language Program and all comparison groups have taken either the Comprehensive Test of Basic Skills (CTBS) or the Stanford Achievement Test (SAT 9) since first grade. The CTBS was administered district wide until the spring of 1996. The SAT 9 was adopted in spring of 1997 to replace the CTBS.

Table 16.5 Differences in English Reading Ability

Project Group	N	Comparison Group	N	t	p(t)	SD
Grade 3 Cohort						
Korean (Project) Students	24	Korean (District)	345	9.2	< .001	.86
		District (all students)	15,500	120.0	< .0001	.23
English (Project) Students	8	Korean (District)	345	15.9	< .001	1.21
		District (all students)	15,500	315.0	< .001	.60
Grade 4 Cohort						
Korean (Project) Students	25	Korean (District)	303	15.08	< .05	.63
		District (all students)	15,500	272.2	< .0001	.47
English (Project) Students	9	Korean (District)	303	4.8	< .05	.28
		District (all students)	15,500	40.8	<.001	.70

Table 16.6 Korean Reading Scores

		Grade 3 Cohort			
	N	Year One (1994-95)	Year Two (1995-96)	Year Three (1996-97)	
Korean (Project)	17	a	51.1	58.1	
Korean (District)	22	a	44.4	46.2	

		Grade 4 Cohort			
	N	Year One (1993-94)	Year Two (1994-95)	Year Three (1995-96)	Year Four (1996-97)
Korean (Project)	18	85.2	89.6	a	90.1
Korean (District)	21	37.4	45.6	a	59.9

Note: Scores expressed in Normal Curve Equivalents (NCEs)
[a]Figures unavailable.

Claim 4: Student Academic Achievement (Korean Language)

Table 16.6 displays the Korean reading scores of the Grade 3 and 4 cohorts. By year three, Grade 3 Korean (Project) students showed a 12-point lead in Korean reading over their Korean (District) counterparts. Similarly, Grade 4 cohort Korean (Project) students consistently outperformed their Korean (District) peers in EO programs, maintaining a 30- to 50-point advantage in reading scores.[21] Korean (Project) students demonstrated competence in Korean reading from first grade, a result of instruction in primary language literacy that began in kindergarten.

Claims A and B: Supporting Evidence of Academic Achievement

Table 16.7 displays the math scores of the Grade 3 and Grade 4 cohorts expressed in NCEs. Prior to academic year 1996–97, there are no notable difference in scores between the Korean (Project) and Korean (District) students for either cohort.[22]

Table 16.7 Math Scores

		Grade 3 Cohort			
	N	Year One (1994-95)	Year Two (1995-96)	Year Three (1996-97)	
Korean (Project)	24	86.9	82.7	84.7	
English (Project)	8	79.6	78.2	75.1	
Korean (District)	345	a	80.6	69.5	
District	15,500	52.1	47.9	52.1	

		Grade 4 Cohort			
	N	Year One (1993-94)	Year Two (1994-95)	Year Three (1995-96)	Year Four (1996-97)
Korean (Project)	17	70.1	74.7	63.5	89.6
English (Project)	9	82.7	89.6	74.7	78.2
Korean (District)	303	68.7	75.9	68.6	67.1
District	15,500	52.1	54.2	54.2	54.8

Note: Scores expressed in Normal Curve Equivalents (NCEs)
[a]Korean (District) students were not tested in Year One per District policy, which generally disallows testing of students who have a language other than English. For the Korean (Project) students, a waiver was requested and granted to allow testing in Year One.

However, in 1996–97, the district adopted the SAT 9. Correspondingly, during years three and four, the Korean (Project) students displayed noticeable gains over their Korean (District) counterparts. The Grade 3 project cohort's scores rose slightly while those of their district counterparts dropped by 1a NCEs. Similarly, the Grade 4 cohort's scores rose over 26 NCEs while their District counterparts' scores dropped slightly. Grade 3 and Grade 4 cohort English (Project) students also maintained their lead over their District counterparts during years 3 and 4. This lead, which began in first grade, is a result of a curriculum design that moves students through grade level content a year ahead of their peers. Overall, it is likely that the format of the SAT 9 advantaged the Korean (Project) students, who had received as much as 65% of their total instructional time in Korean and had developed problem solving skills in their native language.

Educational Significance of the Data Supporting Claims

In sum, the data demonstrate that in the KDLP program:

1. English language development is accelerated.
2. Academic achievement is improved.
3. Korean-speaking students maintain and develop their Korean language skills.
4. English-speaking students acquire a second language.

The district baseline data give us a benchmark against which to measure the success of the KDLP English (Project) students. English (District) students in other programs performed below their English counterparts in the KDLP. Similarly, the Korean (District) comparison group shows the average achievement of ethnic Koreans throughout the district, who have received instruction only in English or in English with minimal primary language support, and who performed significantly worse than their counterparts in the KDLP.

The following outline of features is deemed critical to program success.

1. Students begin reading programs in both languages in kindergarten.
2. Beginning in first grade, all subjects are delivered in both languages.
3. Translation is not used.
4. The two languages are strictly separated. A single lesson is conducted in one language only.
5. Content taught in one language is not taught in the other language; however, content delivered in one language may augment content delivered in the other language.[23]
6. Students are grouped homogeneously (by language and language ability) for language arts; instruction is tailored to meet the needs of each group.
7. Students are grouped heterogeneously (by language and language ability) for all other subjects.

Study Two: Fourth- and Fifth-Grade Korean/American Students

Methodology

Study One demonstrates that on tests of English reading, language, and math, Korean-speaking ELLs in the KDLP outperform their Korean-speaking peers in the LAUSD's EO programs. However, it does not shed light on the extent to which social factors (e.g., family income, social status, attitudes towards bilingual education, attendance at Saturday school) may contribute to the development of language and academic proficiency. Study Two examined these factors.

Five elementary schools representing EO, MB, and KDLP programs were selected for the study. Two San Fernando Valley schools, Castlebay Lane Elementary School and Andasol Elementary School, supplied the cohort of EO students. Twenty Korean subjects came from EO programs at Castlebay, while nine students came from Andasol. Wilton Place (26 students) and Cahuenga Elementary Schools (6 students) provided subjects in the MB program. Finally, subjects from the KDLP program were provided by Cahuenga Elementary School (9 subjects) and Denker Avenue School (15 subjects).

The SAT 9 test scores for all participant groups are shown in Table 16.8. The two EO programs have much higher reading, math, and language scores than the other schools in this study. These results seem to be related to a sociolinguistic factor: the two schools with the EO programs are located in upper-middle-class areas, whereas the other programs are offered by schools in the inner city area, including Koreatown in Los Angeles.

Data included information provided by parents, students' Korean language proficiency scores, and SAT 9 test results. Parents were asked about their education, income, social status, attitudes about the Korean language and bilingualism, and their children's extracurricular activities. Parents were also asked to identify which language they spoke at home, as well as how often they read to their children, and in which language. Next, a Korean language proficiency test was administered based on a series of visual illustrations, measuring communicative and grammatical competence.[24] Research assistants from UCLA recorded interviews with each subject and collected speaking samples from a total of 84 randomly selected students. Student reading and writing samples were also collected from all subjects. Finally, SAT 9 test results were collected for all fourth-grade students who took the test.

Table 16.8 SAT 9 Scores

School	Program	N	Reading	Math	Language
Wilton Place	MB	26	33	51	45
Cahuenga	MB	6	33 [a]	45 [a]	41 [a]
	KDLP	9			
Denker	KDLP	15	27	29	33
Castlebay	EO	20	71	74	72
Andasol	EO	9	56	57	55

[a] Disaggregated scores by type of program are not available for the Cahuenga cohort.

Table 16.9 Mean Korean Language Proficiency and SAT 9 Reading Scores

Program	Korean Language Proficiency	SAT 9 Reading Scores
KDLP	70.15	60.13
MB	45.20	42.27
EO	42.71	63.00
Total Group	**52.68**	**55.13**

Findings

Results on the Korean proficiency test were based on a 5-point rating scale. SPSS was used to examine correlations between Korean language proficiency and institutional programs as well as correlations between Korean language proficiency and other forms of academic achievement. Variables such as the use of private tutors, attendance at Korean weekend schools, educational level of parents, and socio-economic status were also investigated.

The Korean test group mean scores for Korean language proficiency and SAT 9 Reading are summarized in Table 16.9.[25] Students in the KDLP in Grades K–4 had the highest Korean language proficiency means of students in all programs while EO students had the lowest. For all groups, listening scores were higher than reading and writing scores (Sohn & Shin, 2007).[26] As expected, students whose parents speak mostly Korean at home scored noticeably higher in reading skills than those whose parents use both languages at home (Table 16.10). KDLP students also significantly outperformed peers in the MB programs in Stanford 9 English Reading and Math (Table 16.11). Moreover, KDLP students scored far ahead of MB and weekend students in Korean reading and writing. Our analysis of writing samples from Grade 4 KDLP students indicates a consistently higher level of Korean than for students in other programs, particularly in the usage of spelling rules, honorific forms, and speech.

We found a correlation between Korean language ability and English language skills, where KDLP students outperformed students in MB programs

Table 16.10 Korean Test Score by Parent Language

Parent Language	Korean Test Score	Distribution of Students			
		Total	KDLP	MB	EO
Both	45.51	47.2%	33.3%	43.5%	56.0%
Korean Only	58.31	52.8%	66.7%	56.5%	44.0%

Note: Scores expressed in Normal Curve Equivalents (NCEs)

Table 16.11 Korean Proficiency and SAT 9 Test Scores

Program	Korean	English Reading	Math	English Language
KDLP	70.15	60.13	72.14	66.05
MB	45.20	47.27	57.06	54.70

Note: Scores expressed in Normal Curve Equivalents (NCEs)

Table 16.12 Math SAT 9 Scores

Program	English Reading	Math
KDLP	60.13	72.14
MB	47.27	57.06
EO	63.00	74.23

Table 16.13 Parent's Income and Children's Academic Achievement

Parents' Income	Korean Test Score	Total	Dual	Modified bilingual	English only
Less than $50K	53.97	47.1%	50.0%	60.9%	29.2%
$50K-75K	51.45	30.9%	27.8%	30.4%	33.3%
$76K-100K	52.73	11.8%	16.7%	4.3%	16.7%
More than $100K	43.99	10.3%	5.6%	4.3%	20.8%

on standardized tests of English. There was, however, no significant difference between the scores of KDLP and EO program students in language, reading or math (Table 16.12).

There appeared to be no significant relationship between parents' income and students' Korean language performance (Table 16.13). While more than 70% of the parents are educated beyond the college level, neither their educational level nor their socio-economic status is shown to have an effect on academic performance as measured by these instruments.

Almost half of the subjects (47.7%) attended Korean language classes offered by local Korean churches, which typically offer classes for three hours per week on Saturday or Sunday. Attendance at Saturday school and Korean test scores by program (KDLP, MB, and EO) has little impact on the acquisition of Korean proficiency or academic achievement (Table 16.14). In fact, students who did not attend Saturday school scored better on average than those who did.

Significance

The juxtaposition of Studies One and Two clearly demonstrates the KDLP's effect over time and the tremendously positive influence that it has on maintaining the Korean language proficiency of participating Korean/Americans. Together, the studies also offer insight into the Korean communities in which the KDLP is situated.

Table 16.14 Attendance at Saturday School and Korean Test Scores

	Korean test scores				Distribution of students			
	Total	KDLP	MB	EO	All	KDLP	MB	EO
Attended	49.55	66.58	46.06	44.30	47.7%	45.8%	71.4%	62.1%
Didn't attend	57.73	76.81	37.25	45.31	29.5%	33.3%	28.6%	24.1%

Note: Language Proficiency measured on authors' 100-point scale.

The study's major findings show:

1. A positive correlation between higher levels of Korean language proficiency and placement in the KDLP
2. A positive correlation between higher levels of Korean language proficiency and parents who spoke Korean at home
3. No statistically significant difference in English language skills between KDLP and EO program students as measured by the SAT 9
4. Significantly lower scores in Korean language and general academic skills for MB students than for students in the dual language program
5. No correlation between attendance at Saturday Korean school and increased Korean
6. No correlation between socio-economic status and performance in English or Korean. However, parents with lower incomes and education levels were more likely to value the development of primary language skills.

Implications of Studies One and Two

K–12 Education

Although these studies did not examine EO programs, they indicate that Korean-speaking ELLs may be at risk in such programs because they enter school at a linguistic disadvantage vis-à-vis their English native-speaker peers, are not given support mechanisms to help them in the second language "sink or swim" environment, and are deprived of continued development in their home language, which has been shown to support and enhance second language literacy skills (see Collier, 1987, 1992, 1994).

The results do show that the MB programs for Korean-speaking ELLs are not effective. Their Korean language scores are not statistically different from those of EO program students. The limited use of Korean in a MB program neither enhances English language learning nor promotes Korean literacy. Moreover, students in these programs perform well below their dual language and EO program counterparts on standardized tests of English.

It is likely that the principles informing these bilingual programs are to blame. In these programs, Korean is used only to translate English language material that is not understood. Students make better progress, however, when both the primary language and English are used to teach content. To this end, teachers could be trained to deliver comprehensible lessons in English so that translation is not necessary.[27] Moreover, MB program students do not receive systematic instruction in Korean. In sum, the MB program curriculum is not designed to develop proficiency in either language.

Students in "modified" programs such as the one in this study would benefit from instructional strategies found in the more successful bilingual and dual language programs, including separation of languages, no translation, and the development of literacy skills in both languages.

These studies make clear that dual language programs provide the greatest benefit to participating students. Students in dual language programs not only develop English language skills on a par with peers in EO programs, but they also maintain and develop their Korean language skills.

Korean Saturday Schools

It is not clear why there is no correlation between Korean language development and attendance at Saturday school. The instructional program offered at Saturday schools varies from school to school and is largely unknown. If the poor showing of students in Saturday school is a result of instructional practice, it is unclear what that practice is, and more research is needed to explain it.

It is conceivable in principle that students in the dual language program had more knowledge of Korean than Saturday school attendees did when each group started school. However, virtually all parents in the study are first generation, and we would expect the Korean language ability of any group of five-year-old children of first generation parents to be comparable unless more than one language was spoken at home. The gap is more likely explained by programmatic differences, in that Saturday Korean schools focus on cultural enhancement rather than proficiency-oriented language instruction (Hadley, 2001).

Given that Saturday schools may not be the best environment to promote Korean language development, they could be encouraged to adopt effective strategies that allow students to communicate thoughts and feelings in the language, rather than merely talk about the language. These would include strategies outlined above for the MB programs, and those that employ the language for communicative tasks. It is the conjecture of this project's researchers that Korean is not used for communicative purposes in Saturday school programs. That is, Korean is not used to communicate real thoughts, ideas, or feelings. It is the content of lessons that separates knowledge of a language from its use as a communicative tool.

Conclusions

The findings of these studies can help to guide second language curriculum development efforts, by showing the need both to strengthen K–12 language and content instruction and to articulate goals. Furthermore, this research makes clear the urgent need for building Korean language study as a distinct academic discipline.

Educating language minority students is complex and controversial. Proponents of Proposition 227 (Clark, 1999; Unz & Tuchman, 1997), which in essence eliminated bilingual education programs in California, maintain that EO programs are the only way to educate ELLs (English for the Children, n.d.), while advocates of bilingual education insist that development of the primary language enhances SLA (Crawford, n.d.; Hakuta, n.d.; Krashen, n.d.; Krashen

& McQuillan, 1999).[28] This study supports the position that instruction in the primary language is beneficial when it is consistent and includes literacy development as in the dual language program. Because students in MB programs performed poorly on all academic and language indicators, an examination of instructional strategies used in these programs is warranted. Parents of children in EO programs need to know that their children not only may not develop better English skills but they also run a high risk of losing the precious resource of their primary language proficiency.

Acknowledgments

We are greatly indebted to Jesus Salazar of LAUSD's Program Evaluation Branch for the collection and analysis of data in Study One. We also wish to acknowledge the assistance of Ms. Hee Ju and Ms. Mi-Kyung Kim in the interviewing of Korean subjects in this project.

Notes

1. The LAUSD MB program is an early exit program, from which students transition to an English-only setting. This approach differs from the one used in traditional bilingual programs conducted in Spanish, which use Spanish for instruction throughout the day and have as their aim to develop literacy in the primary language. The rationale for the modified Korean bilingual program was that there were not enough Korean language instructional materials to teach core subjects and develop literacy in Korean.
2. The KDLP's success has led to the recognition and inclusion of dual language programs in the District Master Plan for the education of English language learners (Los Angeles Unified School District Board of Education, 1996). Most recently, the U.S. Department of Education has identified the KDLP as one of only six exemplary foreign language programs nationwide (Duncan, 2002).
3. The California Office of Bilingual Bicultural Education (1982) and California State Department of Education (1981, 1984) provide a useful summary of the relevant SLA theories.
4. Verbs in Spanish are conjugated according to 1st, 2nd, or 3rd person, singular or plural, whereas Korean conjugates verbs according to social position in relation to the speaker, listener, and third person referent.
5. Scaffolding refers to an instructional process of introducing material in a way that builds upon information presented earlier. Teachers are careful to introduce material in context with prior learning. Using themes to organize lessons across the curricula and developing instructional units are ways of scaffolding instruction.
6. The term "LEP" to designate ELLs is retained here due to its use in District guidelines. The two terms are roughly synonymous, although it should be noted that ELL is the preferred terminology today.
7. According to California educational code, credentialed teachers must possess one of the following certificates: the Crosscultural Language and Academic Development (CLAD), the Bilingual, Crosscultural Language and Academic Development (BCLAD), or the California Teacher of English Learners (CTEL) (California Teacher of English Learners, n.d.).
8. Specially Designed Academic Instruction in English/Korean is a phrase used in California public education to describe content courses taught to second language learners. The practice is more commonly known as sheltered instruction. See Brinton, Snow, and Wesche (2003), Echevarria and Graves (2003), and Rosen and Sasser (1997) for more information.
9. A program change is defined as entry into a dual language or bilingual program at any grade other than kindergarten, exiting a dual language program, or exiting a bilingual program for reasons other than redesignation.
10. It is important to note that students are identified as EO in kindergarten. However, these chil-

dren may have Korean language backgrounds. The label EO simply indicates that the student is fluent in English when entering school.

11. In this study, data for the Grade 4 cohort are reported for a 4-year period beginning in Grade 1 (1993–94 academic year); data for the Grade 3 cohort are reported for a 3-year period, also beginning in Grade 1 (1994–95 academic year).

12. The CTBS was administered until the spring of 1996. The SAT 9 was adopted in the spring of 1997.

13. Korean-speaking LEP students were granted a special waiver to take the exam even though they did not qualify for examination according to District guidelines. Their scores on these tests were disaggregated from school and District scores.

14. UCLA has used this test to measure the Korean language proficiency of project Korean and English-speaking students, and of non-project Korean-speaking students in Los Angeles and Seoul, Korea.

15. According to District and State guidelines (Los Angeles Unified School District Board of Education, 1996), redesignation requires that Korean LEP students demonstrate minimum levels of English language development as measured by the LAUSD Criteria for Addition of Reading in English (CARE) checklist (Los Angeles Unified School District Board of Education, 1996), read at a level no more than six months below grade level, score at or above the 36th percentile on language and reading components of the CTBS/SAT 9, and pass the reading and writing components of the English CARE test. Students in a dual language program who are redesignated do not exit that program (Los Angeles Unified School District Board of Education, 1996).

16. The instrument used to identify language proficiency was either the Pre-LAS (kindergarten) (CTB/McGraw Hill, n.d.) or the LAS (Grades 1–6) (CTB/McGraw Hill, n.d.), both nationally recognized evaluation instruments of English language ability. Based on the results of these tests, students receive one of four designations: Non, Limited, Functional, or Proficient.

17. These data are based on 12 of 14 Grade 3 cohort students who were in Grade 4 in 1997–98 and had redesignated. The other two Korean LEP students who had not redesignated had not passed all LAS (CTB/McGraw Hill, n.d.) read/write testing requirements.

18. These data are based on 16 of 21 LEP students who were in Grade 5 in 1997–98 and had redesignated. The other five LEP students who had not redesignated had not passed all LAS (CTB/McGraw Hill, n.d.) read/write testing requirements.

19. This may well be explained by the fact that KDLP students received less instruction in English than their peers.

20. A standard deviation difference is equivalent to an effect size difference. Effect size differences (standard deviation differences of .20 or greater) are generally considered to be educationally significant. The findings show that the differences are both statistically and educationally significant.

21. Although this difference is not statistically significant, it is practically or educationally significant (Kirk, 1996).

22. All cohorts showed a dip in scores in 1995–96, the year when the District adopted a new math program.

23. For example, in a unit on shapes, the following sequence of lessons might occur: lesson on circles (in Korean); lesson on squares (in English), lesson on triangles (in Korean).

24. This test measured all four skills. For the listening test, students were asked to listen to a taped story and match the narrative to a series of illustrations.

25. This test, consisting of listening, speaking, reading, and writing subsections, was based on a 5-point scale for each skill. The total score was converted to 100 points for the purpose of data analysis.

26. These scores are consistent with the knowledge of heritage speakers, who often can converse but tend to lack literacy skills in their home language. See Sohn and Shin (2007) for the characteristics of Korean heritage speakers.

27. Cloud, Genesee, and Hamayan (2000) and Echevarria and Graves (2003) are excellent teacher training resources.

28. Excellent online archives of material both for and against Proposition 227 are maintained by the University of Southern California's Center for Multilingual, Multicultural Research (USC Center, n.d.).

References

Bae, J. (2000). *The construct validation of certain components of English and Korean writing ability in children participating in either a two-way immersion program or monolingual classes: A writing assessment and latent variable approach.* Unpublished doctoral dissertation, University of California, Los Angeles.

Bae, J. (2001). Cohesion and coherence in children's written English: Immersion and English-only classes. *Issues in Applied Linguistics, 12,* 51–88.

Bae, J., & Bachman, L. F. (1998). A latent variable approach to listening and reading: Testing factorial invariance across two groups of children in the Korean/English two-way immersion program. *Language Testing, 15,* 380–414.

Brinton, D. M., Snow, M. A., & Wesche, M. (2003). *Content-based second language instruction* (classics ed.). Ann Arbor: University of Michigan Press.

California Office of Bilingual Bicultural Education. (1982). *Basic principles for the education of language minority students: An overview.* Sacramento: California State Department of Education.

California State Department of Education. (1981). *Schooling and language-minority students: A theoretical framework.* Los Angeles, CA: Evaluation, Dissemination and Assessment Center, California State University.

California State Department of Education. (1984). *Studies on immersion education: A collection for United States educators.* Los Angeles: Evaluation, Dissemination and Assessment Center, California State University.

California Teacher of English Learners. (n.d.). 2005–2006 CLAD/BCLAD/CTEL examinations. Retrieved May 21, 2006, from http://www.ctel.nesinc.com/index.asp

Campbell, R. N. (1984). The immersion education approach to foreign language teaching. In *Studies on immersion education: A collection for United States educators* (pp. 114–143). California State Department of Education. Los Angeles: Evaluation, Dissemination and Assessment Center, California State University.

Campbell, R. N. (1996). New learners and new environments: Challenges and opportunities. In R.C. Lafayette, (Ed.), *National standards: A catalyst for reform* (pp. 97–117). Lincolnwood, IL: National Textbook Company.

Campbell, R. N., Snow, A., Rhodes, N., & Gray, T. (1984). *Comparative evaluation of elementary school foreign language programs.* Washington, DC: Center for Applied Linguistics.

Carrasquillo, A. L., & Rodríguez, V. (2002). *Language minority students in the mainstream classroom* (2nd ed.). Philadelphia: Multilingual Matters.

Clark, K. (1999, June). From primary language instruction to English immersion: How five California districts made the switch. Retrieved May 21, 2006, from http://www.ceousa.org/READ/kclark.html

Cloud, N., Genesee, F., & Hamayan, E. (2000). *Dual language instruction: A handbook for enriched education.* Boston: Heinle & Heinle.

The College Board. (n.d.). *The Stanford Achievement Test, Ninth Edition* (SAT 9). New York: Author.

Collier, V. P. (1987). Age and rate of acquisition of second language for academic purposes. *TESOL Quarterly, 21,* 617–641.

Collier, V. P. (1992). How long? A synthesis of research on academic achievement in a second language. *TESOL Quarterly, 23,* 509–531.

Collier, V. P. (1994, March). *Promising practices in public schools.* Plenary address presented at the annual meeting of Teachers of English to Speakers of Other Languages, Baltimore, MD.

Crawford, J. (n.d.). *Issues in U.S. language policy.* Retrieved May 21, 2006, from http://www.humnet.ucla.edu/humnet/linguistics/people/grads/macswan/unz.htm

CTB/McGraw-Hill. (n.d.). Comprehensive test of basic skills (CTBS). Monterey, CA: Author.

CTB/McGraw-Hill. (n.d.). Language assessment scales (LAS). Monterey, CA: Author

CTB/McGraw-Hill. (n.d.). Pre-language assessment scales (Pre-LAS). Monterey, CA: Author.

Cummins, J. (1981). The role of primary language development in promoting success for language minority students. In *Schooling and language-minority students: A theoretical framework* (pp. 3–49). Los Angeles: Evaluation, Dissemination and Assessment Center, California State University.

Cummins, J. (1984). *Bilingualism and special education: Issues in assessment and pedagogy.* San Diego, CA: College-Hill.

Cummins, J., & Swain, M. (1986). *Bilingualism in education: Aspects of theory, research and practice.* New York: Longman.

Duncan, G. (2002). *Building upon success: The impact of FLAP grants.* Washington, DC: U.S. Department of Education, Office of English Language Acquisition, Language Enhancement and Academic Achievement for Limited English Proficient Students.

Echevarria, J., & Graves, A. (2003*). Sheltered content instruction: Teaching English-language learners with diverse abilities* (2nd ed.). Boston: Allyn & Bacon.

English for the Children. (n.d.) Retrieved September 9, 2004, from http://www.onenation.org/

Galvan, J., & Campbell, R. N. (1979). An examination of the communicative strategies of two children in the Culver City Spanish Immersion Program. In R. Andersen (Ed.), *Acquisition and use of Spanish and English as first and second languages: Selected papers from the twelfth annual convention of Teachers of English to Speakers of Other Languages* (pp. 133–150). Washington, DC: Teachers of English to Speakers of Other Languages.

Hadley, A. O. (2001). *Teaching language in context* (3rd ed.). Boston: Heinle & Heinle.

Hakuta, K. (n.d.). *Declaration of Kenji Hakuta.* Retrieved May 21, 2006, from http://www.humnet. ucla.edu/humnet/linguistics/people/grads/macswan/hakuta2.htm

Kirk, R. E. (1996) Practical significance: A concept whose time has come. *Educational and Psychological Measurement, 56*(5), 246–259.

Krashen, S. (1981). *Second language acquisition and second language learning.* Oxford: Pergamom.

Krashen, S. (1982). *Principles and practice in second language acquisition.* Oxford: Pergamom.

Krashen, S. (1984). Immersion: Why it works and what it has taught us. *Language and Society, 12,* 61–64.

Krashen, S. (1985). *The input hypothesis: Issues and implications.* London: Longman.

Krashen, S. (n.d.). *Essays on the anti-bilingual initiative.* Retrieved May 21, 2006, from http://www-rcf.usc.edu/~cmmr/EssayPage_Krashen.html

Krashen, S., & McQuillan, J. (1999). *Structured immersion falls short of expectations: An analysis of Clark (1999).* Retrieved May 21, 2006, from http://ourworld.compuserve.com/homepages/ jWCRAWFORD/Krashen5.htm

Los Angeles Unified School District Board of Education (1996). *The master plan for the education of limited-English proficient students.* Los Angeles, CA: Author.

Rosen, N. G., & Sasser, L. (1997). Sheltered English: Modifying content delivery for second language learners. In M. A. Snow & D. M. Brinton (Eds.), *The content-based classroom: Perspectives on integrating language and content* (pp. 35–45). White Plains, NY: Longman.

Snow, M. A., Galvan, J., & Campbell, R. N. (1983). The pilot class of the Culver City Spanish Immersion Program: A follow-up report, or: Whatever happened to the immersion class of '78? In K. Bailey, M. Long, & S. Peck (Eds.), *Second language acquisition studies* (pp. 115–125). Rowley, MA: Newbury House.

Sohn, S-O., & Merrill, C. (2000). Korean language development and academic achievement of Korean-Americans in the Los Angeles Unified School District. University of California, Santa Barbara: Linguistic Minority Research Institute (No. 98-06G-LA). Availabe at: http://www. lmri.ucsb.edu/research/lmri-grants/database/

Sohn, S-O., & Shin, S-K. (2007). True beginners, false beginners, and fake beginners: Placement strategies for Korean heritage learners. *Foreign Language Annals, 40*(3), 353–364.

University of Southern California's Center for Multilingual, Multicultural Research. (n.d.) *Archives on Prop. 227.* Retrieved May 21, 2006, from http://www-rcf.usc.edu/~cmmr/archives_227.html

Unz, R., & Tuchman, G. (1997). *California proposition 227: English language education for children in public schools.* File No. SA 97 RF 0009.

17
Enhancing Academic Language Proficiency in a Spanish Immersion Classroom[1]

ANDREW D. COHEN AND TANIA GÓMEZ

Introduction

Research on L2 (second language) immersion programs has found that students' use of what is known as *academic language* (Cummins, 1991) is not as developed as their overall L2 proficiency would suggest. For example, Allen, Swain, Harley, & Cummins (1990) found that the overwhelming majority (over 80%) of French immersion student utterances from Grade 3 and 6 study participants were one clause or shorter in length. Other studies of immersion classrooms have shown that students do not partake of extended academic discourse in the target language (Broner, 2001; Fortune, 2001; Genesee, 1987; Lapkin, Swain, & Shapson, 1990; Swain, 1996). In general, it has been observed that immersion students in upper grades tend to use the everyday or vernacular language when discussing academic content.

Immersion educators both in Canada and in the United States have found linguistic gaps in immersion learners' foreign language proficiency. Immersion students have been observed to rely on basic language forms because they have a reduced list of academic vocabulary and structures at their command. For example, a study of U.S. immersion students in the upper elementary grades at a Minneapolis school showed that the students seemed to have little or no ability to produce certain complex verb tenses such as those necessary for conditionals and subjunctives in Spanish (Félix-Brasdefer, 2001). Likewise, research into French immersion has shown that, in spite of several years of comprehensible input, students' spoken and written French contains numerous morphological, syntactic, and lexical deviations from native-speaker norms (Genesee, 1987; Lapkin, Swain, & Shapson, 1990). In addition, Genesee (1987) has concluded that students in bilingual and immersion programs fail to exhibit continuous growth in both their repertoire of communicative skills and their formal linguistic competence, because they are able to get by in school using a limited set of functional and structural skills. Genesee (1987) has also noted that in the upper elementary grades, there is pressure to increase English-medium instruction to prepare students for their standardized district examinations.

In response to these findings, researchers have explored methodologies that focus on the production of academic grammar and vocabulary. Swain (2000) makes the case, for example, that students need not only to have access to comprehensible input but also to produce output. Laplante (2000) conducted an output-oriented study of sixth-grade students in two French immersion classrooms. During the study, students were taught to observe chemical reactions, write experimental procedures, and formulate conclusions while conducting experiments. The results showed that the students learned to incorporate elements characteristic of scientific discourse into their own discourse. While their general ability to talk about science improved, the students still made numerous grammatical errors. Laplante recommended that greater emphasis be placed on contextualizing the academic language structures.

Day and Shapson (1991) conducted an experimental study of seventh-grade immersion students in French, to determine the results of providing them opportunities to use and improve their knowledge of the conditional form. Although the experimental group did not make gains in spoken use of conditionals, their written use of conditionals improved significantly. Several other studies have demonstrated the effectiveness of "language-sensitive content instruction" (see Harley, 1989, and Lyster, 1994, for further evidence in French).

Since the early years of immersion instruction, grammar instruction has typically been de-emphasized especially in the early grades, both because of an assumption that students will lose interest in it, and because experts have believed that grammatical forms would be acquired over time without formal instruction (see Cohen & Swain, 1976, p. 48, for an early statement of this principle).

Especially in the early years of immersion, the programs tended to be evaluated in terms of the foreign language proficiency achieved (see, for example, California State Department of Education, 1984). Until more recent years, little attention had been paid to the processes students use to operate in the second language. Cohen (1998) found that fifth and sixth-grade Spanish language immersion students in a St. Paul school used English more often than Spanish to solve word problems in math.[2] de Courcy's (2002) study investigated the processes involved in the acquisition of French by students in late immersion programs in Australia. She found that acquisition occurs as a result of a balance of input and output, mediated by private speech.

Many cognitive processes are verbalized either in the form of inner, or private, speech or social, or public, speech. In the first language (L1), inner speech or the *inner voice* (Tomlinson, 2000) develops at the same time as the external voice and mediates thinking. Tomlinson asserts that an L2 version of the inner voice can play an important role in L2 learning. Despite the potential for the development of an L2 inner voice, Tomlinson maintains that in L2 classrooms the external voice usually is given dominance from the very beginning, and that it inhibits development of the L2 inner voice.

A small corpus of empirical research has shown that advanced L2 learners do use an L2 inner voice for a number of language functions (Guerrero, 2005). In addition, de Courcy (1993) describes late immersion students spontaneously using their L2 inner voice. She found that students speak to themselves in French to achieve the following goals: (1) for positive reinforcement of their answer, (2) to avoid losing face by calling out a potentially wrong answer, (3) to make sense of the question itself, and (4) to get more practice in using the language. This report revealed that internalized speech plays a crucial role in language acquisition. This internal speech as reported by the students is much more than just rehearsal, or practicing of form.

To our knowledge researchers have not explored the benefits of developing the inner voice in L2 among early immersion students. The aim of this study was to give immersion students the opportunity to enhance the development of their inner voice. The portion of the study reported on in this chapter addressed the following research question: What are the effects of L2 inner voice development among immersion students on their oral academic language performance in science?

The Study

Two instructors were involved in the study: a teacher with immersion experience and a research assistant, both of whom were native speakers of Spanish.

The sample group consisted of 21 5th-grade students (age 10 to 11) at the Adams Spanish Immersion Elementary School in St. Paul. All but one student had attended full immersion Spanish classes since kindergarten. Two were native speakers of Spanish and spoke Spanish at home, and seven students had at least one relative with whom they spoke Spanish. The remaining twelve students spoke Spanish only at school. Based on the instructors' observations, approximately four proficiency levels were represented in the class: two native Spanish speakers; four students with high-level proficiency relative to the other nonnatives; seven students of intermediate proficiency; and nine students of low-proficiency.

At the beginning of the study the students completed two surveys in English: the *Learning Style Survey for Young Learners: Evaluating your Own Learning Styles* (Cohen & Oxford, 2001a) and the *Young Learners' Language Strategies Survey* (Cohen & Oxford, 2001b). The style preference data provided the teacher with information on how to group students for class activities.

Instrumentation

The Treatment

Before the study began, the research assistant and the instructor modeled think-aloud and inner voice protocols to demonstrate problem solving in the target language. This frequently repeated activity also gave the students an opportunity to hear two adults conversing about the science experiments and expressing opinions. Their additional goal was to model the use of appropriate academic language. During the modeling of the Spanish inner voice, the instructors explicitly focused on the language strategies they used. They also drew students' attention to the academic language that they used. In order to enhance use of their L2 inner voice, the instructors taught students to talk to themselves in L2 academic language using cardboard cell phones, conduct conversations with themselves while looking at themselves in a pocket mirror, use puppets, and write postcards to themselves in the L2 (which they then mailed to themselves).

At the beginning of the study, the students were not aware that they already used an inner voice in English to solve problems. They learned that they could use an L2 inner voice as a vehicle both for solving academic problems and when employing metacognitive strategies to monitor their vocabulary and grammar.

For this study, thirty lessons were planned according to the school curriculum in science and history. Each lesson emphasized the use of academic language and complex structures, in particular the subjunctive and the conditional moods, since native speaking children at that age control these structures but immersion children do not (Félix-Brasdefer, 2001).

Before each problem solving activity, the teacher modeled the use of the inner voice for solving the problem (see Cohen & Gómez, 2004, Appendix A, for a list of the activities and a sample lesson plan). At the end of each lesson, the instructors discussed the use of academic language in class.

Students were encouraged to pay attention to the strategies used in performing academic language tasks (see Cohen & Gómez, 2004, Appendix B, for sample language learning strategies associated with each activity). Strategies included creating mental linkages, repeating, highlighting, using synonyms, asking for clarification or verification, and collaborating or co-constructing responses with their classmates.

To acquire vocabulary, the students were taught to use the pattern provided in class, by consulting the dictionary, or by asking their peers. Students were also encouraged to draw pictures of new words in their notebooks or to create a mental picture of the words. The new academic vocabulary introduced in a given lesson was recycled in a subsequent lesson. Students were taught to employ speaking strategies by saying new vocabulary words to themselves and then repeating them out loud. They were also encouraged to plan ahead what they wanted to say and to ask their peers to help them in planning. Some of the activities included role-plays, skits, or presentations to the class. Students were also taught reading strategies that focused on explaining the meaning of text and vocabulary acquisition (see Cohen & Gómez, 2004, Appendix C for a sample of a vocabulary lesson activity). To practice writing, the students were shown how to make a record of the materials, the procedures, and the results for each experiment (see Cohen & Gómez, 2004, Appendix D, for a sample activity).

Data Collection Procedures

The data for the study were collected over a five-month period from October 2001 to February 2002. The initial surveys along with the pre- and post-measures were collected during regular class periods. Each measure took approximately 15 to 30 minutes to complete.

The pre-measure of oral academic language for science was administered in October 2001, prior to the onset of the intervention, and the post-measure was administered in February, immediately after completion of the intervention. The measures of oral academic language in science were administered by the research assistant (RA) and tape-recorded. All classroom sessions were audio-taped and some were video-taped, and the data from these recordings were transcribed. During the intervention, the RA took detailed notes after each class on the students' use of academic language, their development, and the teachers' input.

Data Analysis Procedures

Rating sheets were used to take pre- and post-measures of spoken language. The rating sheets consisted of four subscales: (1) facility in describing the problem in comprehensible Spanish, (2) quantity and quality of academic vocabulary, (3) quantity and quality of complex grammatical forms (e.g., use of the imperative, tenses, and mood), and (4) ability to define academic terms in Spanish. Each subscale had five points, with 5 = high ability and 1 = low ability. These quantitative ratings served as a preliminary indicator of whether individual students made gains in their academic Spanish over the period of the study. The final analysis, and the one presented in this chapter, was qualitative in nature and focused on the development of academic language according to the above categories over the course of the study.

Results

The results of the study suggest that the modeling of academic language by the instructors led to gains in students' use of such language. The interaction between the teacher and the research assistant provided the students with considerable comprehensible input. While the teacher noted that at first she felt "a bit silly" thinking out loud, once she got used to it, the think-aloud protocol became part of her routine. While the students also initially felt inhibited about using their inner voices in Spanish, in time they appeared to enjoy it. By the end of the intervention, the students were convinced that using their L2 inner voice helped them improve their L2 academic language production.

Development of the L2 inner voice appeared to improve students' ability to describe academic problems, use academic vocabulary, and define academic terms. At the same time, it appeared to have a negligible effect on students' ability to use complex grammatical forms (see Cohen & Gómez, 2004, for the details).

Several examples of pre- and post- intervention differences in the oral description of problems and in the definition of science terms follow.

Pre-Intervention Discussion of Science Problems

The following examples are taken from lessons about airplanes. The data were gathered from students at three different proficiency levels in an early session. The transcript shows that the descriptions from this period were lacking in detail and were sometimes incomplete:

RA: *Cuando trabajaste en grupos, ¿qué variables decidieron aplicar al avión?* 'When you worked in groups, what variables did you decide to apply to the plane?'

Cristina [low-proficiency]: *Inclinación y ah! peso y…* 'Incline and, ah!, weight and...'

RA: *Y ¿por qué aplicaron esas variables?* 'And why did you apply these variables?'

Cristina: *No sé.* 'I don't know.'

RA: *¿Qué querían saber con esta variable?* 'What would you want to know by using this variable?'

Cristina: *¿Cuántos vueltas necesitábamos para el movimiento de…* 'How many turns did we need for the movement of…'

RA: *Recuerdas cuales fueron los resultados del experimento?* 'Do you remember what the results of the experiment were?'

Cristina: *Fue 35 para todo y 19 para–* 'It was 35 for all and 19 for–'[3]

RA: *¿Sabes para qué sirve la hélice?* 'Do you know what function the propeller has?'

Paul [intermediate-proficiency]: *Si, para el aire para pasar, ir para cuando hacer rodear girar y el aire pasar y el avión y puedes hacer como un–xx.* 'Yes, for the air to pass, to go for when making it turn around and the air passes and the plane and you can make like a–xx.'

RA: *Cuando trabajaste en grupos ¿qué variable decidieron aplicar?* 'When you worked in groups, what variable did you decide to apply?'

Paul: *Si, ¿qué pasa si nosotros *pone[4] una cinta en un marcador y pone en *la[5] avión y pone cinta como en unos lápices y cosas así.* 'Yes, what happens if we put some tape in a marker and put it on the plane and put tape like on pencils and things like it?'

RA: *¿Cuál es el trabajo o función de la hélice?* 'What is the role or function of the propeller?'

Lucía [high-proficiency level]: *Se mueve muy rápido y da la energía para que el avión pueda volar.* 'It moves very fast and produces the force so that the plane can fly.'

RA: *Cuando trabajaste en grupos, ¿qué variable decidieron aplicar?* 'When you worked in groups, what variable did you decide to apply?'

Lucía: *Mire *el[6] línea suelto.* 'I look at the lose line.'

RA: *Y ¿por qué decidieron aplicar esta variable?* 'And why did you apply this variable?'

Lucía: *Porque ha va a ser como diciendo que es una variable más distinto que...* 'Because it is going to be like saying that it is a different variable from...'

RA: *¿Qué querían saber con esta variable?* 'What would you want to know by using this variable?'

Lucía: *Si vuela más rápido o más despacio.* 'Whether it flies faster or slower.'

Post-Intervention Discussion

The transcript of the discussion held at the end of the study, about pulleys, shows that students were able to describe solving the problem in a more meaningful, organized, and complete manner:

RA: *¿Cómo usarías una polea si tuvieras que rescatar un carro o un coche que se ha quedado atrapado en el lodo?* 'How would you use a pulley to rescue a car or a bus that has become stuck in the mud?'

Cristina [low-proficiency]: *Un carro polea como que tiene esfuerzo y entonces tiene un camión grúa y se levanta y la grúa va a levantar y no va a necesitar como no mucho esfuerzo pero *pequeño[7] esfuerzo. No pequeño pero como medio esfuerzo porque los dos son--xx, pero éste es como más pesado.* 'A car (acting as a) pulley is more likely to be strong and then you have a tow truck and it lifts and the tow truck lifts (it out) and it won't need a lot of effort but a little. Not a little but some effort because both--xx, but this is heavier.'

Paul [intermediate-proficiency]: *Si tiene un carro de grúa que tiene una polea para* attach *más o menos el otro y puede jalar el carro. Y si hay una muy grande polea entonces pueden *atacharlo[8] al carro.* 'If you have a tow truck that has a pulley to attach to the other (car) and you can pull the car. And if there is a bigger pulley, then they can attach it to the car.'

RA: *¿Cómo? ¿En dónde colocarías la polea?* 'How? Where would you place the pulley?'

Paul: *En la parte de arriba, delantera del carro y para levantar del lodo.* 'At the bottom part, in the front part of the car and lift from the mud.'

RA: *¿Y la otra parte de la polea?* 'And the other part of the pulley?'

Paul: *En otra parte que no sea en el lado que se atacho la otra.* 'In the other part that is not on the side where the other was attached.'

Lucía: *Puedes amarrar un lado de la polea al coche y después tú puedes como jalar en el otro lado de la cuerda y con menos esfuerzo peso levantando el coche.* 'You can tie the pulley to the car and then you can pull from the other side of the rope and then with less effort you can lift the weight of the car.'

Oral Definitions of Science Terms

Pre-Intervention

At the beginning of the intervention students defined academic terms using short sentences, everyday words, or simple tenses. They were unable to give a precise and comprehensible definition of the term. Students also tended to give examples to explain the term instead of supplying a definition. For example, when asked to define the word *oscilación,* 'oscillation' they responded that *es como un swing* 'it's like a swing', and when asked to define *una brújula* 'compass', they would respond: *es como un reloj para ubicar* 'it's like a watch for finding where we are.' Other students preferred to define it by miming: *es como esto, Tania* [while swinging his finger] 'It's like this, Tania.'

The following are transcripts of students of various proficiencies discussing the definition of *variable* in a science experiment:

RA: *Podrías decirme que entiendes por variable?* 'Could you tell me what you understand by variable?'

Robert [low-proficiency]: *Variable es como decir algo que cambia, y como constante es algo que no cambia. El longitud del hilo.* 'Variable is like saying something that changes, and like a constant is something that does not change. The length of the thread.'

RA: *¿Qué entiendes por variable?* 'What do you understand by variable?'

Paul [low-proficiency]: *Es que cambia.* 'It changes.'

RA: *¿Qué es una brújula?* 'What is a compass?'

Rosa [low-proficiency]: *Es como un reloj.* 'It is like a clock.'

RA: *¿Podrías decirme que entiendes por variable?* 'Can you tell me what you understand by "variable"?'

Susana [intermediate-proficiency]: (no answer)

RA: *¿Sabes que es una variable?* 'Do you know what "variable" means?'

Susana [intermediate-proficiency]: *Es un ... yo pienso es un cosa de que usas como variable...el peso, los ingredientes, el tamaño, esas cosas.* 'It is a...I think it is a thing that you use as a variable... the weight, the ingredients, the size, those things.'

Some definitions were confusing to the point of unintelligibility:

RA: *¿Podrías decirme qué entiendes por variable?* 'Would you tell me what you understand "variable" to mean?'

William [intermediate proficiency]: *Es algo que cam... No eso es. Si eso es lo otro. Es como los yo pienso que es una variable algo los materiales, los cosas que hiciste necesita, que quiere hacer, que quieres hacer que cambia, que tu quieres que sea así que cambia que tu quieres cambiar. No sé.* 'It is something that change... No, it's not that. Yes, it is the other thing. It is like the...I think that is a variable, something like materials—the things that you did need, that you want to do, that you want to make change, that you want to be this way, that changes, that you want to change. I do not know.'

RA: *¿Sabes qué es una variable?* 'Do you know what a "variable" is?'

Lucía [high-proficiency]: *Si, es una cosa que haces diferente en un experimento.* 'Yes, it is something we do different in a scientific experiment.'

RA: *Y podrias decirme ¿qué entiendes por variable?* 'And could you tell me what do you understand by "variable"?'

Andrea [native speaker]: *Es lo que cambia.* 'It is what changes.'

As seen from these examples, the students provided brief definitions of the terms and in most cases used the word *cosa* (thing.) A special session was devoted to teaching the students to define terms more precisely; they also were given lessons in producing complete sentences and were provided reinforcement in class.

Post-Intervention

The transcripts of discussions held after the intervention show that intermediate-proficiency students were able to give definitions of terms with more confidence and accuracy than they had previously. The intermediate-proficiency students began to replace simple terms like *cosa* or *algo* with more sophisticated academic vocabulary such as *instrumento or objecto*. Moreover, most of the intermediate proficiency students tried to plan, organize, and produce better definitions after the intervention. The following are examples of how Susana and William defined academic terms in Spanish after the intervention, while working on a science experiment with pulleys:

RA: *¿Qué entiendes por fulcro?* 'What do you understand "fulcrum" to mean?'

Susana [intermediate-proficiency]: *Un fulcro es el punto de la polea que puede mover de lado a lado. Es el punto medio para balancear.* 'A fulcrum is the point on the pulley that can move from side to side. It is the middle point for balancing.'

William [intermediate-proficiency]: *Es la parte de una palanca que se balancea como la pesa.* 'It is the part of a pulley that balances the weight.'

The low-proficiency students were also planning, organizing, and producing more complete utterances after the treatment, as the following example shows:

RA: *¿Qué entiendes por fulcro?* 'What do you understand "fulcrum" to mean?'

Paul [low-proficiency]: *El fulcro es la* [instead of the masculine article el] *objeto que balancea la palanca.* 'The fulcrum is an object in which the pulley swings.'

As can be seen, the oral academic language used in these latter utterances was more complete and comprehensive when the students were following the model studied for producing academic language with more precision.

Discussion and Conclusions

The aim of this study was to determine whether students' academic language could be improved. An intervention was planned which involved: (1) exposing the students to modeling by the instructional staff on solving science and history problems in Spanish academic language, and (2) enhancing the students' inner voice in academic Spanish. The intervention emphasized problem solving in academic Spanish using the L2 inner voice and collaborating with classmates.

The students' development of their inner L2 voice appeared to assist them in solving problems in science and history. In addition, the qualitative analysis of Spanish academic language performance over time provided some evidence that the treatment may have had a positive effect on language development. Students tended to show some improvement over the course of the intervention in their ability to describe academic problems in Spanish and define academic terms with greater accuracy (see Cohen & Gómez, 2004, for more detailed examples).

Limitations and Recommendations for Future Research

Because several innovations were applied at the same time, it was not possible to determine the extent to which any particular innovation had more impact than another. In addition, because the sample included only one fifth-grade classroom, it is difficult to generalize the findings across immersion classrooms in the same school and across different immersion programs. The size of the sample group did not allow for the use of more rigorous statistical analysis. Finally, it could be seen as a limitation of the study that there was an extra adult in the classroom for five months, who would not be present in the average immersion classroom and who therefore created an intervening variable. As a result, the students received more individual attention than usual and may have spent more time on task in Spanish.

It would be beneficial to replicate this study, correcting for its limitations by administering only one type of intervention in separate immersion classes, and by ensuring that only one adult was in the classroom. Ideally, the sampling of immersion students would be large enough to allow for differing treatments.

Conclusions

The results of this study suggest that when students are provided with explicit strategies for developing their knowledge of academic language, their knowledge is improved. In addition, the necessity to use academic language in assigned tasks either helped students retain their knowledge of the language or led them to remember that there was specific language for what they needed.

What could be considered a contribution in this research was the combination of innovations (e.g., teacher modeling and supporting students' inner voice development in Spanish). These innovations, as well as the presence of two native speakers of Spanish in the classroom, appeared to bring about a classroom environment in which immersion students improved their ability to use Spanish academic language.

Notes

1. We would like to acknowledge and thank the following people: Martha Bigelow, for input regarding the design and implementation of the study; Annie Ericson, for assistance with data analysis; and Concha Fernández del Rey and her students, for their participation in the study; Merrill Swain for helpful input in the planning of the study; and Emily Acosta-Thompson, Principal of the Adams School, for her enthusiastic support. The study was funded through a National Language Resource Center grant to the Center for Advanced Research on Language Acquisition, University of Minnesota. We would also like to acknowledge Elaine Tarone's insightful feedback on earlier write ups of this study.
2. While the data collectors in that study were native English speakers, the data were collected over a series of months in different class situations, so the switch to using English in math problems was not simply a function of the language of the data collector.
3. "–"indicates that the last word was inaudible on the tape, and "–xx" indicates that the student was cut off without finishing the utterance
4. The standard form is *ponemos.*
5. The masculine noun *avión* requires the article *el.*
6. Instead of *la línea suelta*, with the article and adjective in the feminine.
7. This construction calls for the adverb *poco* rather than the adjective *pequeño.*
8. This context would require *amarrarlo* instead of **atacharlo.*

References

Allen, P., Swain, M., Harley, B., & Cummins, J. (1990). Aspects of classroom treatment: Towards a more comprehensive view of second language education. In B. Harley, P. Allen, J. Cummins, & M. Swain (Eds.), *The development of second language proficiency* (pp. 57–81). Cambridge: Cambridge University Press.

Broner, M. (2001). *Impact of interlocutor and task on first and second language use in a Spanish immersion program* (CARLA Working Paper #18). Minneapolis, MN: University of Minnesota, Center for Advanced Research on Language Acquisition.

California State Department of Education (1984). *Studies on immersion education: A collection for United States educators.* Sacramento, CA: Publication Sales, California State Department of Education.

Cohen, A. D. (1998). *Strategies in learning and using a second language.* Harlow, England: Longman.

Cohen, A. D. & Gómez, T. (2004). *Enhancing academic language in a fifth-grade Spanish immersion classroom* (CARLA Working Paper #24). Minneapolis: University of Minnesota, Center for Advanced Research on Language Acquisition. Retrieved August 19, 2007 from http://www.carla.umn.edu/bibliography/documents/cohen_gomez.pdf

Cohen, A. D. & Oxford, R. L. (2001a). *Learning Style Survey for Young Learners: Evaluating your Own Learning Styles.* Experimental measure. Minneapolis: University of Minnesota, Center for Advanced Research on Language Acquisition. Retrieved August 9, 2005, from http://www.carla.umn.edu/about/profiles/CohenPapers/Young_Style_Survey.doc

Cohen, A. D. & Oxford, R. L. (2001b). *Young Learners' Language Strategies Survey.* Experimental measure. Minneapolis, MN: University of Minnesota, Center for Advanced Research on Language Acquisition. Retrieved August 9, 2005, from http://www.carla.umn.edu/about/profiles/CohenPapers/Young_Lg_Strat_Srvy.doc

Cohen, A. D., & Swain, M. (1976). Bilingual education: The `immersion' model in the North American context. *TESOL Quarterly, 10*, 45–53.

Cummins, J. (1991). Interdependence of first- and second language proficiency in bilingual children. In Bialystok E. (Ed.), *Language processing in bilingual children*. New York: Cambridge University Press.

Day, E., & Shapson, S. (1991). Integrating formal and functional approaches to language teaching in French immersion: An experimental study. *Language Learning, 41*(1), 25–58.

de Courcy, M. C. (1993). Making sense of the Australian French immersion classroom. *Journal of Multilingual and Multicultural Development, 14*(3), 173–185.

de Courcy, M. C. (2002). *Learners' experiences of immersion education*. Clevedon, England: Multilingual Matters.

Félix-Brasdefer, C. (2001). Exploring the grammatical performance of dual immersion students at the end of fifth grade. Paper presented at University of Minnesota.

Fortune, T. (2001). *Understanding immersion students' oral language use as a mediator of social interaction in the classroom*. Unpublished doctoral dissertation, University of Minnesota, Minneapolis.

Genesee, F. (1987). *Learning through two languages: Studies of immersion and bilingual education*. Cambridge, MA: Newbury House Publishers.

Guerrero, M. C. M. de. (2005). Guerrero, M. C. M. de. (2005). *Inner speech – L2: Thinking words in a second language*. New York: Springer.

Harley, B. (1989). Functional grammar in French immersion: A classroom experiment. *Applied Linguistics, 10*(3), 331–359.

Lapkin, S., Swain, M., & Shapson, S. (1990). French immersion research agenda for the 90's. *Canadian Modern Language Review, 46*(4), 638–667.

Laplante, B. (2000). Apprendre en sciences, c'est apprendre à «parler sciences»: Des élèves de l'immersion nous parlent des réactions chimiques. *The Canadian Modern Language Review, 57*(2), 245–271.

Lyster, R. (1994). The effect of functional-analytic teaching on aspects of French immersion students' sociolinguistic competence. *Applied Linguistics, 15*(3), 263–387.

Swain, M. (1996). Integrating language and content in immersion classrooms: Research perspectives. *Canadian Modern Language Review, 52*(4), 529–549.

Swain, M. (2000). The output hypothesis and beyond: Mediating acquisition through collaborative dialogue. In J. P. Lantolf (Ed.), *Sociocultural theory and second language learning* (pp. 97–114). Oxford: Oxford University Press.

Tomlinson, B. (2000). Talking to yourself: The role of the inner voice in language learning. *Applied Language Learning, 11*(1), 123–154.

18

"Oh, I Get It Now!"
From Production to Comprehension in Second Language Learning

MERRILL SWAIN AND SHARON LAPKIN[1]

Introduction

In the late 1980s, we began the task of developing a research agenda for French immersion education in the 1990s, an agenda that was eventually published in 1990 after much feedback from colleagues, parent groups, and various professional organizations (Lapkin & Swain, 1990). At that time, as now, it was stated that with respect to *listening comprehension*, French immersion students attain native-like levels of performance. Even then, however, cautionary qualifications were made. Lightbown (as cited in Lapkin & Swain, 1990) for example, wrote:

> ...I think lots of us are increasingly uncomfortable with general statements about comprehension skills and look forward to more sophisticated studies which will probe the limits of immersion students' comprehension abilities so that, eventually, gaps in these abilities can be taken into account in teacher training and curriculum planning. (p. 644)

Lightbown's call for studies probing the limits of French immersion students' comprehension have gone unheeded, and indeed, the study we are reporting in this chapter was conducted to continue our exploration of how language production mediates second language learning. In this chapter, however, we focus on how production mediates comprehension. We chose this focus because, as we analyzed our data, we discovered that the short story we had asked students to listen to turned out to be more difficult for them to understand than we had anticipated. Yet, by the end of the multi-stage task, students had come to understand some things that, by their own admission, they initially had not understood. How did this happen?

Theoretical Premises

We base this chapter on two theoretical premises. The first premise is that one entry into language learning is through language production. Wertsch and Stone (1985) point out that:

…it is possible to produce [external sign forms] without recognizing the full significance that is normally attached to them by others. As a result, it is possible for a child [a language learner] to produce seemingly appropriate communication behavior before recognizing all aspects of its significance as understood by more experienced members of the culture. (p. 167)

In other words, language learners often say, or write, more than they realize they are saying or writing, and it is through coming to understand what is meant by what they produced that language learning occurs. This occurs through interaction with others and the self. Anna,[2] one of the 12-year-old students in the study we will shortly describe, expressed this idea rather succinctly. While she listened to a story being read aloud, she had made notes that were later incorporated into a written version of the story. Later, when she was interviewed, Anna talked about how she had written down things she had heard, even though she did not understand them: "I was like, "What is that?", and then after [we were finished], it was sort of, "Oh, I get it now!" (Anna, interview, turn 150).

We will consider what happened between the "What is that?" and the "Oh, I get it now!" in more detail below, but the important point here is to note that Anna, in spite of not knowing what the phrase meant, produced something nevertheless. The interaction she had with others gave it meaning, moving Anna along considerably in understanding what she had originally produced without comprehension.

The second premise is that through talking or writing, we may reach a new or deeper understanding. Von Kleist (as cited in Appel & Lantolf, 1994) wrote, in the early 19th century, a paper titled "On the gradual working out of one's thoughts in the process of speaking." His advice at that time, which is relevant to the theoretical premise under discussion, is as follows:

If you want to understand something and can't figure it out by pondering, I would advise you, my dear ingenious friend, to speak of it to the next acquaintance who happens by. It certainly doesn't have to be a bright fellow: that's hardly what I have in mind. You're not supposed to ask him about the matter. No, quite the contrary, you are first of all to tell him about it yourself. (p. 132)

In other words, by externalizing one's inner speech (e.g., Swain, 2000; Talyzina, 1981), ideas are crystallized and sharpened, and inconsistencies become more obvious. This externalized speech is an object about which questions can be raised and answers can be explored with others or with the self. When questioned by the researcher, Sue, another 12-year-old in our study, put considerable time and effort into providing incorrect and inconsistent explanations for why she used the pronoun *se* in the way she did (see below). She finally said: "I think…I don't know. I don't really get why you do need *se*" (Sue, Stimulated Recall, turn 88).

In trying to state her rule for the use of the pronoun *se* for the researcher,

Sue began to recognize the inconsistencies in what she was saying and, having heard what she herself said, realized that it did not make sense.[3] Interaction with another person prompted her realization, and interaction with the self readied her for an explanation that was different from her original misconceptions.

Study Design

In asking how language production mediates the process of comprehension, we are moving in a different direction from the research questions posed by others, for example Gass (1997) and Long (1996), as to whether conversational moves such as comprehension checks and confirmation requests make input more comprehensible. Instead, we want to demonstrate here that at least some language learning proceeds from production to comprehension, rather than what is usually argued, from comprehension to production. The role that interaction plays in this process will become clear as we present our examples.

The data presented in this chapter come from four of 12 students in a Grade 7 early French immersion class who participated in a study we conducted during the spring of 2000. The participants were drawn from a single class in a middle school in the greater Toronto area where most students come from middle-income families. The teacher of the four students judged the students to be "average." That is, on a 7-point scale, where "7" indicates a high level of overall proficiency in French, Emma was judged a "5," Sue and Anna "4s," and Jim a "3." Emma and Sue worked individually, and Jim and Anna worked together, on a multi-stage task that began with listening to a story and writing it out (a dictogloss task).[4]

For each of the task sessions, the students (individually or in pairs) came to a small room in the school where tape- and video-recorders were set up. Data were collected over a period of two school weeks in the following stages/sessions (the language of each session and the approximate length of time it took to do each session appear in parentheses for each stage):

Stage 1: Writing (Pretest in French; 30 minutes)

At the beginning of this session we showed the students a five-minute video-taped lesson focusing on pronominal verbs in French (*les verbes réfléchis*).[5] Jim and Anna then saw a segment of the video in which two students working in a pair modeled a dictogloss task (for details, see Swain & Lapkin, 2001). Sue and Emma were each shown a segment of the video where the same dictogloss task was modeled by a single student thinking aloud as he wrote. The video ended with the instructor reading a short story (see Appendix 18.1), twice, at normal speed. The students took notes while the story was read. These notes helped the students to reconstruct the story as they worked individually or in pairs. The students who worked individually (Sue, Emma) talked aloud while they wrote.

An adult native speaker of French reformulated each text in preparation for the next stage (for details, see Lapkin, Swain, & Smith, 2002). The reformulator had been asked "to revise the students' text to reflect target-language usage while preserving the students' original meaning."[6]

Stage 2: Noticing (in French; 10 minutes)

Two days later, the students were handed the story they had written, now typed. They were also given a typed copy of the reformulated version of their story. The students were asked to notice aloud differences between the two texts.

Stage 3: Stimulated recall (in English; 40 minutes)

Two days later, we showed the students the videotape that had been made of them during the noticing session, stopping the tape at each feature where they had noticed a difference between the story they had written and the reformulated version. The students were asked their opinions of the changes and why they thought they had been made. To prepare for this stage, the research team watched the videos of the noticing sessions, locating where students had verbalized differences between the two texts. In the stimulated recall session, then, one research assistant operated the video, stopping at each relevant location. A second researcher operated tape recorders and a third identified the changes and interacted with the participants. Although the latter research assistant was asked to play no instructional role, this proved to be an unrealistic request, as will be seen in the examples below.

Stage 4: Posttest (15 minutes)

Four days later, the students were given a typewritten copy of their original story (pretest) and asked to write it again (posttest), making any changes they wanted. At this stage the students worked independently.

Stage 5: Interview (in English; 15–20 minutes)

A day later, the students were interviewed individually to elicit their perceptions of all stages in the task.

Findings

We analyzed three extended examples from the transcribed data, one each from Emma, Jim and Anna, and Sue. We selected these examples because they were representative of learners moving from production to comprehension. We adopted several conventions in the presentation of the examples:

1. For each student or pair, a figure at the beginning of the relevant section of the chapter presents the pretest, the reformulation of the pretest, a translation of the reformulated text, and the posttest(s). Within the figure, we have bolded the text that we focus on.
2. None of the French errors the students made in their writing have been corrected. When we transcribe speech, we spell it correctly; for non-words (e.g., *pil*) we use the best approximation.
3. We do not provide translations of French in our text except in cases where the reader cannot infer the meaning from consulting the texts in (1) above. Where translations are given, translated text is put in braces ({}).
4. With the exception of French text in the figures, French words or phrases appear in italics.
5. French excerpts quoted in the main text are italicized. English excerpts quoted in the main text are placed in quotation marks.
6. Abbreviations in the examples include the following: W = writing stage; N = noticing stage; SR = stimulated recall stage; I = interview. The letters representing participants are: E-Emma, J-Jim, A-Anna, S-Sue, and R-Researcher. A sequence that appears as follows: SR-S. 34: should be read as Stimulated Recall, Sue, turn 34.
7. Other transcription conventions are: a) ... indicates a pause; b) - indicates an unfinished utterance; c) indented text indicates overlapping turns; d) [...] indicates omitted words or phrases; e) glosses and transcribers' comments are enclosed in square brackets; f) a space between lines of a transcript indicates that some turns in the sequence have been omitted.

Finally, viewing the videotapes leaves no doubt that all participants were engaged in all stages of the task. They cooperated with the researchers, paid attention to the mini-lesson and task modeling, and worked industriously either on their own or with each other and the researcher.

Emma[7]

In the pretest, reformulation, and posttest (see Figure 18.1), we have highlighted in bold the sentences that constitute the discourse problem that Emma focuses on throughout the multi-stage task.

In her interview, when asked to assess her story in comparison to the reformulation, Emma states: "...I got the main idea, I just had to reverse some sentences." Indeed Emma did get the story line, but her ordering of the bolded sentences in the pretest represents a logical inconsistency because she does not comprehend the meaning of the second sentence (*Le plume sort de réveille à 6:02*) which she produces nevertheless. In the writing stage, as Emma thought aloud while writing her story based on the notes she had taken as the dictogloss

Pretest
Martine lève le matin, mais elle ne veut pas se levé. Elle a des beaux rêves. **Finalement elle se lève. Le plume sort de réveille à 6:02.** Puis elle brosses se dents et commence d'aller à l'école.

Reformulation	Translation of Reformulation
Martine se réveille le matin, mais elle ne veut pas se lever. Elle fait de beaux rêves. **La plume sort du reveil à 6:02. Finalement, elle se lève.** Puis elle se brosse les dents et part pour l'école.	Martine wakes up in the morning, but she doesn't want to get up. She is having sweet dreams. **The feather comes out of the alarm clock at 6:02. Finally she gets up.** Then she brushes her teeth and leaves for school.

Posttest
Martine lève le matin, mais elle ne veut pas se lever. Elle fait des beaux rêves. **Le plume sort du réveille à 6:02. Finalement elle se lève.** Puis, elle brosse ses dents et part pour l'école.

Figure 18.1 Emma's Pretest, Reformulation and Translation, Posttest.

was read, she signaled a lack of comprehension of the key idea that the feather comes out of the clock:

W-E. 13: *Elle a …des beaux rêves…um, finalement……elle se lève……um, Je ne comprends pas vraiment ce qui arrive alors… le plume sssort…* [She is having sweet dreams…um, finally……she gets up……um, I don't really understand what happens next…the feather comes out…]

Given the opportunity four days later to compare her text with the reformulation (during the noticing session), Emma reconfirms that lack of understanding:

N-E. 16: Oh, ok…um… *C'est presque la même chose…ok, um…Ok, um, je ne comprends pas ce que 'la plume sort du réveil' veut dire.* [looks at researcher and smiles] *J'ai juste écrit,* um…Ok, *je vais écrire la différence…um…* [writing on her sheet]. *De rév…de…*[stops writing] *puis…finalement, elle se lève…C'est presque la même chose mais l'ordre est différent…* {Oh, Ok… um… It's almost the same thing…Ok, um, Ok, um I don't understand what "the feather comes out of the alarm clock" means. [looks at researcher and smiles] I just wrote…OK, I'm going to write down the difference…um,…[writing on her sheet] Of the ala…of …[stops writing] then …finally she gets up…It's almost the same thing but the order is different…]

Emma gets help with the problematic sentence from the researcher during the stimulated recall session:

SR-R. 5: [snippet of video] Ok. Were you able to hear that?
SR-E. 6: Uh-huh.

SR-R. 7: Do you remember what you were asking about?

SR-E. 8: Yeah. I didn't really understand what the *plume* thing was all about.

SR-R. 9: So in the story, or - ?

SR-E. 10: Yeah, yeah.

SR-R. 11: Ok, do you want to ask about that?

SR-E. 12: Yeah [laughing]. I don't understand what it means.

SR-R. 13: Ok. So there was a mechanical arm

SR-E. 14: Yeah.

SR-R. 15: That came out of the clock.

SR-E. 16: Oh. [beginning to understand]

SR-R. 17: With a feather.

SR-E: 18: OH!

SR-R. 19: So, yeah, you were right, it did...the *plume*, the feather did come out.

SR-E. 20: OH! Ok.

SR-R. 21: So you did get it correct.

SR-E. 22: Ok. It's sort of like...I sort of wrote like what I like heard.

SR-R. 23: Um-hum.

SR-E. 24: Even though I didn't understand it.

In turn 8 Emma tells the researcher that she did not understand what the *plume* sentence meant. Given some encouragement to ask for more information (turn 11), in turn 12 Emma reiterates that she does not understand what it means. The researcher supplies relevant idea units in the turns that follow: "a mechanical arm" (turn 13), "that came out of the clock" (turn 15). Emma begins to understand in turn 14, and when the researcher supplies the key lexical item, "feather" (turn 17), Emma finally comprehends completely (turn 18). She explains further, in turn 20, that she wrote what she heard (as she listened to the dictogloss), "even though I didn't understand it" (turn 22).

Once she fully understands, she is then able to address a problem at the discourse level of her story:

SR-E. 39: *Alors j'ai écrit que le plume sort après qu'elle lève. Mais maintenant je comprends...* [So I wrote that the feather comes out after she gets up. But now I understand...] I understand that it doesn't make sense. Here it is the other way around.

SR-R 40: OK, so it makes more sense that way?

SR-E.41: Yeah. Uh-huh.

As we saw in N-E.16, in the noticing session, Emma had noticed a difference in the ordering of two pieces of information between her original story and the reformulation. The reformulator had revised a logical inconsistency by reversing two ideas so that the feather's emergence (and the implied tickling) preceded Martine's[8] getting up. Having accepted this change in Stage 2, Emma explains in stage 3 (SR, turn 39) that "I wrote 'the feather comes out after she gets up' and that "here (i.e. in the reformulated text), it is the other way around." In the posttest, Emma adopts the re-ordering of the reformulation.

In the course of noticing and verbalizing the difference between the reformulation and her own text and her interaction with the researcher in the stimulated recall, Emma comes to grips with the logical inconsistency, stating in turn 39 of the stimulated recall: "I understand that it doesn't make sense." Her understanding is confirmed in her correction of the order of events in the posttest. Once the researcher supplied the meaning of the lexical item *plume* (see above, turns 17 and 19, stimulated recall), Emma could turn her attention to the discourse problem and successfully re-order two key events in the story. Here is what she says about the process in her interview:

I-R.103: …Did you try to figure out why one version was better than the other?

I-E.104: Yeah, because the *plume* thing, I get it now. But I'd no idea what it meant before.

I-R.105: So that was something about the story that you weren't sure about?

I-E.106: Yeah, yeah.

I-R.107: Because your French with that part was really good.

I-E.108: Ah [laughs] 'cause I kind of just tried to copy what I saw, what I heard on TV [the video], but I didn't really understand it.

Jim[9] and Anna[10]

In the next example, we see Jim and Anna working together and producing a text including at least one unanalyzed "chunk" that they gradually come to understand. The multi-stage task provides multiple opportunities to revisit the problematic phrase that is bolded in Figure 18.2. In the excerpts that follow, the adverbial phrase in question will not be translated: it is, in the original dictogloss, *la tête au pied du lit et les pieds sur l'oreiller* {her head at the foot of the bed and her feet on the pillow}.

In her interview, Anna signals an initial lack of comprehension of this idea unit [head at the foot of the bed]:

I-A. 148: …And then there was a part with like *tête au pied*, I think I talked to you about that. I didn't get that part, you know.

I-R. 149: So that was something that you'd heard in the story.

I-A. 150: Yeah. Yeah. Like I'd written down *pil* or *pied* and stuff like that, [...] and then after I was like: 'what is that?' and then after it was sort of "Oh, I get it now!". So, you see, that worked.

I-R. 151: You had heard something.

I-A. 152: Yes, I'd heard them and I'd written them down [...]

Pretest (collaboratively written)
Il est 6:00 heure du matin, quand le révaille sonne. **Tête a pil d'oreille**, Martime ne veut pas révaillé. Elle ferment le révaille en sendors encore. A 6:02 un main méchanique tien un plume au pied du Martime est la révaille. Finalement elle sort du lit, elle sabille pour un autre jour d'école.

Reformulation	**Translation of Reformulation**
Il est 6 h du matin quand le réveil sonne. **La tête au pied, et la tête sous l'oreiller**, Martine ne veut pas se réveiller. Elle éteint la sonnerie du réveil et se rendort. A 6 h 02 une main mécanique chatouille le pied de Martine avec une plume, et la réveille. Finalement, elle sort du lit, et elle s'habille pour un autre jour d'école.	It is 6 a.m. when the alarm clock rings. **Her head at the foot, and her head under the pillow**, Martine does not want to get up. She stops the ringing of the alarm clock and falls asleep again. At 6:02 a mechanical hand tickles Martine's foot with a feather, and wakes her up. Finally, she goes out of the bed and she gets dressed for another day of school.

Posttest – Jim
Il est 6h du matin quand le révaile sonne. **Têt au pied du lit sous l'oreille**, Martine ne veut pas révailler. Elle étaient la sonnerie et se rendort encore. A 6:02 un main mécanique tien un plume au pied de Martine est la révaille. Finalement elle sort du lit et elle s'abille pour un autre jour d'école.

Posttest – Anna
Il est 6h du matin quand le revaille sonne est Martine ne veux pas révaillé. **Tête au pied du pil et tête su l'oreille**, elle étainnent le sonnerie et se rendors. À 6:02 une main mécanique chatouille le pied de Martine avec une plum. Finalement elle sort du lit, elle s'habille pour un autre jour d'école.

Figure 18.2 Jim and Anna's Pretest, Reformulation and Translation, Posttest.

Indeed in the writing stage (stage 1), Anna insisted that the mysterious phrase from the notes she took as she listened to the dictogloss be included in the text. Her persistence extends over 16 turns in the three excerpts that follow:

W-A. 48: Ok...his ...so I think something about the *tête à pil de* something....*A pil de...* cause his head was on the pillow...*à pil de*.

W-J. 49: Oh, um -

W-A. 50: [whispering] *tête à pil de* something.

W-J. 51: *A six heures...deux?*

W-A. 52: no, no, no. No, no, no...This is before it.

W-A. 60: No, you have to write *son tête à pil de* something. How do you say pillow?

W-J. 61: *Plume.*

W-A. 62: No! That's feather...*couche d'oreille.*

W-J. 63: [very softly] *couche.*

W-A. 64: *couche d'oreille.*

W-J. 65: *couche...couche...couche...couche de...* I don't know. Ok.

W-A. 66: *Oreiller?...oreiller?...*that's-

[Jim is re-reading their story]

W-J. 243: *A six heures deux, un main mécanique tient un plume aux pieds*
W-A. 244: *tête à pil!!* No, we need to put *tête à pil de* something [taps pen emphatically on the table]... *pil d'oreille*, I think it's *tête à pil d'oreille*.
W-J. 245: No, but if we don't know-
W-A. 246: Yeah but at least it's better than not writing it ... right?

In turn 48, Anna is working out the idea that Martine's head (*tête*) is on the pillow ("à *pil de* something"). When Jim tries to skip over this part of the narrative in turn 51 ("*A six heures deux*" {at 6:02}, Anna (turn 52) insists that the component of the story she is working on comes before the sentence Jim is trying to introduce. Later in turn 60, Anna asks for help with the lexical item pillow and Jim supplies an incorrect lexical item, *plume*. Anna correctly points out in turn 61 that *plume* means feather and proposes an incorrect lexical item *couche d'oreille*.[11]

In turn 63 Jim repeats *couche*, and in turn 64 Anna repeats her new-found lexical item *couche d'oreille*. Jim then tries this item out, repeating *couche* four times (turn 65) before acknowledging "I don't know." Unexpectedly, Anna comes up with the correct word for pillow, *oreiller* (turn 66), though she does not use it in subsequent stages of the task. Toward the end of the writing stage as Jim re-reads their jointly constructed story, he again (turn 243) skips over what Anna insists be included (turn 244): "No, we need to put *tête à pil de* something ... *tête à pil d'oreille*."

In turn 245 Jim wonders elliptically if they should write down a phrase that they do not fully understand, and in turn 246 Anna declares: "at least it's better than not writing it...right?" As we will see, the fact that the phrase appears in their written story ensures that it is reformulated, and allows for it to be noticed (noticing stage) and discussed in the stimulated recall. Undoubtedly, this is why both students include the relevant idea units in their posttests.

In the reformulation, the idiosyncratic phrase *tête a pil d'oreille* is changed to *La tête au pied [du lit], et la tête sous l'oreiller*. Jim and Anna notice the difference between their original story and the reformulation in two places during the noticing stage:

N-A. 26: [...] *tête* [laughs]
N-J. 27: *tête* [laughs] oh.
N-A. 28: *A pied... Il a ...* yeah. *Tête sous l'oreiller...* that was close.
N-A. 60: *la... tête au pied... au pied...* comma, comma... *au pied?...* comma... *et, et la tête sous l'oreiller.*
N-J. 61: *sous l'oreiller.*
N-A. 62: *et... la... tête...* with an *e*.

In turns 27 and 28, Anna and Jim are noticing the reformulated phrase (*la tête sous l'oreiller*) and Anna (turn 28) thinks they came close to getting the phrase right in their original story. Later when the pair writes the reformulator's changes onto the typewritten copy of their original story, Anna repeats the reformulated phrase word for word (turn 60) as she transfers the changes.

Referring to turn 60 above, during the stimulated recall, the researcher asks Jim and Anna what they were thinking:

SR-R. 26: When you said on the tape *la tête au pied* and you were looking at the two texts? What were you thinking?

SR-A. 27: What do you mean? I don't understand like... Well, I had the word *pied* written on my study thing [i.e., in her notes] but I didn't know. Like I just wrote down key words sort of and I didn't remember uh I remembered *tête à* or *'au'*, whatever, *pi* something. I thought it was *pil de pied*, but I didn't write *pied* because it didn't sound right.

Later in the stimulated recall session, the researcher helps the students construct the meaning of this difficult adverbial phrase:

SR-J. 252: And for, for, uh, uh, *tête au pied*. What is that?

SR-A. 253: Yeah, I don't get that one either. *Tête au pied ... sous l'oreiller* and uh whatever.

SR-J. 254: *et la tête*.

SR-R. 255: The complete sentence was la tête au pied du lit. Does that make more sense?

SR-A. 256: Yeah, yeah. That wasn't written in the text you gave me, us, was it?

SR-R. 257: No, no it wasn't, but—

SR-A. 258: That was—

SR-R. 259: What the man said in the first place.

SR-A. 260: Ok.

SR-R. 261: Does that make more sense? [A is thinking.] *La tête au pied du lit.*

SR-A. 262: Ok, but then how could it ... Ok, if it, Oh! Yeah! His head is at the bottom of the bed and then ... I guess that makes sense.

SR-R. 263: So it's the way she's sleeping.

SR-A. 264: Yeah. So is her pillow at the bottom with her? Because it says that her head is—

SR-R. 265: Had to be, yeah.

SR-A. 266: Ok. This is uh ... Yeah that makes sense.

This dialogue occurs with very little overt participation by Jim who initiates it in turn 252 and intervenes on only one other occasion, in turn 254. Yet, in the posttest, Jim arguably comes closer to the reformulation (*têt au pied du lit sous l'oreille*) than does Anna (*tête au pied du pil et tête su l'oreille*). In Anna's case we find it surprising that her posttest response is not more accurate, because in turn 253 she repeats word for word the reformulated (accurate) phrase.

In turn 255, the researcher supplies *du lit* (*au pied du lit*), thereby helping to provide a context for the confusing phrase 'head at the foot.' Anna (turn 256) remarks that *du lit* was not in the reformulated text, the researcher agrees (turn 257) and asks (turn 261) "Does that make more sense?" and adds a further explanation in turn 263: "So it's the way she's sleeping ..." Anna asks for further clarification in turn 264 ("So is the pillow at the bottom [of the bed] with her?") and the researcher confirms that interpretation in turn 265.

The above excerpts, taken together, suggest that the students come to understand the meaning of *la tête au pied du lit et la tête sous l'oreiller* through using a version of it well before they comprehend it. That meaning develops through their interaction with the notes taken while listening to the dictogloss, with each other during the writing stage and throughout the task, with the reformulated text, and with the researcher—a lengthy and complex process.

Sue[12]

In the previous two examples, we have seen how the students used language before they knew its meaning. They told us that they wrote something down without understanding it. Over time, through interaction with the reformulated text, the researcher and themselves, they constructed the meaning of what they had written, reaching an understanding of their own text. In the example we discuss below, Sue also attempts to understand something she has written, but fails. She does, however, talk herself into understanding that she does not understand, an important step in the learning process.

What Sue wrote but did not understand was the pronoun *se* as in, for example, *il se pense.*[13] Like Emma, Sue wrote her story alone, thinking aloud while she did. During her think-aloud and stimulated recall, Sue externalizes the meaning she attributes to *se*, but as she talks, her confusion becomes clear to herself. As we will see, Sue talks herself into understanding that she does not understand.

During the think aloud following, Sue is reading over a sentence she has written: "*Mais il se pense de ne pas être en retard.*" [But he thinks of not being late.][14]

W-S: *Mais il se pense*…no, that doesn't make sense. *Mais il pense de ne pas être en retard*…Don't I need to have a verb?…*réfléchir*? [...] *Mais… il…se…pense*…past. So, ok. *Mais il se pense de pas être, de ne pas être en retard…d'être en retard. Mais il se pense de…se pense…mais il se pense de pas être en retard…il se pense de…* Ok, so he's thinking that he doesn't wanna be late. *Mais il se pense de ne pas être en retard.*

In this excerpt of Sue's think aloud, we see Sue struggling with two issues: whether she should write *il pense* or *il se pense* (the latter is not possible in this context), and whether she should say *pas être, ne pas être,* or *être.* Here we focus only on the former issue.

Sue tries out *il se pense* and thinks that it "doesn't make sense." She then tries the correct form, *il pense*, but wonders if she needs to use a reflexive verb ("need to have a verb?... *réfléchir*?"). When she then repeats the phrase using *se*, she indicates that it is now a verb in the "past," leading us to think that Sue thinks of *se* as a tense marker. This interpretation is validated in the stimulated recall session (see below), though in the latter session, Sue does not appear to think that *se* marks *past* tense, but rather progressive aspect. Towards the end of the segment of the think-aloud shown above, Sue says in English what she is trying to say in French, probably as a means of checking the meaning she has produced in French. Her English translation, "So, he's thinking that he doesn't wanna be late" suggests she thinks *se* is a progressive marker.[15] For Sue, there is a one-to-one parallel between "he is thinking" and *il se pense*; that is, the verb "is" directly matches *se*.

In the noticing stage, although Sue reads aloud the reformulation of the sentence in bold in Figure 18.3, *Mais elle pense à ne pas être en retard*, she does not appear to notice the reformulation; that is, she does not comment on it in the protocol.

Following are excerpts from the stimulated recall session with Sue, which reinforce the interpretation that Sue thinks that *se* is a marker of tense or aspect. In the first excerpt, the researcher has asked about an infinitive, *se lever* {to get

Pretest

C'était 6h du matin. Martin se dormait tranquillement. Il fesait de beaux rêves. C'était temps de se lever et le soleil se brillait mais il ne vouler pas, alors il se rend au lit encore et se rendort tout suite. **Mais il se pense de ne pas etre en retard.** Il a dormit encore. Quelqun a pris le plume et à chatouillé sa pied. Alors il se lève, brosse les dents, beinge les cheveux, et a mis des vêtements. C'était encore un autre belle journee.

Reformulation	Translation of Reformulation
Il etait 6 h du matin. Martine dormait tranquillement. Elle faisait de beaux reves. C'etait l'heure de se lever et le soleil brillait, mais elle ne ne voulait pas se lever, alors elle se recouche et se rendort tout de suite. **Mais elle pense à ne pas être en retard.** Elle dort encore. Quelqu'un prend une plume et lui chatouille le pied. Alors elle se lève, se brosse les dents, se peigne les cheveux, et s'habille. C'est encore une autre belle journée.	It was 6 o'clock in the morning. Martine was sleeping soundly. She was having sweet dreams. It was time to get up and the sun was shining, but she did not want to get up, so she lay down again and fell asleep again immediately. **But she thought about not being late.** She is still sleeping. Someone takes a feather and tickles her foot. Then she gets up, brushes her teeth, combs her hair, and gets dressed. It's another beautiful day.

Posttest

C'était 6h du matin et Martin dormait tranquillement. Il fesait de beaux rêves, mais c'était temps de se lever. Le soleil brille très fort et Martin rendormit pensent qu'il ne veut pas être en ratard. Quelqun prend une plume et chatouille sa pied. Martin se lève, se brosse les dents, se peigne les cheveux et s'habille. C'était encore une autre beau journée.

Figure 18.3 Sue's Pretest, Reformulation and Translation, Posttest.

up}. In her response, Sue focuses on *se*, implying that it serves to mark a periphrastic future:

SR-S. 48: […] because I thought it meant like he was going to. So he was *se lever*, which means like in a moment, not exactly right away.

In the next excerpt (turn 49) the researcher's intention was to focus on a difference in lexical meaning between the non-targetlike *il se rend au lit* (literally, he goes back to bed) and the 'correct' *il se recouche* (literally, he lies down again). Sue, however, does not focus on lexical meaning, but on the tense of the verb, the periphrastic future, marked by "gonna" (turns 50 and 52):

SR-R. 49: […] *Il se rend au lit* was changed to *se recouche*. Do you know why? What's the difference?
SR-S. 50: Uh no. But personally I think that they are the same thing because *couche* […] means he's gonna go to sleep, and […] *il se*, you said *il se rendort*, the thing I put?
SR-R. 51: *Il se recouche*.
SR-S. 52: Oh, *il se recouche?* Oh, it means…they both mean that he's gonna go back to sleep.

In the following excerpt, Sue interprets the non-pronominal form of the verb *brosser* {to brush}, written in the present tense (*il brosse*), as a past tense (turn 74): "when you take off the *se*, it's like so he brushed his teeth". She thinks that the pronominal form (*il se brosse …*) realizes progressive aspect (turn 74: "because when you say *se brosse les dents*, it's kind of like um he is brushing his teeth").

SR-R. 73: Do you see a difference between the two? (*se brosse les dents* and *brosse les dents*)
SR-S. 74: Uh…yeah, because when you say *se brosse les dents*, it's kind of like um he is brushing his teeth and then he's gonna comb his hair. But when you take off the *se*, it's like so he brushed his teeth, combed his hair, and then kind of left.

Sue provides a similar explanation for the *se* in *se peigner* in turn 80, suggesting that *se* marks progressive aspect ("He's doing it…").

SR-S. 80: So it's probably like my other um answer, *il se brosse les dents, se peigne les cheveux*. He's doing it and then he is doing it again. Instead of just kind of uh he did this and that and that so it's a better form of saying it by adding the *se*. It's more French.

Thus, we see that Sue interprets *se* as part of the verb, claiming inconsistently that it marks the future tense or the progressive aspect. Earlier in the stimulated recall, Sue suggested that a wish to be consistent motivated her (over)use of *se* in the pretest:

SR-R. 27: [...] Is what you were saying *le soleil se brillait?*
SR-S. 28: Uh-huh.
SR-R. 29: Why would you say *se?*
SR-S. 30: Uh, I think because I used *se dormait.*
SR-R. 31: Uh-huh.
SR-S. 32: So, to make it the same. I think I put *se* in front of almost all of them.

Across these excerpts, we see Sue generating different explanations of the role of the pronoun *se*, and becoming increasingly confused. Finally, she acknowledges that she simply does not understand:

SR-R. 77: [...] Why would you need *se?*
SR-S. 78: Um I think...I don't know. I don't really get why you do need *se?*

Sue has talked herself into understanding that the use of *se* in French is a complete mystery to her. The inconsistency in her explanations is evident. Interestingly, her verb forms improve between pretest and posttest; in fact, in the posttest, Sue uses pronominal and non-pronominal verbs appropriately throughout, with one exception.[16] It would appear that Sue's ability to articulate rules that apply to the use of pronominal verbs is limited. However, her ability to learn from the reformulation appears quite good, and may be explained by reference to her interview. When the researcher asked if Sue thought about the changes the reformulator made to her pretest story, Sue indicated that she tended to accept changes made by someone with greater expertise:

I-R. 79: Ok. Uh, did you try to remember any of the things that you thought were better afterwards?
I-S. 80: No, not really.
I-R. 81: Ok, so you didn't think about it after you'd completed the activity?
I-S. 82: No, because in class, you know, when the teacher corrects it, then you have to do it that way.
I-R. 83: Um-hum.
I-S. 84: So I kind of did the same, if that's how it was then I just accept it.

Conclusions and Discussion

We had originally classified our participants into two categories: those who worked individually and those who worked collaboratively. We assumed that students working together would assist each other, thereby enhancing their task performance. However, the multiple stages of the task provided numerous opportunities for our learners to interact and in a sense, they never worked alone. In the writing stage, students made notes for their later use, and they interacted with those notes, themselves or their partner as they reconstructed the story. In the noticing stage, the reformulation was a source of expertise that they sometimes questioned or struggled to make sense of; at other times they readily accepted it. During the stimulated recall stage and the interviews, the researcher questioned and prompted the students, and sometimes provided them with information that helped them to solve a linguistic problem they had been unable to solve on their own.

In Sue's case, she talked herself into understanding that she did not understand the meaning of *se*, and she was not provided with the outside help she needed to progress further. In the case of Jim and Anna, Anna persisted in using a phrase recorded in the notes she had taken while listening to the dictogloss. The fact that she "retained" the phrase meant that it could be given meaning through interaction with those for whom it meant something—in the example provided, the reformulator and the researcher. For Emma too, producing what she did not understand provided her with the opportunity of finding out what it meant, and deepening her understanding of the storyline.

The changes the students made to their rewrite of their original story are in many cases directly traceable to what the students noticed in the reformulation relative to their own text and the talk that focused on these changes in the stimulated recall sessions (see also Swain & Lapkin, 2002). In essence, these interactional episodes afforded the students opportunities to learn something about the language they needed in order to convey the meaning they wanted to express.

The examples we have provided demonstrate the important role that language production played in the process of language learning. The process started with the production of language not yet understood. The examples include single vocabulary items, complex phrases, and system-wide rules. In each case, production mediates comprehension in two ways. First, what is produced provides a hook to hang meaning on, as in the case of "the *plume* thing," the "*tête à pil de* something" and the "more French *se*." Second, the talk about that "hooked meaning" shapes the further understanding of it.

We make no claim that all learning proceeds from production to comprehension; clearly this is not the case. However, we do wish to claim that one way in which language is acquired is through use: by producing language we can find out what it means, and of what it consists.

Notes

1. This research was made possible through a grant from the Social Sciences and Humanities Research Council of Canada to Merrill Swain and Sharon Lapkin, for which we are grateful. Additionally, we would like to thank members of our research team—Carole Bracco, Lindsay Brooks, and Agustina Tocalli-Beller—who helped in the collection, transcribing and coding of

Appendix 18.1 Text of Dictogloss

Le réveil-matin de Marline:

Il est six heures du matin et le soleil se lève. Martine dort tranquillement dans son lit. Elle fait de beaux rêves, la tête au pied du lit et les pieds sur l'oreiller. Quand le réveil sonne, Martine ne veut pas se lever. Elle sort son pied et avec le gros orteil, elle ferme le réveil. Elle se rendort tout de suite. Mais elle a le réveil qu'il faut pour ne pas être en retard. À six heures et deux minutes, une main mécanique tenant une petite plume sort du réveil et lui chatouille le pied. C'est efficace! Finalement Martine se lève. Elle se brosse les dents, se peigne les cheveux et s'habille pour prendre le chemin de l'école. Encore une journée bien commencée!

Translation: Martine's Alarm Clock

It's six a.m. and the sun is rising. Martine is sound asleep in her bed. She's having sweet dreams, her head at the foot of the bed and her feet on the pillow. When the alarm clock rings, Martine doesn't want to get up. She sticks her foot out, and with her big toe, she shuts off the alarm. She falls asleep again immediately. But she has the kind of alarm clock you need to prevent being late. At 6:02, a mechanical hand holding a small feather comes out of the alarm clock. It tickles her foot. To good effect! Finally Martine gets up. She brushes her teeth, combs her hair and gets dressed to go to school. Another great start to the day!

data; the principal, teachers and students of the school where we gathered the data; and Alister Cumming, Birgit Harley, David Ishii, Toshiyo Nabei, Katherine Rehner, Monika Smith, Linda Steinman, and Miles Turnbull for their reading of an earlier draft of this chapter.

2. All names used are pseudonyms.

3. This created a "teachable moment"—a perfect opportunity to provide Sue with an appropriate rule.

4. A dictogloss task (Wajnryb, 1990) is one in which a text is read at normal speed while students take notes; the learners then work in pairs or small groups to reconstruct that text in writing from their notes.

5. Connors and Ouellette (1996) state "the possible readings for French pronominal-verbal constructions are (a) reflexive; (b) reciprocal; (c) intrinsic; and (d) passive" (p. 213). The mini-lesson our participants saw focused mainly on reflexive verbs of personal care, and the term immersion students are familiar with for pronominal verbs is *les verbes réfléchis*. (For complete information on the mini-lesson, see Lapkin & Swain, 2000.)

6. Sometimes, the students' reconstruction diverged in meaning from the original dictogloss. The reformulator was asked to respect the students' meaning. Thus it is possible that using the dictogloss and reformulation procedures as we did in this study confused the students in that the meaning they heard in the original dictogloss contradicted the meaning in the reformulation.

7. Emma does not speak French outside of school, though she did go on an exchange in a small town in Québec, where she had to use French all the time, the year before data collection. She enjoyed doing the activities with our research team because it was "one on one" and so "you worked a lot" (interview, turn 12), but she did not like being videotaped. She was not sure how the same activity could happen in class because "I can tell like you make questions like just for me, like, just on what I wrote and it would take a long time for the teacher to write questions for everybody in the class" (interview, turn 56). When asked if she liked working alone for this activity, she said she did. Asked if she would rather have worked in a pair, she said "It doesn't really matter" (interview, turn 22).

8. Martine is the protagonist of the dictogloss story; see Appendix 18.1 for the text of the dictogloss.
9. Jim doesn't use French outside of school except to help his younger sister who is in grade one French immersion with her homework. He enjoyed doing the activities with our research team, but found the team a bit intimidating. He said that if the team hadn't stayed in the room, "I would've been able to talk a little more because I wouldn't be so worried about like if you guys go "Oh! What did you say or something?" (interview, turn 53). When asked if he liked working in a pair, he said he did "Because it's not all concentrated on one person. It's divided up [...] and you can share thoughts and stuff with the other person" (interview, turns 43 and 45). When asked if it would have been better if the corrections had been made on his own copy, he was firm in his response that "you wouldn't learn anything because [...] you say "Oh right, that's the way it is" instead of actually writing it yourself. [...] Instead of just looking it up, you're doing it [mimes writing]" (interview, turns 95, 97, 99). When asked what he thought when he saw the changes between their story and the revised one, Jim said "I thought it was actually...that Anna and I did pretty well" (interview, turn 101).
10. Anna rarely uses French outside of school except to do her homework. She thought the activities were "fun", and was definitely not intimidated by the research team. About working in a pair, she said "It's sort of cool to have a person you know that you can sort of talk to and like say oh you know "is this right?" [...] they can help you, guide you sort of. And you guide the other person. It sort of feels good and you know what you are doing and then the other person is just like "I don't know what I'm doing" and then you can help them. That's why it feels good" (interview, turn 54). When asked how she felt when she saw the reformulated version of their text, she said "I thought we'd done pretty good. We had pretty much gotten most of it" (interview, turn 148).
11. *La couche* means layer in French; *se coucher* means to lie down; *oreille* is the word for ear, while *oreiller* is the word for pillow.
12. Sue speaks another language (unrelated to French or English) at home, and told us that the only time she uses French outside of school is when she is doing homework on the phone with her friends. She said that being videotaped "makes you feel a bit more pressured...it's hard to relax" (interview, turns 42, 45). She was conscientious about her work with us, asking the researchers at the end of the stimulated recall session if it had been okay that she had spoken in English. About her work with us, Sue said she "could have been a bit more careful with my mistakes. But, also it made me feel like I am OK for Grade 7 [...] like that I didn't have too many mistakes" (interview, turns 68, 70). Sue told us that she would have preferred to work with somebody else because "what I picked up could be useful and also what she picked up, because I could've missed a few things and she could've had them. So, if we had put them together, maybe we'd have, we, we would have remembered more from the video" (interview, turn 20).
13. The verb *penser* (to think) in French is pronominalized on rare occasion in the attributive construction with the meaning "He thinks himself intelligent/handsome" etc. (*Il se pense intelligent...*). Otherwise, *penser* cannot be pronominalized.
14. This sentence is difficult to translate. When *penser* {to think}is followed by a complement, that complement can be introduced by either *à* (*je pense à mon enfance* {I am thinking about my childhood}), *de* (*Que penses-tu de la situation au Moyen Est?* {What do you think about/What is your opinion about the situation in the Middle East?}), or *que* (*Je pense que tu as tort.* {I think that you are wrong}). Therefore, the translation that appears here is our best approximation of what Sue meant.
15. On reading this section of the chapter, one of our graduate students, Katherine Rehner, reported the following: "In teaching a grade 10 core French class in an Etobicoke high school I became aware that several students in the class were operating under a common misconception of the function and meaning of 'se' in pronominal verbs. When the students would use the pronominal form of one verb in a paragraph, the majority of the remaining verbs in their paragraph would be in pronominal form, whether or not such a form was possible according to the rules of standard French. When asked to explain the meaning and function of 'se', the students said that it creates the "be+-ing" form of a verb (e.g., *elle s'habille parce qu'elle *se part dans dix minutes* ({she is dressing because she is leaving in ten minutes}). The students were able to create numerous examples of 'se' to perform this function, but they were not able to recall where they had learned this 'rule'" (Katherine Rehner, personal communication).
16. Sue uses *rendormit*, but should have used the verb *se rendormir*, as this verb occurs only in the pronominal form in French.

References

Appel, G., & Lantolf, J. P. (1994). Speaking as mediation: A study of L1 and L2 text recall tasks. *Modern Language Journal, 78*, 437–452.

Connors, K., & Ouellette, B. (1996). Describing the meanings of French pronominal-verbal constructions for students of French-English translation. *Language Sciences, 18*(1-2), 213–226.

Gass, S. (1997). *Input, interaction, and the second language learner*. Mahwah, NJ: Lawrence Erlbaum.

Lapkin, S., & Swain, M. (1990). French immersion research agenda for the 90s. *Canadian Modern Language Review, 46*(4), 638–674.

Lapkin, S., & Swain, M. (2000). Task outcomes: A focus on immersion students' use of pronominal verbs in their writing. *Canadian Journal of Applied Linguistics, 3*, 1001–1017.

Lapkin, S., Swain, M., & Smith, M. (2002). Reformulation and the learning of French pronominal verbs in a Canadian French immersion context. *Modern Language Journal, 86*(4), 485–507.

Long, M. (1996). The role of linguistic environment in second language acquisition. In W. C. Ritchie & T. K. Bhatia (Eds.), *Handbook of second language acquisition* (pp. 413–468). San Diego, CA: Academic Press.

Swain, M. (2000). The output hypothesis and beyond: Mediating acquisition through collaborative dialogue. In J. P. Lantolf (Ed.), *Sociocultural theory and second language learning* (pp. 97–114). Oxford: Oxford University Press.

Swain, M., & Lapkin, S. (2001). Focus on form through collaborative dialogue: Exploring task effects. In M. Bygate, P. Skehan, & M. Swain (Eds.), *Researching pedagogic tasks: Second language learning, teaching and testing* (pp. 99–118). Harlow, England: Longman.

Swain, M., & Lapkin, S. (2002). Talking it through: Two French immersion learners' response to reformulation. *International Journal of Educational Research, 37*, 285–304.

Talyzina, N. (1981). *The psychology of learning*. Moscow: Progress Press.

Wanjryb, R. (1990). *Grammar dictation*. Oxford: Oxford University Press.

Wertsch, J. V., & Stone, C. A. (1985). The concept of internalization in Vygotsky's account of the genesis of higher mental functions. In J. V. Wertsch (Ed.), *Culture, communication and cognition: Vygotskian perspectives*. Cambridge: Cambridge University Press.

19

Locating and Utilizing Heritage Language Resources in the Community
An Asset-Based Approach to Program Design and Evaluation

BRIAN K. LYNCH

Introduction

Language and language learning are inevitably tied to various senses of community. In the mid-1990s, the National Science Foundation funded the Human Capital Initiative (HCI), which originated as a project designed by scholars from the social and behavioral science disciplines. The concept of "capital" in this context was expanded to include social and cultural resources, and the project focused on six areas: the workplace, education, families, neighborhoods, disadvantage, and poverty. In response to the larger HCI report (Blank, 2003), the HCI Working Panel on Linguistics[1] outlined a research agenda for linguistics and applied linguistics that would respond to the six areas of emphasis (Wolfram & Schilling-Estes, 1995). The panel's response identified "building strong neighborhoods" as one of the key areas for research: "…the essential nature of and interrelationships among social networks, the geographic neighborhood, the larger speech community, and the national language populace need to be explicated" (Wolfram & Schilling-Estes, 1995, p. 5).

In connection with the above research agenda, heritage language (HL) learning, identified by scholars (e.g., Brecht & Ingold, 1998) as a part of the social and cultural resources available to the United States, has a particularly important connection to the concept of neighborhood and community. The Heritage Language Research Priorities Conference (University of California, Los Angeles, 2001) concluded that "conserving this resource is a matter of urgency not only for the nation, but also for individuals, families, and communities" (p. 3). The conference report further specifies that HL communities need to be located and profiled through systematic research. Like the response to the HCI, the UCLA conference outlined a research agenda, with specific categories for "the family" and "the community," proposing that research questions focus on the following:

1. The general attitude of the HL community toward HL maintenance;
2. The degree of support the HL community could provide;

3. The motivation for such support (e.g., socioeconomic, religious, political, or cultural); and

4. Optimal ways to incorporate community-based needs and desires in the design of HL programs.

Under the categories of "policy" and "programs," the UCLA conference research agenda also identified "the availability and quality of programs" and "the assessment of learning and evaluation of programs" (p. 5) as key research questions. Under policy, the agenda makes it clear that HL programs must have clear and realizable objectives, and that the policy formulation for creating these programs must include provisions for participation from the HL community: "Unless the heritage language community is motivated and supportive of programs, these programs are doomed to failure" (p. 11). The HL community must understand and must have helped create the goals of the program in order for the results of assessment and evaluation to be informative and motivating. Under programs, the research agenda asks the question: "What are the most efficient and effective means of evaluating the success of programs for heritage speakers?" (p. 13).

This chapter seeks to contribute to HL research by outlining an approach to program evaluation rooted in the concept of community. I begin by briefly sketching the underlying rationale for evaluation and by presenting an overview of the commonly used methods or designs. I next outline what counts as evidence for different program evaluation audiences. This leads to a discussion of needs analysis as the traditional basis for establishing and evaluating language program objectives. Finally, I introduce an asset-based approach to language program development and evaluation. This approach provides an important alternative to needs analysis in that it underscores the value of community participation in the evaluation process.

Language Program Design and Evaluation

In addition to the support of the community, HL programs usually need the support of some funding entity external to the community, e.g., a federal, state, and/or local government agency. A constant companion to such funding is the requirement of formal program evaluation. Models of evaluation for HL programs will therefore be called upon both to meet the expectations of the funding agency and to satisfy the need for informing the HL community stakeholders.

In the 1990s, language program evaluation received a good deal of attention (Alderson & Beretta, 1992; Lynch, 1996; Rea-Dickins & Germaine, 1992; Weir & Roberts, 1994). The models for evaluation presented in this research include the traditional, scientific, or "positivistic" approaches (e.g., Cook & Campbell, 1979; Fitz-Gibbon & Morris, 1987) along with alternative, qualitative, or "naturalistic" approaches (e.g., Parlett & Hamilton, 1976; Eisner, 1991). These approaches reflect different research paradigms, each with distinct assumptions as to what constitutes the object of inquiry, how inquiry is carried out, and how knowledge concerning the object of inquiry is established.[2]

In program evaluation, what counts as evidence is often determined by the primary audiences for the evaluation. The most important of these is the funding agency (including federal, state, and local governments), which generally requires evidence fitting the "positivistic" paradigm. In particular, as García (2000) points out, the program evaluation required for these agencies "has a commitment to *causal inference* [italics added] and a need to optimize the clarity of the inference. Description is not enough" (p. 108). This paradigm embodies the traditional, scientific view of research, with its central objective being the identification of causal relationships. What counts as evidence here is unambiguously experimental (or quasi-experimental) and quantitative. For language program evaluation, this means establishing that the program caused observed improvement in language ability or proficiency through the use of a design comparing the program group of students to a control group, while controlling for pre-existing differences between the two. The conceptual and methodological problems with conducting this type of research have been presented by García (2000). However, since government policy makers are unlikely to accept evidence outside this positivistic, causal framework, García argues for establishing a "community of mutually critical applied social scientists" (p. 109) who can argue against a blind and simplistic faith in such research and who can also develop and conduct more sophisticated research to provide the most thorough evidence possible within this paradigm.

It seems likely that a community of researchers such as that proposed by García would also include those who do their research within alternative paradigms. Even if we agree that language program evaluation must be positivistic and oriented toward causal inference, there remains the possibility for those causal inferences to be better elaborated and understood. That is, alternative research paradigms should be able to provide the sorts of data and analysis that will go beyond simple description, to provide the sort of "thick description" called for by Geertz (1973, pp. 6–20). This thick description should also enable program evaluators to explain their results more effectively to audiences beyond the funding agencies, including the HL community. It may not be enough, for example, to tell the HL community that the program group significantly outperformed the control group, or that a causal relationship between the program and increased language proficiency has been established. Research results that describe and explain what the program actually means, what it does, how program participation results in particular language abilities, and what those abilities mean would surely be a useful addition to the traditional evaluation reports. The challenge, then, is to provide evidence that speaks to the multiple audiences or stakeholders for HL program evaluation. This means positivistic, causal inference evidence for the funding agency as well as evidence that will speak to the HL community.

To accommodate these different evaluation audiences and goals, a model that draws on both positivistic and alternative paradigms, as well as multiple strategies for data gathering, is suggested (Lynch, 1996). This model would necessarily require active participation from participants in the program and the wider HL community, in terms of defining evaluation goals as well as providing evaluation data and interpretations of that data. The evaluators' role thus becomes one of facilitation in a "multiple perspective negotiation" (Lynch, 1996, pp. 62–63). However, this collaborative approach to evaluation is not without its own potential problems (see, for example, Nunan & Lewkowicz, 1999). Its successful use presumes that the varying audiences, particularly the HL community, have been consulted during the program development stage. In other words, there is a connection between the design of the program and its objectives, and the design of the evaluation and its goals. All stakeholders, including the HL community, need to have been a part of the formulation of both. Keeping these needs in mind for HL program development and evaluation, we will proceed to a discussion of the role that needs analysis might play.

Needs Analysis in Program Development

Needs analysis has played a central role in language program development since the 1970s and the growth of language for specific purposes (Johns & Price-Machado, 2001). As a means for defining program objectives, needs analysis uncovers what is lacking, or what needs to be developed in the individuals who will participate in the language program. A language program is then developed to provide what is needed, with the objectives of the instructional curriculum deriving from the needs analysis.

Since the 1960s, a "needs-based" approach to the design of educational programs, especially in North America, has been required by government funding agencies. This use of needs analysis was part of a systematic approach to define programs in terms of measurable objectives and outcomes, and to provide data that could be assessed in relation to the causal inferences required for evaluation evidence, as discussed above. As Berwick (1989) observed, "This positivistic faith in the power of applied science to secure new knowledge and to protect us from the unreliable application of mere 'common sense' has very much made its mark in planning language-for-specific purposes" (pp. 51–52).

Conducting needs analysis requires that the concept of needs first be defined. A variety of definitions has been offered over the past two decades. Initial work done in association with the Council of Europe distinguished between *objective needs* and *subjective needs* (Richterich, 1975; Richterich & Chancerel, 1980; Richterich, 1983), with objective needs seen as those established from factual information about the learners and their language use, resulting in learning goals expressed as linguistic content. Subjective needs, on the other hand, were seen as those based on the perceptions and expressed wants of the learners, resulting in information that could be used to guide the learning process.

Subsequent work in the field has further contributed to the definition of needs. Hutchinson and Waters (1987) critique the early attempts at providing needs analysis that focus on objective, or "target" needs, claiming that when carried to their logical conclusion, these attempts revealed "the ultimate sterility of a language-centred approach to needs analysis" and how little could be learned from a "… 'scientific' needs analysis" (p. 54). They call, instead, for a focus on more subjective "learning needs" (p. 54).[3] Berwick (1989) points out that referring to needs as objective is misleading, since all expressions of learner needs are the result of interpretation and thus reflect particular values and beliefs. He further identifies a distinction between those needs established by teachers or other experts (*perceived needs*) and those that come from the learners (*felt*, or *expressed needs*) and argues for including the various stakeholders in the program design and planning stages (i.e., to achieve a consensus on what the goals and strategies for reaching those goals should be). Finally, Brindley (1989) also questions the objectivity of needs, but nonetheless retains the terms objective and subjective for distinguishing between teacher/expert-defined needs and learner-defined needs. However, he argues that "reconciling teacher-diagnosed objective needs with learner-perceived subjective needs is of crucial importance in a learner-centred system" (p. 74). Acknowledging that such a reconciliation is difficult, he nevertheless maintains that its negotiation is possible.

Brindley's recommendations for needs analysis in relation to learner-centered curricula and Berwick's recommendation for consensus among program stakeholders and planners in defining needs and objectives both argue for an approach to program development and evaluation that is inclusive of the HL community. However, all definitions of needs analysis, including Robinson's (1991) use of *target situation analysis* (what the learners need to know/do at the end of the language program) and *present situation analysis* (what the learners are like at the beginning of the program) imply a gap, or deficit (e.g., between target and present situations) as the basis for program objectives. The next section will outline an approach that focuses on identifying assets, rather than deficits, as the starting point for program development and, ultimately, program evaluation.

Asset-Based Approach

My colleagues on the Scholarship of Teaching and Research Team at Portland State University suggested that work in the area of public policy and planning might be useful in developing a community-based approach to HL program design and evaluation. The work of those who focus on neighborhood and community-based development seemed to hold great potential, in particular the approach developed by Kretzmann and McKnight (1993). These researchers critique the deficit model inherent in needs-based approaches to community development and replace it with an assets-based approach that focuses on identifying the existing abilities and resources of community residents and local associations. Although Kretzmann and McKnight's approach was designed primarily for development work in economically disadvantaged neighborhoods, its principles are applicable to the context of HL program development, regardless of the economic status of the community in which it is taking place.

The asset-based approach represents a counter proposal to the traditional needs-based approach, or "deficiency" model. Needs-based program planning tends to result in funding to service providers rather than to members of the community. It also results in solutions that do not build community solidarity and cohesiveness. Instead, it builds a model where only outside experts can determine the needs and ameliorate the deficiencies, thus creating a cycle of dependence for the community upon the outside experts (both for defining the needs, and ultimately the community's identity, and for providing solutions).

The asset-based approach begins by identifying the range of existing community resources and assets. It next investigates ways to connect these resources. This means identifying the special abilities, knowledge, and capacities of individuals in the community and their local associations. As these community members and groups begin to develop their effectiveness and to articulate projects, the process is extended to more formal institutions, such as businesses and social service providers in the community. While the focus is on the community, this type of planning allows for use of additional help or resources from the outside. However, the view informing this approach is that "outside resources will be much more effectively used if the local community is itself fully mobilized and invested, and if it can define the agendas for which additional resources must be obtained" (Kretzmann & McKnight, 1993, p. 8).

One of the tools used in the asset-based approach to program design is that of *mapping*, or the location of relevant resources within a community space (see Kretzmann & McKnight, 1993). Figure 19.1 represents a possible asset-based map for a community development project. The mapping process begins by locating resources relevant to a HL program design and evaluation. It continues by identifying resources in more detail at the three levels of local institutions, community associations, and community individuals. The map is then constructed

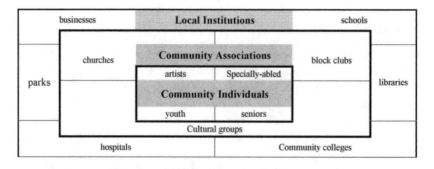

Figure 19.1 An Asset-Based Map for a Community. Source: Kretzmann, J. P., & McKnight, J. L. (1993, p. 7). Adapted with permission.

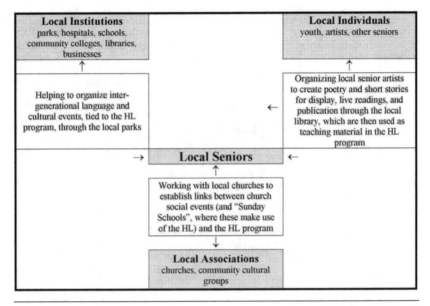

Figure 19.2 An Asset Map for Local Seniors. Source: Kretzmann, J. P., & McKnight, J. L. (1993, p. 63). Adapted with permission.

to show the potential for connections from each of the three levels to the other two, or from particular elements of one level with all three.

For example, at the level of community individuals, we could map the elderly, or local seniors, as resources in relation to each level. In the HL community, local seniors whose first language is the HL represent a key resource and perspective for program design and evaluation. Their linguistic and cultural knowledge could be drawn upon in a number of ways, including those depicted in Figure 19.2.

Other examples of potential assets and partnerships are:

- Using seniors' experience and connections with local businesses to raise funds for the HL program;
- Involving seniors in oral history, life narrative sessions at local cultural associations, where their individual stories and connections with HL culture are told;
- Having HL students from local schools visit the seniors as a field trip or conduct interviews with them;
- Getting seniors to mentor and tutor local youth as an adjunct to the HL program.

At the level of community associations, churches and cultural groups represent an important cluster of resources for the HL program. Churches, for example, usually have personnel with training for community building and facilitation, as well as the background and expertise resident in the parish. Space and facilities

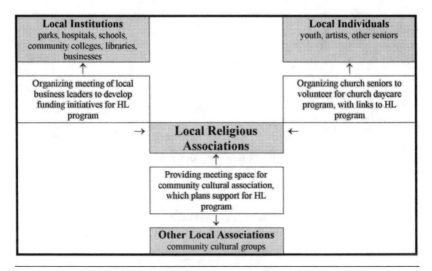

Figure 19.3 An Asset Map for Local Associations. Source: Kretzmann, J. P., & McKnight, J. L. (1993, p. 157). Adapted with permission.

owned by the church may be used for HL programs, as well as materials and equipment (from display boards to electronic media equipment). Where there is a connection between the local church and the HL culture, collaboration with HL learning programs can be an important asset-sharing component for supporting the HL program and maintaining the HL in the community. Figure 19.3 presents an example asset map for this set of resources.

Local religious associations also have other important assets to be drawn upon, such as the ability to:

- Recruit volunteer tutors or teaching assistants for HL learning programs based in the schools or community colleges.
- Provide teachers, materials, and space for HL instruction (pre-HL program or adjunct).
- Coordinate with local cultural associations for promoting HL-based community celebrations and events.

Larger institutions located or represented in the HL community are the final level of asset mapping. Like the local religious associations, institutions such as libraries have important assets to offer. Their staff have special skills that can be of use in HL program design, e.g., locating instructional materials, and applying for grants and other forms of financial support. The local library also represents another community space and set of facilities, materials, and equipment. Because libraries have traditionally been forced to provide their services on restricted budgets, they can be experienced and empathetic partners in the cause of HL

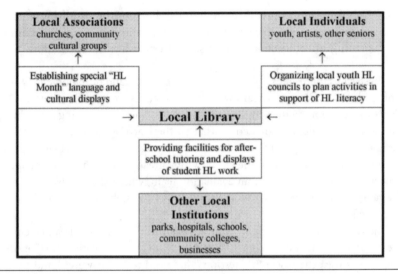

Figure 19.4 An Asset Map for Local Institutions. Source: Kretzmann, J. P., & McKnight, J. L. (1993, p. 203). Adapted with permission.

learning program development, evaluation, and maintenance. Figure 19.4 displays potential assets for this level of community mapping.

Other possibilities for using local library resources include:

- Providing a permanent housing space for local HL senior oral histories.
- Coordinating with local businesses to recycle computer equipment for HL learning use.
- Researching historical information for local cultural associations.

The preceding examples of asset mapping are generic, intended to illustrate the potential of this approach. How would asset mapping be applied to an actual HL community context? The following steps, adapted from Kretzmann and McKnight (1993) suggest a process for identifying resources in the HL community and beginning to build connections among the three levels of stakeholders.

1. Conduct an asset inventory for each of the three levels (individuals, associations, institutions) in the HL community, identifying abilities, experience, and resources related to the HL and its culture.
2. Use the results of the asset inventory to locate and map (see Figures 19.1 to 19.4) areas of overlap and complementarity. For example, there may be HL teaching and learning already taking place across the levels—at a local church, library, and school—that could benefit from coordination and integration with the HL program being designed and evaluated. This step aims at forming partnerships and building a collaborative dialogue that can strengthen the sense of HL community.

3. Elaborate and support the community collaborations by identifying possible mutual resource exchanges within the community and means of obtaining funding and other support from sources external to the community.

These steps represent stages in HL program design and development, which would ideally be done by a team with representatives from all three levels. Designing or developing the program should also include establishing procedures for gathering evaluation evidence. That is, the learning goals and objectives designed for the program will become the starting point for articulating goals for subsequent evaluation. If the HL program already exists, this asset mapping process can be conducted by an evaluation team, which should also represent the range of stakeholders across the three levels, to establish goals for the program evaluation.

The role of asset mapping in program evaluation is to provide a principled means of involving the HL community directly in the formulation of HL evaluation goals (i.e., the research questions that need to be answered) and in the gathering of the evidence needed to reach those goals. The same techniques used for conducting needs analysis are applicable to asset analysis; however, the focus shifts to language and cultural resources that exist in the community rather than to the identification of needs.

Several models or frameworks have been advanced for language program evaluation (Lynch, 1996; Rea-Dickins & Germaine, 1992; Weir & Roberts, 1994). In adapting any of them for use with the asset-based approach, the following primary steps would need to be included:

1. The program stakeholders appoint an evaluation "facilitation team." This team can consist of any combination of stakeholders that is appropriate or required for the particular evaluation context. For example, an evaluation mandated by a funding agency may stipulate the evaluators; in other contexts, community leaders and HL educators may decide on the facilitation team.

2. The facilitation team first constructs asset inventories for the individuals, associations, and institutions that the HL program serves and then maps these assets (see Figure 19.2, Figure 19.3, and Figure 19.4). Even if this mapping has been done previously (e.g., to define program objectives), it is important for the facilitation team to do their own asset mapping in order to understand the program context more fully and to update the asset information.

3. The facilitation team forms an evaluation "audience panel" from representatives of the community levels and any external stakeholders (such as funding agencies). In its interaction with the audience panel, the team presents and discusses the asset maps in terms of potential evaluation goals (e.g., "Has the HL program taken advantage of partnerships with local seniors?").

4. In consultation with the audience panel, the facilitation team forms specific evaluation goals. These goals will represent questions concerning the degree to which the program objectives (which are originally derived from asset mapping) have been met and the processes by which the program pursues the objectives.

5. In consultation with the audience panel, the facilitation team creates a design for establishing evidence to meet the evaluation goals (see Lynch, 1996; Rea-Dickins & Germaine, 1992; Weir & Roberts, 1994). The inclusion of a representative audience panel will result in the HL community having a voice in what counts as evidence. This may result in "mixed designs" (see Lynch, 1996) and multiple strategies for gathering evidence. For example, as discussed above, funding agencies will traditionally require quantitative evidence for causal inferences. Other stakeholders in the HL community, however, may require more in-depth, explanatory case studies that document qualitatively how certain assets within the community contribute to attaining the overall program objectives.

The facilitation team reports the evaluation findings. Several reports may need to be produced, articulated differently for different elements of the evaluation audience. Some of the reporting may also take the form of a discussion held in the HL community, which could further elaborate the understanding of the evaluation findings or suggest directions for further evaluation work.

Conclusion

In arguing for an asset-based approach to HL program development and evaluation, I am not advocating the total abandonment of needs analysis. In fact, much of what has been written about needs analysis fits nicely with the asset-based approach. Brindley's (1989) setting of needs analysis within the learner-centered language syllabus incorporates the notion of setting objectives for the language program in consultation with learners. This underscores some of the recommendations above for representing the HL community in objectives and evaluation goal setting. Robinson's (1991) formulation of target situation and present situation analysis includes reference to an "ecological approach" to needs analysis (citing Holliday & Cooke, 1983, pp. 123–143) where the local culture's patterns of thinking and learning are made part of the analysis. In addition to the previously discussed references on needs analysis, Shaw (1997) has argued for the primacy of needs as expressed by language program participants over those perceived by non-participant stakeholders such as government ministers and planners.

Some of these definitions of needs and their analysis, however, portray a suspicion of policy and an attempt (especially Shaw, 1997) to keep the objectives and goals that result from needs analysis (or asset analysis) separate from the objectives and goals of language policy. That is, language policy is seen as placing control of the program in the hands of language planners and policy makers, rather than keeping needs analysis as a separate activity where "the client will retain control of the program." (Shaw, 1997, p. 240). An alternate view of this relationship is the one expressed by García (2000), where the importance of participant involvement in the research and evaluation (and, by extension, needs analysis) of bilingual education programs is seen as necessary for the formulation of governmental policy that will continue to support these language programs.

Given the continuing importance of government funding and policy support for language programs, including HL programs, it seems wise to follow García's view and to acknowledge the need for evidence that can support claims of a causal connection between the language program and outcomes that demonstrate the program's objectives are being met. However, it is important to remember, as previously mentioned, that HL programs will not survive without the understanding and support of the HL community. This calls for evidence that is complementary to outcomes-based, experimental and quasi-experimental design evaluation, evidence that assists García's "clarity of the inference" (2000, p. 108) as well as capturing the complexity and promise of a HL program that is discovered through asset mapping.

The development and evaluation of language programs will still need to draw upon aspects of a needs-based approach. The asset-based approach, however, helps program developers and evaluators to keep the HL community at the center of the enterprise. It starts with what is present, not what is missing, and gives primary importance to the local definition of the HL program's goals and how they should be judged.

Notes

1. Members of the panel included: John Baugh, Courtney Cazden, Ceil Lucas, Charles Perfetti, Dennis Preston, Bambi Schieffelin, Carmen Silva-Corvalán, Richard Tucker, and Walt Wolfram. Natalie Schilling-Estes was the Recorder and Project Assistant.
2. What counts as evidence across these research paradigms differs (Lynch, 1996; Hamp-Lyons & Lynch, 1998). Since establishing validity concerns evaluating the evidence for our knowledge claims, standards for judging the validity of research findings in these paradigms differ as well.
3. This critique echoes Widdowson's (1981) distinction between goal-oriented (objective) and process oriented (subjective) definitions of language learning needs.

References

Alderson, J. C., & Beretta, A. (Eds.). (1992). *Evaluating second language education.* Cambridge: Cambridge University Press.

Berwick, R. (1989). Needs assessment in language programming: From theory to practice. In R. K. Johnson (Ed.), *The second language curriculum* (pp. 48–62). Cambridge: Cambridge University Press.

Blank, Rebecca. (2003). *Investing in human resources: A strategic plan for the human capital initiative.* National Science Foundation. Retrieved June 15, 2006, from http://www.nsf.gov/sbe/ses/soc/works1.jsp

Brecht, R. D., & Ingold, C. W. (1998). Tapping a national resource: Heritage languages in the United States. *ERIC Digest.* Washington, DC: ERIC Clearinghouse on Languages and Linguistics.

Brindley, G. (1989) The role of needs analysis in adult ESL programme design. In R. K. Johnson (Ed.), *The second language curriculum* (pp. 63–78). Cambridge: Cambridge University Press.

Cook, T. D., & Campbell, D. T. (1979). *Quasi-experimentation: design and analysis issues for field settings.* Boston: Houghton Mifflin.

Eisner, E. W. (1991). *The enlightened eye: Qualitative inquiry and the enhancement of educational practice.* New York: Macmillan.

Fitz-Gibbon, C. T., & Morris, L. L. (1987). *How to design a program evaluation.* Newbury Park, CA: Sage.

García, E. E. (2000). Treating linguistic and cultural diversity as a resource: The research response to the challenges inherent in the Improving America's Schools Act and California's Proposition 227. In R. Dueñas González with I. Melis (Eds.), *Language ideologies: Critical perspectives on the official English movement* (pp. 90–113). Mahwah, NJ: Lawrence Erlbaum/Urbana, IL: NCTE.

Geertz, C. (1973). *The interpretation of culture.* New York: Basic Books.

Hamp-Lyons, L., & Lynch, B. K. (1998). Perspectives on validity: A historical analysis of language testing conference abstracts. In A. J. Kunnan (Ed.), *Validation in language assessment* (pp. 253–276). Mahwah, NJ: Lawrence Erlbaum.

Hutchinson, T., & Waters, A. (1987). *English for specific purposes.* Cambridge: Cambridge University Press.

Johns, A., & Price-Machado, D. (2001). ESP: Tailoring courses to student needs—and to the outside world. In M. Celce-Murcia, (Ed.), *Teaching English as a second or foreign language* (3rd ed., pp. 43–54). Boston: Heinle & Heinle.

Kretzmann, J. P., & McKnight, J. L. (1993). *Building communities from the inside out: A path toward finding and mobilizing a community's assets.* Evanston, IL: Northwestern University Center for Urban Affairs and Policy Research, Neighborhood Innovations Network.

Lynch, B. K. (1996). *Language program evaluation: Theory and practice.* Cambridge: Cambridge University Press.

Nunan, D., & Lewkowicz, J. A. (1999). The limits of collaborative evaluation. *TESOL Quarterly, 33,* 681–700.

Parlett, M., & Hamilton, D. (1976). Evaluation as illumination: a new approach to the study of innovatory programs. In G. V. Glass (Ed.), *Evaluation studies annual review, vol. 1,* (pp. 140–157). Beverly Hills, CA: Sage.

Rea-Dickins, P., & Germaine, K. (1992). *Evaluation.* Oxford: Oxford University Press.

Richterich, R. (1975). The analysis of language needs: Illusion-pretext-necessity. *Education and Culture, 28,* 9–14.

Richterich, R. (Ed.) (1983). *Case studies in identifying language needs.* Oxford: Pergamon Press.

Richterich, R., & Chancerel, J. L. (Eds.) (1980). *Identifying the needs of adults learning a foreign language.* Oxford: Pergamon Press.

Robinson, P. (1991). *ESP today: A practitioner's guide.* New York: Prentice Hall.

Shaw, S. L. (1997). The political nature of needs. In B. Kenny & W. Savage (Eds.), *Language and development: Teachers in a changing world* (pp.231–240). New York: Addison Wesley Longman.

University of California, Los Angeles. (2001). *Heritage language research priorities conference report.* Los Angeles, CA: Author. Available at: http://www.cal.org

Weir, C. & Roberts, J. (1994). *Evaluation in ELT.* Oxford: Blackwell.

Widdowson, H. G. (1981). English for specific purposes: Criteria for course design. In L. Selinker, E. Tarone, & V. Hanzeli (Eds.), *English for academic and technical purposes: Studies in honor of Louis Trimble* (pp. 1–11). Rowley, MA: Newbury House.

Wolfram, W., & Schilling-Estes, N. (1995). *Linguistics and the Human Capital Initiative.* Available at: http://www.cal.org

In Conclusion

20
Salvaging Heritage Languages

TERRY KIT-FONG AU

Introduction

When children lose their heritage languages, everyone loses something. The children and their parents may be unable to bond in a language that both are most comfortable with, the community loses its cultural heritage and the nation loses human resources much needed in bridging cultures within communities and across nations.

Historically, heritage language loss has typically taken place over three generations—with the immigrants most at ease with their heritage language, their children speaking both the heritage language and the majority language, and the grandchildren speaking primarily the majority language (Fishman, 1978; Krashen, 1996; Veltman, 1983). Today in the United States, heritage language loss often happens over just two generations (Fillmore, 1991; Kouritzin, 1999). Such rapid loss could mean that parents may have to raise their children using a language that they themselves have not fully mastered. They may have to endure their children's good-natured (and sometimes not-so-good-natured) teasing about their "funny" accent and grammatical mistakes. It is challenging enough for parents to raise children in a new home country and in an unfamiliar culture; it is doubly hard to do so if they feel inept whenever they open their mouths to speak.

Worse still, when the parents' English is not good enough even for everyday communication, they may have no choice but to speak to their children in the heritage language, whereas the children may speak back in English. When the parents and children do not even share a language, sharing family and cultural values will require overcoming not only a generation gap but also a language barrier. It is no wonder that when immigrant parents and their adolescent children speak in different languages to each other, the children feel that their family is less cohesive and report less family discussion than those who share a language with their parents (Tseng & Fuligni, 2000). I once saw first-hand what such a language chasm could do to parent-child bonds. Back in my college days, a friend of mine claimed that she and her mother (a garment worker in Chinatown) could not really talk to each other as she could not speak Chinese and her mother could not speak English. I never quite believed it. Sure enough, upon visiting her family, I heard her speak to her mother in Chinese. When I challenged her, she replied,

"I wouldn't call 'What's for dinner, Mom?' or 'I can't come home this weekend; too much homework!' real talking." And, of course, she was right.

The human costs of rapid heritage language loss extend beyond immigrant families. Despite the influx of immigrants who bring with them a rich collection of heritage languages to the United States, this nation remains overwhelmingly monolingual. According to Census 2000, about 82% of the people living in the United States speak only English at home (U.S. Census Bureau, 2000). When a community loses its heritage language, its cultural heritage is also at risk. With globalization proceeding at full speed, we find ourselves coming into contact with people from many cultures, including business partners or customers, clients receiving government services, partners in international diplomacy, or adversaries in international hostility. When immigrant children lose their heritage languages, our nation also loses human resources much needed in bridging cultures within our nation and across nations. What can be done to salvage this much underappreciated national treasure?

One strategy is to capitalize on childhood exposure to heritage languages, even if they are incomplete or discontinued, to help adults learn or re-learn their heritage language with greater success. This chapter will review research on how childhood experience with two heritage languages (Spanish and Korean) may help adults learn or re-learn the language they once knew. The chapter will compare two kinds of heritage language learners—childhood hearers and childhood speakers—with native speakers of the language and with typical late second language (L2) learners who had no regular exposure to the language until adolescence. Once the strengths and weaknesses of various kinds of heritage language learners are better understood, language educators may have a better chance of helping them master their heritage language.

Childhood Exposure to a Heritage Language

Childhood language experience seems to have a special status in language acquisition. When children are deprived of language input (due to deafness, child abuse/neglect, etc.), they generally do not fully acquire a language even when input is available later (e.g., Koluchova, 1972, 1976; Fromkin, Krashen, Curtiss, Rigler, & Rigler, 1974; Curtiss, 1977, 1989; Skuse, 1984a, 1984b; Newport, 1990, 1991; Mayberry, 1993). While late learners can still master important aspects of a language, the later the language input begins, the less native-like their ultimate proficiency will be—especially in phonology and morphosyntax. A similar story plays out in L2 acquisition. Research on the onset of exposure suggests that late L2-learners typically do not fully master L2 phonology (e.g., Oyama, 1976; Williams, 1980; Flege, 1987, 1991; Bialystok & Hakuta, 1994; Flege, Yeni-Komshian, & Liu, 1999) and morphosyntax (e.g., Snow & Hoefnagel-Hohle, 1978; Johnson & Newport, 1989, 1991; but c.f. Birdsong & Molis, 2001).

Note that many heritage language learners in high school and college have had some exposure to the target language during early childhood. The special status of childhood language experience, especially experience during the first 6 or 7 years of life, leads us to question whether such childhood language experience can be drawn upon to help high-school and college students learn or re-learn their heritage language. Because of massive pruning of synapses and brain cell death in early brain development (e.g., Rakic, Bourgeois, Zecevic, Eckenhoff, & Goldman-Rakic, 1986), childhood language memory might not survive with little or no exposure to the language. Even if such memory survives, will childhood language memory become inaccessible in adulthood?

One study suggested that the answer might be yes: Monolingual adult speakers of French who had been adopted as monolingual Korean children from Korea to France between the ages of 3 and 8 years seemed to have forgotten Korean entirely (Pallier et al., 2003). When these adult adoptees listened to Korean sentences mixed with sentences in Polish, a language completely unfamiliar to them, they could not tell which sentences were in Korean and which were in Polish. Likewise, brain activation patterns revealed no sign of recognition: the adoptees' event-related fMRI (functional magnetic resonance imaging) activation patterns did not differ while listening to Polish or Korean. Moreover, their activation patterns for French and Korean did not differ from those of native French speakers who had no prior exposure to Korean. It seems, then, that a childhood language can become inaccessible when language input ends entirely after early childhood.

On the other hand, some studies suggest that childhood language memory can remain accessible through adulthood. English-speaking adults who had heard Hindi regularly during the first 2 years of life could distinguish Hindi speech sounds much better than those who had no prior exposure to Hindi (Tees & Werker, 1984). Indeed, their Hindi speech sound perception was quite native-like. Anecdotally, Penfield (1959) has observed that after having a German governess for 2 years during early childhood, his four children re-acquired German in high school and college with good pronunciation (for more examples, see Wode, 1981; Yamada, 1995).

Why does childhood language experience show lasting benefits in some cases but not in others? My colleagues and I (Oh, Au, & Jun, 2002; Oh, Jun, Knightly, & Au, 2003) suspect that the distinction between storage strength and retrieval strength of long-ago memory holds at least part of the answer. Storage strength for a memory depends on how well something was learned originally, and retrieval strength depends on current usage (R. Bjork & E. Bjork, 1992; E. Bjork & R. Bjork, 1996). Storage strength for Korean might be quite strong for the adoptees in Pallier et al.'s study (2003), but retrieval strength was probably minimal because they stopped hearing Korean upon adoption. By contrast, in Tees and Werker's (1984) study, the Hindi hearing infants grew up in Hindi-Canadian communities and probably continued to hear Hindi phonemes in accented English, thereby maintaining substantial retrieval (as well as storage) strength for Hindi phonemes.

Intriguingly, several hypnosis case studies suggest that a childhood language can become accessible when childhood speakers of a heritage language are age-regressed under hypnosis (e.g., Ås, 1962; Au & Romo, 1997; Fromm, 1970). In one case, Fromm (1970) reports the case of a Japanese-American adult who was not only unable to recall (i.e., speak) his childhood language or recognize (i.e., understand) it, but who did not even know that he had once spoken it. When age-regressed under hypnosis to age 3 or 4, he spontaneously and unexpectedly spoke Japanese. However, at all age-regression levels above age 4, he spoke only English. As it turned out, his family had been sent to a Japanese American internment camp during WWII. When his family was released from the camp, they decided to bury that part of the family history, along with the 4-year-old child's linguistic heritage. It seems possible, then, that language abilities acquired during early childhood can last for many years, even though it may require drastic means such as hypnosis to retrieve them. Such abilities may have become practically un-retrievable due to inhibition and interference by new learning, but their storage strength may remain substantial (cf. R. Bjork & E. Bjork, 1992; E. Bjork & R. Bjork, 1996).

How, short of age-regressed hypnosis, can seemingly lost memory of a childhood language be salvaged? Re-learning may be an ecologically more meaningful and certainly much less drastic alternative. For adult re-learners of a childhood language such as Penfield's children (1959), retrieval strength could be built up again through re-learning the language (see E. Bjork & R. Bjork, 1996, on re-learning). The effort saved in re-learning is an extremely sensitive measure of early memory, much more so than recall or recognition measures (e.g., Ebbinghaus, 1964; Kruger, 1929; Luh, 1922). Re-learning even something that seems to have been completely forgotten takes much less time than learning for the first time. For example, many new parents may find their memory for childhood lullabies, songs, and nursery rhymes rather sketchy after years of not hearing, reciting, or singing them; however, re-learning such old favorites tends to be much easier than learning new songs or rhymes. Similarly, even if childhood heritage language speakers seem to have forgotten their childhood language like the Korean adoptees in Pallier et al.'s study (2003), they may still be able to access their childhood language memory once again if they try to re-learn the language.

My colleagues and I have been exploring long-lasting benefits of childhood language experience for adult language learners. Our basic approach is to compare childhood hearers and childhood speakers of a heritage language with typical late-L2-learners in the United States. who had no regular exposure to the target language until their high-school or college language classes. These adult learners are also compared to adult native speakers to see how native-like their command of the target language is. The two target languages we have examined thus far are Spanish and Korean.

Overhearing Spanish during Childhood

Not so long ago, deaf parents with limited resources were, and probably some still are, advised that their children with normal hearing ability would benefit from spoken language input by watching television. Similarly, children living in border towns can and do overhear many conversations in foreign languages by tuning into television broadcasts from across the border. In both cases, popular wisdom would have us believe that the children can learn language simply by watching television broadcasts. However, research indicates that overhearing a language on television seems to do little good—that is, if one is concerned only with how well the children can speak or understand the overheard language (Snow et al., 1976; Sachs, Bard, & Johnson, 1981; Rice, 1983). Thus, the prevailing wisdom among language development researchers is that children cannot learn a language merely by overhearing it (e.g., Pinker, 1994).

But these observations say little about other possible benefits of childhood overhearing, such as the benefits that may exist vis-à-vis later acquisition of the overheard language. My colleagues and I set out to explore this possibility by studying adult learners of Spanish who had overheard Spanish as a heritage language for at least several years during childhood (Au, Knightly, Jun, & Oh, 2002; Knightly, Jun, Oh, & Au, 2003). Our study focused on phonology and morphosyntax because they seem easy for children yet difficult for adults to acquire. We hypothesized that these aspects of language would therefore be good candidates for revealing the lasting effects of childhood overhearing.

Phonology

Infants learn about the characteristic intonational and rhythmic patterns of the ambient language by hearing it before learning to speak it (Mehler, Dupoux, Nazzi, & Dehaene-Lambertz, 1996; Dehaene-Lambertz & Houston, 1998). During their first year of life, infants learn to group distinct speech sounds into consonants and vowels that are relevant to their ambient language (Eimas, Siqueland, Jusczyk, & Vigorito, 1971; Werker & Tees, 1984; Kuhl & Iverson, 1995; Jusczyk, 1997). For instance, Japanese-learning infants lose interest in the distinction between /r/ and /l/ at about 1 year age, whereas English-learning infants continue to care about this distinction. That is, English-learning infants who have become bored by hearing, say, the /r/ sound repeatedly respond when the sound changes to an /l/ sound. By contrast, Japanese-learning infants act like English-learning infants until age 6 months or so, but by their first birthday, they become quite indifferent to changes from /r/ to /l/ (or vice versa). It is as if they have learned that the distinction between /r/ and /l/ does not matter in their ambient language. Infants also have to grasp new distinctions that they do not yet notice at birth. For example, Spanish-learning infants learn to grasp the distinction between the Spanish /b/ and /p/ whereas English-learning infants act as if sounds on both sides of the Spanish /b/ and /p/ boundary belong to the same category. Importantly, once acquired or consolidated, such speech sound categories seem to persist even years after exposure to the language has ended due to, for instance, emigration (Tees & Werker, 1984).

Accurate speech perception can offer a mental model that helps language learners modify their speech to emulate native speakers (Best, 1994; Flege, 1995; Kuhl & Meltzoff, 1982). If overhearing a language during childhood results in more native-like speech perception, can it help adult learners attain near-native pronunciation as well? There is actually some compelling evidence for a link between speech perception and production. An intensive regimen designed to train Japanese adults to distinguish English /r/ and /l/ improved both their perception and their production of these consonants (Bradlow, Pisoni, Akahane-Yamada, & Tohkura, 1997; Bradlow, Akahane-Yamada, Pisoni, & Tohkura, 1999). If overhearing a language during childhood helps children develop a good ear for the language, and if such perceptual ability lasts for years (Tees & Werker, 1984), then childhood overhearers of a language may indeed learn to speak that language with more native-like pronunciation later in life.

If childhood overhearing has lasting and measurable benefits for phonology, childhood overhearers should sound better than typical late-L2-learners. To test this hypothesis, my colleagues and I (Au et. al., 2002; Knightly et al., 2002) compared adult learners of Spanish who overheard Spanish regularly during childhood with learners who had no regular exposure to Spanish until around age 14. We also compared the pronunciation of these two groups to native speakers of Spanish who served as a standard for how native-like the childhood overhearers and typical late-L2-learners sounded.

Language Background Assessment

To identify childhood overhearers and typical late-L2-learners, we screened over 200 college students enrolled in second-year Spanish language classes at the University of California, Los Angeles with a detailed language background questionnaire and follow-up interview. We identified 15 childhood overhearers and many more typical late-L2-learners. The childhood overhearers reported that they had overheard informal Spanish spoken by native speakers for at least several hours a week and for at least 3 years between birth and age 6; they all overheard Spanish much less frequently afterwards. Ethnographies reveal that childhood overhearers in the United States rarely interact with relatives who speak little or no English, even when they are together (e.g., Kouritzin, 1999). This was also the case in our study. The childhood overhearers reported that they had spoken and had been spoken to in Spanish minimally (e.g., occasional Spanish words or short phrases embedded in English utterances) until they started taking Spanish classes at about age 14.

The typical late-L2-learners had minimal exposure (i.e., spending less than an hour each week, if at all, around someone who uttered at most isolated Spanish words or short phrases in Spanish) or had no regular exposure to Spanish until they started taking Spanish classes at about age 14. Fifteen typical late-L2-learners were randomly selected to match the gender composition, Spanish instruction, and number of years of Spanish classes in high school (about 4 years) and in college (somewhat less than 1 year). Fifteen native speakers of Spanish were also recruited from the same university to serve as another comparison group.

Self-reports of childhood Spanish language experience corresponded well with independent reports from informants who were familiar with the participants' childhood experience with Spanish. Further corroboration came from the participants' knowledge of childhood slang in Spanish. Because childhood slang is typically used by native speakers around children, mastery of childhood slang could be an indicator of childhood experience with a language. To assess knowledge of childhood slang in Spanish, we asked the participants to translate English expressions such as *cry baby, pacifier,* and *dry crust in the eyes* orally into informal Spanish (production test). We also asked them to listen to childhood slang terms in Spanish (e.g., *chiqueado* for "spoiled child," *las escondidas* for "hide-and-seek") and translate them into English (comprehension test). As expected, the native speakers passed the test with flying colors (80% or better correct). The overhearers did significantly worse than the native speakers but still reliably better than the typical late-L2-learners (about 20% and 3% correct, respectively). The overhearers' childhood experience with Spanish in terms of speaking and understanding seemed rather limited.

Phonology Assessment

Participants read aloud 36 Spanish sentences "Diga [target word] por favor" (English translation: "Say [target word] please."), each with a different target word, presented on a computer screen. The target words contained voiceless stops /p, t, k/ and voiced stops /b, d, g/ in either word initial (e.g., *tacos; beso*) or word medial position (e.g., *notar; jabón*).

We measured voice onset time (VOT) for /p, t, k/ because this measure has been productively used in assessing phonology in first and second language acquisition (e.g., Eimas et al., 1971; Williams, 1977). VOT refers to the time from the release of a stop consonant (e.g., when the lips open in saying /p/) to the onset of voicing (vocal cord vibration) of the following vowel. The VOT for /p, t, k/ is typically 30–50 msec longer in English than in Spanish (e.g., Lisker & Abramson, 1964). If overhearing Spanish during childhood helps an adult learner's Spanish pronunciation, overhearers should produce /p, t, k/ with more native-like, and hence shorter, VOT than typical late-L2-learners. This turned out to be the case, documenting systematically for the first time the benefits of childhood overhearing for adult learners' pronunciation.

We examined lenition for /b, d, g/. When a Spanish voiced stop appears between two vowels, it becomes lenited (i.e., the air flow is only partially blocked) both within a word (e.g., the /b/ in *sabor*) and across word boundaries (e.g., the /b/ in *Diga beso…*). To an untrained ear of a native English-speaker, a lenited Spanish /b/ sounds somewhat like a "v," and a lenited Spanish /d/ sounds somewhat like the "th" in the English word *this*. Importantly, these rules do not exist in English.

If childhood overhearing helps adult learners master these rules, overhearers should produce Spanish /b, d, g/ as lenited consonants in intervocalic contexts more often than typical late-L2-learners. This too was exactly what we found.

To see if any benefit of childhood overhearing could be detected by the average native speaker, we asked native speakers to rate participants' pronunciation on the "Diga ...por favor" sentences and also on samples of more natural speech elicited with a wordless children's book in a story-telling task. Although their pronunciation was not rated as highly as that of native speakers, the childhood overhearers were rated as having reliably better pronunciations than the typical late-L2-learners.

Taken together, these findings suggest that overhearing Spanish regularly for a few years during early childhood helps adult learners of Spanish speak with more native-like pronunciation when compared to adult learners who had no regular exposure to Spanish until about age 14.

Morphosyntax Assessment

Like phonology, morphosyntax is easy for children to acquire and difficult for adults to master. Can childhood overhearers learn the small grammatical markers (e.g., number and gender markers in nouns, adjectives, and determiners; number and tense/aspect markers in verbs) in the same way that they attain good pronunciation?

To assess morphosyntactic production, we elicited noun phrases, verb phrases, and narratives using a variety of tasks. We asked participants to complete simple jigsaw puzzles verbally, requiring the use of noun phrases that varied in number and gender to specify the puzzle pieces (e.g., "Pon los pianos blancos en cuatro, pon la vaca negra en tres...." English translation: "Put the white pianos in four, put the black cow in three."). We elicited verb phrases by asking participants to describe pictures in complete sentences in Spanish. We elicited narratives by asking participants to tell a story with a wordless picture book. After thousands of hours of transcribing, coding, checking, and rating, our data revealed no childhood overhearing advantage whatsoever. A better knowledge of morphosyntax, then, seems to require more than merely overhearing a language during childhood.

Childhood overhearers seem to have no advantage over other L2 learners in receptive mastery of morphosyntax. The participants listened to a set of grammatical sentences in Spanish that alternated with similar but ungrammatical sentences. They were asked to judge, one at a time, whether the sentences were grammatical. Each ungrammatical sentence contained an error in one of these morphosyntactic categories: number or gender agreement in noun phrases (e.g., *la flores[1]; *el carro blanca), number or person agreement in verbs (e.g., *Marta corren; *nosotros comienzan), tense/aspect marking in verbs (e.g., *Dentro de cuatro años, soy un abogado), negation (e.g., *El conoce a nadie), or indirect object (e.g., **El enseña a nosotros*) marking. As in the morphosyntax production tasks, the childhood overhearers were reliably worse than the native speakers and no better than the typical late-L2-learners.

Hearing and Speaking Korean during Childhood

What are the advantages of speaking another language in early childhood? In a second study, we explored what happens when children become virtually mono-lingual in a second language and then try to re-learn their first language as adults (Oh, Au, & Jun, 2002; Oh, Jun, Knightly, & Au, 2003). We focused on childhood speakers of Korean and their mastery of Korean phonology as adult learners. These childhood speakers have spoken exclusively or predominantly Korean prior to starting school around age 5 and very little Korean afterward. Importantly, their shift from Korean to English took place within the critical/sensitive period for phonology acquisition (e.g., Williams, 1980; Long, 1990).

Childhood speakers of Korean were compared with the following groups: (1) novice adult learners to assess the benefits of childhood exposure to Korean; (2) childhood hearers of Korean to compare the benefits of childhood speaking with childhood hearing; and (3) native Korean speakers to assess how native-like the childhood speakers' phonology was. All non-native speakers of Korean were recruited from first year Korean language classes at the University of California, Los Angeles (UCLA), about 4 months into the academic year; the native speakers were also recruited from UCLA. All participants were tested on their perception and production of Korean phonemes.

Language Background Assessment

After completing a detailed language background questionnaire and follow-up interview, the participants were categorized as:

1. Native speakers who were born in Korea, immigrated to the United States after elementary school, and spoke Korean regularly (n = 12).
2. Childhood speakers who had spoken Korean regularly for at least 3 years during early childhood (n = 15).[2]
3. Childhood hearers who had regularly heard Korean during childhood but had spoken it rarely, if at all (n = 6).
4. Novice learners who had no experience with Korean until college Korean classes (n = 10).

As in the Spanish study, the participants' actual knowledge of childhood slang corroborated with their self-reports. Novice learners had the lowest scores (0% correct), followed by childhood hearers (about 30%), childhood speakers (about 45%), and finally native speakers, who had the highest scores (about 65%).[3]

Phonology Assessment

While there is a two-way contrast in English for alveolar stop consonants, there is a three-way contrast in Korean, referred to here as plain, aspirated, and tense consonants (/t/, /tʰ/, and /t'/ respectively). A primary distinguishing feature among these consonants in both English and Korean is voice onset time (VOT). In Korean, aspirated stop consonants have the longest VOT, and tense ones have the shortest (Lisker & Abramson, 1964; Han & Weitzman, 1970).

For phoneme perception assessment, participants heard a native Korean speaker say nine words from three minimal triplets (e.g., /taN/, /tʰaN/, and /t'aN/, meaning "a crowd," "hot water," and "the earth," respectively). Within each triplet, words varied only on the target consonant. In each trial, participants heard a word, saw the entire triplet presented in Korean orthography on a computer screen, and were asked to indicate which word they heard by pressing a button. The childhood hearers and childhood speakers performed as well as the native speakers did. All three groups outperformed the novice learners. These results suggest that hearing a language during childhood suffices to help adult learners of the language hear important phonemic contrasts characteristic of the language.

For phoneme production assessment, participants saw the same nine stimulus words used in the perception test presented in Korean orthography ("igon/igae [target word] ipnita," meaning "this is a [target word]."). They were asked to read the sentences aloud. Their utterances were audiotaped and digitized for VOT measurements. The results were straightforward. The childhood and native speakers reliably distinguished among all three Korean alveolar stop consonants whereas the childhood hearers and novice learners did not reliably contrast any of them. Native speakers judged the pronunciation of the childhood speakers as more native-like than that of the childhood hearers or the novice learners.[4]

Korean Spoken Beyond Early Childhood

All childhood speakers began to speak significantly less Korean at about age 5. However, some continued to speak Korean occasionally whereas others spoke virtually none. We wondered how their Korean pronunciation might be related to the *quantity* (e.g., hours per week speaking) and *quality* (e.g., isolated words versus sentences; amount of mixing with English) of Korean spoken after the sharp drop in the use of Korean (i.e., during elementary, middle, and high school). The quantity of their post-drop spoken Korean turned out not to predict the quality of the adult re-learners' pronunciation. By contrast, the quality of their post-drop Korean did. Pronunciation rating scores were reliably correlated with the quality of spoken Korean during elementary school and high school. Analogous analyses with VOT data revealed no reliable correlations.

We were equally curious to find out what childhood speakers who spoke virtually no Korean beyond early childhood (i.e., except for isolated Korean words or short phrases embedded in English sentences) sound like. We found six such childhood speakers whose self-reports of prior speaking experience were corroborated by their scores on the childhood slang test. These speakers turned out to know fewer Korean childhood slang terms than the remaining nine childhood speakers (around 30% vs. 45% correct, respectively). Importantly, this sub-sample reliably contrasted aspirated and tense consonants, almost reliably contrasted aspirated and plain consonants, but did not reliably contrast plain and tense consonants. Like the full sample of 12 childhood speakers, this sub-sample of childhood speakers was rated to be reliably better than the novice learners and worse than the native speakers. But unlike the full sample, they were not reliably better than the childhood hearers.

Taken together, these findings suggest that hearing Korean during childhood helps adult learners distinguish important Korean phonemic contrasts and that speaking Korean for a few years during early childhood suffices to help adult learners speak Korean with good pronunciation. As sensible as these findings sound, they probably do not reveal the whole story. In other words, additional variables undoubtedly also play a role in the ability of adult learners to re-learn childhood languages. For example, the duration of re-learning may play a significant role. Recall that childhood overhearing experience can also have lasting benefits for phonology production in Spanish (Au et al., 2002; Knightly et al., 2003). The childhood overhearers of Spanish had 4 to 5 years of Spanish classes during high school or college, whereas the childhood hearers of Korean had only 4 months of Korean instruction. Recall that storage strength for a memory depends on how well something was learned originally, and retrieval strength depends on current usage. Perhaps it takes several years of re-learning and using a childhood language to build up sufficient retrieval strength to access the ambient language of the childhood years. As with the study involving Spanish, hearing Korean during childhood may benefit phonology production for adults who have gone through several years of re-learning and using the language. The relative difficulty of the phonemic contrasts in the two languages may also play a role. While Spanish, like English, observes a two-way contrast in stop consonants (although with different VOT boundaries), Korean observes a three-way contrast. Mastery of this three-way contrast may require childhood speaking experience. These seemingly contradictory findings from our two studies highlight how the nature of language experience could affect language acquisition.

Concluding Remarks

My research team's findings offer a window—albeit a narrow one—into how childhood language experience may help adults learn or re-learn their heritage language. To acquire and maintain a heritage language, children need to speak it beyond early childhood. Speaking a heritage language for a few years during early childhood seems sufficient to help adult re-learners speak with good, if not entirely native-like, pronunciation. Even merely overhearing a language for several years during early childhood can, in some cases, result in adult learners acquiring good pronunciation in the language. Specifically, childhood overhearers of Spanish who have had several years of Spanish language classes in high school or college speak with more native-like pronunciation than their classmates with no childhood exposure to Spanish. But these benefits seem limited to phonology. No benefits to morphosyntax have been detected thus far. If the ultimate goal is the mastery of a heritage language grammatically as well as phonologically, it is crucial to find ways to foster an environment that supports heritage-language speakers' regular and active use of the language beyond the preschool years. In short, Plan A for salvaging heritage languages is to get children to speak them regularly beyond early childhood.

Failing that, Plan B will be to identify the strengths and weaknesses of older heritage language learners and re-learners through research such as that reported here. A case in point: given that childhood speakers and, in some cases, childhood hearers manage to attain fairly high levels of pronunciation as adult learners, language instructors may want to help them master more subtle aspects of phonology to develop even more native-like pronunciation. By contrast, since no analogous benefit for morphosyntax has been detected so far, language instructors may have to work harder to help childhood speakers and hearers master the grammar of the target language.

They may have to work harder not only on the mastery of morphosyntax compared to phonology, but also in teaching heritage speakers compared to typical late-L2-learners. While childhood exposure to a heritage language may help adult learners acquire higher levels of pronunciation, it may also cause them to have a somewhat inflated "feeling-of-knowing" and hence a false sense of security about their knowledge of the language. More than one high school/college language instructor has remarked that students who earned A's in their classes tend to be typical late-L2-learners rather than heritage learners, as if the heritage language learners are overconfident and hence study less hard. Meanwhile, diligent typical late-L2-learners may be so in awe of the heritage language learners, especially by their pronunciation and their knowledge of slang terms if our research findings are any guide, that they tend to study extra hard in order to compete. Whether these speculations will turn out to be true requires further research. Nonetheless, our research to date suggests that language instructors and students alike cannot take for granted that childhood exposure to the language will translate into a morphosytactic advantage for adult learners. In short, Plan B for salvaging heritage languages is to know your (or your students') strengths and weaknesses, build on the strengths, and deal with the weaknesses squarely.

Acknowledgments

The research reported here was supported by NIMH Grant MH56118 and seed grants from the UCLA Institute of American Cultures and the UC Linguistic

Minority Research Institute (Au), NIMH traineeships USPHS MH19926 (Knightly and Oh), and a National Science Foundation Graduate Fellowship (Oh). I am very grateful to my collaborators, Sun-Ah Jun, Leah Knightly, and Janet Oh, my many dedicated research assistants, my colleagues in the Spanish and Korean language programs at UCLA, and the research participants. The preparation of this chapter was supported by research funds from the Vice Chancellor's office and the University Research Committee at the University of Hong Kong.

Notes

1. The asterisks indicate incorrect forms.
2. After age 5, their Korean, if they spoke it at all, was mostly limited to isolated words and short phrases.
3. The native speakers' less than perfect performance seemed to be due to their limited proficiency in English. While they may have known the Korean childhood slang terms, they had difficulty coming up with an English translation in the comprehension test and/or understanding the English expressions in the production test.
4. Note that none of the groups approached true native-like pronunciation.

References

Ås, A. (1962). The recovery of forgotten language knowledge through hypnotic age regression: A case report. *American Journal of Clinical Hypnosis, 5,* 24–29.

Au, T. K., Knightly, L. M., Jun, S.-A., & Oh, J. S. (2002). Overhearing a language during childhood. *Psychological Science, 13,* 238–243.

Au, T. K., & Romo, L. F. (1997). Does childhood language experience help adult learners? In H.-C. Chen (Ed.), *The cognitive processing of Chinese and related Asian languages* (pp. 417–441). Hong Kong: Chinese University Press.

Bialystok, E., & Hakuta, K. (1994). *In other words: The science and psychology of second language acquisition.* New York: Basic.

Best, C. T. (1994). The emergence of native-language phonological influences in infants: A perceptual assimilation model. In H. C. Goodman & H. C. Nusbaum (Eds.), *The development of speech perception: The transition from speech sounds to spoken words* (pp. 167–224). Cambridge, MA: MIT Press.

Birdsong, D., & Molis, M. (2001). On the evidence for maturational constraints in second-language acquisition. *Journal of Memory Language, 44,* 235–249.

Bjork, E. L., & Bjork, R. A. (1996). Continuing influences of to-be-forgotten information. *Consciousness and Cognition: An International Journal, 5,* 176–196.

Bjork, R. A., & Bjork, E. L. (1992). A new theory of disuse and an old theory of stimulus fluctuation. In A. Healy, S. Kosslyn, & R. Shiffrin (Eds.), *From learning processes to cognitive processes: Essays in honor of William K. Estes* (vol. 2, pp. 35–67). Hillsdale, NJ: Erlbaum.

Bradlow, A. R., Pisoni, D. B., Akahane-Yamada, R., & Tohkura, Y. (1997). Training Japanese listeners to identify English /r/ and /l/: IV. Some effects of perceptual learning on speech production. *Journal of the Acoustical Society of America, 101,* 2299–2310.

Bradlow, A. R., Akahane-Yamada, R., Pisoni, D. B., & Tohkura, Y. (1999). Training Japanese listeners to identify English /r/ and /l/: Long-term retention of learning in perception and production. *Perception & Psychophysics, 61,* 977–985.

Bjork, R. A., & Bjork, E. L. (1992). A new theory of disuse and an old theory of stimulus fluctuation. In A. Healy, S. Kosslyn, & R. Shiffrin (Eds.), *From learning processes to cognitive processes: Essays in honor of William K. Estes* (vol. 2, pp. 35–67). Hillsdale, NJ: Erlbaum.

Curtiss, S. (1977). *Genie: A psycholinguistic study of a modern-day "wild child."* New York: Academic Press.

Curtiss, S. (1989). The independence and task-specificity of language. In A. Bornstein & J. Bruner (Eds.), *Interaction in human development* (pp. 105–138). Hillsdale, NJ: Erlbaum.

Dehaene-Lambertz, G., & Houston, D. (1998). Faster orientation latencies toward native language in two-month-old infants. *Language & Speech, 41,* 21–43.

Eimas, P. D., Siqueland, E. R., Jusczyk, P., & Vigorito, J. (1971). Speech perception in infants. *Science, 171,* 303–306.

Ebbinghaus, H. (1964). *Memory: A contribution to experimental psychology* (H. A. Ruger & C. E. Bussenius, Trans.). New York: Dover. (Original work published 1885)

Fillmore, L. W. (1991). When learning a second language means losing the first. *Early Childhood Research Quarterly, 6,* 323–346.

Fishman, J. A. (1978). *Language loyalty in the United States.* The Hague: Mouton.

Flege, J. (1987). A critical period for learning to pronounce foreign languages? *Applied Linguistics, 8,* 162–177.

Flege, J. (1991). Age of learning affects the authenticity of voice-onset time (VOT) in stop consonants produced in a second language. *Journal of the Acoustical Society of America, 89,* 395–411.

Flege, J. (1995). Second language speech learning: Theory, findings, and problems. In W. Strange (Ed), *Speech perception and linguistic experience: Issues in cross-language research* (pp. 233–277). Baltimore: York.

Flege, J. E, Yeni-Komshian, G. H., & Liu, S. (1999). Age constraints on second-language acquisition. *Journal of Memory & Language, 41,* 78–104.

Fromkin, V. A., Krashen, S., Curtiss, S., Rigler, D., & Rigler, M. (1974). The development of language in Genie: A case of language acquisition beyond the "critical period." *Brain and Language, 1,* 81–107.

Fromm, E. (1970). Age regression with unexpected reappearance of a repressed childhood language. *International Journal of Clinical and Experimental Hypnosis, 18,* 79–88.

Han, M. S., & Weitzman, R. S. (1970). Acoustic features of Korean /P,T,K/, /p,t,k/, and /pʰ,tʰ,kʰ/. *Phonetica, 22,* 112–128.

Johnson, J. S., & Newport, E. L. (1989). Critical period effects in second language learning: The influence of maturational state on the acquisition of English as a second language. *Cognitive Psychology, 21,* 60–99.

Johnson, J. S., & Newport, E. L. (1991). Critical period effects on universal properties of language: The status of subjacency in the acquisition of a second language. *Cognition, 39,* 215–258.

Jusczyk, P. W. (1997). *The discovery of spoken language.* Cambridge, MA: Massachusetts Institute of Technology Press.

Knightly, L. M., Jun, S.-A., Oh, J. S., & Au, T. K. (2003). Production benefits of childhood overhearing. *Journal of the Acoustical Society of America, 114,* 465–474.

Koluchova, J. (1972). Severe deprivation in twins: A case study. *Journal of Child Psychology and Psychiatry, 13,* 107–114.

Koluchova, J. (1976). The further development of twins after severe and prolonged deprivation: A second report. *Journal of Child Psychology and Psychiatry, 17,* 181–188.

Kouritzin, S. G. (1999). *Face[t]s of first language loss.* Mahwah, NJ: Erlbaum.

Krashen, S. (1996). *Under attack: The case against bilingual education.* Culver City, CA: Language Education Associates.

Kruger, W. C. F. (1929). The effects of the degree of overlearning on retention. *Journal of Experimental Psychology, 12,* 71–78.

Kuhl, P. K., & Iverson, P. (1995). Linguistic experience and the "perceptual magnet effect." In W. Strange (Ed.), *Speech perception and linguistic experience: Issues in cross-language research* (pp. 121–154). Baltimore: York.

Kuhl, P. K., & Meltzoff, A. N. (1982). The bimodal perception of speech in infancy. *Science, 218,* 1138–1141.

Lisker, L., & Abramson, A. S. (1964). Cross-language study of voicing in initial stops: Acoustical measurements. *Word, 20,* 384–422.

Long, M. H. (1990). Maturational constraints on language development. *Studies in Second Language Acquisition, 12,* 251–285.

Luh, C. W. (1922). The conditions of retention. *Psychology Monograph, 32,* 1–87.

Mayberry, R. I. (1993). First-language acquisition after childhood differs from second-language acquisition: The case of American Sign Language. *Journal of Speech and Hearing Research, 36,* 1258–1270.

Mehler, J., Dupoux, E., Nazzi, T., & Dehaene-Lambertz, G., (1996). Coping with linguistic diversity: The infant's viewpoint. In J. L. Morgan & K. Demuth (Eds.), *Signal to syntax: Bootstrapping from speech to grammar in early acquisition* (pp. 101–116). Mahwah, NJ: Erlbaum.

Newport, E. (1990). Maturational constraints on language learning. *Cognitive Science, 14,* 11–28.

Newport, E. (1991). Contrasting conceptions of the critical period of language. In S. Carey & R. Gelman (Eds.), *The epigenesis of mind: Essays on biology and* cognition (pp. 111–130). Hillsdale, NJ: Erlbaum.

Oh, J. S., Au, T. K., & Jun S.-A. (2002). Benefits of childhood language experience for adult L2-learners' phonology. In A. H.-J. Do, L. Domínguez, & A. Johansen (Eds.), *Proceedings of the 26th annual Boston University Conference on Language Development* (pp. 464–472). Somerville, MA: Cascadilla Press.

Oh, J. S., Jun S.-A., Knightly, L. M., & Au, T. K. (2003). Holding on to childhood language memory. *Cognition, 86*, 53–64.

Oyama, S. (1976). A sensitive period for the acquisition of a non-native phonological system. *Journal of Psycholinguistic Research, 5*, 261–185.

Pallier, C., Dehaene, S., Poline, J.-B., LeBihan, D., Argenti, A.-M., Dupoux, E., & Mehler, J. (2003). Brain imaging of language plasticity in adopted adults: Can a second language replace the first? *Cerebral Cortex 13*, 155–161.

Penfield, W. (1959). The learning of languages. In W. Penfield & L. Roberts (Eds.), *Speech and brain mechanisms* (pp. 235–257). Princeton, NJ: Princeton University Press.

Pinker, S. (1994). *The language instinct.* New York: Morrow.

Rakic, P., Bourgeois, J. P., Zecevic, N., Eckenhoff, M. F., & Goldman-Rakic, P. S. (1986). Concurrent overproduction of synapses in diverse regions of the primate cerebral cortex. *Science, 232*, 232–235.

Rice, M. (1983). The role of television in language acquisition. *Developmental Review, 3*, 211–224.

Sachs, J., Bard, B., & Johnson, M. L. (1981). Language learning with restricted input: Case studies of two hearing children of deaf parents. *Applied Psycholinguistics, 2*, 33–54.

Skuse, D. H. (1984a). Extreme deprivation in early childhood-I: Diverse outcomes for 3 siblings from an extraordinary family. *Journal of Child Psychology and Psychiatry, 25*, 523–541.

Skuse, D. H. (1984b). Extreme deprivation in early childhood-II: Theoretical issues and a comparative review. *Journal of Child Psychology and Psychiatry, 25*, 543–572.

Snow, C. E., Arlman-Rupp, A., Hassing, Y., Jobse, J., Joosten, J., & Vorster, J. (1976). Mothers' speech in three social classes. *Journal of Psycholinguistic Research, 5*, 1–20.

Snow, C., & Hoefnagel-Hohle, M. (1978). The critical period for language acquisition: Evidence from second language learning. *Child Development, 49*, 1114–1128.

Tees, R. C., & Werker, J. F. (1984). Perceptual flexibility: Maintenance or recovery of the ability to discriminate non-native speech sounds. *Canadian Journal of Psychology, 34*, 579–590.

Tseng, V., & Fuligni, A. J. (2000). Parent-adolescent language use and relationships among immigrant families with east Asian, Filipino and Latin American backgrounds. *Journal of Marriage & the Family, 62*, 465–476.

U.S. Census Bureau. (2000). United States census 2000. Available at: http://www.census.gov/

Veltman, C. (1983). *Language shift in the United States.* Berlin: Mouton.

Werker, J. F., & Tees, R. C. (1984). Cross-language speech perception: Evidence for perceptual reorganization during the first year of life. *Infant Behavior & Development, 7*, 49–63.

Williams, L. (1977). The perception of stop consonant voicing by Spanish-English bilinguals. *Perception & Psychophysics, 21*, 289–297.

Williams, L. (1980). Phonetic variation as a function of second-language learning. In G. H. Yeni-Komshian, J. F. Kavanagh, & C. A. Ferguson (Eds.), *Child phonology: Vol. 2. Perception* (pp. 185–215). New York: Academic Press.

Wode, H. (1981). *Learning a second language: An integrated view of language acquisition.* Tübingen, Germany: Gunter Narr.

Yamada, R. A. (1995). Age and acquisition of second language speech sounds: perception of American English /r/ and /l/ by native speakers of Japanese. In W. Strange (Ed.), *Speech perception and linguistic experience: Theoretical and methodological issues* (pp. 305–320). Baltimore: York.

About the Editors and Contributors

Terry Kit-fong Au received her A.B. in Psychology & Social Relations from Harvard University in 1982 and her Ph.D. in Psychology from Stanford University in 1987. She was previously an Associate Professor at Brown University and a Professor at UCLA, and is currently Professor and Chair of the Department of Psychology at the University of Hong Kong. She has served as Associate Editor of *Developmental Psychology* and an editorial board member of several other international journals (e.g., *Child Development, Cognition, Journal of Memory & Language, Psychological Science*). Her research interests include language and cognitive development, and health, science and language education.

Susan Bauckus is a staff researcher at the UCLA Center for World Languages and the managing editor of the *Heritage Language Journal*. She co-edited *The Learning and Teaching of Slavic Languages and Cultures* (Bloomington, IN: Slavica, 2000) which received an award from the American Association of Teachers of Slavic and East European Languages in 2001. Bauckus teaches Russian language at several colleges in the Los Angeles area.

Joseph Lo Bianco holds the Chair of Language and Literacy Education at The University of Melbourne and was formerly Director of the National Languages and Literacy Institute of Australia. He has worked on language policy, peace education, literacy planning, bilingualism and multicultural education in several countries, including Australia, Sri Lanka and Scotland. His recent books include: *Australian Literacies: Informing National Policy on Literacy Education*, with P. Freebody, 2001; *Australian Policy Activism in Language and Literacy*, with R. Wickert, 2001; *Voices from Phnom Penh, Development and Language*, 2002; *Teaching Invisible Culture: Classroom Practice and Theory*, with C. Crozet, 2003, all published by Melbourne: Language Australia Publications; and *Language Policy in Australia* (Strasbourg: Council of Europe, 2004). For his research and policy work he was elected Fellow of the Australian Academy of the Humanities and Fellow of the Australian Council of Educators, and has been awarded the Order of Australia, the Centenary Medal and the title of *Commendatore nell'ordine di merito della repubblica Italiana*.

Donna M. Brinton recently retired as Lecturer in Applied Linguistics and as the Associate Director of UCLA's Center for World Languages to pursue her interest in international teacher development. She is currently Professor of TESOL at Soka University of America in Aliso Viejo, California. She has taught a variety of graduate level classes and trained and supervised teaching assistants. She is the co-author and co-editor of several professional texts including Content-Based Second Language Instruction (University of Michigan, 2003), The Content-Based Classroom (Longman, 1997), Teaching Pronunciation (Cambridge, 1996), New Ways in Content-Based Instruction (TESOL, 1997), and New Ways in ESP (TE-SOL, 1998). She has also co-authored several English language textbooks and numerous journal and book articles. From 1994-2002, she served as co-editor of The CATESOL Journal. Brinton has conducted short-term international teacher training in North America, Central and South America, Asia, Africa, Central Asia, and the Middle East. Her interests include materials and curriculum development, program evaluation, teaching methodology, and Content-based Instruction as well as English for Special Purposes.

Donna Christian is President of the Center for Applied Linguistics (CAL) in Washington, DC. Her work focuses on language in education, including issues of second language learning, dialect diversity, and language education policy. Publications include the co-authored or co-edited volumes *Educating English Language Learners: A Synthesis of Research Evidence* (Cambridge University Press, 2006), *What Teachers Need to Know About Language* (CAL/Delta Systems, 2002), *Bilingual Education* (TESOL, 2001), *Dialects, Schools, and Communities* (Lawrence Erlbaum, 1999) and *Profiles in Two-Way Immersion Education* (CAL/ Delta Systems, 1997). She serves on numerous boards, including the Editorial Board of the *Heritage Language Journal*, the Advisory Board of the Hispanic Family Literacy Institute, and the Board of Directors of the TESOL International Research Foundation.

Andrew D. Cohen is Professor of Applied Linguistics and Chair of the English as a Second Language Program at the University of Minnesota, Minneapolis, where he received the Scholar of the College award for 2002–2005. He was also recipient of the American Association for Applied Linguistics Distinguished Scholarship and Service Award for 2006. Cohen was evaluator of two pioneering language programs: the first two-way bilingual Spanish-English program in the United States, in Redwood City, California (1969–1972), and a full-immersion Spanish program in Culver City, California (1972-1975). He has published articles on the learning, teaching, and assessment of a second language, research methods, and speech acts in pragmatics. His books include authored and edited volumes on bilingual education, language learning strategies, language assessment, and research methods. His latest books are a co-edited volume with D. Boxer, *Studying Speaking to Inform Second Language Learning* (Multilingual Matters, 2004) and another with E. Macaro, *Language Learner Strategies: 30 Years of Research and Practice* (Oxford University Press, 2007).

Masako O. Douglas is Associate Professor of Japanese at California State University, Long Beach. She earned her doctoral degree in Education from the University of Southern California. Her research focuses on acquisition and pedagogy of Japanese as a heritage language for young learners and college students. She is also interested in the theory and practice of teaching Japanese as a foreign language. Douglas has presented and published papers on curriculum design, needs analysis, content-based language learning, and acquisition of literacy skills by learners of Japanese as a heritage or foreign language. She is a coordinator of the Japanese as a Heritage Language Special Interest Group of the Association of Teachers of Japanese, and is a co-manager of the JHL listserv.

Patricia A. Duff received a Ph.D. in Applied Linguistics from the University of California, Los Angeles in 1993. She is Professor of Language and Literacy Education at the University of British Columbia. Her research on second language acquisition and socialization, task-based interaction, L2 education, and research methods in applied linguistics have appeared in several dozen journals and edited volumes. Her recent publications include three books (two of which are co-edited): *Case Study Research in Applied Linguistics, Inference and Generalizability in Applied Linguistics,* and *Language Socialization* (*Encyclopedia of Language and Education, Vol. 8*). Duff's great fondness and admiration for Russ Campbell, her former professor and colleague at UCLA, and his wonderful legacy in language education, inspired her to write this chapter.

Debra Friedman earned her B.A. in Slavic Languages from the University of California, Berkeley, and her M.A. in Teaching English as a Second Language and Ph.D. in Applied Linguistics from the University of California, Los Angeles. She is Assistant Professor in Second Language Studies at Michigan State University. Her research interests include language education, especially heritage language education, and ideologies of language and identity. Her doctoral dissertation focused on the role of Ukrainian language education in the revitalization of the Ukrainian language and the construction of national identity in the newly emerging nation state of Ukraine.

Dania López García is Assistant Professor of Hispanic Linguistics at the University of Texas at Brownsville. She is a doctoral candidate at Stanford University, where she is completing her dissertation, entitled *¿Tan cubanos como siempre? The Cultural Evolution of a Cuban American Family in the United States.* Her areas of interest are sociolinguistics and applied linguistics, particularly language maintenance and language shift, bilinguals and bilingualism, language diversity, the teaching of Spanish to Hispanics as a heritage language, and the teaching of Spanish to monolingual English speakers.

Tania Gómez is a Ph.D. student of Hispanic Linguistics in the Spanish and Portuguese Department at the University of Minnesota, Minneapolis. She has worked in a Spanish Immersion school where she helped students work on their use of learning strategies and styles appropriate for the immersion environment. Currently, she is working on an analysis of the strategies Spanish speakers use in making apologies and on the inclusion of those strategies in the teaching curriculum.

Sonia V. González is Assistant Professor of Spanish in the Department of Foreign Languages and Literatures at Purdue University. She obtained her Ph.D. in Spanish from Stanford University, and wrote her dissertation on the poetry of Lorna Dee Cervantes. Her areas of interest are Chicana/o literature and the teaching of Spanish to heritage language students. Her current research project focuses on the acquisition of high registers by advanced heritage speakers. She is also working on a book on the poetics of loss and recovery of cultural memory in the poetry of Lorna Dee Cervantes. In 2004, González started the Spanish for Heritage Speakers Program at Purdue University. She teaches undergraduate classes for heritage students as well as a graduate seminar on teaching Spanish to heritage students.

Tomomi Hasegawa received her Ph.D. in Second Language Acquisition from the University of Hawaii at Manoa and is Assistant Professor in the Faculty of Education and Human Sciences at Yokohama National University, Japan. She has B.A. and M.Ed. degrees in Japanese as a second language and has taught Japanese as a second/foreign language in elementary schools in Japan and middle schools in the United States. Her current research interest is the acquisition of Japanese as a second language, especially by child second language learners. Her article on child heritage language proficiency measurement appears in *Teaching Chinese, Japanese, and Korean Heritage Language Students: Curriculum Needs, Materials, and Assessment edited by* K. Kondo-Brown and J. D. Brown (Lawrence Erlbaum, 2007)

Nancy H. Hornberger is Professor of Education at the University of Pennsylvania. She investigates multilingual language and education policy and practice, combining methods and perspectives from anthropology, linguistics, sociolinguistics, and policy studies. Her special focus is comparative work on indigenous and immigrant heritage language education, grounded in her in-depth and long-term experience in Andean South America and urban Philadelphia. A three-time Fulbright Senior Specialist Awardee, Hornberger has also served as consultant for the U.S. Department of State, UNICEF, and the United Nations Development Program and has taught, lectured, and advised on multilingualism and education throughout the world. Author/editor of a dozen books and over 100 articles and chapters, her recent volumes include *Continua of Biliteracy: An Ecological Framework for Educational Policy, Research, and Practice in Multilingual Settings* (Multilingual Matters, 2003), and *Heritage/Community Language Education: US and Australian Perspectives* (Multilingual Matters, 2005). Hornberger co-edits an international book series and is General Editor for the 10-volume *Encyclopedia of Language and Education* (Springer, 2008).

Keiko Ikeda is Associate Professor at Nagoya University, Japan. She has a Ph.D. in Japanese Language from University of Hawaii at Manoa. She also holds a Master's degree in Teaching English to Speakers of Other Languages from Portland State University. Her research interests include the role of oral communication in social networks; intercultural and cross-cultural communication; relationships between media, communication, and politics in Japan; popular culture (dialect revival, commercialization of the term "hometown") in Japanese society; debate and argumentation; sociolinguistics; conversation analysis; and foreign language pedagogy.

Yasuko Ito is Assistant Professor in the Department of English at Kanda University of International Studies in Chiba, Japan. She has an M.A. in Education and an M.S. in Applied Linguistics. She received her Ph.D. in Second Language Acquisition from the University of Hawaii at Manoa. Her academic interests include teaching of listening and speaking, second language acquisition, second language phonology and syntax, and psycholinguistics.

Olga Kagan is Director of the Title VI National Heritage Language Resource Center. Since 2002 she has directed the UCLA Center for World Languages founded by Russ Campbell (originally called the Language Resource Program). She is Coordinator of the Russian Language Program in the UCLA Slavic Department. She has co-edited a book on teaching Russian as a Foreign Language (Moscow: Russian Language Publishers, 2005) and five Russian language textbooks, including a second-year Russian textbook (Prentice Hall, 2005) and the first textbook for heritage speakers of Russian *Russian for Russians* (Bloomington, IN: Slavica, 2003), which received an award from the American Association of Teachers of Russian and Eastern European Languages (AATSEEL) for the Best Contribution to Pedagogy. She also received an AATSEEL award for co-editing *The Teaching and Learning of Slavic Languages and Cultures* (Slavica, 2000). Kagan is co-editor of the *Heritage Language Journal*.

Kazue Kanno is Associate Professor of Japanese in the Department of East Asian Languages and Literatures, and a faculty member of the Ph.D. program in Second Language Acquisition at the University of Hawaii at Manoa. She has also taught at the University of Calgary in Canada. She received her Ph.D. in Linguistics from the University of Hawaii in 1992. Her research interests include second language acquisition, syntax and semantics, and Japanese pedagogical grammar and sentence processing. She has published a number of book chapters and articles on the acquisition of Japanese as a second or foreign language. She is the editor of *The Acquisition of Japanese as a Second Language* (John Benjamins, 1999).

Sharon Lapkin is Professor Emerita in the Modern Language Centre and Second Language Education Program of the Ontario Institute for Studies in Education at the University of Toronto. Her research projects center on French second language education in Canada and range from evaluations of core French and immersion programs to qualitative studies of language learning in progress through detailed analysis of transcribed learner dialogues. From 1995 to 2004 she was co-editor of the *Canadian Modern Language Review* and she is currently co-President of the Canadian Association of Applied Linguistics.

Michael H. Long is Professor of Second Language Acquisition (SLA) and Director of the School of Languages, Literatures, and Cultures at the University of Maryland, College Park, where he teaches in the M.A. and Ph.D. programs in SLA. He is the author of over 100 articles and several books, and in 1991 was co-recipient of TESOL's International Research Prize. He serves on the Editorial Boards of *Studies in Second Language Acquisition, JACET Bulletin, Porta Linguarium, Estudios de Linguistica Aplicada,* and *Revista Nebrija de Lingüística aplicada a la enseñanza de lenguas,* and is co-editor of the *Cambridge Applied Linguistics Series.* His current research includes work on theory change in SLA, negative feedback, sensitive periods, needs analysis, Task-based Language Teaching, and a longitudinal study of stabilization/fossilization in the interlanguage of a Japanese immigrant to Hawaii. His recent publications include *The Handbook of Second Language Acquisition* co-edited with Catherine Doughty (Blackwell, 2003), *Second Language Needs Analysis* (Cambridge, 2005), and *Problems in SLA* (Lawrence Erlbaum, 2007).

Brian K. Lynch received his Ph.D. in Applied Linguistics from the University of California, Los Angeles in 1987. He has been active in teaching, research, program evaluation and testing in China, Mexico, the United States, Armenia, Costa Rica, and Australia. His academic appointments include UCLA (Adjunct Assistant Professor & Director of ESL Service Courses), the University of Melbourne (Senior Lecturer in Applied Linguistics & foundation Director of the Centre for Communication Skills and ESL), and Portland State University (Professor of Applied Linguistics). He credits his professional success to the support, mentoring, and friendship he received from Russ Campbell. Lynch retired in 2006 to pursue poetry and political activism.

Patricio Márquez is a first generation Mexican American and a heritage speaker of Spanish. He completed his undergraduate and graduate studies in Spanish at Stanford University. Following completion of his Master's degree, he attended the Columbia University School of Law and is currently an attorney in Los Angeles.

Scott McGinnis received his Ph.D. from Ohio State University, Columbus in 1990. He is the Academic Advisor and Professor at the Defense Language Institute, Washington Office, in Arlington, Virginia. Between 1999 and 2003, he served as Executive Director of the National Council of Organizations of Less Commonly Taught Languages at the National Foreign Language Center. His twenty two years in the language teaching profession have included a decade of experience as supervisor of the Chinese language programs at the University of Oregon and University of Maryland. McGinnis has authored or edited five books, and over 40 book chapters, journal articles and reviews on language pedagogy and linguistics for the less commonly taught languages in general, and Chinese and Japanese in particular. He previously served two terms as President of the Chinese Language Teachers Association, and as chair of The College Board Chinese Language Test Development Committee for the Educational Testing Service.

Mary McGroarty is Professor in the Applied Linguistics Program of the English Department at Northern Arizona University, Flagstaff, and a former faculty member and colleague of Russ Campbell's at the University of California, Los Angeles. Her research and teaching interests include second language learning and teaching, bilingualism, language policy, and assessment. Over a twenty-year period, she has trained language teachers in Arizona, California, China, Hungary, Italy, Morocco, Peru, Tunisia, and Venezuela, and also worked on research projects related to different types of assessment for English, Spanish, and Navajo. Her articles on aspects of heritage language learning, assessment, and applicability to contexts outside schools have appeared in *Annals of the American Academy of Political and Social Science, Applied Linguistics, Language Learning, TESOL Quarterly*, and other journals, newsletters, and collections. A past president of the American Association for Applied Linguistics, she is Editor-in-Chief of the *Annual Review of Applied Linguistics*.

Craig C. Merrill is a Ph.D. student in the Department of Asian Languages and Cultures at the University of California, Los Angeles. His area of research is child acquisition of honorifics in Korean. He worked as a bilingual teacher and advisor in the Los Angeles Unified School District for twelve years, during which time he assisted with implementation of the Korean/English Dual Language Program. He authored reports and presentations that led to recognition of the program as an Exemplary Bilingual Program by the California Department of Education and designation by the U.S. Department of Education as one of six exemplary foreign language programs nationwide. Merrill was a visiting professor in the Department of Korean Language Education at Seoul National University in 2002–2003. He is also the recipient of numerous grant awards in the United States and Korea for innovative projects that incorporate technology and long distance learning to facilitate language learning and acquisition.

Claudia Parodi is Professor in the Department of Spanish and Portuguese at the University of California, Los Angeles, where she has been on the faculty since 1991. Her research focuses on historical linguistics, historiography of linguistics, dialectology, philology, applied linguistics, literature, and generative syntax. She has published in Mexico, Holland, and the United States. Her book *Orígenes del español americano* (UNAM, 1995), deals with Spanish dialect contact in sixteenth-century Latin America. Her book *La lingüística en México* (El Colegio de México,1998), co-authored with R. Barriga, is a historiography of Mexican linguistics. Her most recent work deals with language and culture in Colonial Mexico and Chicano Spanish in Los Angeles. She is particularly interested in Spanish language teaching and education of Chicanos.

Joy Kreeft Peyton is Vice President of the Center for Applied Linguistics (CAL) in Washington, DC, and Director of the Center for Adult English Language Acquisition (CAELA). She is interested in ways that teachers implement educational innovations, particularly writing methodologies, and factors that influence their success. She is co-editor (with D. Ranard and S. McGinnis) of *Heritage Languages in America: Preserving a National Resource* and (with P. Griffin, W. Wolfram, and R. Fasold) of *Language in Action: New Studies of Language in Society*. She is a member of the editorial boards of *Language Learning and Technology*, the *Heritage Language Journal*, and the *Modern Language Journal*.

Maria Polinsky is Professor of Linguistics at Harvard University. Her research focuses on language universals, syntax-to-information structure interface, and heritage languages. She combines her work in linguistic theory with an interest in psycholinguistic explanations for language universals and language change. Her work on heritage languages explores recurrent grammatical patterns across different languages and competence-based differences between heritage and non-heritage speakers. She is associate editor of the journal *Natural Language and Linguistic Theory* and a member of the editorial board of the *Heritage Language Journal*. In 2000, she founded the Heritage Language Program at the University of California, San Diego, where she was then a professor of Linguistics. Her recent publications on heritage languages include articles on incomplete grammar, heritage acquisition of Russian, and gender analysis.

Sung-Ock S. Sohn is Professor in the Department of Asian Languages and Cultures at the University of California, Los Angeles. She received her M.A. and Ph.D. degrees in Linguistics at the University of Hawaii. Her research includes functional/cognitive linguistics, grammaticalization, discourse and grammar, language acquisition, and bilingual education. She is the author/co-author of six books including *Integrated Korean* (University of Hawaii Press, 2000/2001) and *Tense and Aspect in Korean* (University of Hawaii Press, 1995). She has also published more than fifty articles on Korean language and linguistics. As coordinator of the Korean language program at UCLA, she oversees one of the largest Korean programs in North America, and supervises undergraduate as well as graduate students majoring in Korean. She received UCLA's Distinguished Teaching Award in 1997.

Merrill Swain is Professor Emeritus in the Department of Curriculum, Teaching and Learning at the Ontario Institute for Studies in Education of the University of Toronto. Her interests include bilingual education, particularly French immersion, and communicative second language learning, teaching and testing. Her present research focuses on the role of collaborative dialogue in second language learning. She was president of the American Association for Applied Linguistics in 1998–1999, and is currently a member-at-large of the International Association of Applied Linguistics (AILA). She is recipient of the 2003 Prix Robert Roy Award, which is given to an outstanding Canadian language educator. She is also the recipient of AAAL's 2004 Distinguished Scholarship and Service Award. Her most recent book, co-edited with M.Bygate and P.Skehan is *Researching Pedagogic Tasks: Second Language Learning, Teaching and Testing* (Longman 2001).

G. Richard Tucker received his Ph.D. from McGill University, Montreal. He is the Paul Mellon Professor of Applied Linguistics and former Head of the Modern Languages Department at Carnegie Mellon University. Prior to joining Carnegie Mellon, he served as President of the Center for Applied Linguistics (1978–1991), and as Professor of Psychology and Linguistics at McGill University (1969–1978). He has published more than 200 books, articles, and reviews concerning diverse aspects of second language learning and teaching. In addition to his work in North America, he has spent a number of years living and working as a Language Education advisor for the International Division of the Ford Foundation in Southeast Asia and in the Middle East and North Africa. Tucker is the only applied linguist to have been recognized for his contributions by all of the major North American language education associations—NABE in 1995, ACTFL in 1997, TESOL in 1998, and AAAL in 2003.

Alfredo Urzúa is Assistant Professor of English and Applied Linguistics at Old Dominion University, Norfolk, Virginia, where he teaches graduate and undergraduate courses in TESL and English Linguistics. He has been involved in language teaching, teacher education, curriculum development, and program administration in Mexico and the United States. He was Chair of the Department of Modern Languages at the University of Guadalajara for seven years. He served on the national committee of Mexico's TESOL organization. He has an M.A.in TESL from the University of California, Los Angeles and a Ph.D. in Applied Linguistics from Northern Arizona University. His research interests include reflective discourse, second language teacher development, and language use in schools and in the workplace. In 2008 he is assuming the position of Coordinator of ESOL Programs and Assistant Professor of Languages and Linguistics at the University of Texas, El Paso.

Guadalupe Valdés is the Bonnie Katz Tenenbaum Professor of Education at Stanford University and has a joint appointment as a Professor of Spanish and Portuguese. Valdés works in the area of applied linguistics. Much of her work has focused on the English-Spanish bilingualism of Latinos in the United States and on discovering and describing how two languages are developed, used, and maintained by individuals who become bilingual in immigrant communities.

Her recent work includes two books entitled *Learning and not Learning English* (Teachers College Press, 2001) and *Expanding Definitions of Giftedness: Young Interpreters of Immigrant Background* (Lawrence Erlbaum, 2003). Two other books include: *Bilingualism and Testing: A Special Case of Bias* (Ablex Publishing Co., 1994) and *Con Respeto: Bridging the Distance Between Culturally Diverse Families and Schools* (Teachers College Press, 1996).

Shuhan C. Wang received her Ph.D. in Educational Linguistics from the University of Pennsylvania. She is Executive Director for the Chinese Language Initiative at the Asia Society. From 1998 to 2006, she worked for the Delaware Department of Education. She serves on numerous national committees, including the Editorial Board of *Foreign Language Annals*, the Board of Directors for the Chinese Language Teachers Association (CLTA), and the Leadership Teams of the Alliance for the Advancement of Heritage Languages and the STARTALK Project under the National Security Language Initiative. Her most recent publications include Building Societal Capital: Chinese in the U.S. (special issue of *Language Policy*, Volume 6, Springer, 2007), *Creating a Chinese Language Program in Your School: An Introductory Guide* (Asia Society, 2006), and *Expanding Chinese Language Capacity in the United States: What would it take to have 5% of high school students learning Chinese by 2015?* (Asia Society, 2005)

Terrence G. Wiley is Professor of Applied Linguistics and Educational Policy Studies in the Division of Educational Leadership and Policy Studies at Arizona State University, Phoenix, where he conducts doctoral seminars on heritage and community language education, literacy/biliteracy, language policy, and education in global contexts. He is author of *Literacy and Language Diversity in the United States* (Center for Applied Linguistics, 2005), co-editor of *Ebonics in the Urban Education Debate* (Multilingual Matters, 2005) and author of numerous articles on language policy and politics, literacy/biliteracy, and language diversity. Wiley co-edits the *Journal of Language, Identity, and Education* and the *International Multilingual Research Journal* and has guest edited/co-edited special issues of the *International Journal of Sociology of Language* and the *Bilingual Research Journal*. He serves on the editorial boards of the *Heritage Language Journal, International Journal of Bilingual Education and Bilingualism, Current Issues in Language Planning, Education Policy Analysis Archives, and the Journal of Southeast Asian American Education.*

Index